WRITING & GRAMMAR

9

second edition

for Christian Schools®

TEACHER'S EDITION

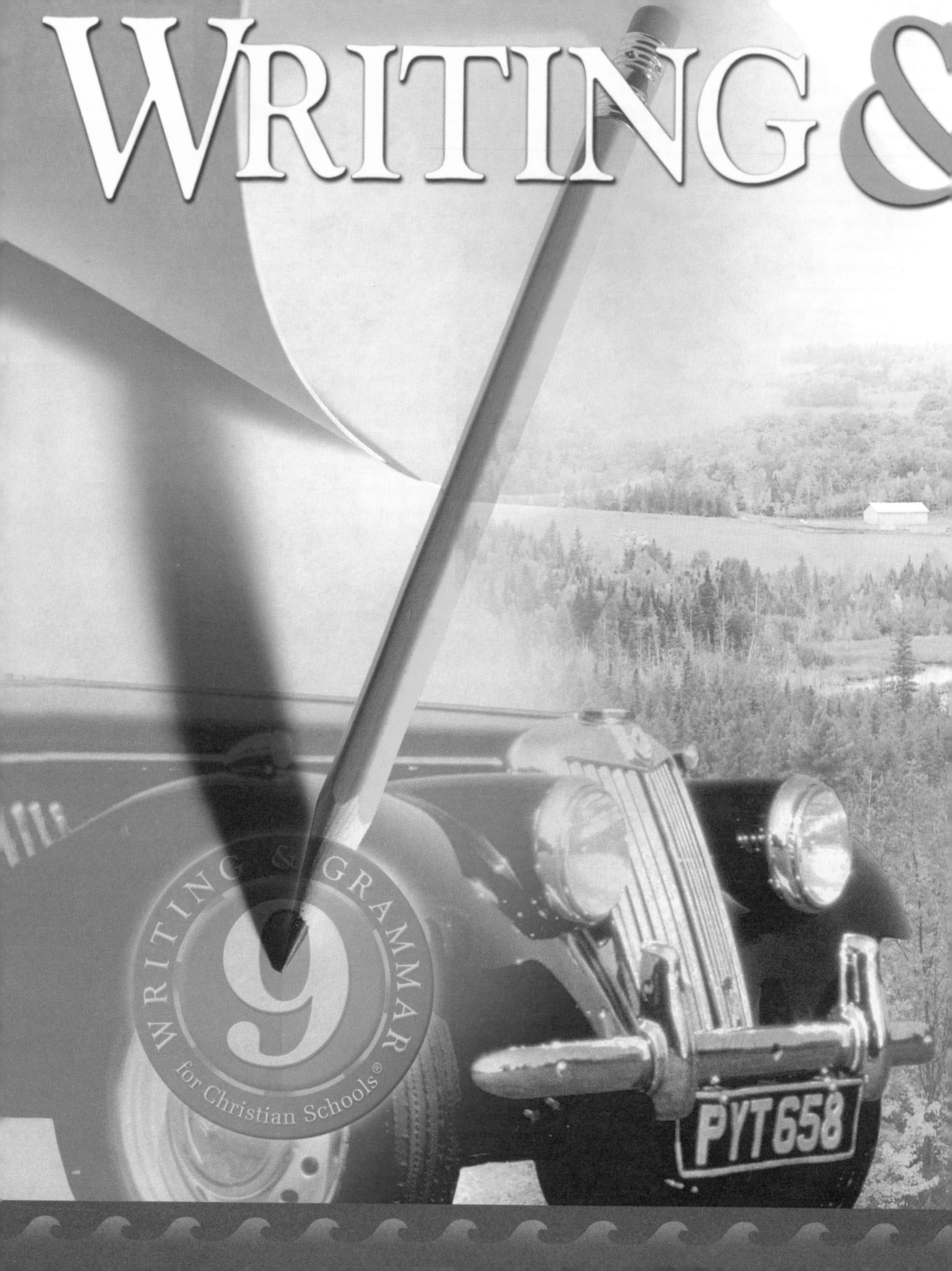
WRITING&
WRITING & GRAMMAR
9
for Christian Schools®
PYT658

GRAMMAR

for Christian Schools®

Teacher's Edition
second edition

Dana Denise Gage

Denise L. Patton

Elizabeth Rose

Dawn L. Watkins

Bob Jones University Press
Greenville, South Carolina 29614

1.800.845.5731 • *www.bjup.com*

NOTE:
The fact that materials produced by other publishers may be referred to in this volume does not constitute an endorsement by Bob Jones University Press of the content or theological position of materials produced by such publishers. The position of Bob Jones University Press, and of the University itself, is well known. Any references and ancillary materials are listed as an aid to the student or the teacher and in an attempt to maintain the accepted academic standards of the publishing industry.

WRITING AND GRAMMAR 9 for Christian Schools® Teacher's Edition, Book 1
Second Edition

Coordinating Authors
Dana Denise Gage, M.A.
Denise L. Patton
Elizabeth Rose, M.Ed.
Dawn L. Watkins, M.Ed., M.A.

Contributing Authors
Alicia M. Bernson, M.A.
Eileen M. Berry, M.A.
Sarah Miller, M.A.
Kimberly Y. Stegall, M.Ed.

Melanie N. Suydam
Danielle J. Sweede
Denise C. Zutter, M.Ed.

Consultants
June W. Cates
Grace Collins Hargis, Ph.D.
*Chairman of the Departments of
Linguistics and English Education,
Bob Jones University*
Coart Ramey, M.A.
Steven N. Skaggs
*Product Development Coordinator,
Secondary Level,
Bob Jones University Press*

Editor
Shelby J. Morris

Compositor
Kelley Moore

Cover Design
Elly Kalagayan
Duane A. Nichols

Designer
Duane A. Nichols

Photo Acquisition
Cindy Mauk

Illustrators
Timothy Banks
Paula Cheadle
Johanna Ehnis
Justin Gerard
Cory Godbey
Preston Gravely Jr.
Dyke Habegger
Jeremy Jantz
Stefanie Kubina
John Muessen
Scotty Pruitt
John Roberts
Lynda Slattery
Del Thompson
Sanela Tutaris

Produced in cooperation with the Bob Jones University Division of English Language and Literature of the College of Arts and Science, the School of Education, and Bob Jones Academy.

for Christian Schools is a registered trademark of Bob Jones University Press.

© 2001 Bob Jones University Press
Greenville, South Carolina 29614
First Edition © 1985 Bob Jones University Press

Printed in the United States of America
All rights reserved.

ISBN 1-57924-528-5

15 14 13 12 11 10 9 8 7 6 5 4 3

Table of Contents

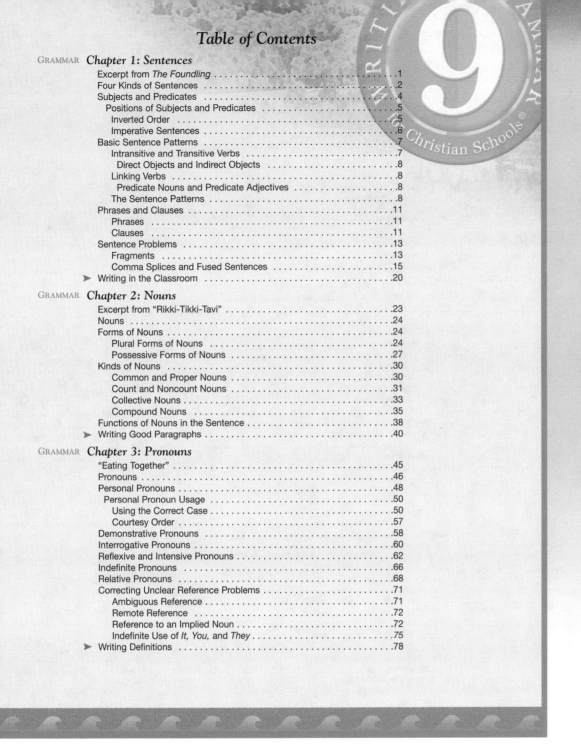

To the Teacher

WRITING AND GRAMMAR 9 for Christian Schools, Second Edition, provides students with a basis for forming a clear understanding of basic English grammar and for increasing their proficiency in the use of English. Further, the text seeks to present material in an engaging, manageable style. Plentiful examples and exercises cover topics of interest to ninth-grade students. Special features and a wide variety of writing opportunities enrich the learning experience.

Teachers or students coming to this textbook series for the first time will find that the grammatical terms and concepts are largely familiar. The text seeks to emphasize the orderliness of language. This emphasis helps students understand that language, a gift from God, reflects the orderliness of His nature. In addition, the grammar is constructive, not only pulling sentences apart to see how they work but also helping students to build clear sentences of their own.

Writing instruction and assignments take students through the writing process as it applies to informative writing, personal narrative, descriptive writing, creative writing, persuasive writing, and report writing.

Features of the Student Text

The student text contains three units: **Grammar, Usage,** and **Reference.**

Each chapter in the Grammar unit (Chapters 1-8) begins with a literature excerpt, a model of good writing featuring the part of speech taught in that chapter. Each chapter in the Usage unit (Chapters 9-12) begins with an optical illusion linking communication skills to other areas of knowledge. In both units, discussion questions draw students into the chapter.

Every section of new material closes with an **In Summary** review of the concepts, followed by **Practice the Skill, Review the Skill, Use the Skill,** or **Cumulative Review** exercises.

Chapters 1-8 each end their grammar instruction with discussion questions that refer to the opening literature selections. These questions allow students to see how grammar aids effective written communication.

Both the Grammar unit (Chapters 1-8) and the Usage unit (Chapters 9-12) include **writing instruction** and assignments that guide students through the writing process.

The third unit, Reference (Chapters 13-15), includes information that will benefit students throughout the school year.

Throughout the text, **Combine the Skills** flags identify related information that may be found elsewhere in the book. The teacher can use these flags to combine instruction of skills from one chapter with related skills from another chapter. A student can use the flags to find information to aid his

understanding of the concept he is studying. A flag marked with a *G* refers to pages in the Grammar unit; *U* refers to the Usage unit; *R* refers to Chapter 13 or 14 in the Reference unit; and *W* refers to the writing instruction in Chapter 15. **ESL** notes provide in-depth information for the student whose native language is not English. *(ESL is a widely used acronym for English as a Second Language.)*

Features of the Teacher's Edition

The Teacher's Edition consists of two volumes. Book 1 contains reduced student text pages as well as lesson support. Book 2 contains reproducible blackline masters that supplement the lessons in Book 1. For more information about the contents of Book 2, see "To the Teacher" on page iv of that volume.

Lesson Plans for each chapter offer inductive teaching strategies, efficient yet thorough methods of evaluation, and helpful sources for further information.

- A list of *Objectives* states the outcome of instruction in terms of student behavior.
- *Lesson Support* sections list the applicable pages from the student text as well as from the Teacher's Edition, Book 1 and Book 2, for that lesson.
- *Teaching Strategy* sections suggest procedures for instruction.
- *ESL Strategy* paragraphs offer suggestions for individualized instruction of the student whose native language is not English.
- *Link* strategies suggest ways to connect the grammar and usage instruction to other disciplines, such as literature, writing, speech, and history.
- *Scriptural Application* ideas point to biblical principles drawn from the lesson content.
- *Reinforcement* suggestions offer methods for reinforcing the concepts in the lesson, including homework suggestions.

- *Evaluation* ideas present ways to assess students' grasp of the material presented.
- *Enrichment* activities supplement the basic lesson plans with additional, enjoyable activities to reinforce lesson concepts.
- Many activities include an alternative *One on One* activity for those teachers who are working with only one student.
- Lists of *Additional Resources* recommend other sources of information for students and teachers.

The suggested **Teaching Schedules** on pages 437-41 show how the material in WRITING AND GRAMMAR 9 *for Christian Schools,* Second Edition, can be taught in one semester or in two semesters. The schedules are flexible, allowing for adaptation to individual needs.

The sketches of the suggested **Bulletin Boards** on pages 443-52 offer visual ideas for informative displays, interactive reinforcement of concepts, and exhibits of student work.

The sentence **Diagram Answers** on pages 453-68 correspond to those sentences in the student text marked with the diagram symbol. This symbol indicates that students should be able to diagram correctly the sentence elements that they have studied up to that lesson. Practices not marked with the diagram symbol may contain elements that students will not encounter until later lessons or may not learn how to diagram this year.

If you choose to teach diagramming, you may wish to refer to "Sentence Diagrams," which begins on page 287 of *The Writer's Toolbox,* for sample diagrams of various sentence elements.

Making Writing Assignments

Getting a good writing assignment from a student starts long before the student picks up a pen or sits down at a computer. It starts with the teacher's making a thorough plan for the year, then carrying it through, and adapting and revising as needs and opportunities arise.

A good curriculum, of course, is a solid place to start; but every student, every class, is unique, and only the teacher can really determine what is best. Beyond a general plan, a teacher also needs to make good, specific assignments.

An assignment that gets a good response needs to be focused, inviting, and clear. "Write about your summer vacation" is not going to prompt the kind of polished writing that pleases. It is too general, too broad, and too overwhelming, even for the eager writer. "Write a paragraph describing the most interesting place where you ate on your vacation" is better. It narrows the assignment; it engages the interest of the student; it looks possible, even to the least eager writer.

In clarifying the topic, it is possible, however, to put too many parameters on the as-

signment. "Write a five-sentence paragraph using five adjectives to describe the way the restaurant looked" is too limiting. Nor is it advisable to use writing to teach a particular grammar principle. For example, "Write two paragraphs on your favorite sport, using four complex sentences" not only does not teach the grammar well but also encourages poor style.

Writing assignments should prompt good writing and should communicate messages that are important to the writer. An assignment given with definition and clarity helps engender a writing assignment of purpose

Acknowledgments

A careful effort has been made to trace the ownership of selections included in this textbook in order to secure permission to reprint copyrighted material and to make full acknowledgment of their use. If any error or omission has occurred, it is unintentional and will be corrected in subsequent editions, provided written notification is made to the publisher.

CHAPTER 1
Excerpt from *The Foundling* by Linda Hayner. Copyright © 1997 by Bob Jones University Press.

CHAPTER 3
LI-YOUNG LEE: "Eating Together" © 1986 Li-Young Lee. Reprinted from ROSE, poems by Li-Young Lee, with the permission of BOA Editions, Ltd.

CHAPTER 4
Excerpt from "Blues Ain't No Mockin' Bird" from GORILLA, MY LOVE by Toni Cade Bambara. Copyright © 1960, 1963, 1964, 1965, 1968, 1970, 1971, 1972 by Toni Cade Bambara. Reprinted by permission of Random House, Inc.

CHAPTER 5
"The Most Dangerous Game" by Richard Connell. Copyright © 1924 by Richard Connell. Copyright renewed © 1952 by Louise Fox Connell. Reprinted by permission of Brandt & Brandt Literary Agents, Inc.

CHAPTER 6
Excerpt from "Their Finest Hour" by Winston S. Churchill. Copyright Winston S. Churchill. Reproduced by permission of Curtis Brown Group Ltd., on behalf of Winston S. Churchill.

CHAPTER 8
Excerpt from *Men of Iron* by Howard Pyle. Copyright © 1993 by Bob Jones University Press.

Photograph Credits
The following agencies and individuals have furnished materials to meet the photographic needs of this textbook. We wish to express our gratitude to them for their important contribution.

BJU Press Files
George R. Collins
Corbis Images
Corel Corporation
Digital Stock
Gene Fisher
Joe Golden
National Aeronautics and Space Administration (NASA)
National Center for Atmospheric Research/National Science Foundation (NCAR/NSF)
National Oceanic and Aeronautic Administration (NOAA)
PhotoDisc, Inc.
Royal Canadian Mounted Police
Unusual Films
www.arttoday.com
www.sandlotscience.com

Front Cover
Digital Stock (both)

Back Cover
PhotoDisc, Inc.

Title Page
PhotoDisc, Inc. ii (top); Corel Corporation ii (bottom); Digital Stock iii

Chapter 1
PhotoDisc, Inc. 2, 9, 11, 15; Corel Corporation 3; George R. Collins 5; Digital Stock 7; www.arttoday.com 13, 14, 16, 17, 20, 21; Unusual Films 19

Chapter 2
PhotoDisc, Inc. 25, 27, 29; www.arttoday.com 26, 31, 33, 34, 35, 39, 40, 42, 43; Unusual Films 30; Royal Canadian Mounted Police 36; BJU Press Files 37

Chapter 3
www.arttoday.com 46, 47, 49, 51, 52, 53, 54, 55, 56, 60, 61, 66, 69, 71, 73, 74, 76, 78; Corel Corporation 48; PhotoDisc, Inc. 79

Chapter 4
www.arttoday.com 83, 85, 95, 97; NOAA, photo by Joe Golden 88; PhotoDisc, Inc. 92, 106; BJU Press Files 99; NCAR/NSF 101; Corel Corporation 104

Chapter 5
NASA 115, 118, 120, 124, 130, 132; PhotoDisc, Inc. 126, 129, 136; Corel Corporation 138

Chapter 6
www.arttoday.com 142, 154, 161; Unusual Films 144, 148, 152, 167; Gene Fisher 149; Corbis Images 158; Corel Corporation 162

Chapter 7
PhotoDisc, Inc. 171, 181; www.arttoday.com 172, 180; Corel Corporation

175, 179, 182, 186; George R. Collins 185

Chapter 8
Corel Corporation 193, 194, 197, 201, 204, 206; PhotoDisc, Inc. 195; www.arttoday.com 198; Digital Stock 205

Chapter 9
www.sandlotscience.com 208; PhotoDisc, Inc. 210, 217, 219, 225; Corel Corporation 212, 215, 227

Chapter 10
PhotoDisc, Inc. 237, 240; Corel Corporation 238, 245, 249, 251; Digital Stock 242, 247, 252

Chapter 11
www.sandlotscience.com 256; www.arttoday.com 258, 268; PhotoDisc, Inc. 260, 271; Digital Stock 262; Corel Corporation 267

Chapter 12
www.sandlotscience.com 272; Corel Corporation 274; PhotoDisc, Inc. 278, 286, 292, 314; www.arttoday.com 281, 305; Digital Stock 283, 297, 309

Chapter 13
Digital Stock 320; NASA 328; PhotoDisc, Inc. 332

Chapter 14
PhotoDisc, Inc. 336, 355

Chapter 15
PhotoDisc, Inc. 358; www.arttoday.com 360

and energy. Then the evaluation of the work is far more enjoyable and useful to both the student and the teacher.

Grading Writing Assignments

The only thing harder than getting a student to write is grading the writing he produces. The task seems overwhelming. Sometimes, perhaps, it seems easier just to cut back on the amount of writing altogether—less hassle all around.

To aid your grading, this curriculum offers reproducible **Rubrics** for each major writing assignment. The purpose of the Rubrics is twofold: to inform the students of the teacher's expectations and to give the teacher a method for evaluating fairly yet quickly.

Additional Resources

THE WRITER'S TOOLBOX: A WRITING AND GRAMMAR HANDBOOK for Christian Schools is a valuable supplement for students and teachers.

Another useful supplement for teachers who want to include additional research writing assignments is *WRITING FROM RESEARCH for Christian Schools.*

Both *The Writer's Toolbox* and *Writing from Research* are available from Bob Jones University Press.

Teachers who want a fuller understanding of the aims of Christian education should consult the following publications from Bob Jones University Press: *The Christian Philosophy of Education, Christian Teaching and Learning, Christian Educational Methods,* and *The Christian Teaching of English.*

To the Student

Why do we study English? We learn how to understand and how to speak English while we are very young. Why, then, do we spend so much of the rest of our lives studying something we already know?

English is a living language. It changes—constantly. New words appear; obsolete words fade away as they are no longer needed. Usage patterns change; even rules occasionally change. We need to learn to speak and to write so that others can understand. Without a thorough understanding of English, we cannot communicate effectively.

English is also a flexible language. We use different levels of formality for different audiences. We speak to our friends differently than we speak to our pastor or teacher. We use one style for a letter to a friend and another style for a research paper to be graded by a teacher.

WRITING AND GRAMMAR 9 for Christian Schools®, Second Edition, will help you learn to communicate in English more effectively. The first step toward the goal of better speaking and writing is to acquaint yourself with the text. Take a few minutes to look through the book and become familiar with these features:

- Flags in the margin point you to other pages in the text with more information about the topic. Each flag indicates the category of material to which that flag refers.

  - A **Grammar** flag refers to a concept that appears in one of the first eight chapters.

  - A **Usage** flag sends you to material in Chapters 9-12 dealing with correct usage or mechanics.

  - A **Reference** flag refers to the library skills and study skills in Chapters 13 and 14.

  - A **Writing** flag indicates that the material will be an important writing concept in Chapter 15 or one of the writing activities throughout the book.

- ESL notes explain in detail the concepts that can be difficult for students from another language background (*ESL* is an abbreviation for *English as a Second Language*). Every student can learn more about English from these helpful explanations.

Mastering the concepts in this book will increase your appreciation for language. If you learn to use English correctly and to value the beauty of English, you will enjoy the satisfaction of becoming a more effective communicator.

1 SENTENCES

Objectives

Students will

1. identify and compose the four kinds of sentences and use correct end marks with each kind.

2. identify the complete and simple subject.

3. identify the complete and simple predicate.

4. identify compound subjects and compound predicates.

5. determine whether written sentences contain transitive or intransitive verbs.

6. distinguish between direct and indirect objects.

7. analyze inverted sentences to locate subjects and verbs.

8. determine the sentence pattern of a given sentence.

9. classify word groups as phrases, independent clauses, or dependent clauses.

10. revise fragments, comma splices, and fused sentences.

11. evaluate and revise a piece of writing containing a variety of sentence errors.

The Foundling

by Linda Hayner

One morning in January 1644, four-year-old Willy is abandoned at a parish church in London. The parish constable finds him, and Willy begins an unlikely journey for a foundling. First Willy lives in the home of Master Perry, under the care of two servant girls, Marie and Gillian.

Cook peered at Willy. "Needs his hair cut." She nodded to Marie. "Mind this floor, girl." Cook shuffled to the table. "His breakfast is ready. He'd best be here on time tomorrow. I'll not make a second breakfast again."

Another maid entered with a small basketful of rags. "Some nanny you are," she said to Marie. "If you don't quiet him soon, Mistress will be here laying us all by the ears." She kneeled before the fire. One by one the rags went into the flames.

"Nasty things, so worn we can't even use them for cleaning. Look at this shirt!" She held it up with thumb and forefinger. "No child should have to wear such as this." She tossed the shirt into the fire.

"Mine! My shirt!"

"You'll have more shirts and better. And cleaner." She added more clothes to the fire.

"Mine!" Willy ran to the basket and grabbed at his belongings. Marie dragged Willy back. "Oh, do give him a shirt, Gillian. We can wash it. Or give him those breeches." Marie pointed. "I don't want to hear much more of his wailing."

"No, they're to be burned, all of them."

Willy screamed. He kicked at Marie's legs, but she was too quick and her skirts hid his target.

"Give him whatever's cleanest," she said. "I won't be scolded because of a screaming brat." Marie caught up the blue shawl and shoved it in Willy's face. "Now be still," she hissed.

Willy grabbed his mother's shawl and wadded it up against his chest.

Mistress Perry swept into the kitchen. The maids jumped up and curtseyed, standing with their eyes lowered and their hands clasped before them. Cook merely looked up for a moment.

"What is going on here? The whole house is disturbed." Mistress Perry's foot tapped impatiently. She addressed the younger girl. "Gillian?"

"Yes, mum?" Gillian curtseyed again.

"Why is that child carrying on so?"

"I suppose because I'm burning his old clothes. He wants them, mum."

The basic structure of written English is the sentence. In order to be a good writer, you must first learn to create complete, well-crafted sentences.

- *Which character uses the most imperative sentences?*
- *Whose speech has the most exclamations?*
- *What questions does Mistress Perry ask?*

The kinds of sentences characters use reveal their relationships with other characters. For example, we know that Marie is probably in a slightly higher position than Gillian because she uses imperatives (gives orders) to Gillian frequently. Sentence types in dialogue can also indicate a character's motives. Do you think Mistress Perry is merely gathering information, or is there more meaning behind her questions? This chapter will help you become more familiar with sentences, the basic tool of writing.

ESL: "Laying us . . . by the ears" is an idiom, probably meaning "to box our ears," or to hit very hard on the ears (a common form of punishment during the Middle Ages for young servants and children).

ESL: "Mum" is a dialectal form of *ma'am*.

ESL: "Carrying on" is an idiom describing someone's bad behavior, usually an informal description of someone making a lot of noise.

- *Marie*
- *Willy's*
- *"What is going on here?" and "Why is that child carrying on so?"*

Lesson Support

Student Text
Chapter 1 Review—pp. 397-98

Teacher's Edition, Book 1
Bulletin Boards—p. 445

Teacher's Edition, Book 2
Pretests—pp. 1-2

Teaching Helps—p. 37

Concept Reinforcements—pp. 87-90

Preparation

Before beginning lesson preparation, read through Chapter 1 completely to acquaint yourself with the scope of the chapter. Assign Chapter 1 Pretest (Book 2, pp. 1-2) as a tool to help you determine the students' skill levels before they study the chapter. Use this information to plan the emphasis of your lessons.

Literature Link

Use the literature selection at the beginning of each grammar chapter as a springboard for speech and writing activities. After reading the selection aloud, discuss the questions with your students.

Four Kinds of Sentences

Sentences can be classified according to their purpose, that is, by what they do. A writer may choose a particular kind of sentence to emphasize a message or to give a certain tone to his work.

A **declarative** sentence makes a statement and ends with a period.

> In 1871 reporter Henry Stanley confirmed that missionary and explorer David Livingstone was still alive in Africa.

An **interrogative** sentence asks a question and ends with a question mark.

> Have you ever been to the top of the Sears Tower?

An **imperative** sentence gives a command or request and most often ends with a period. It may sometimes end with an exclamation point.

> Place these cups and saucers in the china cabinet. Be careful!

An **exclamatory** sentence expresses strong emotion and always ends with an exclamation point.

> The water is getting higher! The bridge is washed out!

In English, one of the major differences in the types of sentences is the rising and falling pitch, called the *intonation*. Intonation of a sentence can be a hint about what type the sentence is.

- Declarative sentences have falling intonation at the end.
- Many interrogative sentences have rising intonation at the end.
- Imperative sentences have falling intonation at the end.
- Exclamatory sentences are stated at a higher pitch than other sentences or with a greater difference between the high and the low pitches.

in summary

A **declarative** sentence makes a statement and ends with a period.

An **interrogative** sentence asks a question and ends with a question mark.

An **imperative** sentence gives a command or request and most often ends with a period.

An **exclamatory** sentence expresses strong emotion and ends with an exclamation point.

1-1 PRACTICE THE SKILL

In the blank, label each sentence *declarative, exclamatory, imperative,* or *interrogative*. Place the appropriate punctuation mark at the end of the sentence.

interrogative 1. Can people grow plants without soil?

declarative or exclamatory 2. They certainly can. *or* !

Teaching Strategy: Introduction

Materials
- an unusual object

Bring an unusual object to class and tell students to comment on the object aloud. Write selected responses for display. After you have written the sentences, ask students to group the sentences according to purpose by using the information on page 2 of their texts. Encourage students to share their groupings with the class.

Teaching Strategy: Participation

Write the following sentence for display: *Look out the window.* Ask several class members to read the sentence aloud, each reading the sentence to produce a different meaning (e.g., one a command, one a question, one to show strong emotion). Elicit from the students the conclusion that although each sentence has the same words, each has a different meaning.

ESL Strategy

Use the ESL note on page 2 to explain American intonation patterns. ESL students will usually use what would sound correct to them in their native language. Different languages vary at least slightly (and usually quite widely) in the importance and nature of changes regarding pitch. Read the example sentences on page 2 aloud to allow your ESL students to hear the correct intonation.

<u>interrogative</u>   3. Have you ever heard of *hydroponics*?

<u>declarative</u>   4. *Hydro-* indicates that water plays a part in this technique.

<u>imperative</u>   5. Mix the solution carefully.

<u>declarative</u>   6. The water must contain the right amount of nutrients.

<u>exclamatory</u>   7. Wow, those plants have grown another inch already!

<u>imperative</u>   8. Watch out for that hose. *or !*

<u>interrogative</u>   9. Does that hose pump oxygen into the water solution?

<u>declarative</u>   10. Those plants have been placed in peat instead of dirt.

1-2 REVIEW THE SKILL

In the blank, label each sentence *declarative, exclamatory, imperative,* or *interrogative.* Place the appropriate punctuation mark at the end of the sentence.

<u>interrogative</u>   1. Do you know about the Great Wall of China?

<u>imperative</u>   2. Look carefully at those pictures.

<u>interrogative</u>   3. Can you see the Great Wall of China?

<u>exclamatory</u>   4. That is amazing!

<u>declarative or exclamatory</u>   5. The vast span of the Great Wall of China is incredible. *or !*

<u>exclamatory</u>   6. Wow, the wall is over four thousand miles long!

<u>declarative</u>   7. In 221 B.C. the oldest section of the wall was begun.

<u>interrogative</u>   8. Was building the wall dangerous?

<u>declarative or exclamatory</u>   9. Over one million people died building a three-thousand-mile section. *or !*

<u>declarative</u>   10. Some of the sections of the Great Wall have been restored.

Scriptural Application

Ask the students to look for all four kinds of sentences in the Bible. Perhaps divide the class into four groups and assign each group one of the four sentence types. Encourage each group to find twenty examples of its assigned sentence type in Scripture. Encourage them to note the context in which the sentence type appears and to be ready to explain why that sentence type is appropriate in that context.

One on One

Assign your student two of the four sentence types and take the other two for yourself. Compete to find ten examples of each type by the end of a time limit. Ask your student to examine the context of several sentences and to explain why that sentence type is appropriate.

Reinforcement

Using Practice the Skill 1-1 on pages 2-3, ask students to find the simple subjects and the simple predicates. Guide students toward the subject by asking them whom or what the sentence is about and toward the predicate by asking them what the subject is doing. Point out the variations in subject-predicate position within the exercise (e.g., 1, 3, 9—inverted; 5, 8—understood *you*).

List the four types of sentences and compose your own example of each. Be sure to punctuate the sentences correctly. *(Sentences will vary.)*

1. _____declarative_____

_____

_____

2. _____interrogative_____

_____

_____

3. _____imperative_____

_____

_____

4. _____exclamatory_____

_____

_____

Subjects and Predicates

The **subject** and the **predicate** are the two basic parts of every sentence. The subject tells whom or what the sentence is about. The predicate is the part that makes a statement about the subject.

The main word or words of the subject make up the **simple subject.** The simple subject is usually a noun or pronoun.

> My next-door **neighbor** writes long letters to her cousin in New York.

The **complete subject** includes the simple subject and all the words that modify the subject.

> A blue **notebook** with calendar pages and an index of phone numbers keeps Cettina's busy life somewhat organized.

The main word or words of the predicate make up the **simple predicate.** The simple predicate is always a **verb.**

> After dinner, Anthony **plays** basketball in the driveway with his dad.
> We **can hear** them out there now.

The **complete predicate** includes the simple predicate, or verb, and all the other words that tell what the subject is or what the subject is doing.

> A few diamonds **appeared** in jewelry and clothing for the first time in the thirteenth century.

> According to a law of King Louis IX of France, only the king **could own** a diamond.

U
USAGE

Chapter 9: Subjects and Predicates
p. 209

G
GRAMMAR

Chapter 4: Recognizing the Complete Verb
p. 82

4   Chapter 1

Teaching Strategy: Participation

Instruct students to fold a sheet of notebook paper in half lengthwise. Ask them to write *subject* on the left side and *predicate* on the right side. Tell half of the students to write three subjects down the left side of their papers and tell the other half to write three predicates down the right side. Collect and trade papers, giving each student the opposite of what he wrote (e.g., a student who wrote three subjects should receive a paper with three predicates). When students receive the switched papers, instruct them not to look at the side that has been written on but to fill in the blank side with the required part: subject or predicate. After writing, students should unfold the papers and match subjects and predicates. Ask for volunteers to read the combined sentences aloud. (*Note:* If you have an odd number of students, fill out a sheet yourself.) Discuss with your students why some sentences made sense and others did not. Talk about the elements that make up subjects and predicates. Ask the students what differentiates a subject from a predicate.

One on One

Let your student choose to start with subjects or predicates and you take the other. Make lists of sentence parts as described above. Trade papers with your student and read the combined sentences aloud.

> **Word Order:** In English, the subject almost always comes before the verb.
>
>   **S   V**
> China has one of the longest recorded histories of any country today.
>   **S**   **V**
> Americans often think of them as a Communist country, but the current
>   **S**   **V**   **V**
> government has really only begun.
>   **S**   **V**
> The Communist government has been here only since 1949; many
>   **S**   **V**
> Chinese dynasties, however, lasted for centuries.

Both subjects and predicates can be compound. A compound subject or predicate has at least two parts, often joined by the word *and.* A **compound subject** is two or more nouns or pronouns functioning as subjects of the same verb. A **compound predicate** has two or more verbs.

SIMPLE COMPOUND SUBJECT	A long book **report** and an extra reading **assignment** in history will keep Eric busy this weekend.
COMPLETE COMPOUND SUBJECT	**A long book report** and **an extra reading assignment in history** will keep Eric busy this weekend.
SIMPLE COMPOUND PREDICATE	Because of their hardness, diamonds **cut, grind,** and **polish** other hard substances.
	Jewelers **purchase** diamonds and **place** them in attractive settings.
COMPLETE COMPOUND PREDICATE	Jewelers **purchase diamonds** and **place them in attractive settings.**

Positions of Subjects and Predicates

Inverted Order

In most sentences, the subject comes before the verb. In some cases, however, the sentences are in inverted order, with the subject coming after the verb or between the two parts of the verb.

> In her usual chair with a hot cup of tea *sat* **Amy.**
> **Amy** *sat* in her usual chair with a hot cup of tea.

The inverted order of subjects and verbs appears in many interrogative sentences.

> Did **you** *write* down the study questions for the test?
> **You** *did write* down the study questions for the test.

Other types of sentences with inverted order are those that begin with *there* or *here.* You can rearrange these sentences to help you find the correct subject and verb.

> Here *are* the study **questions.**
> The study **questions** *are* here.

Chapter 9: Inverted Order
p. 216

ESL Strategy

Use the ESL note on page 5 to teach normal word order for English sentences. Explain that the order is altered only in certain kinds of sentences (interrogatives and some declaratives, as listed in the section on "Inverted Order" on page 5). If your ESL students are using other word orders in their sentences, they may be reverting to the sentence word order of their first language. For example, in German the verb occupies the second position in a present-tense sentence regardless of what comes before or after. In Korean and Japanese, the verb comes at the end of the sentence.

Remind your ESL students that the subject must always be present, except in a few kinds of sentences. For example, some imperatives such as "Get away from there!" and some nonstandard interrogative forms used in casual conversation (e.g., "Got any money?") do not overtly state their subjects since the subject *you* is understood. Students' first language may not require the subject to be present since many languages rely on the cases of conjugated verbs to indicate the appropriate subjects by using different verb endings to indicate person and/or number.

When English inverts the normal word order to form a question (an interrogative sentence), the subject changes places with the auxiliary verb, not with the main verb.

He *is going* to the beach this summer.
Is **he** *going* to the beach this summer?

He *has been* there many times.
Has **he** *been* there before?

Chapter 4: Imperative
p. 107

Imperative Sentences

When a command or request is addressed directly to the person being spoken to, often the subject is not stated. The subject of an imperative sentence is not missing; it is the understood word *you.*

Be home before ten.
(You) *be* home before ten.

in summary

The **subject** tells whom or what the sentence is about.

The **simple subject** is the main word or words of the subject; the **complete subject** includes the simple subject and the words that modify the subject.

The **predicate** makes a statement about the subject.

The **simple predicate** (a verb) is the main word or words of the predicate; the **complete predicate** includes the simple predicate and the words that modify the predicate.

Inverted order occurs when the subject comes after the predicate or between two parts of the predicate.

1-4 PRACTICE THE SKILL

Underline the simple subject(s) once and the simple predicate(s) twice. If the subject is understood *you,* write *you* to the left of the number.

1. What do you know about fencing?

2. This swashbuckling art exists today as an Olympic sport.

3. Here are three types of swords used in fencing: the foil, the épée, and the saber.

you 4. Look at the different blade shapes of the three kinds of swords.

5. Fencing rounds usually last a maximum of six minutes.

6. Both men and women must wear special clothing for competitions.

7. Every fencer in a match should have a special mesh mask for his face.

ESL Strategy

Use the ESL note on page 6 to explain word inversion to your ESL students. Some students may have difficulty grasping the fact that it is not the main verb but the auxiliary that inverts with the subject. Refer to the information about auxiliaries on page 100 for further explanation of inversion in negative sentences.

ESL Strategy

If you notice that your ESL students are making imperatives such as "Leaves the room" or "She go away," explain that imperatives are tenseless (no present or past) and cannot have a subject other than the understood *you.* Imperatives also do not take modals as auxiliaries, but the auxiliaries *do* and *be* can occur with imperatives. (See pages 82-83 of the student text for more information about modals.)

8. One <u>contestant</u> <u>might</u> <u>join</u> with another contestant and <u>may</u> <u>fence</u> on a team.

9. In épée fencing, any <u>portion</u> of the fencer's body <u>constitutes</u> a valid target.

10. Sabre <u>fencing</u> and foil <u>fencing</u> <u>do</u> <u>not</u> <u>permit</u> touches on specific parts of the body.

1-5 REVIEW THE SKILL

Underline the simple subject(s) once and the simple predicate(s) twice. If the subject is understood *you*, write *you* to the left of the number.

1. <u>Samson</u> <u>ruled</u> as an Israelite judge for twenty years.

2. Samson's <u>parents</u> <u>knew</u> about Samson's special call before his birth.

3. The <u>angel</u> of the Lord <u>visited</u> Samson's father, Manoah, and his wife and <u>told</u> them God's message.

4. Samson's distinctive Nazarite <u>vow</u> <u>should</u> <u>have</u> <u>determined</u> his actions.

you 5. <u>Notice</u> Samson's disobedience to his vow.

6. <u>He</u> <u>ate</u> the honey from a dead lion and <u>drank</u> strong drink.

7. <u>He</u> <u>revealed</u> the secret of his strength to Delilah.

8. The <u>Lord</u> severely <u>punished</u> Samson for his disobedience.

9. The <u>Philistines</u> <u>gouged</u> out Samson's eyes.

you 10. <u>Remember</u> the consequences of sin.

Basic Sentence Patterns

The complete predicate in a sentence may include complements. A complement completes the thought of the sentence. The kind of verb in a predicate depends on the type of complement that follows it.

Intransitive and Transitive Verbs

Two kinds of verbs are **intransitive** and **transitive.** An intransitive verb does not have an object.

The lesson *began.*   The home team *scored* first.

A transitive verb has one or more objects.

The guard opened the *gate.*   She plays the *piano* and the *flute.*

G
GRAMMAR

Chapter 4: Intransitive Verbs
p. 86

Teaching Strategy: Induction and Discussion

Write the words *take* and *come* for display. Ask students to volunteer sentences using these two verbs. *(I take a bath. She came to the party with me.)* Write a selection of their sentences under the appropriate word. Ask students to comment on similarities and differences between the sentences. The students' comments should include the fact that *take* always has an object, but *come* never does.

Teaching Strategy: Discussion

After reading the material on pages 7-8, refer to the sentences written for display from the previous induction and discussion section. Ask students to identify each sentence as transitive or intransitive.

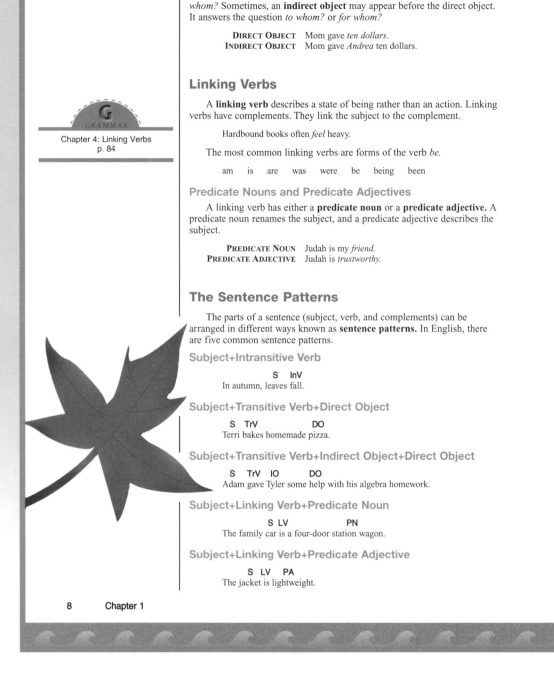

Direct Objects and Indirect Objects

A transitive verb has a direct object. The **direct object** appears after the verb and receives the action of the verb. It answers the question *what?* or *whom?* Sometimes, an **indirect object** may appear before the direct object. It answers the question *to whom?* or *for whom?*

DIRECT OBJECT Mom gave *ten dollars.*
INDIRECT OBJECT Mom gave *Andrea* ten dollars.

Linking Verbs

A **linking verb** describes a state of being rather than an action. Linking verbs have complements. They link the subject to the complement.

Hardbound books often *feel* heavy.

The most common linking verbs are forms of the verb *be.*

am   is   are   was   were   be   being   been

Predicate Nouns and Predicate Adjectives

A linking verb has either a **predicate noun** or a **predicate adjective.** A predicate noun renames the subject, and a predicate adjective describes the subject.

PREDICATE NOUN Judah is my *friend.*
PREDICATE ADJECTIVE Judah is *trustworthy.*

The Sentence Patterns

The parts of a sentence (subject, verb, and complements) can be arranged in different ways known as **sentence patterns.** In English, there are five common sentence patterns.

Subject+Intransitive Verb

S   InV
In autumn, leaves fall.

Subject+Transitive Verb+Direct Object

S   TrV   DO
Terri bakes homemade pizza.

Subject+Transitive Verb+Indirect Object+Direct Object

S   TrV   IO   DO
Adam gave Tyler some help with his algebra homework.

Subject+Linking Verb+Predicate Noun

S   LV   PN
The family car is a four-door station wagon.

Subject+Linking Verb+Predicate Adjective

S   LV   PA
The jacket is lightweight.

Teaching Strategy: Demonstration

If the example sentences from the previous activity contain indirect objects, instruct students to find and distinguish between the direct objects and the indirect objects.

Teaching Strategy: Discussion

Remind students that the prefix *in* frequently means "not" and that *intransitive* indicates a verb that does *not* have a receiver of action.

Teaching Strategy: Discussion

Talk with students about their favorite or least favorite animals. Ask them why they like or dislike those animals. Display the responses that fit the sentence patterns taught thus far. *(Dogs are obedient. I can ride a horse. Cats scratch.)* Then ask the students to identify the sentence patterns for those answers. *(S-LV-PA, S-TrV-DO, S-InV)*

in summary

An **intransitive verb** does not have an object.

A **transitive verb** has one or more objects.

A **direct object** appears after a transitive verb and receives the action of the verb. It answers the question *what?* or *whom?*

An **indirect object** appears before a direct object. It answers the question *for what?* or *for whom?*

A **linking verb** describes a state of being rather than an action.

A **predicate noun** follows a linking verb and renames the subject.

A **predicate adjective** follows a linking verb and describes the subject.

1-6 𝒫RACTICE THE 𝒮KILL

Label the sentence patterns *S-InV*, *S-TrV-DO*, or *S-TrV-IO-DO*. Above each word of the sentence pattern, write its label.

1. (S) Changes in the weather (TrV) give (IO) many people (DO) allergic symptoms.

2. (S) Some people (InV) react abnormally to normally harmless substances.

3. (S) Pollen and other (S) substances can also (TrV) cause (IO) allergy sufferers allergic (DO) reactions.

4. (S) Symptoms may (TrV) include (DO) sneezes, (DO) watery eyes, and a (DO) runny nose.

5. (S) Hay fever (TrV) affects approximately twenty to forty million (DO) Americans.

6. Unfortunately, many severe allergy (S) sufferers should not (InV) go outside for extended periods of time during allergy season.

7. (S) Cold weather often (TrV) relieves (DO) people's symptoms of hay fever.

8. How can (S) doctors (TrV) give (IO) people (DO) help for their allergies?

9. (S) Doctors can (InV) help in the diagnosis of allergies.

10. (S) They (TrV) use (DO) skin tests and (TrV) prescribe (DO) medicine according to the test results.

Teaching Strategy: Introduction

Write the following phrases for display:

- in the house
- could be problematic
- the talented freshman student
- of a play

Ask students what these groups of words are called. *(phrases)* Ask them what makes these word groups phrases. *(Each group contains more than one word, and the words within each group are related.)*

If students have trouble with this concept, write or say aloud a group of unrelated words like *car, yesterday, the, asparagus, gone.* Ask the students whether these words together constitute a phrase. *(no)* What is different about the phrases and the words? *(The words in the phrases are related; the random words are not.)*

Evaluation

If you have assigned sentence diagramming with Practice the Skill 1-6, check students' answers using page 455.

Label the sentence patterns *S-LV-PN* or *S-LV-PA*. Above each word of the sentence pattern, write its label.

     S LV PA
1. The day feels beautiful.

      S LV PA
2. Yes, but looks can be deceptive.

     S LV   PA
3. Weather is often unpredictable.

        S LV PA
4. Does the weather forecast sound favorable?

     S   LV   PN
5. My brother has become a meteorologist.

     S   LV   PN
6. Computers remain a vital source of weather information.

       S LV   PA
7. A short-term forecast can be fairly accurate.

      S LV   PA
8. Longer forecasts seem more difficult because of the complexities of

weather.

        S   LV PN
9. Modern weather instruments have become necessities in the improve-

ment of forecasting.

    S LV   PN
10. Weather is indeed a complex phenomenon.

Label the sentence patterns *S-InV, S-TrV-DO, S-TrV-IO-DO, S-LV-PN,* or *S-LV-PA*. Above each word of the sentence pattern, write its label.

     S LV   PA
1. Modern Olympic games are very different from ancient Olympics.

     S TrV   DO
2. The early Olympics had fewer events.

       S LV PN
3. An unusual Olympic game was pankration.

     S LV PN
4. Pankration was a combination of boxing and wrestling.

       S LV   PA
5. Due to a lack of rules, pankration was extremely dangerous.

        S   TrV DO
6. In this particular sport, the competitors did not wear gloves on their

hands.

Evaluation

If you have assigned sentence diagramming with Practice the Skill 1-7 or Review the Skill 1-8, check students' answers using pages 455-56.

7. Before an Olympic competition, athletes trained for ten months in

     Olympia.

$$\overset{S}{} \quad \overset{InV}{}$$

8. Women did not compete in the earliest Olympics.

$$\overset{S}{} \quad \overset{TrV}{} \quad \overset{IO}{} \quad \overset{DO}{}$$

9. A winner gave his city fame in the ancient Greek world.

$$\overset{S}{} \quad \overset{LV}{} \quad \overset{PN}{} \quad \overset{PN}{}$$

10. Other ancient games were the Isthmian games, the Pythian games, and

     the Nemean games.

Phrases and Clauses

Phrases

    A **phrase** is a group of related words that does not have both a subject and a predicate. A phrase may contain a subject or a verb, but not both. A group of related phrases together can become a sentence. The following sentence contains several phrases.

In winter, Canada geese fly southward over the lake.

Chapter 8: Phrases and Clauses
p. 192

Clauses

    A **clause** is a group of related words that has both a subject and a verb. The following sentence has two clauses.

The Canada geese fly south where the weather is warmer.

Independent and Dependent Clauses

    If the clause expresses a complete thought and can stand alone, it is an **independent clause** (sometimes called a main clause). A clause that must be part of another sentence is a **dependent clause** (sometimes called a subordinate clause).

INDEPENDENT The geese fly south.
DEPENDENT where the weather is warmer

in summary

A **phrase** is a group of related words that does not have both a subject and a predicate.

A **clause** is a group of words that has both a subject and a predicate.

An **independent clause** can stand alone as a sentence.

A **dependent clause** cannot stand alone but must be part of another sentence.

Sentences   11

Teaching Strategy: Induction

Write the following word groups for display: *I wanted a new bike* and *although I couldn't afford one.* Ask the students these questions:

- Are these word groups different from the phrases you examined earlier? *(yes)*
- What is different? *(These word groups have subjects and verbs.)*
- Are both of them sentences? *(no, only the first one)*

- Why is the second one not a sentence? *(It does not express a complete thought because it contains a subordinating word; it must be part of another sentence.)*

Teaching Strategy: Participation

Materials
- four blank slips of paper for each student

Pass out four slips of paper to each student and ask the students to write a clause on each slip: two examples of a dependent clause and two examples of an independent clause. Collect the slips. Allow each student to pick a slip and to identify the clause it contains as dependent or independent. After each student has identified a clause, ask him to find another student whose clause will combine with his to make a complete sentence. Allow students to read the newly formed sentences aloud.

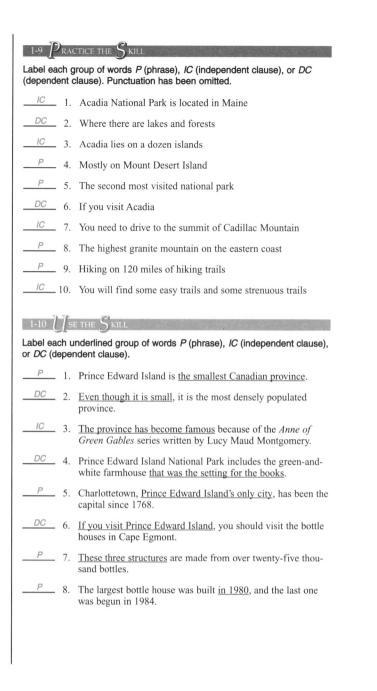

Label each group of words *P* (phrase), *IC* (independent clause), or *DC* (dependent clause). Punctuation has been omitted.

_IC_ 1. Acadia National Park is located in Maine

_DC_ 2. Where there are lakes and forests

_IC_ 3. Acadia lies on a dozen islands

_P_ 4. Mostly on Mount Desert Island

_P_ 5. The second most visited national park

_DC_ 6. If you visit Acadia

_IC_ 7. You need to drive to the summit of Cadillac Mountain

_P_ 8. The highest granite mountain on the eastern coast

_P_ 9. Hiking on 120 miles of hiking trails

_IC_ 10. You will find some easy trails and some strenuous trails

Label each underlined group of words *P* (phrase), *IC* (independent clause), or *DC* (dependent clause).

_P_ 1. Prince Edward Island is <u>the smallest Canadian province</u>.

_DC_ 2. <u>Even though it is small</u>, it is the most densely populated province.

_IC_ 3. <u>The province has become famous</u> because of the *Anne of Green Gables* series written by Lucy Maud Montgomery.

_DC_ 4. Prince Edward Island National Park includes the green-and-white farmhouse <u>that was the setting for the books</u>.

_P_ 5. Charlottetown, <u>Prince Edward Island's only city</u>, has been the capital since 1768.

_DC_ 6. <u>If you visit Prince Edward Island</u>, you should visit the bottle houses in Cape Egmont.

_P_ 7. <u>These three structures</u> are made from over twenty-five thousand bottles.

_P_ 8. The largest bottle house was built <u>in 1980</u>, and the last one was begun in 1984.

12   Chapter 1

Reinforcement

Use Practice the Skill 1-9 to compose independent clauses from dependent clauses. After the students have completed the exercise, instruct them to change all of the dependent clauses to independent clauses by adding the necessary information.

Evaluation

Check the students' answers to the previous reinforcement exercise to evaluate whether they understand what makes a clause dependent or independent.

Enrichment

Materials
• three slips of paper for each student

Divide the class into at least two teams and pass out three slips of paper to each student. Instruct each student to write a phrase on the first slip, an independent clause on the second slip, and a dependent clause on the third slip. The phrases and clauses should all be related to a topic that you assign. Each team will then use its slips of paper to create a paragraph. A representative from each team will read its paragraph aloud. To

use this activity as a contest, assign points: five points for each phrase in the paragraph, ten points for each independent clause, and fifteen points for each dependent clause. The students should be able to identify these elements in their paragraphs.

One on One
Allow your student to complete two sets of paper slips while you complete two sets. Use the twelve slips to create a paragraph. Ask your student to identify the phrases, independent clauses, and dependent clauses in the paragraph.

_DC_   9. The final structure is a chapel, <u>which includes pews and an altar</u>.

_IC_   10. While visiting the island, <u>you can eat plenty of lobster</u>, the most valuable catch of the nation's fishing industry.

Sentence Problems

Knowing how to recognize and correct sentence errors is a necessary writing skill for a good writer. Be careful to avoid these common sentence problems in your own writing.

Fragments

A **fragment** is an incomplete sentence wrongly punctuated as if it were a complete sentence. A fragment can be a phrase, missing a subject or a verb. Sometimes a fragment is a dependent clause that is written as a sentence.

> Charles Dickens, a popular novelist.
> Because the auditions are tomorrow afternoon.

Correct a fragment either by adding a subject or a verb or by joining the dependent clause to a complete sentence.

FRAGMENT	The cat, in the stream of sunlight coming through the glass door.
CORRECT	The cat lay in the stream of sunlight coming through the glass door.
FRAGMENT	After her computer erased her essay.
CORRECT	Janae began making backup disks after her computer erased her essay.

in summary

A **fragment** is an incomplete sentence wrongly punctuated as if it were a complete sentence.

1-11 PRACTICE THE SKILL

A. In the blank, label each group of words _S_ (sentence) or _F_ (fragment).

_S_   1. The story of David and Abigail is fascinating.

_F_   2. Abigail, whose name means "beauty that is more than skin deep."

_S_   3. Abigail's husband, Nabal, was a foolish and wicked man.

_S_   4. Nabal did not give David and his soldiers any hospitality.

Teaching Strategy: Introduction

Use a newspaper or magazine to discuss sentence fragments. Ask students to locate examples of sentence fragments in the headlines of the newspaper or magazine.

Teaching Strategy: Discussion

Remind students that a word group's length, the group's beginning with a capital letter, or its having end punctuation does not make it a sentence. Review the definitions of *fragment* and *sentence* with the students.

Evaluation

If students did not write sentences for the reinforcement activity on page 12, instruct them to rewrite the fragments in Practice the Skill 1-11 to make them complete sentences.

_F_ 5. David, who was angry over the insult from Nabal.

_S_ 6. David planned to attack Nabal and destroy his house.

_F_ 7. Abigail with food and presents for David.

_S_ 8. Abigail interceded for Nabal and her entire household.

_S_ 9. David listened to and accepted Abigail's petition.

_S_ 10. David married Abigail after Nabal's death.

B. Rewrite the fragments from Part A, making them complete sentences. If a group of words is already a sentence, write _C_ in the blank. _(Answers may vary.)_

1. _C_

2. _Abigail means "beauty that is more than skin deep."_

3. _C_

4. _C_

5. _David was very angry over the insult from Nabal._

6. _C_

7. _Abigail brought food and presents for David._

8. _C_

9. _C_

10. _C_

Rewrite the following paragraph, revising each fragment to make it a complete sentence. There are five errors. *(Answers may vary.)*

Archery, like fencing, began as an important battle skill. Today, however, sporting events and hunting being the primary uses of archery. Sometimes people use bows and arrows in pursuit of game. For instance, fish below water. Also, both men and women participate in archery competitions. Which often have targets with bands of five different colors. The outside white ring worth one point, the black ring worth three points, the blue ring worth five points, the red ring worth seven points, and the innermost circle worth nine points. This circle is better known as the bull's-eye. And is the target's golden center.

Archery, like fencing, began as an important battle skill. Today, however,

sporting events and hunting are the primary uses of archery. Sometimes

people use bows and arrows in pursuit of game. For instance, experienced

hunters shoot fish below water. Also, both men and women participate in

archery competitions, which often have targets with bands of five different colors.

The outside white ring is worth one point, the black ring is worth three points,

the blue ring is worth five points, the red ring is worth seven points, and

the innermost circle is worth nine points. This circle is better known as the

bull's-eye and is the target's golden center.

Comma Splices and Fused Sentences

A **comma splice** is two sentences incorrectly joined by only a comma. A **fused sentence** is two sentences incorrectly joined without any punctuation. To correct these errors, use one of the following methods: (1) Separate the two sentence parts with a period or a semicolon. (2) Combine them correctly with a comma and coordinating conjunction. (3) Change one of the sentences into a dependent clause.

Chapter 12: Commas in a Series
of Independent Clauses
p. 279

COMMA SPLICE	Tray grabbed his books, he was late for class.
TWO SENTENCES	Tray grabbed his books. He was late for class.
SEMICOLON	Tray grabbed his books; he was late for class.
CONJUNCTION	Tray grabbed his books, but he was late for class.
DEPENDENT CLAUSE	Tray grabbed his books because he was late for class.

Sentences   15

Teaching Strategy: Induction

Write the following sentences for display: *The navigator spotted an approaching ship. He quickly warned the captain of the submarine.* After reading the sentences aloud, ask the students to identify two ways that the two independent clauses can be combined without changing any words. *(with a comma and a coordinating conjunction or with a semicolon)* Ask the students to identify possible combination errors. Several answers are possible. If students mention using a comma without a conjunction or neglecting both the comma and the conjunction, identify these errors as comma splices and fused sentences respectively.

Teaching Strategy: Discussion

Discuss the terms *comma splice* and *fused sentence.* Tell students that both are sentence errors that involve two or more sentences incorrectly written as one. They can remember the difference by thinking that the comma splice contains a comma. A fused sentence has no punctuation to show that its two parts are independent clauses.

Enrichment

Use Teaching Help 1 (Book 2, p. 37) as additional practice in avoiding sentence errors by joining clauses correctly.

FUSED SENTENCE	Jordan was tired he had worked hard that day.
TWO SENTENCES	Jordan was tired. He had worked hard that day.
SEMICOLON	Jordan was tired; he had worked hard that day.
CONJUNCTION	Jordan was tired, for he had worked hard that day.
DEPENDENT CLAUSE	Jordan was tired after he had worked hard that day.

in summary

A **comma splice** is two sentences incorrectly joined by only a comma.

A **fused sentence** is two sentences incorrectly joined without any punctuation.

1-13 PRACTICE THE SKILL

A. In the blank, label each group of words *S* (sentence), *FS* (fused sentence), or *CS* (comma splice).

CS 1. The gyrfalcon is one of the most beautiful falcon species, these birds often appear white with black speckled stripes on their backs.

FS 2. Gyrfalcons live in areas frequently covered by snow the coloration, therefore, serves as good camouflage.

FS 3. Gyrfalcons live in regions such as Iceland, Sweden, and Siberia other areas such as Canada, Alaska, and Greenland also contain gyrfalcons.

S 4. Usually two feet in length, gyrfalcons are larger than any other falcon species.

CS 5. Gyrfalcons are more persistent than peregrine falcons, gyrfalcons will follow game over a large expanse of territory.

S 6. These birds prey on creatures such as ptarmigan, mink, and rabbits.

CS 7. Gyrfalcons sometimes land to seek out hiding prey, they also like to hunt by surprise.

FS 8. Noblemen once used gyrfalcons in falconry the birds were highly prized creatures.

FS 9. Kings especially liked gyrfalcons the birds' rarity made the creatures special treasures.

S 10. Today gyrfalcons remain one of God's loveliest creations.

B. Rewrite Part A, revising each fused sentence or comma splice to make it a correct sentence. If a group of words is already a sentence, write *C* in the blank. *(Answers may vary.)*

1. *The gyrfalcon is one of the most beautiful falcon species; these birds often appear white with black speckled stripes on their backs.*

2. *Gyrfalcons live in areas frequently covered by snow; the coloration, therefore, serves as good camouflage.*

3. *Gyrfalcons live in regions such as Iceland, Sweden, and Siberia. Other areas such as Canada, Alaska, and Greenland also contain gyrfalcons.*

4. *C*

5. *Gyrfalcons are more persistent than peregrine falcons because gyrfalcons will follow game over a large expanse of territory.*

6. *C*

7. *Gyrfalcons sometimes land to seek out hiding prey. They also like to hunt by surprise.*

8. *Noblemen once used gyrfalcons in falconry; the birds were highly prized creatures.*

9. *Kings especially liked gyrfalcons. The birds' rarity made the creatures special treasures.*

10. *C*

1-14 REVIEW THE SKILL

A. In the blank, label each group of words *S* (sentence), *F* (fragment), *FS* (fused sentence), or *CS* (comma splice).

S   1. Elijah was a prophet of Israel who prophesied about the impending drought in Israel.

FS   2. Elijah prophesied against King Ahab and Queen Jezebel they were angry toward Elijah.

F   3. The wicked king and queen of Israel.

Reinforcement

Ask students to exchange texts after they have completed Practice the Skill 1-13, Part B. Tell each student to identify which method his classmate has used to correct the sentence errors of Part A. Then ask each student to correct the sentences again on his own paper, using a method different from the one already chosen by his classmate.

18   Chapter 1

_____S_____ 4. Because of the wrath of Ahab and Jezebel, God hid Elijah near the brook Cherith.

_____CS_____ 5. Birds brought food, the river provided water.

_____S_____ 6. Later, Elijah lived with a widow woman and her son.

_____CS_____ 7. God performed a miracle, the woman had enough oil and grain throughout the whole drought.

_____F_____ 8. The oil and grain container that never ran dry.

_____FS_____ 9. Elijah also defeated the prophets of Baal he proved that God was the true God.

_____S_____ 10. Elijah passed on his mantle to Elisha.

B. Rewrite Part A, revising each fragment, fused sentence, or comma splice to make it a correct sentence. If a group of words is already a sentence, write _C_ in the blank. _(Answers may vary.)_

1. _C_

2. _Elijah prophesied against King Ahab and Queen Jezebel. They were angry toward Elijah._

3. _Ahab and Jezebel were the wicked king and queen of Israel._

4. _C_

5. _Birds brought food, and the river provided water._

6. _C_

7. _God performed a miracle. The woman had enough oil and grain throughout the whole drought._

8. _The oil and grain container never ran dry._

9. _Elijah also defeated the prophets of Baal. He proved that God was the true God._

10. _C_

Taking Notes

Lesson Support

Teacher's Edition, Book 2
Writing Worksheets—p. 133

Introduction

Tell the students that each person has his own style of taking notes. Some people record everything in rigid outlines on neatly lined paper. Others make charts and diagrams. Preferring unlined paper, more artistic note takers often use arrows and symbols and may even include creative drawings in their notebooks (point out that this does not include doodling). You may want to ask some of the students to show the class an example of their own notes.

Discussion

Ask the students to give examples of occasions when taking notes is especially important. _(class lectures, sermons, important meetings)_ Remind them that taking notes is often beneficial and sometimes necessary when reading books.

Direct the students to read the introduction and the text material about taking notes in school. Direct a discussion about the example, pointing out how the ideas in the paragraph were summarized.

Objectives

Students will

1. take notes on a paragraph the teacher reads.

2. organize their notes clearly and efficiently.

Overview of the Writing Process

Planning—gathering supplies

Drafting—taking notes

Revising—reading over notes and amending for clarity

Publishing—not applicable

Rewrite the following letter, revising each fragment, fused sentence, or comma splice to make it a correct sentence. There are five errors.

(Answers may vary.)

Dear Gwen,

　Here is the information about Lady Jane Grey. I hope that this material from my history class helps, some extra books may help you with your project too. These facts are all that I'm sure about.

　Lady Jane Grey lived during the sixteenth century she was actually queen of England for a little more than a week. Lady Jane knew five languages. Hebrew, one of these languages, Greek another. She was very devout, and many feel she died as a martyr, which seems especially sad because of her young age. Lady Jane was only sixteen. When she died at the hand of her Catholic cousin, Mary I.

　Perhaps you can expand on these facts for your paper I'd really like to read it when you finish.

　　　　　Yours truly,
　　　　　Katrina

Dear Gwen,

　Here is the information about Lady Jane Grey. I hope that this material from

my history class helps; some extra books may help you with your project too.

These facts are all that I'm sure about.

　Lady Jane Grey lived during the sixteenth century. She was actually queen of

England for a little more than a week. Lady Jane knew five languages. Two of

these languages were Hebrew and Greek. She was very devout, and many feel

she died as a martyr, which seems especially sad because of her young age.

Lady Jane was only sixteen when she died at the hand of her Catholic

cousin, Mary I.

　Perhaps you can expand on these facts for your paper. I'd really like to

read it when you finish.

　　　　　Yours truly,

　　　　　Katrina

　Look at the selection from *The Foundling* again.
*   *Which type of sentence does the narrator use?*
*   *Why do you think she uses only that one?*

* *declarative*
* *to maintain an objective point of view*

Planning and Drafting

Materials
*   a paragraph of your choosing that is clearly organized and concrete

Direct the students to listen carefully and to take notes as you read the paragraph you have chosen. Encourage them to refer to the example in the text as a guide.

Revising

Instruct the students to read over their notes and to make any brief amendments necessary for clarity. Ask volunteers to share how they organized their notes.

Scriptural Application

Ask the students to recall a time when they forgot something important. Because the Lord knows that we are forgetful, He commands us to write down and actively strive to remember the things that He tells us. Discuss Deuteronomy 11:18-20 and Proverbs 7:1-3. The purpose of taking notes is to remember. We may hear and read good material, but if we do not remember it, then we are simply wasting our time. Discuss James 1:25. Disciples of Christ must act on the truth, but they cannot if they do not first remember the truth.

Evaluation

Check to see that the assignment has been completed but do not grade it.

Enrichment

Distribute a copy of the Writing Worksheet (Book 2, p. 133) to each student. Encourage the students to use the worksheet as they take notes in class. They may wish to make several copies—one for each class.

Writing in the Classroom

Taking Notes

An old proverb says, "The palest ink is better than the best memory." How well do you remember things? Do you find you can remember things that interest you more easily than those you don't find as interesting?

Even people with so-called photographic memories have to write things down to remind themselves of appointments, grocery lists, and birthdays. The skill is knowing what to write down.

You probably have been taking notes in your classes for some time. You are learning by experience how to decide which things need to be written down exactly, which can be summarized in your own words, and which do not need to be written down at all. If you try to copy down every word a speaker says, you will have to be an expert in shorthand. And even if you are the fastest writer in the West, you do not want a twenty-volume set of notes from every class. Learn to be selective, precise, and legible. Then you will glean the most important facts from lectures—facts that make your studying easier and that increase the probability of good grades.

Taking Good Notes in School

1. Get dates, times, and names exactly right. There is, for instance, a significant difference between January 13 and January 31.

2. Try to follow the outline of a printed source, a speech, or a lecture, getting down main headings but leaving out most of the examples.

3. Summarize main ideas in your own words. For example, the main point of an entire paragraph might be recorded in a few fragments.

Suppose, for example, you wanted to research nicknames. The following paragraph comes up in a computer search you did. What would you write down if you were taking notes?

> Nicknames develop for several reasons. Some people get a nickname because of some physical characteristic: redheads are sometimes called "Red," and lanky fellows are sometimes called "Slim." Other nicknames come from a person's ability or talents. For example, a skillful pianist might be called "Fingers." Still other nicknames are derived from birthplaces or places of residence—a Texan may be called "Tex." These are only a few reasons people get nicknames.

Your notes might read like this:

> Why people get nicknames
>
> • how they look ("Red" for redhead)
> • what they do ("Fingers" for pianist)
> • where they live ("Tex" for Texan)

The main ideas are there, as well as just a few examples to help jog your memory later.

Your Turn

Listen as your teacher reads you a paragraph. Take notes on what you hear, following the suggestions above.

Writing an Essay Answer

Lesson Support

Teacher's Edition, Book 2
Rubrics—p. 147

Introduction

Try to create a realistic environment for the in-class essay assignment. If possible, allow enough time to complete the entire activity in one class period. Introduce the topic of essay answers by comparing it to basketball practice. At practice, players demonstrate to the coach what they have learned.

Ask students the following question: Why is it important to show the coach how well you've learned your basketball skills? *(so he will know you are ready to play in the game)* Likewise, the skills needed to answer an essay question will serve in many of life's challenges, not just in getting a good grade in one class.

Discussion

Direct the students to read the introduction and the text material about writing an essay answer. Encourage them to pay special attention to the examples in Steps 4-7. Refer them to the sections in Chapter 15 about essay writing. Answer any questions they may have after reading this material.

Writing an Essay Answer

Usually when you are asked to write an essay, you have a few days to think it over. There may be times, though, when you have just a few minutes to plan an essay. (This need for swift, efficient planning should not result from putting off doing your homework until the hour before it is due!)

The essay test, surprising as you may find this, was not developed during the Middle Ages as a torture device. It is simply another form of test. Unlike most objective tests, the essay lets you show connections among the facts you present. And once you learn how to use it, the essay form may be less intimidating than true-false or fill-in-the-blank forms.

1 Assuming, of course, that you have studied the material you are to be tested over, the first thing you should do is carefully read the directions and the question (or questions, if you are given several to choose from).

2 On a separate piece of paper jot down the main ideas you will use in your answer. Write down any dates, names, or places that you don't want to leave out. This step is often called a scattergram.

3 When you have sketched out the information to include, look it over. What is most important? What is least important? Mark all points that seem to belong together, that deal with the same idea. (Use a different mark for each group.) You now have a rough outline.

4 Write a thesis statement. The easiest way is to turn the question into a declarative sentence. For example:

> QUESTION Why are ants a superior insect?
> ANSWER Ants are a superior insect because they are numerous, adaptable, and long-lived.

5 Write a topic sentence that covers the first point on your scattergram (Step 2) and that ties into the thesis statement. For example:

> Ants are a dominant group because they can adapt to changes in weather, food, and location.

6 Write and thoroughly support a topic sentence for each of the main points on your scattergram. Give as many clear details as you can within your time limits. Do not assume that the reader will accept a statement without sufficient proof.

> Ants are a superior group partly because they live longer than most insects. Worker ants live from four to seven years, and queens live from thirteen to fifteen years. Because ants live so long, their colonies are rather stable and can last twenty or thirty years.

7 Conclude the essay with a restatement of the thesis—saying the thesis another way, not merely copying it down again.

> Because ants are plentiful, flexible, and able to live a long time, they have become a very prosperous group.

Your Turn

Write an essay in response to a question your teacher will give you.

Planning and Drafting

Materials
- Create a handout containing an essay question (consult the history or science teacher for some ideas). Include instructions such as "Read the following question and respond with an essay of three to five paragraphs."

Distribute the essay question. Remind the students of the importance of planning (Steps 1-3). Inform them of any time limit. Allow students to write their essays.

Revising

Instruct the students to read over their essays and to make any changes for clarity and correctness. Notify them when they have only ten minutes left to work.

Publishing

Collect the essays.

Scriptural Application

Pose this theoretical essay question: "How does a child of God respond correctly to life's trials?" Read Psalm 23 as David's "in-class" response to this question.

Evaluation

For help in grading this assignment, see "Grading Writing Assignments" (p. x) and Rubric 1 (Book 2, p. 147).

Enrichment

Encourage the students to transfer these essay writing skills to their other classes when in-class responses are called for.

2 NOUNS

Objectives

Students will

1. identify words in sentences as nouns.

2. form the singular and plural forms of nouns.

3. correct misused plural forms of nouns in sentences.

4. form the possessive forms of nouns.

5. evaluate and revise a paragraph to include possessive nouns.

6. distinguish between common and proper nouns.

7. distinguish between count and non-count nouns.

8. identify nouns as collective and determine whether a collective noun is singular or plural.

9. determine the correct forms for compound nouns.

10. distinguish between compound and collective nouns.

11. determine the function of a noun in a sentence.

12. write sentences using nouns in various functions.

13. evaluate and revise a piece of writing for errors in noun form and usage.

Rikki-Tikki-Tavi

by Rudyard Kipling

This is the beginning of a story about a brave and resourceful mongoose. Set in India, the story recounts how Rikki-tikki-tavi returns the kindness of the family who saved his life.

He was a mongoose, rather like a little cat in his fur and his tail, but quite like a weasel in his head and his habits. His eyes and the end of his restless nose were pink. He could scratch himself anywhere he pleased with any leg, front or back, that he chose to use. He could fluff up his tail till it looked like a bottle brush, and his war cry as he scuttled through the long grass was: *Rikk-tikk-tikki-tikki-tchk!*

One day, a high summer flood washed him out of the burrow where he lived with his father and mother, and carried him, kicking and clucking, down a roadside ditch. He found a little wisp of grass floating there, and clung to it till he lost his senses. When he revived, he was lying in the hot sun in the middle of a garden path, very draggled indeed, and a small boy was saying, "Here's a dead mongoose. Let's have a funeral."

"No," said his mother, "let's take him in and dry him. Perhaps he isn't really dead."

They took him into the house, and a big man picked him up between his finger and thumb and said he was not dead but half choked. So they wrapped him in cotton wool, and warmed him over a little fire, and he opened his eyes and sneezed.

"Now," said the big man (he was an Englishman who had just moved into the bungalow,) "don't frighten him, and we'll see what he'll do."

It is the hardest thing in the world to frighten a mongoose, because he is eaten up from nose to tail with curiosity. The motto of all the mongoose family is "Run and find out," and Rikki-tikki was a true mongoose. He looked at the cotton wool, decided that it was not good to eat, ran all around the table, sat up and put his fur in order, scratched himself, and jumped onto the boy's shoulder.

- *What two other animals is a mongoose compared to? What is the mongoose's tail compared to?*

- *What words in the story help you identify the setting?*

- *What words would you use to change the setting to Siberia?*

You probably used mostly nouns to answer these questions. Without nouns, we could not communicate. (Your first word was probably a noun.) Nouns and verbs are the main parts of a sentence. In the excerpt you just read, nouns help us not only to see the place but also to determine the time and to understand the characters.

- *a cat and a weasel; a bottle brush*

- *mongoose, long grass, summer flood, roadside ditch, garden path, bungalow*

- *Answers will vary.*

Lesson Support

Student Text
Chapter 2 Review—pp. 399-401

Teacher's Edition, Book 1
Bulletin Boards—p. 445

Teacher's Edition, Book 2
Pretests—pp. 3-4

Teaching Helps—pp. 38-39

Concept Reinforcements—pp. 91-93

Literature Link

Read aloud (or ask a student to read aloud) the excerpt from "Rikki-Tikki-Tavi"; lead a discussion using the questions in the student text.

Nouns

A **noun** names a person, place, thing, or idea. Nouns make up the largest group of words in the English language.

PERSON	*Thomas Edison* invented the light bulb.
PLACE	*Vatican City* is the smallest *country* in the *world*.
THING	Let's put a *candle* on the dinner *table*.
IDEA	A godly person's speech is characterized by *kindness*.

Forms of Nouns

Nouns appear in different forms: singular, singular possessive, plural, and plural possessive. Most nouns can appear in all four forms.

SINGULAR	The *dog* has proved himself to be a friend of man.
SINGULAR POSSESSIVE	A *dog's* friendship is constant and dutiful.
PLURAL	*Dogs* have performed many amazing tasks.
PLURAL POSSESSIVE	Throughout history, many *dogs'* acts of loyalty have been recorded.

Plural Forms of Nouns

A **singular** noun names only one person, place, thing, or idea. A **plural** noun indicates that there is more than one. Use the following rules to change singular nouns to plural.

Regular Plural Formation

Add *s* to the singular form of most nouns.

bone	bones
tail	tails

Add *es* to singular nouns ending with *s, x, z, ch,* and *sh.*

bus	buses
box	boxes
buzz	buzzes
church	churches
dish	dishes

If the word ends in *y* preceded by a consonant, change the final *y* to *i* and add *es.*

cry	cries

If a noun ends in a *y* preceded by a vowel, add only *s.*

essay	essays

If a noun ends in *f* or *fe,* consult your dictionary. For some nouns, add *s;* for others, change the *f* to *v* and add *s* or *es.*

reef	reefs
wife	wives

Chapter 10: Rules for Spelling Singular Present-Tense Verbs and Plural Nouns p. 236

ESL: Students may have difficulty understanding that most English nouns do not show different genders; many languages (such as Spanish, French, and German) change the form of their nouns based on the nouns' grammatical classification as masculine, feminine, or neuter. English has gender in only a few nouns whose meanings are innately masculine or feminine (e.g., *actor/actress, widower/widow, host/hostess*).

ESL: Some languages do not have plural noun forms or do not pronounce them. Even after learning how to form and use English plurals, ESL students often leave them off in their writing and speech.

Teaching Strategy: Introduction

Materials
- several small objects on a tray

Bring in a tray full of small objects (a set of keys, an egg, a small car, coins, a postcard, a family portrait, etc.). Allow students to view the objects for thirty seconds and then cover the tray. Give students one minute to list as many objects as they can remember. Ask for a volunteer to read his list aloud. (*Note:* Try to have at least one item that could be considered a representation of an idea; for example, a heart could represent love.)

Teaching Strategy: Participation

Use the items from the lists generated above to spell the plural forms of nouns. Instruct students to write the plural of each of the words on their lists. Or instruct them to trade lists and write the plurals of someone else's list.

Teaching Strategy: Discussion

Point out that the plural forms of most singular nouns adhere to the first two spelling rules on page 24.

If a noun ends in *o,* consult your dictionary. For some nouns, add *s;* for others, add *es.*

memo	memos
tornado	tornadoes

Irregular Plural Formation

Some nouns have identical singular and plural forms.

sheep	sheep
moose	moose
deer	deer

Some nouns have unusual plural forms.

woman	women
goose	geese
louse	lice

Add *'s* to make a letter or word plural.

one *t*	many *t*'s
one *the*	many *the*'s

Add only *s* to make a number plural.

1900	1900s

Pronunciation of Plurals and Possessives

English has three different pronunciations for its plural and possessive noun forms.

- Plurals after voiceless consonants (consonants that you form only with your mouth, but do not say with your vocal cords, such as *f, k, p,* or *t*) are pronounced /s/.
  Examples: *cats, ropes, larks, cuffs*
- Plurals after vowel sounds and voiced consonants (consonants that you both form with your mouth and pronounce with your vocal cords, such as *b, d, g, l, m, n, r, v,* or *w*) are pronounced /z/.
  Examples: *dogs, dolls, cans, cows, arias.*
- Plurals after s, *x, z, ch,* or *sh* sounds (sounds very similar to the /s/ sound of the plural and possessive endings) are pronounced /ez/.
  Examples: *buses, boxes, quizzes, churches, dishes.*

---

in summary

A **noun** names a person, place, thing, or idea.

Most nouns can appear in four different forms: **singular, singular possessive, plural,** and **plural possessive.**

Add *s* or *es* to most singular nouns to form the plural.

Some nouns have irregular forms for the plural.

Teaching Strategy: Induction

Ask students to think of additional words that follow the other spelling rules on pages 24-25. *(e.g., sentry, prey, muff, knife, solo, potato, beef, child, mouse)*

One on One

Assist your student in making up a spelling bee for the family (or for younger siblings).

Reinforcement

Remind students that most plurals are not made with an apostrophe.

Change each underlined noun to its plural form and write it in the blank.

_____*l's*_____ 1. Fala (spelled with only one *l*) was a Scottish terrier belonging to Franklin D. Roosevelt.

_____*Scotties*_____ 2. This adorable <u>Scottie</u> received plenty of publicity and now enjoys a special place in history because of his renown.

_____*1940s*_____ 3. Margaret Suckley, Roosevelt's cousin, gave Fala to the president in <u>1940</u>.

_____*sheep*_____ 4. Roosevelt had owned dogs before; instead of chasing <u>sheep</u>, his spirited German shepherd once chased Britain's prime minister.

_____*dogs*_____ 5. Fala, though, became the most famous <u>dog</u>; he was on the *Augusta* when the commander in chief and Churchill signed the Atlantic Charter.

_____*limousines*_____ 6. Fala frequently rode in the president's <u>limousine</u>.

_____*men*_____ 7. A <u>man</u> from the Secret Service had to evict a resentful Fala from the car when the Scottie tried to join Roosevelt for his third inauguration.

_____*ways*_____ 8. As a <u>way</u> to accuse Roosevelt of wasting money, Republicans once condemned his deploying a navy ship to the Aleutian Islands to pick up a forgotten Fala.

_____*wives*_____ 9. In a well-known fireside chat, Roosevelt claimed that the rumor angered Fala; the president said he could understand charges against him and his <u>wife</u> but not against his dog.

_____*Cemeteries*_____ 10. Unlike one of Roosevelt's dogs buried in the Rosedale Dog <u>Cemetery</u>, Fala has his grave in New York beside the president.

Underline the nouns. Correct any incorrect plurals by writing the correction in the blank.

_____*cities*_____ 1. In Edinburgh, one of Scotland's largest <u>citys</u>, stands a statue to a Skye terrier known as Greyfriars' Bobby.

_____ 2. Bobby lived with a poor Scottish man named John Gray during the 1800s.

_____ 3. After Gray died, this small terrier displayed tremendous loyalty because he remained near the grave for at least ten years.

_____ 4. Bobby usually stayed near Greyfriars' Church-yard during the day and reportedly slept on the grave at night.

lunches 5. Though Gray died in 1858, folks say Bobby continued his visits to the place where he and Gray used to eat their lunchs.

_____ 6. In fact, some sources claim that the dog would faithfully pick up his bone around one o'clock.

strays 7. Eventually, Bobby received a collar so that the police would not confuse him with straies wandering the streets.

centuries 8. Baroness Burdett-Coutts provided funds for the fountain containing Bobby's statue so that people in later centurys would remember his faithfulness.

lives 9. Bobby's remarkable story has influenced the lifes of people beyond Scotland.

photos 10. Today tourists desiring special souvenirs of their time in Edinburgh have photoes taken beside this popular memorial.

Possessive Forms of Nouns

The possessive is formed by adding *'s* or just an apostrophe. Use the following rules to form the possessive of nouns.

Add *'s* to the singular form of the noun even if the noun already ends in *s*.

dog   dog's bone
boss   boss's wish

The names *Jesus* and *Moses* are two exceptions. These names traditionally end with only an apostrophe.

Jesus   Jesus' love
Moses   Moses' excuse

Nouns   27

Add only an apostrophe to a plural noun that already ends in *s*.

| bushes | bushes' berries |
| the Millers | the Millers' dogs |

If a plural noun does not end in *s*, add *'s* to form the plural possessive.

| children | children's pets |

in summary

To form the singular possessive, add *'s* to the singular form.

To form the plural possessive, add *'* or *'s* to the plural form.

2-3 PRACTICE THE SKILL

In the blank rewrite each of the italicized phrases to form an equivalent phrase containing a possessive noun.

1. Some of *the most famous figures of literature* have had special canine companions.

   literature's most famous figures

2. Keeper, a mongrel described by some sources as a bulldog and by some as part mastiff, was *the pet of Ellis Bell.*

   Ellis Bell's pet

3. You may know this author by another name, since Ellis Bell was *the pseudonym of Emily Brontë.*

   Emily Brontë's pseudonym

4. Brontë and Keeper often wandered the heaths together because *the atmosphere of the moors* held a special attraction for Brontë.

   the moors' atmosphere

5. When inside, Keeper commonly caused problems by leaving *the dirty prints of his paws* on the clean, white beds.

   his paws' dirty prints

6. The maid once found Keeper taking his nap on a clean bed, and he soon discovered *the displeasure of his mistress.*

   his mistress's displeasure

7. Two ladies watched Brontë chastise the dog severely—a feat evoking *the surprise of the women,* since Keeper was quite intimidating.

   the women's surprise

8. According to the diary of one man, Brontë once put pepper in Keeper's nose to drag the dog from a fight—reportedly evoking *the astonishment of the village men.*

    the village men's astonishment

9. Some sources say Brontë gave *the food of Floss* and Keeper's food to the dogs shortly before she died, but this account seems questionable.

    Floss's food

10. The claim that Keeper was part of *the company of the mourners* when Brontë died and that he then whined outside her bedroom door for days seems more reliable.

    the mourners' company

2-4 REVIEW THE SKILL

Underline any incorrect possessives and rewrite the words correctly in the blanks below the paragraph.

Togo was a Siberian husky who helped save many Alaskans and Eskimos from diphtherias' devastating effects. When the governor decided to use dogsleds to deliver a life-saving antitoxin to Nome, Togo was chosen to lead Leonhard Seppala's team of dogs. During the citys' 1925 diphtheria epidemic, twenty sledders and their dogs carried the serum over 650 miles. The other driver's journeys were 25 to 50 miles, but Togo and Sepalla went 91 miles. Despite blizzard conditions and temperatures well below zero, Togo proved to be as good as any compass' guidance. Togo's trek helped prevent more peoples' deaths. Without Togo, many men's, women's, and childrens' lives would have ended needlessly.

diphtheria's, city's, drivers', compass's, people's, children's

Kinds of Nouns

English has several different kinds of nouns. We describe nouns by placing them into one or more of the following categories.

Common and Proper Nouns

Every noun is either common or proper. A **common noun** names a type of person, place, thing, or idea. A **proper noun** names a specific person, place, thing, or idea. Proper nouns are always capitalized.

COMMON	girl	city	school
PROPER	Maria	Paris	Redwood High

in summary

A **common noun** names a type of person, place, thing, or idea.

A **proper noun** names a specific person, place, thing, or idea. Proper nouns are always capitalized.

2-5 PRACTICE THE SKILL

Label each italicized noun *C* (common) or *P* (proper).

- _C_ 1. The number of products sold for *pets* is incredible.
- _P_ 2. *Zack* pampers his dog with some interesting items.
- _P_ 3. Zack recently purchased *Aldo* a toy box.
- _P_ 4. He also gave Aldo some glow-in-the-dark *Frisbees*.
- _C_ 5. Zack finds new toys on *websites*.
- _C_ 6. My *neighbors* are extravagant too.
- _C_ 7. Mrs. Danton sews special clothes for her *poodle*.
- _P_ 8. The other day, *Mrs. Danton* dressed her poodle in a sweater and boots.
- _C_ 9. Of course, it is *winter*.
- _C_ 10. Well, don't forget gourmet dog cookies, a dog *board game,* or a doggie backpack.

Teaching Strategy: Demonstration

Before discussing page 30, play a game of fast answers. Give students a common noun such as *building* and ask students to respond with a corresponding specific name. *(Chrysler Building)* Give each student a chance to answer. Point out that their answers are proper nouns and that the words you gave were common nouns.

Evaluation

If you have assigned sentence diagramming with Practice the Skill 2-5, check students' answers using page 456.

Underline the common nouns once and the proper nouns twice.

1. Central Park in New York City contains the statue of another dog made famous by the 1925 race to Nome.

2. Balto, a black husky owned by Leonhard Seppala, received tremendous praise for leading the team of Gunnar Kaasen.

3. While many drivers and dogs carried the medicine, Balto and Kaasen received much of the glory because, as the last team, they took the serum into the city.

4. Though Seppala skipped Balto when picking huskies for his team, Balto was a good leader and deserves some honor.

5. For example, Balto continued to lead the team successfully when Kaasen could not see the way during a blizzard.

6. Once during the trip, Balto refused to obey orders. His disobedience stopped the other dogs from freezing their feet in water that had broken through ice on the trail ahead.

7. Following their famous trek of fifty-three miles, Balto and the dogs on his team ended up in the Cleveland Zoo in Cleveland, Ohio.

8. When Balto died, his body was preserved; it is displayed in the Cleveland Museum of Natural History.

9. Today the Iditarod, a famous dogsled race, reminds many people of this race to Nome run by Balto and the other dogs.

10. Some think the genetic accidents taught by Darwinism produced such a fine dog as Balto and gave him the instincts to accomplish his great feat, but Christianity teaches us that dogs were designed by an intelligent Creator.

Count and Noncount Nouns

Every common noun is either a count noun or a noncount noun. **Count nouns** can be made plural. **Noncount nouns** cannot be made plural.

> COUNT *a penny, a few pennies, some pennies*
> NONCOUNT *milk, some milk, plenty of milk*

Some nouns can be used as count nouns or noncount nouns, with a different meaning.

ESL: Many words that are considered noncount in English are count words in other languages. Be aware that mistakes in this area may simply result from a student's applying what his native language does.

Nouns 31

Teaching Strategy: Demonstration

Materials
- several dollar bills

Bring in several dollar bills. Ask students to list various names for the bills. *(dollars, ones, bills, money, cash)* List the words for display and ask the students to use the various words in sentences. *(The teacher has three dollars. She had many ones. I have very little money. I don't have much cash.)* Encourage students to try different types of modifiers (a lot of, a few, a small amount of, several, etc.) with the different words. Ask the students whether they could use the modifier *much* with the word *dollars* or if they could use *three* with *cash.*

Teaching Strategy: Induction

Ask students to make a list of "rules" for the words naming the dollar bills. Ask the students these questions:

- Can the words be divided into categories? *(yes)*
- How many? *(two)*
- How should they be divided? *(dollars, ones, bills; money, cash)*

Review the material on count and noncount nouns on pages 31-32. Ask the students which of their lists contains count nouns and which of their lists contains noncount nouns. *(first—count; second—noncount)*

Teaching Strategy: Discussion

If you have a copy of *The Writer's Toolbox,* compare the students' list of rules about count and noncount nouns with the list in the book.

NONCOUNT	Mom bought some *chocolate*.
COUNT	Would you like a *chocolate*?
COUNT	Do you like *eggs* for breakfast?
NONCOUNT	There's *egg* on your napkin.
NONCOUNT	He washed his *hair*.
COUNT	There are two *hairs* on your jacket.
NONCOUNT	Jim really likes *cheese*.
COUNT	He brought three different *cheeses* for the party.
COUNT	Two *chickens* walked toward the fence.
NONCOUNT	The buffet included ham, *chicken,* and beef.

Although noncount nouns are always singular in form, they cannot have *a, an,* or *one* before them.

WRONG   We breathe an air
We breathe one air.

RIGHT   We breathe air.
We breathe the air.

Noncount nouns use *much* and *a little* rather than *many* and *a few,* which are only for count nouns.

NONCOUNT   How much milk did you buy?

COUNT   How many cans of vegetables did you buy?

in summary

Count nouns can be made plural to show how many.

Noncount nouns are always singular in form.

2-7 PRACTICE THE SKILL

Label each italicized noun *CO* (count) or *N* (noncount).

_CO_ 1. Stubby is a bulldog that became a World War I *hero*.

_N_ 2. His *bravery* was notable, and he received medals given personally by General Pershing.

_CO_ 3. Stubby saved many soldiers' *lives* in the trenches of France and Belgium.

_CO_ 4. He would save the soldiers by barking before a gas *attack* would occur.

_CO_ 5. After Stubby was wounded, he was placed in a Paris *hospital*.

___N___ 6. He gave great *comfort* to the wounded soldiers in the hospital when he walked around to their beds.

___N___ 7. Physicians were amazed at the *therapy* he provided the soldiers and noted how quickly they recovered after a visit from Stubby.

___N___ 8. After the war, Stubby received *honor* by being invited to the White House by two different presidents.

___CO___ 9. With all his *honors,* Stubby led many military parades.

___CO___ 10. Stubby's *death* came in 1926 after a life of service to people.

2-8 PRACTICE THE SKILL

Underline the count nouns once and the noncount nouns twice. (Consider only the common nouns.)

1. A famous dog in American advertising is Nipper.

2. Francis Barraud painted Nipper, his brother's dog, which was looking into and listening to a phonograph.

3. The darkness of the painting dissatisfied Francis, so the painter went to the Gramophone Company Limited of London to borrow a bright brass horn for the phonograph.

4. This company purchased the rights to the work and introduced the painting in their advertisements.

5. Emile Berliner received the rights for a trademark in the United States.

6. In 1901 the Victor Talking Machine Company obtained the trademark's rights.

7. In 1929 RCA purchased the company and received the trademark.

8. Nipper has appeared on millions of products.

9. Because of Nipper's longevity, Nipper has been joined by Chipper, a puppy who represents the future of electronics.

10. Nipper is also a famous landmark on Broadway in Albany, New York.

Collective Nouns

Collective nouns are nouns that name a group. When a collective noun is singular in form, it can be either singular or plural in meaning. Look at the meaning of the sentence to determine whether the noun is referring to the group as a unit or to the individual members of the group.

Advanced students may notice the changes in the verb for collective nouns. Tell them that keeping in mind whether the word is referring to the whole box (the team or family or group) or to the individual circles (the members of the team or family or group) will help them with subject-verb agreement and pronoun-antecedent agreement later.

Teaching Strategy: Demonstration

Use a simple diagram to show the logic behind collective nouns. Draw a square and label it "team." Draw several circles inside the square (perhaps nine for a baseball team) and label them "team" also. Read the example sentences on page 34 aloud and point to the corresponding part of the drawing.

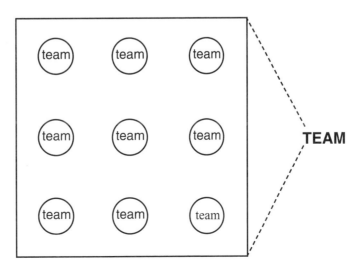

SINGULAR The *team* practices every day after school for the game.
PLURAL The *team* take their jerseys home after the game.

The first sentence refers to the team as a unit. The second sentence refers to the individual members of the team.

in summary

Collective nouns name a group. When a collective noun is singular in form, it can be either singular or plural in meaning.

2-9 PRACTICE THE SKILL

For each category underline the one collective noun.

Example: **Home:** children, mother, <u>family</u>, babies

1. **Sports:** soccer, coach, <u>team</u>, player

2. **Religion:** Bible, <u>congregation</u>, Christian, belief

3. **Government:** <u>Senate</u>, law, judge, courtroom

4. **Education:** <u>class</u>, teacher, pupil, instruction

5. **Birds:** wing, flight, <u>flock</u>, nest

6. **Music:** <u>orchestra</u>, director, player, instrument

7. **Animals:** dog, pet, <u>herd</u>, quadruped

8. **Armed services:** general, corporal, <u>army</u>, barracks

9. **Hospital workers:** <u>staff</u>, doctor, nurse, employee

10. **Fish:** aquarium, catfish, <u>school</u>, shark

2-10 REVIEW THE SKILL

Underline each collective noun. In the blank, label the noun *S* (singular) or *P* (plural) in meaning.

_S_ 1. The <u>community</u> has recognized that stray dogs have become a problem.

_S_ 2. Last week, a <u>pack</u> of dogs was found in the city.

_S_ 3. The general <u>public</u> has raised an outcry to the local government.

_P_ 4. The Gibson <u>family</u> are asking their neighbors to sign a petition.

Teaching Strategy: Participation

Encourage students to come up with their own sentences using other collective nouns. *(group, class, family, etc.)*

  _S_   5. An entire <u>litter</u> of puppies was found in the woods behind their house.

  _P_   6. The neighborhood soccer <u>team</u> are taking the stray puppies to their homes.

  _S_   7. A <u>committee</u> will meet next Monday to form new laws about stray animals.

  _S_   8. An <u>audience</u> will be allowed to sit and listen but not to speak.

  _P_   9. At the second meeting, a <u>group</u> of concerned citizens will be allowed to express their various concerns.

  _S_ 10. This <u>panel</u> will discuss the various solutions it has devised to solve the problem.

Compound Nouns

Compound nouns are formed by combining two or more words. The meaning of a compound word is often a special combination of the meanings of the two original words. Compound nouns can be written as one word, one hyphenated word, or two words.

> staircase
> self-assessment
> high school

To form the plural of a compound noun, change the most important word to its plural form. If you are unsure which part of the compound noun should be made plural, check a dictionary for the correct form.

base+ball	baseball	baseballs
father+in+law	father-in-law	fathers-in-law
bird+dog	bird dog	bird dogs

Notice the intonation difference between compound nouns and adjectives describing nouns.

- Compound nouns in English have their main stress (their loudest syllable) in the first part of the compound: <u>high</u>chair, <u>red</u>head.
- However, when the same two words appear as an adjective and a noun, the noun has the main stress: high <u>chair</u>, red <u>head</u>.

in summary

Compound nouns are formed by combining two or more words.

To form the plural of a compound, change the most important word to its plural form.

Nouns   35

ESL: Using and spelling compound words can often be a problem for ESL students whose native languages do not use compounding to form words. Therefore, students may sometimes come up with awkward English paraphrases such as "blanket of baby" rather than "baby blanket." The most common English compounding patterns are the following:

- noun + noun: *baseball*
- adj + noun: *redhead*
- noun + verb + *er*: *can opener*
- adj/adv + noun + *ed*: *fair-minded*
- prep + verb: *undertake*

As evident from this list, punctuation of compound words is not very consistent. Some words can appear correctly in all three forms (e.g., babysitter, baby sitter, baby-sitter). Encourage your ESL students (and native English speakers) to check their dictionaries when they are not sure of the punctuation of a compound word.

Writing Link

Direct students to work individually or in pairs to combine words to form interesting compound nouns of their own. Remind them that their compound nouns can be one word, two words, or hyphenated words. Ask them to write definitions of their new words. *(leafswing—a swing made of leaves; picture monkey—someone who always goofs off for photographs)* Tell them to illustrate their words and definitions to share them with the rest of the class.

Enrichment

Use Teaching Help 2A (Book 2, p. 38) for more practice in identifying the forms and kinds of nouns.

Underline the singular compound noun in each sentence. In the blank write the correct plural form of the underlined compound noun.

helpmates   1. A dog has always been a special <u>helpmate</u> to man.

battlefields   2. Dogs have often been used for rescue; in fact, many wounded soldiers on the <u>battlefield</u> owe their lives to dogs.

bloodhounds   3. A <u>bloodhound</u> is often used by police in search and rescue because of its keen sense of smell.

policemen   4. A <u>policeman</u> can also use dogs as companions to help ensure safety.

dogsleds   5. Also, adventurers have used dogs and a <u>dogsled</u> to deliver supplies to remote areas during winter and to save lives.

snowstorms   6. All over the world, dogs help people during a <u>snowstorm</u>, especially if a person gets lost in the snow or buried in an avalanche.

service dogs   7. A <u>service dog</u> is a special aid to persons with physical disabilities.

purebreds   8. The owner of a <u>purebred</u> can earn revenue by breeding his pet.

caregivers   9. Many have realized that a dog is a special <u>caregiver</u> to people with health needs.

nursing homes   10. Petting a dog may help a patient in a <u>nursing home</u> feel less lonely.

Underline the compound and collective nouns. Label the nouns *cd* (compound) or *coll* (collective).

coll   1. A <u>pack</u> of dogs may include dogs that vary greatly in physical appearance and in ability.

cd   2. <u>Gundogs</u> include pointers, setters, retrievers, and spaniels; they aid hunters who use guns.

cd   3. Although some dogs use their sense of smell to hunt, the <u>gazehound</u> pursues its game by sight.

coll   4. The collie may be used to keep a <u>flock</u> of sheep from straying.

cd   5. A <u>bulldog</u> and a Dalmatian are examples of nonsporting dogs that are large companion dogs.

cd   6. A Chihuahua may weigh only one to six pounds, but a <u>wolfhound</u> may weigh between 126 and 145 pounds.

coll   7. Your <u>family</u> might prefer a registered dog, but the cost could be high.

cd   8. Dogs have varying lengths of hair, but all dogs have an <u>undercoat</u>, fine hairs that help keep the animal warm.

cd   9. Life <u>spans</u> of dogs vary according to their size; a small breed may live fifteen to sixteen years.

cd 10. German <u>shepherds</u> look similar to wolves in form and coloring.

Nouns   37

Functions of Nouns in the Sentence

A noun can have several different functions in sentences. The word *family* is a noun, and in the sentence *My family owns a station wagon,* the word *family* functions as the subject. Here are several examples of the different noun functions in a sentence.

SUBJECT	The *store* will reopen on Monday.
PREDICATE NOUN	The meeting place is a *store* on North Street.
DIRECT OBJECT	He closes the *store* at 5:00 P.M.
INDIRECT OBJECT	She ordered the *store* new windows.
OBJECT OF PREPOSITION	The front of the *store* needs painting.
NOUN OF DIRECT ADDRESS	*Jeremy,* get the door, please.
APPOSITIVE	My favorite picture, a *photograph* of my dad and me, sits on my dresser.

A noun that names the person to whom you are speaking is called a **noun of direct address.**

Jared, would you like to come over for dinner this evening?
I would be happy to deliver the address, *sir.*

A word or phrase that follows a noun or pronoun and renames it is called an **appositive.**

The winning team, *the Spartans,* will advance to the state competition.
My first-hour class, *Introduction to Computer Science,* is challenging.

A predicate noun has a linking verb before it, but an appositive does not.

PREDICATE NOUN	Jared is Tom's best *friend.*
APPOSITIVE	Jared, Tom's best *friend,* went hiking with him.

in summary

Nouns can function as subjects, predicate nouns, direct objects, indirect objects, objects of prepositions, nouns of direct address, and appositives.

A **noun of direct address** names the person to whom you are speaking.

An **appositive** is a word or phrase that follows a noun or pronoun and renames it.

2-13 PRACTICE THE SKILL

Label the function of each italicized noun *S* (subject), *DO* (direct object), *IO* (indirect object), *OP* (object of the preposition), *PN* (predicate noun), *App* (appositive), or *NA* (noun of direct address).

_NA_ 1. *Class,* do you know anything about a dog in space?

_OP_ 2. In 1957 the Soviet Union sent an artificial satellite with a dog on board to *space.*

Teaching Strategy: Participation

Students should be familiar enough with noun functions to compile a list of the various functions a noun can have in a sentence. Ask them to list as many noun functions as they can. Write their answers for display. After you have written the first five noun functions listed on page 38, ask students to write five sentences using a noun in each of the first five functions. For an added challenge, ask students to use the same word for all five functions.

Teaching Strategy: Induction

Write the following sentences for display: *Frances, please be careful. My favorite room, the underline{library}, is replete with books and comfortable chairs.* Ask students what the underlined words are doing in the sentences. Elicit from the students that the word *Frances* addresses someone and that the word *library* renames *room.* Ask the students what words that function in these two ways are called. *(nouns of direct address, and appositives)*

Evaluation

If you have assigned sentence diagramming with Practice the Skill 2-13, check students' answers using page 457.

App   3. That dog, *Laika,* was a stray from the streets of Moscow.

PN   4. Laika was the first live *creature* in space.

DO   5. Technology at that time did not permit the *return* of space-craft.

S   6. *Laika* could stay calm for extended periods of time.

S   7. *Sputnik II* carried the dog for a week. Then she died from lack of oxygen.

IO   8. The Russians built *Laika* a memorial after forty years.

DO   9. The Soviet Union launched at least thirteen other *dogs* between 1957 and 1961.

PN   10. The use of dogs in space was the *preparation* for the flight of human astronauts into space.

2-14 REVIEW THE SKILL

Write a sentence using the specified noun in the function stated.
(Answers will vary.)

1. brother, *subject:* My brother owns ten dogs.

2. bone, *predicate noun:* My dog's favorite treat is a bone.

3. stick, *direct object:* I threw the stick to my dog.

4. my sister, *indirect object:* My parents gave my sister a puppy for her birthday.

5. house, *object of the preposition:* After the rain, I did not allow my dog in the house.

6. Paul, *noun of direct address:* Paul, did you know that?

7. dog biscuit, *appositive:* I give my dog a prize, a dog biscuit, for good behavior.

Enrichment

Use Teaching Help 2B (Book 2, p. 39). For each specified noun function, the students will identify a noun in the paragraph.

Teaching Strategy: Participation

Ask students to write sentences about a real or an imaginary pet. Tell them to use nouns of direct address and appositives in their sentences.

History Link

Encourage students to read more about the space dog Laika or *Sputnik II.* Allow students to present their findings to the class.

Scriptural Application

Ask students to research what the Bible has to say about dogs. If the students do not have access to a concordance, you may need to direct them to passages such as I Samuel 17:43; I Kings 14:11; Psalm 22:16; Proverbs 26:11; Ecclesiastes 9:4; Isaiah 56:10; Matthew 7:6; Philippians 3:2; and Revelation 22:15. Guide their study by asking them questions that include the following:

- Are dogs usually referred to positively or negatively? *(negatively)*

- Do you think the dogs during the time of the Bible were mostly wild or domesticated? *(wild)* What reasons do you have for your answer? *(They are not named, they do not have owners, and they often appear in packs.)*

- People are sometimes described as dogs in the Bible. What types of people are called dogs? *(people who are deceptive, wicked, or unrighteous)*

- *boy's; bottle brush, war cry, cotton wool (roadside is another compound noun, but it functions like an adjective in this passage); curiosity; Englishman, Rikki-tikki*

- *Answers will vary.*

Rewrite the following paragraph, correcting any fragments, comma splices, fused sentences, incorrect plural noun forms, incorrect possessive noun forms, and incorrect compound nouns. There are five errors.

My family owns an unusual variety of dogs. For example, both of my brother-in-laws own purebred toy poodles. Which they enjoy clipping, trimming, and taking to shows. One of my sisters' dogs is a St. Bernard she actually keeps him in the house! Frankly, I enjoy my dog Mitzi. I found her as a stray in the bushs outside my house, and I have now had her for five years. Despite all the variety, my family loves all of our dogs.

My family owns an unusual variety of dogs. For example, both of my brothers-in-law own purebred toy poodles, which they enjoy clipping, trimming, and taking to shows. One of my sister's dogs is a St. Bernard. She actually keeps him in the house! Frankly, I enjoy my dog Mitzi. I found her as a stray in the bushes outside my house, and I have now had her for five years. Despite all the variety, my family loves all of our dogs.

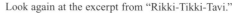

Look again at the excerpt from "Rikki-Tikki-Tavi."

- *Find a possessive noun, a compound noun, a noncount noun, and a proper noun.*

- *What nouns were unfamiliar to you? How did they affect your interest in the story?*

Writing Good Paragraphs

If two sailors want to use flags to communicate between ships, they must understand the shapes and colors of the flags and know how to form the right patterns with the flags. Communicating in writing also requires knowledge of signals and form. To write a good paragraph, a writer needs to follow a certain form. Topic sentences of paragraphs are signals, indicating what the subjects will be. If the writer uses signals and form effectively, the reader will more easily understand the message.

Evaluation

Use Test 2 or prepare your own test from unassigned practices, Chapter Review questions, or Concept Reinforcement questions.

Writing Good Paragraphs

Lesson Support

Teacher's Edition, Book 2
Writing Worksheets—p. 134

Rubrics—p. 148

Introduction

Materials
- computer with Internet access (optional)

If you have access to the Internet in your classroom, you may want to find a site that explains and demonstrates the maritime signal flag system. Allow some time at the beginning of class for students to practice making and deciphering messages.

Discuss the necessity of sending unambiguous messages. When speaking, singing, writing, or sending flag signals, we want our messages to be clear.

A paragraph is a group of sentences that discuss one topic. Here is a paragraph about flag signals:

> The flag hoist system of signaling can send messages in two ways. When flown in groups, special colorful flags with various shapes and designs represent letters of the alphabet. Flown from the masthead and read from the top down, the flags spell words. When flown singly, however, each flag has a code meaning. One flag, for example, is a white *X* on a background of blue. It can stand for *M* or for the message "I have a doctor on board." The same symbol in red on white stands for *V* or "I require assistance."

Is the paragraph above simply about the flag hoisting—or is it really about the way a flag hoist sends messages? Read the first sentence of the paragraph again to answer this question.

Generally, a paragraph begins with a topic sentence. As you might guess from its name, this sentence introduces the topic of the paragraph, the subject that will be discussed. But a good topic sentence does more than merely name the topic. It also gives a general statement of what will be said about the topic. It determines what information the paragraph will give about the subject.

If you had to write a paragraph from a topic sentence given to you, which sentence would you rather start with?

- My neighbor owns a collie.
- Collies make good farm dogs.

Either one might become the topic sentence of a paragraph. But the second one would make your writing easier. Why? The second sentence not only names the topic but also determines what kind of information you should give about that topic.

    S   **V**
Collies make good farm dogs.

The topic is *collies*—the subject of the sentence tells you that. The predicate narrows the topic, keeping it from getting too big to handle. There is much, for example, that could be said about collies. The predicate here, however, directs the paragraph to tell only how collies are useful on farms.

The other sentence, *My neighbor owns a collie,* would not make as good a topic sentence for an informative paragraph as *Collies make good farm dogs.*

    S   **V**
My neighbor owns a collie.

The subject suggests the topic *neighbor,* but the predicate does not determine the kind of information you tell about that topic. *Owns a collie* merely gives a fact about the neighbor. To tell what will be said about the topic, you would probably have to revise the topic sentence.

    S   **V**
My neighbor has trained his collie to help him on the farm.

This sentence is a better topic sentence. Can you tell why?

Discussion

Direct the students to read the introduction and the text material about writing good paragraphs. Then direct a discussion about the example, pointing out how the ideas in the paragraph are supported with examples.

For display, write the topic sentence of the sample paragraph about signal flags. Ask the students to identify the two sentences that introduce the two methods suggested in the topic sentence. *(sentences 2 and 4)*

Discuss how the supporting examples further clarify these categories.

Also refer students to the subsection in Chapter 15 about writing topic sentences. Answer any questions they may have after reading this material.

Planning

Direct the students to read the instructions in "Your Turn."

Allow time for the students to choose one of the listed topics or to select one of their own.

Direct the students as they brainstorm and then help them evaluate possible topic sentences for the listed suggestions. For ex-ample, "My room has a nautical theme in its furnishings" is a good topic sentence. However, "My room is nice" is not a useful beginning.

Remind the students to select details or examples to support their topic sentences.

Drafting

Allow time for students to write their paragraphs in class.

Good Topic Sentences

Like all sentences, topic sentences have subjects and predicates. The subjects and predicates of topic sentences, though, usually have special jobs to perform for the paragraphs they introduce.

Take this sentence for example:

Many Bible heroes suffered persecution.

1. The subject usually names the topic of the paragraph. The grammatical subject—*Many Bible heroes*—is the topic of the paragraph.

2. The predicate controls how much the paragraph can say about the topic. Heroes of the Bible are remembered for many things. This topic sentence, however, limits the discussion. The paragraph will tell how some of the heroes suffered persecution.

A good topic sentence, then, says both what the paragraph will discuss and how it will discuss that topic.

Building Paragraphs

A good paragraph is more than a group of sentences written or printed together with the first line indented. To make a paragraph, the sentences must discuss the same idea and follow each other logically. There is unity and order in a good paragraph.

Some paragraphs are developed with *details*. Descriptive paragraphs, you may remember, are made up of sentences that give details about an object, a person, or a place. What details develop the following paragraph?

He was an excellent athlete. Not only did he hold the local record for the 400-meter, but he was also a forward on the soccer team. He biked to school nearly every day. In the spring, he helped coach Little League. Whenever there was a teen night at the church, he would make all the arrangements for a softball game or a Ping-Pong tournament.

See how the topic sentence is supported or further explained by the sentences that follow? The whole paragraph is built of sentences that discuss the same topic and follow each other smoothly.

Other paragraphs are developed with *examples*. What are the examples in this paragraph?

Israel and Judah have had many godly kings. The most famous, of course, was David. Although David failed many times, God called him a man after His own heart. Another great king was Solomon. God asked him what he wanted most to have; Solomon chose wisdom over wealth and power. Because he chose well, God gave him wealth and power too. Josiah, the son of a wicked king, became a godly ruler. He burned the groves of the false priests and broke the idols into pieces. He followed the Lord with his whole heart. II Kings 23:25 says of him, "And like unto him was there no king before him . . . ; neither after him arose there any like him." These men who followed God's commands are some of the greatest kings of Israel and Judah.

The topic sentence in this paragraph is supported by specific examples: David, Solomon, and Josiah. The sentences all develop the same topic; together they form a good paragraph.

Revising (Peer Response)

Distribute a copy of the Writing Worksheet (Book 2, p. 134) to each student. Direct students to exchange paragraphs with a partner and to fill out the evaluations, returning them to the writer when finished.

Instruct the students to read over their paragraphs and the suggestions from their partners, making any changes for clarity.

Publishing

Ask volunteers to share their paragraphs aloud. Collect the paragraphs.

Scriptural Application

Read I Peter 3:15 aloud. Christians must be able to give reasons for their faith. Ask the students to write a well-developed paragraph giving reasons for their faith.

Evaluation

For help in grading this assignment, see "Grading Writing Assignments" (p. x) and Rubric 2 (Book 2, p. 148).

Enrichment

Direct the students to listen to newscasts or read newspapers and to identify the topic sentences in the news stories.

Look at the paragraph again. Can you find an adjective clause in it? That's right—it's in the last sentence. The sentence is better than this alternative: "These men are some of the greatest kings of Israel. They followed God's commands." Why is it better?

Your Turn

Write a rough draft for a paragraph that is developed by details or examples. You may choose a topic from the list below or find one of your own. Be sure to include a clear topic sentence.

- Describe a room.
- Tell about three inspiring people you know or have read about.
- Describe a person in your family.
- Discuss some ways to spend a Saturday.

3 PRONOUNS

Objectives

Students will

1. identify a pronoun and its antecedent.

2. distinguish a personal pronoun from other pronouns and identify person, number, gender, and case.

3. choose between pronoun cases for both single and compound antecedents.

4. use pronouns to complete sentences.

5. choose the correct case for a pronoun used as an appositive.

6. implement courtesy order when choosing pronoun order.

7. use demonstrative and interrogative pronouns correctly.

8. write sentences using interrogative pronouns correctly.

9. distinguish between intensive and reflexive pronouns.

10. revise sentences to include intensive pronouns.

11. identify indefinite pronouns as singular or plural and use the correct pronoun in a sentence.

12. recognize a relative pronoun and identify its antecedent.

13. correct unclear pronoun reference.

14. recognize the differences between incorrect, informal, and formal uses of indefinite pronouns.

15. evaluate and revise writing to make pronoun reference clear.

Eating Together

By Li-Young Lee

This poem describes a family having a meal together a few weeks after
the father has died.

In the steamer is the trout
seasoned with slivers of ginger,
two sprigs of green onions, and sesame oil.
We shall eat it with rice for lunch,
brothers, sister, my mother who will   5
taste the sweetest meat of the head,
holding it between her fingers
deftly, the way my father did
weeks ago. Then he lay down
to sleep like a snow-covered road   10
winding through pines older than him,
without any travelers, and lonely for no one.

- *What words in the poem convey a feeling of togetherness?*
- *The poem consists of only three sentences. What does each sentence focus on?*
- *Does the lunch they are eating sound good?*

- we, brothers, sister, my mother, *and* my father
- *(1) the trout, (2) the family, and (3) the father*
- *Answers will vary.*

Which words in this poem seem most memorable to you? Was it *trout,
ginger,* or *snow-covered road?* You probably wouldn't choose *it, my,* or *he.*
Pronouns usually do not call attention to themselves. Their presence is not
often noticed, but their absence certainly would be. For example, read line
7, substituting the antecedent for the pronoun *it.* The change spoils the line,
doesn't it? Pronouns not only improve the rhythm and efficiency in writing,
but they also make ideas easier to follow.

Lesson Support

Student Text
Chapter 3 Review—pp. 403-5

Teacher's Edition, Book 1
Bulletin Boards—p. 446

Diagram Answers—pp. 457-58

Teacher's Edition, Book 2
Pretests—pp. 5-7

Teaching Helps—p. 40

ESL Worksheets—pp. 65-66

Concept Reinforcements—pp. 94-99

Literature Link

Allow the students to read the poem
silently. Then read the poem aloud, remembering to pause at the punctuation instead
of at the ends of the lines. Re-read the
poem, changing the pronouns to nouns.
Point out how doing so spoils the flow and
tone of the poem.

Teaching Strategy: Discussion

Instruct students to find the eleven pronouns in the poem "Eating Together" and
ask them what word or words each of the
first nine pronouns in the poem is replac-
ing. *(We—author, brothers, sister, mother;
it—trout; my—author's; who—mother; it—
meat; her—mother's; my—author's; he—
father; him—father) (Note: The last two
pronouns are indefinite, so there is no clear
word being replaced.)*

Pronouns

A **pronoun** is a word that substitutes for a noun. Pronouns help you avoid needless repetition in your writing. Look at the following sentence:

> Dale, Alan, and Ben like the hot dogs at the Timeout Café. *They* eat there often with *their* friends.

The word, phrase, or clause that a pronoun replaces is called the **antecedent**. *Dale, Alan,* and *Ben* are the antecedents of *they* and *their.* Read the second sentence using nouns instead of pronouns.

in summary

A **pronoun** substitutes for a noun.

The word a pronoun replaces is called the **antecedent**.

3-1 PRACTICE THE SKILL

In the blank write the antecedent of each italicized pronoun. Remember that the antecedent may appear in another sentence.

Benedict Arnold   1. Although Benedict Arnold is known as a traitor to the United States of America, *he* was once a fearless and distinguished leader in the Revolutionary War.

parents   2. Benedict lived with his parents until he was fourteen; then he ran away from *them.*

wives   3. During his lifetime, Arnold married two wives, and *they* gave him eight children.

Money   4. Money was one of Benedict Arnold's chief desires, and many believe *it* was one of the motivating factors for his betraying his country.

Congress   5. Congress bestowed due honors on Major General Benedict Arnold, but *it* was extremely late in its bestowment on more than one occasion.

Teaching Strategy: Discussion

Tell the students that the word *antecedent* comes from two Latin words: *ante,* "before," and *cedere,* "to go." An antecedent is a word that usually comes before a pronoun and is the word to which the pronoun refers. Ask the students what the words *antechoir* and *antechamber* might mean. *("in front of the choir" and "a room [i.e., "chamber"] before another room")*

Teaching Strategy: Discussion

Point out that not all antecedents come before the pronouns that replace them. Sometimes the antecedent (i.e., a noun) follows its pronoun in a sentence when the two are closely related. For example, in the sentence "When she heard the news, Laura gasped" the pronoun *she* precedes the antecedent *Laura.* Of course, antecedents can also be in an entirely separate sentence, as in the example on page 46.

decisions   6. Later, Arnold made some quick decisions in battle, and *they* proved to be important to the outcome of those battles.

government   7. However, Benedict Arnold was beginning to show signs that he was frustrated with the government and *its* suspicion of him.

Margaret Shippen   8. In April 1779 he married Margaret Shippen, a daughter of a Loyalist. His marriage to *her* aroused even more suspicion.

Benedict Arnold   9. Benedict Arnold offered to help the British government. Arnold appears to have made *his* infamous decision based on pride and money.

life   10. After his treason, Benedict Arnold's life was filled with unhappiness; *it* was plagued with debt, scorn, and distrust.

3-2 *R*EVIEW THE *S*KILL

In the blank write the antecedent of each italicized pronoun. Remember that the antecedent may appear in another sentence.

Joseph   1. Joseph made the right choices in spite of difficult circumstances, and God honored *him.*

brothers   2. Because Joseph's brothers were jealous and angry, *they* sold him to the Egyptians.

estate   3. Joseph supervised Potiphar's estate, and the Lord caused *it* to prosper.

wife   4. Potiphar's wife tempted Joseph, but he refused to listen to *her.*

Potiphar   5. However, Potiphar listened to *his* wife's lies and put Joseph into prison.

dream   6. Later, Pharoah had a dream, and the Lord enabled Joseph to interpret *it.*

Joseph   7. Because of Joseph's interpretation and advice, *he* became ruler over the land of Egypt.

family   8. Eventually, his family needed help because of a famine, and because of his unique position, Joseph was able to help *them.*

brothers   9. When his brothers came for food, he was not angry over *their* treatment of him.

God   10. Joseph saw the hand of God and knew that *He* had used Joseph's circumstances for good.

Chapter 9: Number and Gender
p. 224

Chapter 9: Special Rules for *Be*
p. 211

Personal Pronouns

The most common type of pronoun is the **personal pronoun.** Personal pronouns have four important characteristics: person, number, gender, and case.

SINGULAR			
	SUBJECTIVE	**OBJECTIVE**	**POSSESSIVE**
FIRST PERSON	I	me	my, mine
SECOND PERSON	you	you	your, yours
THIRD PERSON			
neuter	it	it	its
masculine	he	him	his
feminine	she	her	her, hers

PLURAL			
	SUBJECTIVE	**OBJECTIVE**	**POSSESSIVE**
FIRST PERSON	we	us	our, ours
SECOND PERSON	you	you	your, yours
THIRD PERSON	they	them	their, theirs

Personal pronouns are called *personal* because they are divided into the following three categories of **person:**

FIRST PERSON	the person speaking	I am going to Quebec.
SECOND PERSON	the person(s) spoken to	You are going to Quebec.
THIRD PERSON	any other person or thing	They are going to Quebec.

The **number** of a personal pronoun tells whether it is singular or plural. Second-person pronouns do not show a difference in number.

| SINGULAR | I was invited to have lunch with *her.* |
| PLURAL | We were invited to have lunch with *them.* |

Gender tells whether the personal pronoun is masculine, feminine, or neuter. Only the third-person singular pronouns show a difference in gender.

MASCULINE	He has read several books by that author.
	We followed *his* complicated directions around the city.
FEMININE	*She* will not be coming to the meeting tomorrow.
	Have you given *her* your tickets?
NEUTER	*It* is much larger and more elaborate than I expected.
	Its value is difficult to comprehend.

Teaching Strategy: Induction

Tell students a brief personal anecdote—for example, what you had for breakfast or how your car once broke down. (Include pronouns in the first, second, and third persons.) Ask the students to write down as many pronouns as they hear. Then discuss the students' lists, writing their words for display. Ask a volunteer to attempt to group the words into three separate groups. Discuss his decisions with the class and make any corrections necessary to form a pronoun chart similar to the one on page 48.

Teaching Strategy: Discussion

Ask students to point out differences or similarities between the various pronouns on the chart. Lead them to see differences in number, gender, and case.

Teaching Strategy: Discussion

Point out that, in English, some objects that would otherwise be neuter are sometimes assigned a gender. Countries, ships, and automobiles are often referred to as being female. Animals kept as pets are usually referred to by their genders; however, most other animals are referred to using neuter pronouns.

The **case** of a personal pronoun is its form that shows the way it is used in the sentence. The three cases are subjective, objective, and possessive. Notice how the pronoun changes in the following sentences, even though it always refers to the same antecedent:

SUBJECTIVE   *We* are traveling together in a van.
OBJECTIVE   The van will barely hold all of *us.*
POSSESSIVE   *Our* luggage will not fit in the back.

in summary

Personal pronouns show **person** (first, second, third), **number** (singular, plural), **gender** (masculine, feminine, neuter), and **case** (subjective, objective, possessive).

3-3 PRACTICE THE SKILL

Underline each personal pronoun in the following sentences.

1. We can all learn a lesson from the story of King Midas.

2. King Midas's selfish choices almost destroyed him and his family.

3. Midas was a greedy man who loved his gold and other possessions.

4. In fact, King Midas spent all day admiring them.

5. Taking a look at his palace, you would see that it was full of gold; but Midas was not satisfied.

6. One night, King Midas was granted his wish that everything he touched would turn to gold.

7. The next morning, King Midas tried his gift on the things around him by touching them.

8. However, King Midas could not eat his food because it also turned into gold!

9. Later, when he touched his daughter, she turned into gold.

10. Shocked and grieved, King Midas begged that his gold and his golden touch would be taken away and that his daughter would be given back.

Reinforcement

Instruct students to find the antecedents of the pronouns in Practice the Skill 3-3.

Underline each personal pronoun. Be prepared to state the person, number, gender, and case of each pronoun.

1. Recently, I have been studying the origin of fables.

2. Have you ever read or studied any fables?

3. We can particularly enjoy the lessons and morals in Aesop's fables.

4. "The Swallow's Advice" is one of my favorite fables.

5. I will tell you about the swallow's friends.

6. They would not listen to the swallow's advice.

7. He had warned them about the farmer's evil hemp seed.

8. However, his friends were lazy.

9. The farmer later made nets from the hemp seed, and the birds were trapped in his nets.

10. The birds did not destroy the seed of evil, and it later destroyed them.

Chapter 9: Number and Gender
p. 224

Personal Pronoun Usage

Using the Correct Case

Subjective case pronouns are used primarily for the subjects of sentences.

> *I* must be on time for the rehearsal.
> *She* will have to make arrangements for a substitute.
> Even if Ed has to stay up late, *he* will be finished on time.

Subjective case pronouns may also be used as predicate nouns, which rename the subject of the sentence.

> The guest speaker tonight is *she.*

Objective case pronouns are used for objects: direct objects, indirect objects, and objects of prepositions.

> DIRECT OBJECT   David visited *me* in Salt Lake City.
> INDIRECT OBJECT   I sent *them* a package of nuts and cookies.
> OBJECT OF PREPOSITION   The color of *it* is darker than I remember.

Be careful not to use the objective case for a predicate noun. A predicate noun must always be in the subjective case.

> WRONG   Is it him?   It's him.
> RIGHT   Is it he?   It's he.

The **possessive case** shows ownership or a similar relationship. A possessive case pronoun usually functions as an adjective to modify a noun.

Teaching Strategy: Introduction

Review the functions of nouns. Using the sentences on page 50, show the students that pronouns can have the same functions in sentences.

Teaching Strategy: Demonstration

Write the words *subjective* and *objective* for display. Ask students to guess which column the noun functions they just reviewed go in. Point out that the case of an appositive depends on the case of the renamed word.

Teaching Strategy: Discussion

Ask students to find the possessive pronouns in "Eating Together" on page 45. *(my, her, my)* What words do they modify? *(mother, fingers, father)* Point out that these possessive pronouns are functioning as adjectives in these sentences.

That is *my* coat.
What is *your* idea?
I tried to paint a desert scene, but I liked *his* painting better.

Some possessives can also be used alone as subjects, predicate nouns, and objects. These possessive words are called **independent possessives.**

Yes, it's *yours.*
Theirs is the best idea.
He sold *his* to a local art collector.

in summary

Subjective case pronouns function as subjects and predicate nouns in sentences.

Objective case pronouns function as objects in sentences: direct objects, indirect objects, and objects of prepositions.

Predicate nouns must always be in the **subjective** case.

Possessive case pronouns often show ownership and usually modify nouns.

Possessives that function alone as subjects, predicate nouns, and objects are called **independent possessives.**

3-5 PRACTICE THE SKILL

Underline the correct pronoun from the choices in parentheses.

1. In history class, *(we, us)* studied Peter Salem and Crispus Attucks.

2. Some African-American heroes of the Revolutionary War were *(they, them)*.

3. America attacked the British soldiers and fought *(they, them)* bravely.

4. My friend Dacia gave me *(she, her)* report on Peter Salem.

5. Later I returned the report to *(she, her)*.

6. *(She, Her)* reported that Peter Salem was a hero at Bunker Hill.

7. The British attacked Breed's Hill, and in the fourth charge, *(they, their)* took the hill from the colonists.

8. As British Major Pitcairn led the final charge against *(they, them)*, Pitcairn was shot.

9. The one responsible for wounding Major Pitcairn was *(he, him)*.

10. The last colonists were not captured because of *(he, his)* courage; the British soldiers suffered many casualties in the battle.

Underline the correct pronoun from the choices in parentheses. In the blank, label the function of the pronoun *S* (subject), *DO* (direct object), *OP* (object of the preposition), *IO* (indirect object), *PN* (predicate noun) or *Adj* (adjective).

DO   1. People with faith during great danger amaze *(I, me)*.

OP   2. Many of *(we, us)* have heard of the following reformers: John Huss, John Wycliffe, and Martin Luther.

OP   3. All of *(they, them)* were protesters of the Catholic Church.

IO   4. Some of these men taught the common people and gave *(they, them)* the Bible in their own language.

S   5. John Huss was a priest. However, *(he, him)* publicly preached against the abuses of the church.

Adj   6. Several friends of Huss came to Cardinal Colono. Unfortunately, the cardinal would not listen to *(they, their)* pleas.

PN   7. The instigator of Huss's excommunication was *(he, his)*.

DO   8. The church leaders imprisoned Huss and sentenced *(he, him)* to death.

Adj   9. God worked through *(him, his)* example. Later reformers used his life as an inspiration.

IO   10. The reformers' boldness has given *(I, me)* courage.

Compound Constructions

Choosing the right pronoun case in a compound construction can sometimes be confusing. When determining case, use the same rules for compound constructions as for simple constructions.

SINGLE   *She* is traveling to Europe.
COMPOUND   Sharon and *she* are traveling to Europe.

Ignoring the other half of the compound will make the correct case easier to determine.

COMPOUND   Mom made an appointment for you and *(I, me)*.
SUBJECTIVE   Mom made an appointment for *I*.
OBJECTIVE   Mom made an appointment for *me*.
CORRECT CASE   Mom made an appointment for you and *me*.

In the compound construction, ignore the word *you*. An objective case pronoun is needed because *you* and the pronoun will be the objects of the preposition *for*. The correct choice is the objective case pronoun *me*.

Art and History Link

Look at the picture of John Huss on page 52. Ask students what they know about the reformers discussed in Review the Skill 3-6. Probably the best known of these is Martin Luther, a German monk who was well acquainted with the Scriptures. His studies led him to question the practices of the established church. For example, he knew that salvation is a free gift from God to those who believe on His Son and who ask forgiveness for their sins. Such forgiveness could not be handed out by the church as a reward for good works. Luther protested the abuses of the church by posting his Ninety-five Theses, or statements for debate, regarding the church's sale of indulgences (items sold to replace the sacrament of penance). Luther's actions sparked the Protestant Reformation. Ask students where the word *Protestant* comes from. *(Luther's protest against the church)* Encourage students to learn more about John Huss, John Wycliffe, and Martin Luther.

Evaluation

If you have assigned sentence diagramming with Review the Skill 3-6, check students' answers using page 457.

Teaching Strategy: Introduction

Before going over compound constructions on page 52, ask students to choose the correct pronoun in the following sentence: The coach gave Bryan and *(I, me)* a ride home. Tell the students to ignore the first part of the compound in a compound construction in order to choose the correct pronoun. *Me* is the correct pronoun in the preceding sentence.

in summary

When determining case, use the same rules for **compound constructions** as for simple constructions.

3-7 Practice the Skill

Underline the correct pronoun from the choices in parentheses.

1. Blake and Sonya are studying the biblical view of lying, so I read the story of Ananias and Sapphira to Blake and *(she, her)*.

2. You and *(I, me)* know the story of Ananias and Sapphira.

3. The story has an important lesson for you and *(I, me)*.

4. The church members were selling land to help the poor, and Peter was distributing the money from the land to *(they, them)*.

5. Ananias and *(she, her)* sold a piece of land.

6. Although he told the church members that he was giving all the money from the land, Ananias gave only part of it to Peter and *(they, them)*.

7. Peter asked Sapphira if she were giving all the money, and *(she, her)* lied also.

8. The deceivers were *(she, her)* and her husband.

9. God killed *(they, them)* for their deception.

10. God is warning you and *(I, me)*; we need to be completely honest.

3-8 Review the Skill

Underline the correct pronoun from the choices in parentheses. In the blank, label the underlined pronoun *S* (subject), *PN* (predicate noun), *IO* (indirect object), *DO* (direct object), or *OP* (object of the preposition).

_PN_ 1. Yesterday, Mrs. Canasta asked for a report on the Holocaust for the school paper. The reporters are Ruben and *(I, me)*.

_S_ 2. Fortunately, my grandmother and *(I, me)* have just read a few books on the war.

_PN_ 3. Some residents of Germany during World War II were my grandfather and *(she, her)*.

_IO_ 4. The times were difficult, and the war gave both *(they, them)* and others many challenges.

_S_ 5. Both the Jews and *(they, them)* experienced Nazi terror.

_S_ 6. Grandfather saw his Jewish neighbors sent away to prison camps; *(he, him)* and Grandmother never saw them again.

_IO_ 7. My uncle has given my brother and *(I, me)* some books about the Holocaust.

_OP_ 8. Some non-Jewish Germans were opposed to Nazism, and the Nazis eventually executed many of *(they, them)* too.

_IO_ 9. Mrs. Canasta has spoken to a few local Jewish people, and they are giving *(she, her)* and *(I, me)* an interview.

_OP_ 10. I am interested in the history of *(they, them)* and their families.

3-9 USE THE SKILL

In the blank write an appropriate pronoun to complete the sentence. Use a variety of pronouns. Do not use *you* or *it*. *(Answers may vary.)*

_us_ 1. Mr. Wagner is taking some parents and _?_ on a trip to Plymouth Plantation.

_I_ 2. My parents and _?_ visited there last summer.

them 3. I was studying the Pilgrims with _?_ .

_I_ 4. Admirers of the Pilgrims are my friend and _?_ .

She 5. _?_ and I are looking forward to the trip.

they 6. The chaperones have set the schedule, and we students and _?_ will visit the *Mayflower II* on Tuesday.

_I_ 7. _?_ want to learn more about the Pilgrims' brave choices.

_us_ 8. Mr. Wagner has given _?_ a study guide with questions.

_He_ 9. _?_ and his wife have ancestors who were on the *Mayflower*.

_we_ 10. Last month, _?_ wrote papers about what caused the Pilgrims to leave their homeland.

Appositives

An **appositive** is a noun or pronoun that follows another noun or pronoun and renames it.

> We will be reading selections by the next poet, *William Butler Yeats*.
> We *students* will be taking turns reading aloud.

When determining the case of a pronoun that is followed by an appositive, disregard the appositive noun. The case of the pronoun is not affected by the presence of an appositive.

> The problem was not too difficult for *us* math students.

The pronoun in this sentence is an objective case pronoun because it is the object of the preposition *for.* The subjective case *we* would be incorrect.

If a pronoun is part of an appositive following a noun, determine the case of the pronoun according to the function of the renamed noun.

> The two drivers, Aaron and *he,* will rotate every six hours.

In this sentence *Aaron and he* renames the subject of the sentence, *drivers.* *Drivers* is the subject; therefore, the appositive pronoun needs to be in the subjective case.

in summary

The presence of an appositive does not affect the case of the pronoun it renames.

The case of a pronoun in an appositive is determined by the function of the renamed noun.

3-10 PRACTICE THE SKILL

Underline the correct pronoun from the choices in parentheses.

1. Our teacher read *(we, us)* students the story of Mary and Martha.

2. It was especially instructive for my friends, Lola and *(she, her).*

3. Their choices teach many lessons to *(we, us)* students.

4. Jesus' friends, Martha and *(she, her),* received Christ into their home.

5. The servers were the sisters, Mary and *(she, her).*

6. *(We, Us)* listeners know of Mary's devotion and Martha's busy work.

7. Christ taught the women, Martha and *(she, her).*

8. My friends, Lola and *(she, her),* admire Mary's single-minded devotion.

9. Jesus taught the disciples the importance of Mary's devotion. His lesson applies to all His followers, the disciples and *(we, us)* today.

10. *(We, Us)* students can still learn from Mary's example today.

Teaching Strategy: Discussion

Point out that, unlike other pronouns, the case of a pronoun functioning as an appositive depends on the case of the renamed word. Students can refer to page 90 of *The Writer's Toolbox* for further examples.

Underline the correct pronoun from the choices in parentheses.

1. *(We, Us)* students like our school nurses.

2. Miss Hopkins has worked at our school for ten years, and Mrs. Keade has been a helpful assistant to *(she, her)*.

3. Miss Hopkins and Mrs. Keade are the nicest nurses in town. I always receive the best care from *(they, them)*.

4. Kaili and I admire nurses. *(We, Us)* girls enjoy learning about famous nurses from history.

5. Our teacher told *(we, us)* girls about Florence Nightingale.

6. Because of *(she, her)*, modern nursing methods developed.

7. Florence, along with other nurses, volunteered to care for the wounded during the Crimean War, and she and *(they, them)* helped to save many lives.

8. The other nurses and *(she, her)* had an insufficient supply of basic medical supplies.

9. Her evident concern and care for others challenges *(we, us)* students to be kind to others as well.

10. In 1907 Great Britain's King Edward VII awarded *(she, her)* the Order of Merit.

Archaic Second-Person Pronouns

You probably do not use pronouns such as *thee, thine,* and *thou* in your writing, but you may have read them in the King James Version of the Bible, in the works of Shakespeare, or in other writings of the Early Modern English period (1500-1660). You may see them in hymns you sing today, and some people use them as a sign of respect when addressing God in prayer. These formal-sounding pronouns may seem random, but they actually follow grammatical rules just as our pronouns do today.

ARCHAIC SECOND-PERSON PRONOUNS		
	SINGULAR	PLURAL
SUBJECTIVE	thou	ye
OBJECTIVE	thee	you
POSSESSIVE	thy, thine	your, yours

Music Link

Borrow hymnals from the school chapel or a local church and ask students to find examples of archaic second-person pronouns in the hymn texts. Sing several of the hymns that the students find.

Courtesy Order

In compound pronoun constructions, always mention yourself last. Also, put the second-person pronoun *you* before third-person pronouns or nouns. In other words, always mention your hearer before anyone else.

WRONG	RIGHT
I and Kara will . . .	Kara and I will . . .
Between me and you . . .	Between you and me . . .
Brandon and you . . .	You and Brandon . . .

in summary

Archaic second-person pronouns follow grammatical rules for case.

In compound constructions, mention yourself last and your hearer before anyone else.

3-12 PRACTICE THE SKILL

Underline the correct word from the choices in parentheses.

1. Have *(you, Maria)* and *(you, Maria)* ever visited Costa Rica?

2. Who is asking *(me, him)* and *(me, him)* about Costa Rica?

3. *(I, Juan)* and *(I, Juan)* know that Costa Rica was the first Latin American country to abolish slavery.

4. *(I, Flora)* and *(Flora, I)* learned that the government later became corrupt.

5. Should *(I, Amelia)* and *(I, Amelia)* read about José María Figueres Ferrer?

6. *(You, Enrique)* and *(you, Enrique)* mentioned that Figueres gathered an army in 1948 and defeated the corrupt government.

7. *(I, You)* and *(I, you)* would think that he would have taken power.

8. *(I, Philip)* and *(I, Philip)* read that he handed over power to the winner of the democratic election.

9. Do *(you, Lana)* and *(you, Lana)* know that Figueres was later elected president?

10. *(I, Debra)* and *(I, Debra)* learned much about politics in Costa Rica.

Teaching Strategy: Discussion

Ask the students this question: If you had to summarize *courtesy* in one phrase, what would you say? *(Answers may vary, but elicit the idea that courtesy always includes thinking of others first.)* Tell the students that any pronoun referring to the speaker should be put last in a series of pronouns. If a second-person pronoun is used, that pronoun should always be first. Give students the three words *me, you,* and *Elliot* and ask them which should come first, second, and last in a sentence. *(you, Elliot, me)* Ask them what function this list would have to be in a sentence and why. *(some kind of object because* me *is in the objective case)*

Choose the correct pronoun from the choices in parentheses. In the blank, label the function of the pronoun *S* (subject), *DO* (direct object), *OP* (object of the preposition), *PN* (predicate noun), *App of S* (appositive of subject), or *App of OP* (appositive of object of preposition).

S	1.	(*We, Us*) students are studying church history.
App of OP	2.	Richard Allen is especially interesting to our pastor's children, Marshall and (*she, her*).
S	3.	(*He, Him*) was the founder of a black Methodist denomination.
S	4.	In 1768 (*he, him*) and his family were sold as slaves to Stokely Sturgis.
OP	5.	Sturgis later sold several of (*they, them*) to help pay some of his debts; however, Richard was not sold.
DO	6.	Later the power of the gospel converted both (*he, him*) and Sturgis.
App of S	7.	Two slaves, his brother and (*he, him*), were eventually released.
DO	8.	Richard's ensuing ministry to black Methodists should inspire (*we, us*) Christians.
PN	9.	In 1793 two faithful helpers during a yellow fever epidemic in Philadelphia were Absalom Jones and (*he, him*).
IO	10.	Richard Allen worked on behalf of blacks; he gave (*they, them*) an important voice.

Demonstrative Pronouns

Another kind of pronoun is the **demonstrative pronoun.** Demonstrative pronouns point out specific persons and things. *This* and *these* usually point out persons and things that are near. *That* and *those* point out persons and things that are farther away.

	NEAR	FAR
SINGULAR	this	that
PLURAL	these	those

Teaching Strategy: Induction

Write the following sentences for display:

- Please bring me _____. *(that)* (Point at an object across the room.)
- I need _____. *(these)* (Hold several objects from your desk.)
- I do not need any of _____. *(those)* (Point at several objects across the room.)
- _____ is my favorite pencil. *(This)* (Hold one pencil.)

Instruct students to fill in the correct pronoun as you read the sentences aloud, demonstrating items as indicated above. Ask students to explain why they chose the different pronouns. Then discuss the text on page 58.

This is the table we will use for lunch.
That is Regina's new picnic basket.
Would you like one of *these*?
I'll take one of *those* instead.

in summary

Demonstrative pronouns, *this, that, these,* and *those,* point out specific persons and things.

3-14 PRACTICE THE SKILL

Underline the demonstrative pronouns.

1. <u>This</u> is a book with interesting stories.

2. Yes, I have read <u>those</u>.

3. <u>These</u> are called fables.

4. Oh, <u>those</u> were written by a man named Aesop.

5. All of <u>these</u> use animals to teach a lesson about human mistakes.

6. <u>That</u> is called "The Farmer and the Stork."

7. Yes, <u>this</u> is an interesting fable about choosing friends carefully.

8. The stork made a choice to keep company with the wrong friends; <u>that</u> was a disastrous choice.

9. All <u>these</u> were caught in the net, and the stork begged to be freed.

10. But the farmer would not free him because even though the stork was not guilty, he was caught with <u>those</u> who were.

3-15 REVIEW THE SKILL

Write an appropriate demonstrative pronoun in the blank. *(Answers may vary.)*

These   1. I have read many stories about choices. _?_ often teach me about the choices I make.

Those   2. _?_ in the Bible are full of lessons.

This   3. _?_ is a powerful story about Lot's selfish choosing of the more fertile land.

That   4. _?_ was a choice full of consequences.

those   5. One of _?_ was the death of his wife.

Pronouns   59

	6. _?_ is a story about the results of sin.
This	
This	7. Achan also made a choice to sin. _?_ resulted in serious consequences.
These	8. _?_ were the execution of him and his family and Israel's loss of the battle.
that	9. We can learn a lesson from an incident like _?_ .
This	10. _?_ teaches us that our sin also affects others.

Interrogative Pronouns

The **interrogative pronouns** are *who, whom, whose, which,* and *what.* They are used to ask questions and do not have antecedents.

> *Who* called while I was gone?
> He asked to speak with *whom?*
> *Whose* is that coat lying on the floor?
> *Which* of those books would you like to see?
> *What* is your preference for a vacation?

Who/Whom

The pronouns *who* and *whom* are often misused. Remember that *who* is a subjective case pronoun and *whom* is an objective case pronoun.

> SUBJECTIVE   *Who* is coming tomorrow?
> OBJECTIVE   With *whom* are you going?

In the first sentence, *Who* is the subject of the sentence. In the second sentence, *whom* is the object of the preposition *with.* Use the pronoun *who* for subjects and predicate nouns and the pronoun *whom* for objects.

in summary

The **interrogative pronouns**, *who, whom, whose, which,* and *what* are used to ask questions.

Who is a subjective case pronoun, and *whom* is an objective case pronoun.

3-16 PRACTICE THE SKILL

Underline the interrogative pronouns.

1. In the Scripture, who was rewarded for obedience?

2. To whom did God give a difficult command?

3. Abraham received an unexpected command from God. What was it?

ESL Strategy

The inversion that often occurs in questions that use *wh* words (who, whose, which, what, where, when, why, etc.) often causes problems for ESL students. Refer to the information in Chapter 4 about using auxiliaries to form questions (p. 100) and use ESL Worksheet 4D (Book 2, pp. 70-71) to explain the correct formation of *wh* questions.

Enrichment

Play a game of questions and answers. Divide students into teams and read a set of answers that are unique to your school. Instruct students to give questions that correspond to the answers. (For example, the teacher reads, "Doug and Karl are on the soccer team." The student answers, "Who is on the soccer team?") Encourage them to use interrogative pronouns correctly by paying special attention to the case of *who/whom.*

One on One

Adapt this activity by using members of your family or church youth group and questions about your home or church. You provide the answers; your student should respond with the matching questions using appropriate interrogative pronouns.

4. <u>Whose</u> was the life that Abraham was supposed to take?

5. Abraham waited a long time for a son of his own. <u>What</u> was his son's name?

6. Abraham had two sons: Ishmael and Isaac. <u>Which</u> of the two was he commanded to sacrifice?

7. To <u>whom</u> did Abraham pray?

8. Abraham did not hesitate to obey, and soon he heard a voice. <u>Whose</u> was it?

9. <u>What</u> was the result of Abraham's obedience?

10. God provided an animal to be the sacrifice instead of Isaac. <u>What</u> was it?

3-17 REVIEW THE SKILL

Write in the blank an appropriate interrogative pronoun to complete the sentence. *(Answers will vary.)*

whom   1. The *Book of Martyrs* was written by _?_ ?

Who   2. _?_ was John Foxe?

Which   3. _?_ of the martyrs did he write about?

Who   4. _?_ was killed for his faith?

Whose   5. _?_ was an interesting story?

Who   6. _?_ was Thomas Cranmer, former archbishop of Canterbury?

what   7. The causes of Thomas Cranmer's execution were _?_ ?

What   8. _?_ caused him to renounce his Protestant beliefs?

whom   9. By _?_ was Cranmer's death ordered?

What   10. _?_ caused him to recognize the enormity of the mistake that he had made?

Using interrogative pronouns, write appropriate questions about the sentences given. *(Answers may vary.)*

1. David was called the "man after God's own heart."

   What was David called?

2. Jesse was David's father.

   Who was David's father?

3. As a youth, David was a shepherd.

   What was David as a youth?

4. In his youth, David defeated Goliath.

   Whom did David defeat in his youth?

5. David tried Saul's armor but rejected it.

   Whose was the armor that David tried but rejected?

6. As a man, David became one of the greatest kings of Israel.

   What did David become as a man?

7. David's great sin was his sin with Bathsheba.

   Which was David's great sin?

8. He killed Bathsheba's husband and took her as his wife.

   What did David do?

9. Some of the consequences of David's sin were the death of his first-born son and the rebellion of his son Absalom.

   What were some of the consequences of David's sin?

10. We need to learn from David's experience that we will reap what we sow.

    What do we need to learn from David's experience?

Reflexive and Intensive Pronouns

Reflexive and intensive pronouns are personal pronouns with *self* or *selves* on the end. A **reflexive pronoun** always refers to the same person or thing as the subject. Reflexive pronouns usually function as direct objects, indirect objects, and objects of prepositions.

> Josh gave *himself* a haircut.
> We kept *ourselves* from the cold by taking extra blankets.
> Each person brought a blanket for *himself.*

Intensive pronouns are used for emphasis. An intensive pronoun emphasizes, or intensifies, some noun or pronoun already in the sentence. Grammatically, an intensive pronoun functions as an appositive of the word

**Teaching Strategy:
  Discussion**

Emphasize that reflexive pronouns must have a function in the sentence; intensive pronouns merely emphasize a noun in the sentence. By assigning sentence pattern labels to the sentences they analyze, students can easily distinguish between reflexive and intensive pronouns.

it emphasizes. Because an intensive pronoun does not function as part of the sentence pattern, it can be removed without changing the basic meaning of the sentence.

> Mr. Baker *himself* could not remember where he had stored it.
> I *myself* cannot say that I approve.
> The program allowed Dr. Fagan to explain the procedure *herself*.

	SINGULAR	PLURAL
FIRST PERSON	myself	ourselves
SECOND PERSON	yourself	yourselves
THIRD PERSON	himself, herself, itself	themselves

in summary

Pronouns with *self* or *selves* are **reflexive** or **intensive pronouns**.

Reflexive pronouns always refer to the same person or thing as the subject and usually function as objects in the sentence.

Intensive pronouns emphasize the noun and function as appositives.

3-19 PRACTICE THE SKILL

Label the italicized pronoun *reflexive* or *intensive.*

_____reflexive_____ 1. At certain times, a young person may think only about *himself.*

_____reflexive_____ 2. Kathryn Forbes wrote a story about *herself* and a selfish incident in her youth.

_____intensive_____ 3. The family *itself* did not have much money.

_____intensive_____ 4. Her father *himself* was recuperating in the hospital.

_____reflexive_____ 5. Kathryn and her friends wanted expensive graduation presents for *themselves.*

_____intensive_____ 6. Kathryn's mother did not have the money *herself.* She offered Kathryn her grandmother's heirloom brooch.

_____reflexive_____ 7. Kathryn did not want the brooch. She wanted a new dresser set for *herself.*

_____reflexive_____ 8. Because of Kathryn's selfishness, the dresser set could not bring joy by *itself.*

Evaluation

If you have assigned sentence diagramming with Practice the Skill 3-19, check students' answers using page 458.

intensive   9. Kathryn's mother had sold the precious brooch _herself._

reflexive   10. Kathryn understood _herself_ better by the end of the story.

3-20 REVIEW THE SKILL

Underline the reflexive pronouns once and the intensive pronouns twice. If the pronoun is reflexive, write its function in the blank. If the pronoun is intensive, in the blank write the noun or pronoun intensified.

_DO_   1. Sometimes, a young person may humble himself and give to others.

_IO_   2. At age sixteen Betsy Dowdy gave herself a chance to help the American cause.

_OP_   3. Betsy's neighbors had been talking among themselves about the British soldiers.

soldiers   4. The British soldiers themselves had been attacking in nearby areas and causing great destruction, and they were headed toward Betsy's home.

neighbors   5. Betsy's neighbors themselves knew about the American General Skinner.

General Skinner   6. General Skinner himself had a large number of soldiers about fifty miles away.

_OP_   7. Betsy thought about herself and about her home.

_DO_   8. Ignoring the danger, Betsy steeled herself and successfully rode the fifty miles to warn General Skinner.

ride   9. The ride itself was dangerous and scary.

men   10. Because of the warning, General Skinner's men themselves defeated the British.

Rewrite the sentence, adding intensive pronouns to emphasize certain elements in the sentences below.

1. My brother wanted to visit our friends.
   (Emphasize that the brother wanted to go.)

   My brother himself wanted to visit our friends.

2. My brother and I wanted to go out with our friends.
   (Emphasize that the speaker wanted to go.)

   My brother and I myself wanted to go out with our friends.

3. However, my mother wanted us to finish our work first.
   (Emphasize that the speaker's mother wanted something.)

   However, my mother herself wanted us to finish our work first.

4. However, my mother wanted us to finish our work first.
   (Emphasize the work the speaker needs to finish.)

   However, my mother wanted us to finish our work itself first.

5. I did the work, but my attitude was extremely poor.
   (Emphasize that the speaker did the work.)

   I did the work myself, but my attitude was extremely poor.

6. I did the work, but my attitude was extremely poor.
   (Emphasize the work that the speaker did.)

   I did the work itself, but my attitude was extremely poor.

7. Because of my poor attitude, we were not allowed to go.
   (Emphasize the attitude the speaker had.)

   Because of my poor attitude itself, we were not allowed to go.

8. Because of my poor attitude, we were not allowed to go.
   (Emphasize the importance of the speaker and her brother.)

   Because of my poor attitude, we ourselves were not allowed to go.

9. "I see, Denise," said my father, "that you have learned that your attitude affects not only yourself but also others."
   (Emphasize the importance of the father.)

   "I see, Denise," said my father himself, "that you have learned that your

   attitude affects not only yourself but also others."

10. "I see, Denise," said my father, "that you have learned that your attitude affects not only yourself but also others."
    (Emphasize the importance of the listener.)

    "I see, Denise," said my father, "that you yourself have learned that your

    attitude affects not only yourself but also others."

Chapter 9: Indefinite Pronouns as Antecedents
p. 229

Indefinite Pronouns

We use indefinite pronouns when we want to speak in general terms. Unlike other pronouns, **indefinite pronouns** do not refer to specific persons or things; therefore, they do not have antecedents.

> *Someone* is here.　　　*Anybody* is allowed to come.

Some indefinite pronouns are always singular and some are always plural. Other indefinite pronouns, however, can be either singular or plural.

ALWAYS SINGULAR　someone, anyone, everyone, no one; somebody, anybody, everybody, nobody; something, anything, everything, nothing; each, one, much, little, less

ALWAYS PLURAL　many, several, both, few, fewer

SINGULAR OR PLURAL　some, any, more, most, all, none

To determine whether one of these last pronouns is singular or plural, look at the context of the sentence. Many times the object of the preposition will help you determine whether the pronoun is singular or plural.

SINGULAR　He ate only *some* of the pie, not *all* of it.
PLURAL　Only *some* of the library books, not *all* of them, are overdue.

in summary

Indefinite pronouns do not make specific references and do not have antecedents.

Determine the number of an indefinite pronoun that can be either singular or plural by examining the context of the sentence.

3-22 PRACTICE THE SKILL

Underline the indefinite pronoun. In the blank, label the pronoun *singular* or *plural*.

_____*plural*_____　1. A few of the greatest tragedies in history occurred because of people who did not listen to warnings.

_____*singular*_____　2. One of the deadliest tragedies was the sinking of the *Titanic*.

_____*singular*_____　3. The *Titanic* had been constructed and engineered with all of the technology available in the early 1900s.

Teaching Strategy: Introduction

Ask students to list several things they look for in a friend. After they discuss some of the characteristics, begin writing parts of their descriptions for display. Look for phrases beginning with indefinite pronouns (e.g., *someone* who is kind, a person who is interested in *everything* that interests me, or *anyone* who loves the Lord). Point out that these words are not specific and have no clear antecedents. Look at the list of indefinite pronouns on page 66.

Scriptural Application

Review the biblical characteristics of good friends. You may want to direct the students to the following passages: Proverbs 13:20; 17:17; 27:6, 10; 28:7; John 15:13; Acts 27:3; Hebrews 10:25; and James 4:4. Discuss the importance of the right kind of friends.

ESL Strategy

Use ESL Worksheets 3A and 3B (Book 2, pp. 65-66) for further information about the correct use of *some* as an indefinite pronoun and as an indefinite determiner (see also p. 118).

singular 4. Everyone involved with the building of the ship felt that it was extremely safe and virtually unsinkable.

plural 5. The ship was constructed with sixteen watertight compartments, and several of these compartments would have to flood completely to pose a danger.

singular 6. As the ship was sailing, the crew received warnings about icebergs in their path; however, because of their confidence in the ship, no one gave an order to slow the ship down.

plural 7. The ship hit an iceberg and began to sink; most of the passengers were unaware of the danger at first.

plural 8. In fact, some of the passengers were so confident that they refused to believe the danger even after they were told.

plural 9. Because many of the warnings went unheeded, over fifteen hundred people lost their lives.

singular 10. Each of us needs to learn a lesson from the mistakes of those on the *Titanic* and to listen to advice and warnings given to us.

3-23 REVIEW THE SKILL

In the blank write an appropriate indefinite pronoun to complete the sentence. Do not use any one pronoun more than once. *(Answers will vary.)*

Both 1. _?_ of my parents tell me to be responsible for my choices.

One 2. _?_ of the Bible's commands is to "keep thy heart with all diligence."

Everyone 3. _?_ around me should be able to know that I am a Christian by the choices I make.

no one 4. However, _?_ expects any human to be absolutely perfect.

some 5. We all make mistakes _?_ of the time.

all   6. We can be sure that if we sin, God will listen to our confession _?_ of the time.

None   7. _?_ of our sins are too bad to be forgiven.

each   8. However, _?_ of our choices has consequences that we cannot erase.

Everything   9. _?_ that we do affects our lives and, many times, the lives of those around us.

nothing   10. Nonetheless, _?_ can separate us from God's love, so we should strive to be more Christlike.

Relative Pronouns

The **relative pronouns** are the words *who, whom, whose, which,* and *that.* A relative pronoun relates a dependent clause to the rest of the sentence. The antecedent of the relative pronoun is a noun in the independent clause.

> It was Haley [*who* gave the first presentation.]
> Rob bought a duffle bag [*that* could hold his practice clothes and his gym shoes.]

In the first sentence, the relative pronoun *who* replaces the noun *Haley.* In the second sentence, the relative pronoun *that* replaces the noun *duffle bag.* Both relative pronouns relate the dependent clause to the rest of the sentence. In both sample sentences above, the relative pronoun also functions as the subject of the dependent clause. Relative pronouns may function as subjects, objects, or possessive adjectives within the dependent clauses.

in summary

The **relative pronouns**, *who, whom, whose, which,* and *that,* relate dependent clauses to the rest of the sentence.

3-24 PRACTICE THE SKILL

Underline the relative pronouns in the following sentences.

1. John Bunyan, who wrote *Pilgrim's Progress,* wanted to help other struggling Christians.

2. Bunyan's main character, Christian, is a man with whom believers can identify.

3. Christian represents the common man who is trying to get rid of his guilt and to find the path to heaven.

Teaching Strategy: Induction

Write the following sentences for display: *My grandfather owns an old pickup truck. The pickup truck is often used to take his grandchildren for a ride.* Ask the students to combine the two sentences, making the second one a dependent clause. Answers may vary, but try to elicit the following response: "My grandfather owns an old pickup truck, which he uses to take his grandchildren for a ride." The students will remember the word *which* as an interrogative, but explain to them that here it is being used as a relative pronoun. By combining the sentences themselves, they will better recognize that the relative pronoun *which* replaces *pickup truck.* Therefore, the antecedent is *pickup truck.* You may want to give the students several sentences to combine in this way. Emphasize the meaning of *relative* so that the students can remember that relative pronouns *relate* the dependent clause to the rest of the sentence.

4. His pilgrimage, <u>which</u> is long and difficult, represents a Christian's journey to heaven.

5. Because Christian desperately wants to get rid of the burden <u>that</u> is on his back, he starts on this pilgrimage into the unknown.

6. Evangelist, <u>who</u> represents good counsel, tells Christian the right way to go.

7. However, Christian is sometimes snared by the evil counsel <u>that</u> he receives.

8. One time, Christian listens to Worldly Wiseman, <u>who</u> tells Christian to ignore the Bible and to get off the right path.

9. As Christian begins to travel down the wrong path, the burden <u>that</u> is on his back grows heavier, and flashes of fire come out of the hill that he is traveling beside.

10. Christian is sorry for listening to the evil counsel, <u>which</u> caused him so much trouble.

3-25 PRACTICE THE SKILL

Underline each relative pronoun and write its antecedent in the blank.

choice 1. In *The Knights of the Silver Shield* by Raymond MacDonald Alden, a knight makes a choice <u>that</u> he does not want to make—choosing duty over glory.

knight 2. In the story, any knight <u>who</u> is particularly brave in his deeds receives a golden star on his shield.

person 3. At the time of the story, the lord of the castle was the only person <u>that</u> had already received the golden star.

knight 4. Sir Roland is one knight <u>who</u> desperately wants to fight and prove himself.

Sir Roland 5. The lord of the castle speaks to Sir Roland, <u>whom</u> he has chosen to stand and guard the castle gate.

_____assignment_____ 6. Sir Roland is frustrated with the assignment **that** he has been given, but it is his responsibility to obey.

_____knight_____ 7. After a few minutes, a knight **who** has been wounded tries to get Sir Roland to switch places with him.

_____lady_____ 8. Later, an old lady **who** has been at the scene of the battle mocks Sir Roland for not fighting, but Sir Roland refuses to leave his duty.

_____sword_____ 9. Finally, a magician offers Sir Roland a sword **that** would help him defeat his foes if he would leave and take it to battle.

_____offer_____ 10. Although tempted by the offer **that** he receives, Sir Roland remembers his duty.

3-26 USE THE SKILL

In the blank write an appropriate pronoun as indicated in parentheses. *(Answers may vary.)*

_____What_____ 1. *(Interrogative)* was one of the worst environmental disasters in history?

_____which_____ 2. One of the worst was the Exxon Valdez oil spill, *(relative)* happened on March 24, 1989.

_____that_____ 3. A ship carried a cargo of 1,264,155 barrels of oil; about one-fifth of *(demonstrative)* spilled into Prince William Sound along the coast of Alaska.

_____which_____ 4. Much oil turned into a substance called mousse, *(relative)* will not burn and can be difficult to clean up.

_____Some_____ 5. *(Indefinite)* of the other results of the spill were that wildlife was lost and that the economy of the area was devastated.

_____themselves_____ 6. Several hundred thousand air and sea creatures died, but birds *(intensive)* totaled more than 250,000 deaths.

_____that_____ 7. An alarming result of the spill is more than one thousand miles of coastline *(relative)* was damaged by oil.

One	8. *(Indefinite)* of the most disturbing facts about the disaster was the fact that it was caused by human error.
Who	9. *(Interrogative)* was to blame?
who	10. Many people contributed to the accident, but the person most at fault was the captain, *(relative)* was impaired because of alcohol.
he	11. Because of the impairment, *(personal)* had left his duty.
himself	12. Also, the captain allowed an inexperienced officer to run the ship by *(reflexive)*.
itself	13. Finally, many sources say that the company *(intensive)* could have provided better training and a better crew.
it	14. Many years later, the coastline was checked, and *(personal)* still contained many evidences of oil damage.
ourselves	15. The far-reaching damages exemplify that we need to learn to watch *(reflexive)* and our decisions carefully.

Correcting Unclear Reference Problems

Pronouns unify your writing by providing important links between your sentences and paragraphs. Notice in the sentences below that the second sentence is linked to the first sentence by the pronoun *her.*

Becca's birthday is Saturday.
Today a package for *her* came in the mail.

It is important for each pronoun reference to be clear. Unclear pronoun reference creates sentences that are ambiguous or misleading.

Ambiguous Reference

One problem is having two nearby nouns that are both possible antecedents for the pronoun. Rewrite the sentence in order to have only one noun nearby that is clearly the antecedent of the pronoun.

AMBIGUOUS   When Marshall met Steve at the game, *he* was surprised.

CLEAR   Marshall was surprised when he met Steve at the game.
or
When he met Steve at the game, Marshall was surprised.

In the first sentence, it is unclear whether *he* refers to Marshall or Steve. In the second set of sentences, *he* clearly refers to Marshall.

Writing Link

Return a previous writing assignment or allow the students to choose a journal entry to revise. Tell them to improve their work by rewriting unclear pronoun references.

Another way to correct an unclear reference is to use a direct quotation.

AMBIGUOUS   Olivia told Abby that she was ready to go home.
CLEAR   Olivia told Abby, "I'm ready to go home."

Remote Reference

Reference sometimes becomes unclear when the pronoun is too far away from the antecedent. To make the reference clear, replace the pronoun with the noun or a synonym of the noun.

UNCLEAR   Tomorrow's festivities will be the highlight of this campaign. There will be an outdoor lunch followed by music and speeches. The keynote address will be brought by President Tony Battaglia. *It* will be held as an appreciation for everyone's commitment to and completion of the task.

CLEAR   Tomorrow's festivities will be the highlight of this campaign. . . . *The celebration* will be held as an appreciation for everyone's commitment to and completion of the task.

The pronoun reference in the last sentence of the example is made clear by changing *It* to *The celebration.*

Reference to an Implied Noun

A pronoun should always refer to an actual noun, not an implied noun. We should not assume that our reader knows of whom or what we are speaking.

IMPLIED NOUN   I went to the doctor's office yesterday, and my doctor said that I am healthy. This pleased me.

CLEAR   I went to the doctor's office yesterday, and my doctor said that I am healthy. This good report pleased me.

in summary

To achieve **clear pronoun reference,** do not place more than one possible antecedent near the pronoun.

Do not place the pronoun too far from its antecedent.

Always make the antecedent of a pronoun an actual noun, not an implied noun.

Label each sentence *clear* or *unclear*.

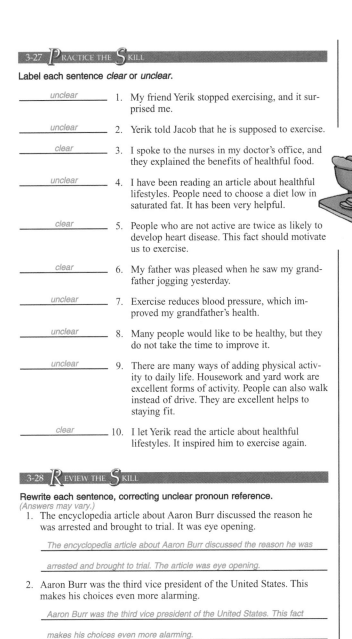

_____unclear_____ 1. My friend Yerik stopped exercising, and it surprised me.

_____unclear_____ 2. Yerik told Jacob that he is supposed to exercise.

_____clear_____ 3. I spoke to the nurses in my doctor's office, and they explained the benefits of healthful food.

_____unclear_____ 4. I have been reading an article about healthful lifestyles. People need to choose a diet low in saturated fat. It has been very helpful.

_____clear_____ 5. People who are not active are twice as likely to develop heart disease. This fact should motivate us to exercise.

_____clear_____ 6. My father was pleased when he saw my grandfather jogging yesterday.

_____unclear_____ 7. Exercise reduces blood pressure, which improved my grandfather's health.

_____unclear_____ 8. Many people would like to be healthy, but they do not take the time to improve it.

_____unclear_____ 9. There are many ways of adding physical activity to daily life. Housework and yard work are excellent forms of activity. People can also walk instead of drive. They are excellent helps to staying fit.

_____clear_____ 10. I let Yerik read the article about healthful lifestyles. It inspired him to exercise again.

Rewrite each sentence, correcting unclear pronoun reference.
(Answers may vary.)

1. The encyclopedia article about Aaron Burr discussed the reason he was arrested and brought to trial. It was eye opening.

   The encyclopedia article about Aaron Burr discussed the reason he was

   arrested and brought to trial. The article was eye opening.

2. Aaron Burr was the third vice president of the United States. This makes his choices even more alarming.

   Aaron Burr was the third vice president of the United States. This fact

   makes his choices even more alarming.

Reinforcement

Instruct the students to rewrite the unclear sentences in Practice the Skill 3-27. *(1, 2, 4, and 7-9).* Remind them to look back at the "In Summary" section for help with their revisions.

3. Aaron Burr and Thomas Jefferson received an equal number of electoral votes for president. However, he was eventually elected by the House of Representatives.

   Aaron Burr and Thomas Jefferson received an equal number of electoral

   votes for president. However, Jefferson was eventually elected by the

   House of Representatives.

4. Alexander Hamilton, a leading Federalist politician, publicly criticized Burr. Burr did not like it and challenged Hamilton to a duel.

   Alexander Hamilton, a leading Federalist politician, publicly criticized Burr.

   Burr did not like the criticism and challenged Hamilton to a duel.

5. Alexander Hamilton and Aaron Burr met on July 11, 1804. One shot killed him.

   Alexander Hamilton was shot and killed by Aaron Burr on July 11, 1804.

   _____

6. The vice president was charged with murder. However, that did not stop him from finishing his term.

   The vice president was charged with murder. The charge, however, did not

   stop him from finishing his term.

7. Many historians believe that Burr wanted personal fame, which later led him into questionable activities.

   Many historians believe that Burr wanted personal fame, a desire that

   later led him into questionable activities.

8. Burr wanted an invasion of Mexico. However, he may also have wanted a secession of some of the United States. It would have made him leader over a large area.

   Burr wanted an invasion of Mexico. However, he may also have wanted a

   secession of some of the United States. If these actions had been success-

   ful, he would have been leader over a large area.

9. General James Wilkinson, a fellow conspirator, betrayed Burr. He was later arrested.

   General James Wilkinson, a fellow conspirator, betrayed Burr. Burr was

   later arrested.

10. Aaron Burr was tried for treason and acquitted. Many believe this did not stop him from continuing to try to enact his plans.

    Aaron Burr was tried for treason and acquitted. Many believe that his

    acquittal did not stop him from continuing to try to enact his plans.

Indefinite Use of *It*, *You*, and *They*

In written English and formal spoken English, do not use *they* as an indefinite pronoun. A personal pronoun should always refer to a definite noun. Usually a specific noun or pronoun will replace the indefinite *they*.

> **INDEFINITE** *They* say that exercise lowers blood pressure.
> **SPECIFIC** *Doctors* say that exercise lowers blood pressure.

The personal pronoun *it* also should have a specific antecedent. Instead of the indefinite "it says," use the specific name or title of the source.

> **INDEFINITE** In the article, it says that prolonged exposure to the sun causes skin damage.
>
> **SPECIFIC** In the article, researcher Angela Tompkins states that prolonged exposure to the sun causes skin damage.
> *or*
> The article says that prolonged exposure to the sun causes skin damage.

In conversation and informal writing, the pronoun *you* often refers to people in general. More formal situations, however, do not allow the indefinite use of *you*.

> **INFORMAL** You may need basic computer skills in order to be successful in the twenty-first century.
>
> **LESS INFORMAL** A person may need basic computer skills in order to be successful in the twenty-first century.
>
> **FORMAL** In order to be successful in the twenty-first century, one may need basic computer skills.

> **Exception:** *It* does not refer to a specific noun in certain common English expressions referring to time, distance, weather, and environment.
>
> **TIME** It's 6:30, and it's already after dark.
> **DISTANCE** It's five miles to the next town. It's not too far away.
> **WEATHER** It's raining. It's going to snow tomorrow.
> **ENVIRONMENT** It can get very busy here during the day, but it's totally deserted at night.

in summary

The pronouns *it* and *they* should always have definite antecedents.

In formal writing and speaking, do not use the personal pronoun *you* as an indefinite pronoun to refer to people in general.

3-29 PRACTICE THE SKILL

Label each sentence correct *(C)* or incorrect/informal *(I)*.

_____*I*_____ 1. In this book, it has a section on Greek mythology.

_____*I*_____ 2. In the section on myths, they say that people invented Greek myths to explain how many aspects of nature came to exist.

Teaching Strategy: Discussion

Discuss the differences between informal, formal, and incorrect language. Remind students that informal language is acceptable in one-on-one conversation and in other informal situations such as e-mail. In speeches or academic writing, however, formal language is preferred. Of course, incorrect language is rarely acceptable. One exception might be the use of incorrect language within the context of a play or a short story in which an author has a character speak incorrectly in order to depict a lack of education or manners.

Reinforcement

Discuss the sentences that the students labeled *I* in Practice the Skill 3-29. *(1-3, 5, 8-9)* Encourage students to differentiate between the incorrect and the informal sentences. Instruct students to rewrite the incorrect sentences to make them correct.

Enrichment

Use Teaching Help 3 (Book 2, p. 40) for more practice with using pronouns.

_I_ 3. Our teacher says that you can learn valuable lessons by studying the myths.

_C_ 4. In many Greek myths, either humans or gods make choices and learn lessons.

_I_ 5. You can learn about pride by reading the story of Niobe.

_C_ 6. Niobe had fourteen children, and they were all extremely beautiful.

_C_ 7. A student can read how Niobe demanded worship from everyone who came to worship the goddess Leto.

_I_ 8. They say that all of her children died because of her pride.

_I_ 9. You can see how her pride affected her.

_C_ 10. Proverbs 16:18 speaks about the effects of pride. It states, "Pride goeth before destruction."

3-30 REVIEW THE SKILL

Rewrite each sentence to make the pronoun-antecedent relationship clear or to express an indefinite subject correctly. *(Answers may vary.)*

1. In *Treasury of Great Hymns and Their Stories,* it tells the story of Fanny Crosby, who was blind.

   Treasury of Great Hymns and Their Stories tells the story of Fanny Crosby, who was blind.

2. Because of it, she memorized much Scripture.

   Because of her blindness, she memorized much Scripture.

3. They say that at the age of eight, Fanny resolved to be content with her situation.

   Biographers say that at the age of eight, Fanny resolved to be content with her situation.

4. Bitterness can take over if you are not content.

   Bitterness can take over if a person is not content.

5. They say that many of Fanny Crosby's hymns come from her own experiences.

   Many of Fanny Crosby's hymns come from her own experiences.

Additional Resources

Students can learn more about great hymn writers like Fanny Crosby from the following source published by Bob Jones University Press: *Treasury of Great Hymns and Their Stories* by Guye Johnson.

6. Your life experiences teach you many important lessons.

   A person's life experiences teach him many important lessons.

7. When she wrote "All the Way My Savior Leads Me," it resulted from God's providing some money at a time of need.

   The writing of "All the Way My Savior Leads Me" resulted from God's

   providing some money at a time of need.

8. In a story about Fanny Crosby, it says that she needed and prayed for five dollars.

   A story about Fanny Crosby says that she needed and prayed for five

   dollars.

9. They say that she received it within minutes.

   She received it within minutes.

10. God can also provide for you.

    God can also provide for anyone who asks.

3-31 Cumulative Review

Rewrite the following paragraph, correcting any fragments, comma splices, fused sentences, incorrect plural noun forms, incorrect possessive noun forms, incorrect compound nouns, incorrect pronoun reference, incorrect case, and incorrect courtesy order. There are ten errors. *(Answers may vary.)*

Alice Hamiltons' achievements as a physician were remarkable. She introduced workers' compensation to the United States. In the early 1900's, workplace conditions were extremely unsafe. With many workers getting ill and even dying from those conditions. This was the reason someone needed to help. Dr. Hamilton researched industrial disease in both American and European countries. She discovered that the United States and them varied greatly in workplace practices. They had more research and insurance programs. Therefore, Alice Hamilton set out to improve conditions in the United States and many new laws were passed because of her research. Furthermore, the first woman on the Harvard University faculty was her. Hamilton continued studying various harmful substances while teaching her study's results continued to improve conditions.

Alice Hamilton's achievements as a physician were remarkable. She intro-

duced workers' compensation to the United States. In the early 1900s, workplace

conditions were extremely unsafe, with many workers getting ill and even dying

from those conditions. These conditions were the reason someone needed to

help. Dr. Hamilton researched industrial disease in both American and European

countries. She discovered that the United States and European nations varied

Reread "Eating Together," this time noticing the pronouns.
- *Which pronouns give the poem a feeling of warmth and togetherness?*
- *Which pronouns give a feeling of distance and isolation?*

Writing Definitions

What Words Mean

What comes to mind when you read the word *game?* Last year's basketball championship? Getting all the expensive properties in Monopoly? A ten-point white-tailed buck? Each of these is a valid definition if the word is presented with no context, no visual clues, and no introduction.

Many words in English have multiple definitions. *Game* has about eleven that come from the same root: the Common Germanic *gam-,* meaning "to enjoy." When you use *game* to mean "lame" (as in, "The horse has a game leg"), however, you are using a word that sounds just like the first word but comes perhaps from the French *gambi* ("crooked").

Better-than-average writers are fully aware of the words they choose. And the best writers make sure that their readers are aware of the words and meanings as well.

Agreeable Terms

It's a good idea when writing an essay or a report (or anything, for that matter) to be sure that everyone knows what you mean by the terms you use. If, for example, you were telling your neighbor about soccer and you said that you were disappointed with the game, he might think you meant the sport itself when you actually meant only the single instance of the sport that your team had just lost. Both are valid meanings of the word.

So what steps should a writer follow when he wants to use just one definition of a word with more than one meaning?

Step 1

Look up the word in the dictionary. You should not simply copy the definition from the dictionary but rather use it to help limit how you will discuss your term. For example, if a writer chooses to define *game* as wild animals hunted for food or sport, he will benefit by knowing what the dic-

---

- we, my
- he, him, no one, any

Objectives

Students will

1. choose a word to define.
2. write a definition of one of its meanings.

Overview of the Writing Process

Planning—choosing a word and limiting the definition

Drafting—writing the definition

Revising—making necessary changes for clarity

Publishing—handing in to the teacher

Writing Definitions

Lesson Support

Teacher's Edition, Book 2
Writing Worksheets—p. 135
Rubrics—p. 149

Introduction

If possible, allow an entire class period for this assignment.

Materials

- a note card for each student

Tell each student to take out a sheet of paper. Direct the students to write the first meaning that comes to mind when you say "game."

Ask several students to read their definitions. Ask the students the following question: Why is it important to be sure that your audience defines words the same way you do? (*so the audience will not misinterpret your message*)

Discussion

Direct the students to read the introduction and the text material about writing defini-

tions. Encourage them to pay special attention to the examples in Steps 3-5. Answer any questions they may have after reading this material.

Distribute a copy of the Writing Worksheet (Book 2, p. 135) to each student and direct the students to evaluate the paragraph. Discuss their responses.

Planning

Direct the students to read the instructions in "Your Turn." Allow time for them to choose a word from the list and to jot down ideas.

tionary says about that meaning. And it will help to know that the dictionary calls the meat from such animals *game* as well.

Step 2

When a dictionary definition is not enough to clarify sufficiently, a writer must extend his meaning. One way is to use example. The writer about wild animals may want to improve on his original attempt.

FIRST TRY   Game is any animal or bird hunted for food or sport.

EXTENDED   Game is any animal or bird hunted for food or sport, such as quail and rabbit.

Another method of extending the definition is to use contrast; that is, to tell what the term does not include.

> Game is any animal or bird commonly hunted for food or sport, not those pursued by only a few people or those accidentally killed. For example, most people would not kill a porcupine for sport, even though someone who was very hungry might kill it for food.

Step 3

Be sure your definition is indeed a definition, not an editorial comment on how you feel about the topic. For example, the following is a description of a feeling, not a definition.

> *Game* is a cruel way to refer to animals that cannot protect themselves from hunters.

Step 4

Check your definition to see that it does not go around in a circle, coming right back to itself.

> *Game* is any animal used as game.

Step 5

Refine the definition to make it compact and concise. Here is the definition of *game* that would introduce an essay on hunting.

> The dictionary broadly defines *game* as any animal, bird, or fish that is hunted for food or sport. Throughout history there have been many animals that fit this category. However, modern practice defines *game* as animals, birds, or fish that are *commonly* hunted, mainly for sport but also for eating. It does not include those animals that only a few eat (most people nowadays do not relish an opossum steak). It would certainly not include endangered species, no matter how high they used to be on the big game lists.

Your Turn

Critique the definition your teacher gives you. Then rewrite it to meet the standards of usefulness and clarity. Or write a new paragraph defining one of the following:

- set
- ring
- walk

Each word above has multiple meanings. Be sure to choose just one meaning and to make it clear to your reader.

Drafting

Allow students time to write their definitions. Inform them of any time limit.

Revising

Instruct the students to read over their definitions when they finish them, making any changes for clarity and correctness.

Publishing

Collect the definitions.

Scriptural Application

Discuss with the students the fact that the Book of Proverbs contains many definitions. In Proverbs 14:9, for example, God defines fools as those who mock sin.

Evaluation

For help in grading this assignment, see "Grading Writing Assignments" (p. x) and Rubric 3 (Book 2, p. 149).

Enrichment

Encourage the students to identify definitions in the Book of Proverbs.

4 VERBS

Objectives

Students will

1. identify auxiliaries and recognize the complete verb in a sentence.

2. identify linking verbs and distinguish between predicate nouns and predicate adjectives.

3. label transitive verbs and their direct and indirect objects.

4. distinguish between transitive, intransitive, and linking verbs.

5. choose the correct principal part of the verb in a sentence.

6. evaluate and revise a paragraph for verb errors.

7. use the present, past, and future tenses correctly.

8. use the present perfect, past perfect, and future perfect tenses correctly.

9. use the progressive tense correctly.

10. use auxiliaries to create emphasis, to make sentences negative, or to form questions.

11. distinguish between active- and passive-voice verbs.

12. revise sentences to make them active or passive.

13. write sentences to include active- or passive-voice verbs.

14. identify the mood of a verb.

15. distinguish between the indicative and the imperative mood.

16. write sentences in the indicative and imperative moods.

Blues Ain't No Mockin' Bird

by Toni Cade Bambara

When two thoughtless cameramen working on a county project invade Granddaddy Cain's farm, they are taught some manners by the dignified owners.

By the time the man with the camera had cut across our neighbor's yard, the twins were out of the trees swingin low and Granny was onto the steps, the screen door bammin soft and scratchy against her palms. "We thought we'd get a shot or two of the house and everything and then—"

"Good mornin," Granny cut him off. And smiled that smile.

"Good mornin," he said, head all down the way Bingo does when you yell at him about the bones on the kitchen floor. "Nice place you got here, aunty. We thought we'd take a—"

"Did you?" said Granny with her eyebrows. Cathy pulled up her socks and giggled.

"Nice things, here" said the man, buzzin his camera over the yard. The pecan barrels, the sled, me and Cathy, the flowers, the printed stones along the driveway, the trees, the twins, the tool-shed.

"I don't know about the thing, the it, and the stuff," said Granny, still talkin with her eyebrows. "Just people here is what I tend to consider."

Camera man stopped buzzin. Cathy giggled into her collar.

"Mornin, ladies," a new man said. He had come up behind us when we weren't lookin. "And gents," discoverin the twins givin him a nasty look. "We're filmin for the county," he said with a smile. "Mind if we shoot a bit around here?"

"I do indeed," said Granny with no smile. Smilin man was smiling up a storm. So was Cathy. But he didn't seem to have another word to say, so he and the camera man backed on out of the yard, but you could hear the camera buzzin still. "Suppose you just shut that machine off," said Granny real low through her teeth, and took a step down off the porch and then another.

"Now, aunty," Camera said, pointin the thing straight at her.

"Your mama and I are not related."

- *How does the author make the dialogue seem like real speech?*
- *How do you know Granny is not pleased?*
- *What words help you hear what is happening in this scene?*

With the exception of *scratchy,* all the other sound words are verbs. How would the words *shuttin, laughed,* and *runnin* change the scene? *(The sounds in the scene would not be as specific.)* Verbs, with nouns, are the meat and potatoes, the essentials of good writing. Notice how all the action verbs give this excerpt life.

- *by dropping the endings on some words and by including interrupted sentences*
- *She cuts the men off in mid-sentence twice, she stops smiling, she raises her eyebrows, and she takes two steps down off the porch.*
- *bammin, scratchy, giggled, buzzin*

Lesson Support

Student Text
Chapter 4 Review—pp. 407-9

Teacher's Edition, Book 1
Bulletin Boards—p. 446
Diagram Answers—pp. 458-59

Teacher's Edition, Book 2
Pretests—pp. 9-10
Teaching Helps—p. 41
ESL Worksheets—pp. 67-72
Concept Reinforcements—pp. 100-102

Literature Link

Read aloud the excerpt from "Blues Ain't No Mockin' Bird" and lead a discussion using the questions in the student text. Point out the various action verbs and discuss the vital importance of verbs in writing. Verbs are like engines in a car: they create action and move the story along. Throughout this chapter, you can select and use other literature pieces of various genres or student writing that relies strongly on verb usage. Show the benefits of using strong, vibrant verbs.

Verbs

Verbs are often the most important words of a sentence. Verbs are necessary to communicate what is happening or to connect the subject with its complement. Look at the following sentence:

> The strong winds *create* rough waves on the water and *bend* small trees along the shore.

The verbs *create* and *bend* communicate what is happening. Learning how to use verbs effectively will give strength and vitality to your writing. Verbs express action or state of being.

ACTION	He *listens* to the news reports.
	The cars *maneuver* on the highway.
	Trash *accumulates* in the bin.

STATE OF BEING	He *is* the president. The waters *are* calm.
	She *has* a cold.
	The house *seems* empty without him.

In the examples, the action verbs communicate physical or mental action. The state-of-being verbs express the continuous state, or condition, of someone or something. All verbs fall into one of three categories: transitive, intransitive, or linking.

Recognizing the Complete Verb

The verb is the main word or words in the predicate. Nearly every verb can have *s* or *ing* added to it without changing the meaning of the verb. Any word that fits the following test frame can be a verb:

He _____ s.	He is _____ ing.
He moves.	He is moving.
It becomes.	It is becoming.

Auxiliaries

Auxiliaries join other verbs to make up the complete verb of a sentence. Auxiliaries are also called helping verbs. A verb may have one or more auxiliaries.

> They **will** *finish* on time.
> I **may be** *arriving* in the evening.

These are the most common auxiliaries in English.

- am, is, are, was, were, be, being, been
- have, has, had
- do, does, did
- will, would, shall, should, can, could, may, might, must

This fourth list is a group of auxiliaries called modals. Modals have only one form; they do not ever take a different ending to agree with the subject or to change tense.

ESL: Watch for recurring mistakes such as "He cans run fast" for "He can run fast." Some ESL students may overgeneralize the rule that requires an *s* on present tense verbs with a third-person singular subject.

Teaching Strategy: Introduction

Write these sentences for display:

- He _____ the ball at the most crucial moment in the game. *(caught, threw, fumbled, hurled)*
- In a sudden storm, the rain _____ the flowers. *(soaks, pelts, bathes)*
- The children _____ in the afternoon. *(sleep, study, play)*

Ask the students to fill in the blanks with a variety of answers. Show them how the verb can change the meaning or tone of the sentence. Stress the importance of learning correct verb usage.

Teaching Strategy: Induction

Write the following sentences for display:

- He leads the battle.
- He is a general.
- The soldiers listen for his orders.
- They are ready for action.

Ask the students to discuss the differences between the verbs in these sentences. (Leads *and* listen *show action while* is *and* are *express a continuous state.*) Tell them that verbs that describe physical or mental action are called action verbs. Verbs that express a continuous state or condition are called state-of-being verbs. Ask the students to form more sentences using either action or state-of-being verbs.

Some verbs can be used either as auxiliaries or as main verbs. For example, *be* can act as a linking verb. *Have* and *do* also can be main verbs.

> Martin *has* a cold today.
> Who will *do* the dishes tonight?

in summary

The **verb** is the main word or words in the predicate.

An **auxiliary** helps the main verb.

4-1 PRACTICE THE SKILL

Underline the complete verb in each sentence. If the complete verb includes an auxiliary, write the auxiliary in the blank.

_has__ 1. Weather has always fascinated man.

_____ 2. The writers of Scripture used weather imagery throughout the Bible.

__is___ 3. Many times nature is used as a metaphor.

__do___ 4. Do you know any weather imagery in the Bible?

_____ 5. The psalms are full of weather and nature images.

__will__ 6. For example, the Lord will lead us beside still waters.

__is___ 7. The writer is talking about God's peace.

_does__ 8. The psalmist does mention weather occurrences such as clouds, rain, and floods.

_____ 9. The heavens declare the glory of God.

__can__ 10. We can learn more about Scripture from the study of weather.

4-2 REVIEW THE SKILL

Underline the complete verb in each sentence. If the complete verb includes an auxiliary, write the auxiliary in the blank.

_____ 1. Between 1980 and 1999, the United States suffered from more than thirty-six large-scale natural disasters.

____have_____ 2. These disasters have cost the United States over one billion dollars each.

Verbs   83

Teaching Strategy: Demonstration

Write these sentences for display: *He _____s. He is _____ing.* Explain that this is a verb test frame. Ask the students to supply verbs and to evaluate them using the test frame. Remind the students that not all verbs (including many state-of-being verbs) will fit the test frame.

Teaching Strategy: Participation

After explaining that auxiliaries, or helping verbs, are often part of the complete verb, ask the students to name common auxiliaries. Write the auxiliaries for display and then refer students to page 82 in their texts for a complete listing of the most common auxiliaries. Ask each student to form one sentence in which an auxiliary acts as the main verb.

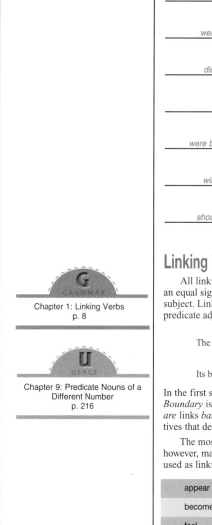

_____ 3. During 1998 alone, seven of these tragedies occurred.

___was___ 4. Almost six billion dollars <u>was spent</u> on repairs to the damage from Hurricane Georges.

___were___ 5. During the same year, the southern states <u>were</u> experiencing a severe heat wave and drought.

___did___ 6. Unbelievably, the cost <u>did surpass</u> thirty billion dollars.

_____ 7. More than two hundred people <u>died</u> because of the weather.

___were being___ 8. Other parts of the world <u>were</u> also being battered with unusual weather conditions.

___will___ 9. Scientists <u>will</u> continually <u>learn</u> more about extreme weather.

___should___ 10. We <u>should</u> always <u>be</u> aware of the powerful force of weather.

Linking Verbs

All linking verbs are state-of-being verbs. A linking verb is similar to an equal sign; it links the subject to a word that renames or describes the subject. Linking verbs have a complement, either a predicate noun or a predicate adjective.

<pre>
       S LV   PN
The river is a boundary between the two states.
</pre>

<pre>
       S LV PA   PA
Its banks are rough and steep.
</pre>

In the first sentence, *is* is a linking verb connecting *river* and *boundary*. *Boundary* is a predicate noun that renames *river*. In the second sentence, *are* links *banks* with *rough* and *steep*. *Rough* and *steep* are predicate adjectives that describe *banks*.

The most common linking verbs are forms of the verb *be*. Other verbs, however, may be used as linking verbs. Below is a list of verbs commonly used as linking verbs.

appear	grow	seem	stay
become	look	smell	taste
feel	remain	sound	

Chapter 1: Linking Verbs
p. 8

Chapter 9: Predicate Nouns of a Different Number
p. 216

Teaching Strategy: Induction

Write this sentence for display: *Our neighbor is _____.* Ask the students to fill in the blank. *(friendly, talkative, a doctor, a teacher, a member of our church)* As they give you answers, group the nouns together and the adjectives together. Then ask the students to identify the two groups. *(nouns and adjectives)* Explain that *is* is a linking verb. Linking verbs are state-of-being verbs that link the subject to a complement. If the complement is a noun, we call it a predicate noun. If it is an adjective, we call it a predicate adjective. Ask the students to identify other linking verbs. (*Note:* Students may fill in the blank with words that end with *ing.* Explain that these words are actually part of the complete verb and that they will be discussed later in the chapter.)

Notice that the *be* verb acts as both an auxiliary and a linking verb. If the *be* verb is followed by another verb, it is an auxiliary, not a linking verb.

 **in summary**

A **linking verb** is a state-of-being verb. Linking verbs have a complement, either a predicate noun or a predicate adjective.

4-3 PRACTICE THE SKILL

Underline the complete verb once. Underline the predicate noun or predicate adjective twice. In the blank, label the complement *PN* or *PA*.

PA   1. The tools of a weather forecaster are interesting and diverse.

PA   2. A thermometer is important in the measurement of temperature.

PN   3. A falling barometer is a sign of stormy weather.

PA   4. Weather satellites have also grown increasingly useful to meteorologists.

PN   5. These satellites have become an especially valuable tool for a worldwide view of weather conditions.

PA   6. Weather equipment remains crucial in the study of various types of weather.

PN   7. The study of snow crystals has been a fascination of some scientists.

PA   8. Every snowflake is unique in its testimony to God's creativity.

PN   9. According to observation, no two snowflakes are duplicates.

PN 10. Plates, needles, and dendrites are types of snow crystals.

4-4 REVIEW THE SKILL

Underline the complete verb once. Underline the predicate noun or predicate adjective twice. In the blank, label the complement *PN* or *PA*.

PN   1. Meteorology is a particular branch of science.

PN   2. Meteorologists are students of the earth's atmosphere.

Verbs   85

Evaluation

If you have assigned sentence diagramming with Review the Skill 4-4, check students' answers using page 458.

_PA_ 3. Many types of instruments are important for weather study.

_PN_ 4. Some of these instruments are weather balloons, hygrometers, and weather satellites.

_PA_ 5. The earth's atmosphere is divisible into distinct regions.

_PA_ 6. Each region feels different in temperature.

_PN_ 7. The troposphere is the lowest region of the earth's atmosphere.

_PA_ 8. Air in the troposphere is never static.

_PN_ 9. The troposphere and the waters beneath it are the home of all of the earth's plant, animal, and human life.

_PA_ 10. The study of the troposphere has become especially interesting and important.

Chapter 1: Intransitive and Transitive Verbs p. 7

Chapter 1: Intransitive and Transitive Verbs p. 7

Transitive Verbs

A **transitive verb** has an object that receives the action of the verb. Transitive verbs transfer their action to receivers called **direct objects.** Direct objects answer the questions *whom?* or *what?* after the verb. Transitive verbs can also have **indirect objects.** An indirect object comes between the verb and the direct object and answers the question *to whom/what?* or *for whom/what?* the action of the verb is done.

       S   TrV   DO
The associate deposited the money.

    S TrV   IO   DO
He gave the teller his account number.

Intransitive Verbs

In some sentences, the verb does not need an object or other complement to complete the meaning. These verbs are called **intransitive verbs.**

       S   InV
The rain suddenly stopped.

      S   InV   InV
The lions stalked and then attacked.

Words may follow intransitive verbs, but these words will not be direct objects, predicate nouns, or predicate adjectives.

             S   InV
In the noisy cafeteria, everyone speaks loudly.

  InV
Please speak into the microphone.

Adverbs and prepositional phrases often follow intransitive verbs.

Teaching Strategy: Induction and Discussion

Write this sentence for display: *My friend gives me _____.* Ask the students to fill in the blank. Discuss with them how the verb *gives* differs from a linking verb. *(It transfers action to an object. It does not link the subject to a complement.)* Tell them that this type of verb is called a transitive verb.

Teaching Strategy: Participation

For a review of direct and indirect objects, tell each student to take out half a sheet of paper and to write a sentence that contains either a direct object or both a direct object and an indirect object. Collect the papers and, reading each sentence aloud, quickly repeat a word in the sentence and ask a student to identify the word as either a direct object or an indirect object. Give each student a chance to answer.

One on One
Generate several sentences with direct and indirect objects. After reading each sentence aloud, repeat either the direct or indirect object; then ask your student to identify the word correctly as a direct object or an indirect object.

in summary

in summary

A **transitive verb** must have an object that receives the action of the verb.

A **direct object** receives the action of a transitive verb.

An **indirect object** comes between the verb and the direct object and answers the question *to whom/what?* or *for whom/what?* the action of the verb is done.

An **intransitive verb** does not have an object.

4-5 PRACTICE THE SKILL

Underline the complete verb in each sentence. Label the sentence patterns *S-InV, S-TrV-DO,* and *S-TrV-IO-DO.* Above each word of the sentence pattern, write its label.

1. The ozone layer in the earth's upper atmosphere blocks the sun's ultra-
    violet rays.
    — S ... TrV ... DO

2. In the lower atmosphere, increases in ozone amounts cause smog.
    — S ... TrV ... DO

3. The upper ozone layer gives humans protection from the ultraviolet
    rays.
    — S ... TrV ... IO ... DO

4. In 1974 M. J. Molina and F. S. Rowland first showed people a decrease
    in ozone amounts.
    — S ... S ... TrV ... IO ... DO

5. The human eye cannot see changes in the ozone layer.
    — S ... TrV ... DO

6. Many scientists argue about the causes of ozone depletion.
    — S ... InV

7. In 1999 ozone levels had decreased to 33 percent of the levels before
    1975.
    — S ... InV

8. Because of this depletion, many countries have reduced the use of
    harmful chemicals.
    — S ... TrV ... DO

9. Natural volcanic eruptions can also decrease the level of ozone.
    — S ... TrV ... DO

10. Extensive investigation has given researchers more information.
    — S ... TrV ... IO ... DO

Teaching Strategy: Discussion and Reinforcement

For display, write sentences that have intransitive verbs. Ask the students to identify the difference between these verbs and the verbs they have studied previously. *(They do not need objects or complements to complete them.)* Remind the students that words may follow an intransitive verb. These words, such as adverbs or prepositional phrases, are not direct objects. Write these sentences for display: *She revised the chapter. She revises on her computer.* Ask students to distinguish between these sentences. Make sure they can see the difference and that they understand that the same verb may be transitive in one sentence but intransitive in another. *(The first sentence pattern is S-TrV-DO. The second is S-InV with a prepositional phrase.)*

Evaluation

If you have assigned sentence diagramming with Review the Skill 4-5, check students' answers using page 459.

Underline the verb in each sentence. In the blank, label the verb *transitive*, *intransitive*, or *linking*.

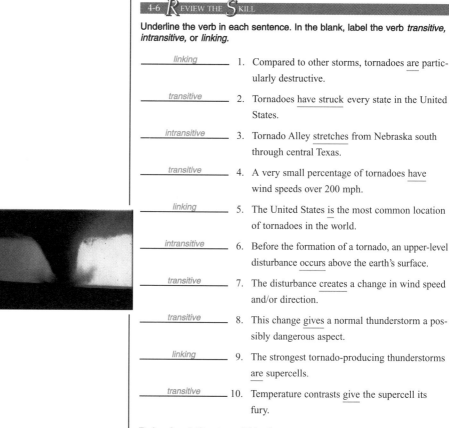

linking	1.	Compared to other storms, tornadoes are partic-ularly destructive.
transitive	2.	Tornadoes have struck every state in the United States.
intransitive	3.	Tornado Alley stretches from Nebraska south through central Texas.
transitive	4.	A very small percentage of tornadoes have wind speeds over 200 mph.
linking	5.	The United States is the most common location of tornadoes in the world.
intransitive	6.	Before the formation of a tornado, an upper-level disturbance occurs above the earth's surface.
transitive	7.	The disturbance creates a change in wind speed and/or direction.
transitive	8.	This change gives a normal thunderstorm a pos-sibly dangerous aspect.
linking	9.	The strongest tornado-producing thunderstorms are supercells.
transitive	10.	Temperature contrasts give the supercell its fury.

Principal Parts of Verbs

Almost all verbs have three basic forms. These basic forms are the principal parts of a verb. The word *principal* here means "main." All the different forms of verbs can be made from these three main forms: present, past, and past participle. The past participle is the form that is used after some form of the auxiliary *have*.

PRESENT	PAST	PAST PARTICIPLE
talk	talked	(have) talked
take	took	(have) taken

Notice that the second and third principal parts of *talk* are the same. All the principal parts of *take*, however, are different. Verbs that form the second and third principal parts by adding *ed* to the first principal part are

ESL: Some ESL students may not realize that the past participle cannot be used alone as a main verb. Emphasize that the past participle must be used with some form of *have* to be a finite verb (the predicate of a clause).

Evaluation

Use Review the Skill 4-6 to determine whether your students can identify verbs as transitive, intransitive, and linking. Students should be able to explain how they distinguished the three types of verbs from one another.

Teaching Strategy: Introduction

Bring a color chart or three colored items (red, blue, and yellow) to class. Explain to the students that many colors are developed from one group of primary colors: red, blue, and yellow. Ask the students to name several colors and to identify the primary colors from which those colors are developed. *(Green is a combination of yellow and blue; orange is a combination of red and yellow.)* Explain that just as there are numerous colors, there are numerous forms of verbs. There are three principal parts of

each verb. Every form of that verb is created from one of the three principal parts.

called **regular verbs.** Verbs such as *take* are called **irregular verbs.** There are various kinds of irregular verbs, but they all form the past and past participle some other way than by adding *ed* to the present form of the verb.

Regular Verbs

The past and the past participle of regular verbs are formed by adding *d* or *ed* to the present form of the verb.

hope	hoped	hoped
walk	walked	walked

These regular verbs are often troublesome.

climb	climbed	climbed
drag	dragged	dragged
drown	drowned	drowned
hang (execute)	hanged	hanged
raise (lift up)	raised	raised
shine (polish)	shined	shined
sneak	sneaked	sneaked

Irregular Verbs

If the past and past participle of a verb are not formed by adding *d* or *ed* to the present form, that verb is irregular. Learning the principal parts will help you avoid mistakes in usage. A dictionary lists the principal parts of any verb right after the pronunciation.

There are three categories of irregular verbs.

•All three principal parts of the verb are the same.

burst	burst	burst
cost	cost	cost
cut	cut	cut
let	let	let
put	put	put
set	set	set

•Two principal parts of the verb are the same.

become	became	become
bring	brought	brought
buy	bought	bought
catch	caught	caught

Teaching Strategy: Induction

Write several verbs for display, including the following: *lift, walk, break,* and *give.* Ask the students to identify other ways that the verbs can appear. *(lifted, walked, broken, gave)* As the students supply these answers, place their responses into one of three columns. Complete the columns and then label them "present," "past," and "past participle" respectively. Identify these forms as the three principal parts of verbs. Students may supply verbs that have *ing* endings. Tell them that you will discuss *ing* verbs (present participles) later. You may want to explain that the present participle is a common form but that it is not a principal part because it is always formed from the first principal part, just as a secondary color is formed from a primary color. Students may question why the past or the past participle forms are principal parts when they are formed by simply adding *ed* to the first principal part. Refer to the verb *break.* The past and past participle are not formed from the first principal part. Point out that verbs whose second and third principal parts are not formed by adding *ed* are called irregular verbs.

Teaching Strategy: Participation

Help the students understand what a participle is. Ask one or several students to look up the word *participle* in the dictionary. Ask someone to explain his findings to the class. Then ask the students to create several sentences using participles.

come	came	come
cling	clung	clung
dig	dug	dug
get	got	got
hang (suspend)	hung	hung
keep	kept	kept
lay (place)	laid	laid
lead	led	led
lose	lost	lost
run	ran	run
shine (emit light)	shone *or* shined	shone *or* shined
sit	sat	sat
swing	swung	swung
teach	taught	taught
tell	told	told
think	thought	thought
weep	wept	wept

•All three principal parts of the verb are different.

begin	began	begun
blow	blew	blown
break	broke	broken
choose	chose	chosen
do	did	done
draw	drew	drawn
drink	drank	drunk
drive	drove	driven
eat	ate	eaten
fall	fell	fallen
freeze	froze	frozen
give	gave	given
go	went	gone
grow	grew	grown

Teaching Strategy: Participation

Materials
• several slips of paper with a verb written on each one (Verbs should represent all the principal parts.)

Display three columns labeled "present," "past," and "past participle." Give each student two or three slips of paper with a verb written on each slip. Ask each student to read at least one of his slips aloud and to identify the column to which his verb belongs. (Some regular verbs may belong in both the past and the past participle columns.) If possible, allow students to actually place their slips of paper in the appropriate columns. Try to include as many irregular verbs as possible.

Teaching Strategy: Discussion

Ask the students if they have ever heard a small child say "I drinked" or "I drawed." Lead a discussion about why a child might do this when he has never heard that word before. Explain that young children quickly discover that the past tense is usually the present tense with *ed*. They often apply this rule to irregular verbs as well.

hide	hid	hidden
know	knew	known
lie (recline)	lay	lain
ride	rode	ridden
rise (go up)	rose	risen
see	saw	seen
shake	shook	shaken
show	showed	shown
sing	sang	sung
sink	sank *or* sunk	sunk
speak	spoke	spoken
swim	swam	swum
take	took	taken
throw	threw	thrown
write	wrote	written

in summary

The three principal parts of the verb are the **present, past,** and **past participle**.

Regular verbs form the second and third principal parts by adding *ed* to the first principal part.

Irregular verbs form the second and third principal parts by some method other than by adding *ed* to the first principal part.

4-7 PRACTICE THE SKILL

Underline the correct verb from the choices in parentheses. Be sure to look for any auxiliary that may go with the verb you have chosen.

1. What are some of the best things you ever *(did, done)* outside?

2. I love ice skating on a lake that has *(froze, frozen)*.

3. Today I just *(laid, lay)* out in the sun and read a book.

4. I have also *(swam, swum)* in the ocean recently.

5. I love hearing birds sing, like the robin that just *(sang, sung)* a beautiful song outside my window.

6. What are some of the lovely things you have *(saw, seen)*?

7. I love seeing fresh snow that has just *(fell, fallen)*.

8. Seeing a sun that has recently *(rose, risen)* is also unforgettable.

9. The lovely roses in my garden have already *(grew, grown)* tall.

10. Yesterday before supper ended, my family had *(ate, eaten)* the last of the vegetables from our summer garden.

11. Last Saturday my friend *(came, come)* over for a hike.

12. I really *(began, begun)* to enjoy the days of beautiful weather.

13. The walk was beautiful with the colored leaves on the trees; I am so glad we had *(chose, chosen)* to go.

14. The wind had *(blew, blown)* down some of the leaves, and we collected some.

15. I have to go in now, before I am *(bite, bitten)* by a mosquito!

4-8 REVIEW THE SKILL

In the blank write the correct past or past participle form of the verb in parentheses.

taught 1. In Matthew 14, Jesus had *(teach)* the multitudes by healing and feeding them.

told 2. After finishing, He had *(tell)* his disciples to get into a ship and to go to the other side.

went 3. Then, Jesus left His disciples and *(go)* to pray.

blew 4. But the wind *(blow)* hard, and the ship was tossed.

became 5. The disciples *(become)* afraid.

shaken 6. The disciples were *(shook)* and troubled.

come 7. Jesus had *(come)* to them, walking on the water.

known 8. Before He spoke, they had not *(know)* who He was.

sank 9. Peter started walking on the water, but when he took his eyes off Jesus, he *(sink)*.

spoke 10. Jesus saved him and *(speak)* gently to him.

Rewrite the following paragraph, correcting any errors in verb forms. There are ten errors.

Men have always knew that the sun has gave the earth light and warmth. Crops and plants have grew because of the sun's life-giving rays. One particular curiosity that has drew scientists is the study of sunspots. With telescopes scientists have began to understand sunspots. Scientists have saw that changes on the sun cause changes in magnetic instruments here on earth. Also, plasma, a hot substance around a sunspot, has bursted up from the sun's surface. Particles from these solar flares have came to the earth in geomagnetic storms. One effect is the northern and southern lights, which have brung enjoyment to many. Scientists have also known sunspots to affect radio transmissions and satellites. The sun has shown many of its effects to all, but it has also hid some of its effects from many.

Men have always known that the sun has given the earth light and warmth.

Crops and plants have grown because of the sun's life-giving rays. One

particular curiosity that has drawn scientists is the study of sunspots. With tele-

scopes scientists have begun to understand sunspots. Scientists have seen that

changes on the sun cause changes in magnetic instruments here on earth. Also,

plasma, a hot substance around a sunspot, has burst up from the sun's surface.

Particles from these solar flares have come to the earth in geomagnetic storms.

One effect is the northern and southern lights, which have brought enjoyment to

many. Scientists have also known sunspots to affect radio transmissions and

satellites. The sun has shown many of its effects to all, but it has also hidden

some of its effects from many.

Verb Tenses

Simple Tenses

English verbs have three simple tenses: present, past, and future.

PRESENT   They *work* today.
PAST   They *worked* yesterday.
FUTURE   They *will work* tomorrow.

Verbs   93

Teaching Strategy:
Introduction

Explain that the three simple tenses do not have a direct correspondence to the three principal parts. Each simple tense, however, is formed from one of the three principal parts.

Present tense verbs express either a state that is true now or an action that occurs habitually. Notice that the present tense is formed from the first principal part of the verb.

The team *has* a good record.
The team *practices* on Saturdays.

Past tense verbs show action that occurred in the past. The past tense of the verb is the same as the past principal part.

Last week, the team *practiced* on Saturday.

Future tense verbs show action that will occur in the future. To form the future tense, add the helping verb *will* (or *shall*) to the first principal part.

The team *will practice* on Saturday.
The law *shall provide* for an educational exemption.

in summary

Present tense verbs express either a state that is true now or an action that occurs habitually.

Past tense verbs show action that occurred in the past.

Future tense verbs show action that will occur in the future.

4-10 PRACTICE THE SKILL

Underline each verb. Label its tense *present, past,* or *future.*

_____present_____ 1. The magnificence of nature teaches us about the magnificence of God.

_____future_____ 2. God will teach us about His power in His Word.

_____past_____ 3. God created the world in six days.

_____present_____ 4. Many natural events show God's greatness.

_____present_____ 5. Lightning is a powerful weather event.

_____past_____ 6. Writers of the Bible referred to lightning many times.

_____future_____ 7. According to Matthew, Jesus will come like lightning.

_____present_____ 8. The psalms also speak of lightning.

<u>past</u> 9. According to Psalm 97, lightning <u>lighted</u> the world.

<u>present</u> 10. God <u>displays</u> His awesome power through lightning.

4-11 *R*EVIEW THE *S*KILL

In the blank write the correct form of the verb in parentheses.

<u>think</u> 1. We often <u>?</u> of radar being used only for weather forecasts. *(think, present)*

<u>used</u> 2. However, people first <u>?</u> radar in World War II to detect enemy planes. *(use, past)*

<u>affected</u> 3. Unfortunately, rain <u>?</u> the radar so that planes could not be seen. *(affect, past)*

<u>discovered</u> 4. Weather forecasters <u>?</u> that radar could be used for weather forecasting. *(discover, past)*

<u>works</u> 5. Radar <u>?</u> by transmitting radio waves. *(work, present)*

<u>will return</u> 6. When the waves hit rain, the signal <u>?</u> to the radar. *(return, future)*

<u>send</u> 7. Many radar units <u>?</u> out approximately one thousand signals per second. *(send, present)*

<u>is</u> 8. Doppler radar <u>?</u> an especially useful type of radar. *(be, present)*

<u>started</u> 9. Doppler radar research <u>?</u> in the mid-1960s. *(start, past)*

<u>will continue</u> 10. Radar <u>?</u> to be beneficial to various types of work. *(continue, future)*

Perfect Tenses

The perfect tenses express completion of an action. Perfect tenses are formed from the third principal part and require a form of the auxiliary *have* to complete them. The name of each perfect tense matches the form of *have* used with the past participle.

Tense	Auxiliary
Present Perfect	have or has
Past Perfect	had
Future Perfect	will have (or shall have)

Verbs 95

Teaching Strategy: Introduction

Ask the students for their definition of the word *perfect*. Most will probably think of it as meaning "without defect" or "superlative." Require a few students to look up the word in the dictionary. Explain to the class that *perfect* also refers to completeness. The following tenses are called perfect tenses because they express action that has been or will be completed by a certain time.

The **present perfect tense** describes an action or state that is completed during the present time period or one that began in the past and has continued up to the present moment. Use the auxiliary *have* or *has* to form the present perfect tense.

> I *have finished* two books already this month.
> They *have talked* all evening.
> The snow *has begun* to fall.

The **past perfect tense** describes an action that was completed (or a state that existed) before a certain time in the past. Use the auxiliary *had* to form the past perfect tense.

> Before my cousin's family arrived, we *had prepared* a bedroom for them.
> We *had waited* for them an hour before they finally arrived.

The **future perfect tense** describes an action that will be completed (or a state that will exist) by or before a certain time in the future. Use the auxiliaries *will have* (or *shall have*) to form the future perfect tense.

> I *will have practiced* five hours before my lesson on Thursday.
> At the end of this vacation, we *will have been* in seven states.

in summary

A **present perfect tense verb** describes an action completed or a state that existed during the present or one that began in the past and has continued up until the present moment.

A **past perfect tense verb** describes an action that occurred or a state that existed before a certain time in the past.

A **future perfect tense verb** describes an action that will occur or a state that will exist by or before a certain time in the future.

4-12 PRACTICE THE SKILL

Underline each complete verb. Label its tense *present, present perfect, past, past perfect, future,* or *future perfect.*

<u>future perfect</u>   1. Before the end of the next thunderstorm, lightning <u>will</u> probably <u>have struck</u> somewhere.

<u>present perfect</u>   2. How <u>have</u> people <u>learned</u> about lightning?

<u>past perfect</u>   3. Before the advent of scientific study, the Greeks and Romans <u>had thought</u> that lightning was a weapon of the gods.

<u>past</u>   4. Other groups of people also <u>had</u> superstitious beliefs about lightning.

Teaching Strategy: Induction

Write the following sentence for display: *We complete the costumes.* Ask the students to identify the tense of the verb *complete.* (present) Now ask them to change the verb into past tense and to repeat the sentence. (*We completed the costumes.*) Now tell them to express that the costumes were completed when the rehearsal began. (*We had completed the costumes when the rehearsal began.*) Tell them that this form of *complete* is in the past perfect tense. Explain that each perfect tense is created using a form of *have* plus the past participle form of the verb. Now encourage the students to use the same basic sentence and to change it into the present perfect tense and the future perfect tense. (*We have finished the costumes. We will have finished the costumes before the rehearsal begins.*)

Reinforcement

Remind the students that all perfect tense verbs require some form of *have* as an auxiliary.

Teaching Strategy: Participation

Display six columns labeled with the three simple tenses and the three perfect tenses. Either give the students slips of papers with sentences on them or read sentences aloud. The students should identify the tenses of the verbs. Write each verb in the appropriate category on the chart.

ESL Strategy

For more practice with perfect tenses, see ESL Worksheets 4A and 4B (Book 2, pp. 67-68).

past perfect   5. Before the end of the 1700s, Benjamin Franklin had proved that lightning was electricity.

present   6. Lightning has many different forms: forked, streaked, ribbon, bead, and ball.

present perfect   7. Some of these forms have been a curiosity for scientific study.

future   8. During the next storm, you will notice that flashes of lightning differ in length.

present perfect   9. Some flashes have been as long as nine miles.

future perfect   10. By the end of this chapter, you will have learned more about lightning.

4-13 USE THE SKILL

In the blank write the correct form of the verb in parentheses.

_is_   1. Ball lightning _?_ a glowing ball of electricity that moves through the air. *(be, simple present)*

have witnessed   2. Few people _?_ an occurrence of ball lightning. *(witness, present perfect)*

had documented   3. Before 1999, forty-three people _?_ accounts of ball lightning penetrating closed rooms. *(document, past perfect)*

reported   4. One woman _?_ actually seeing a ball of light come into her bedroom. *(report, simple past)*

have seen   5. The people who _?_ ball lightning say that it is beautiful. *(see, present perfect)*

lingers   6. Because ball lightning _?_ only a few seconds, many people doubt its existence. *(linger, simple present)*

believe   7. However, many scientists _?_ that it is real. *(believe, simple present)*

have had   8. They simply _?_ not _?_ many experiences for study. *(have, present perfect)*

Will understand   9. _?_ scientists ever _?_ ball lightning any better? *(understand, simple future)*

will have learned   10. We hope that scientists _?_ more about ball lightning by the next decade. *(learn, future perfect)*

Verbs   97

Evaluation

Assign Use the Skill 4-13 to determine if your students can correctly produce verbs with simple and perfect tenses.

Progressive Tenses

Each of the simple and perfect tenses also has a progressive form. The progressive tense of the verb shows continuous action. Use a form of *be* as an auxiliary and the *ing* form of the verb to form the progressive tense.

I *am studying* the Civil War.
I *have been studying* the Civil War for several weeks.

The tense of the first sentence is present progressive, which shows present continuing action. *Am* is the present tense of the verb *be,* and *studying* is the progressive form of *study.* The tense of the second sentence is present perfect progressive, which shows continuing action completed during the present or continuing up until the present. *Have been* is the present perfect tense of *be.* Notice in the examples below that the form of *be* in each sentence reflects the simple or perfect tense of the verb.

TENSE OF VERB	FORM OF *BE*	EXAMPLE
Present progressive (present continuing action)	Present tense of *be*	He *is studying* the Civil War. We *are studying* the Civil War today.
Past progressive (past continuing action)	Past tense of *be*	I *was studying* the Civil War. They *were studying* the Civil War all last week.
Future progressive (continuing action in the future)	Future tense of *be*	I *will be studying* the Civil War next week.
Present perfect progressive (continuing action done during the present time period)	Present perfect tense of *be*	I *have been studying* the Civil War for several weeks now.
Past perfect progressive (continuing action completed before a certain time in the past)	Past perfect tense of *be*	When our reports were due, we *had been studying* the Civil War for two weeks.
Future perfect progressive (continuing action that will be completed before a certain time in the future)	Future perfect tense of *be*	When the semester ends, we *will have been studying* the Civil War for three weeks.

Teaching Strategy: Discussion

The students have learned that the perfect tenses express completed action. Now ask them to describe a verb that would show continuing action. You can help them by giving them a sentence and asking them to fill in the blank. For example, you may want to write the following sentence for display: *Tomorrow I will be _____ all evening for my test. (studying)* Identify the *ing* form as the progressive tense. Explain that each of the simple and perfect tense verbs can be made progressive.

Teaching Strategy: Participation

Give the students several simple or perfect tense sentences. Now ask the students to rewrite each of the sentences in the progressive form. Students may make the mistake of changing perfect tense verbs to the simple progressive form rather than the perfect progressive form. Use such errors as an opportunity to emphasize the differences between simple progressive and perfect progressive forms.

Scriptural Application

Lead a discussion with your students about the concept of time. The concept of time continues to fascinate and baffle the human mind. Writers, scientists, and philosophers have theorized and experimented with the possibility of time travel. As of yet, however, no one has traveled to the future or back to the past. God, who created time, is not bound by time. The Scriptures record two instances of His stopping or changing time. God began time at Creation, and there is coming a day when time will be no more. This concept is difficult even to imagine,

Underline the complete verb. In the blank, label its tense.

<u>present perfect progressive</u>   1. Our science instructor <u>has been teaching</u> weather every day.

<u>future progressive</u>   2. Tomorrow we <u>will be going</u> on a field trip to the National Weather Service regional headquarters.

<u>present perfect progressive</u>   3. Our class <u>has been planning</u> the trip for several months.

<u>future progressive</u>   4. We <u>will be traveling</u> in a Greyhound bus.

<u>future perfect progressive</u>   5. By the time of our arrival, we <u>will have been riding</u> for over four hours.

<u>future progressive</u>   6. The National Weather Service <u>will be giving</u> us information on the equipment for weather forecasts.

<u>past progressive</u>   7. Yesterday before the the end of class, we <u>were looking</u> at weather safety.

<u>past perfect progressive</u>   8. Before our study of safety, we <u>had been researching</u> types of clouds.

<u>present perfect progressive</u>   9. My friend Jesse <u>has been</u> especially <u>enjoying</u> the topic of storms.

<u>future perfect progressive</u>   10. At the end of the semester, my science class <u>will have been studying</u> weather for four weeks.

In the blank write the progressive form of each italicized verb. Do not change the tense of the verb.

<u>will be studying</u>   1. We *will study* the settlement of America in our history class.

<u>are causing</u>   2. Extreme weather conditions *cause* difficulty to many people.

<u>are relating</u>   3. Many historians *relate* the hardships of the settlers of America.

Verbs   99

but there will be a day when we no longer need calendars, watches, or appointment books. For now, though, every human endeavor is subject to time. Even the Bible is written with reference to time. The history books are written in past tense. The Psalms and other biblical poetry are often written in present tense to make the message more personal and to show the endurance of truth. The prophecy books are often in future tense. Tell the students to locate several verses in the Scripture that are written in different tenses. As they use the Bible, ask them these questions:

• What tenses are predominant in the Gospels? *(past and present)* What do these tenses accomplish or what literary value do they have? *(Past tense is the normal tense for recording past, factual information, but the present tense makes the words of Christ individual and timeless.)*

• What is the predominant tense of the Epistles? *(present)* What advantage does this have? *(Answers will vary but may include the following: Present tense makes the passages personal, timeless, and immediate.)*

• What tenses are found in Revelation? *(past, present, and future; much of Revelation is prophecy that is recorded in past tense in the form of a dream.)* Ask the students to give their ideas on why the book was designed this way. *(Answers will vary but may include the following: From God's perspective, these future events have already occurred. The past tense emphasizes the certainty that these things will take place.)*

<u>were causing</u> 4. Poor weather conditions *caused* many of those hardships.

<u>were making</u> 5. At least 90 percent of early American settlers *made* a living through farming.

<u>are having</u> 6. We *have* a hard time imagining how difficult the settlers' lives were.

<u>will be having</u> 7. With the onset of modern technology, we *will* never *have* the same experience.

<u>was having</u> 8. Shipping also *had* a major impact on colonial life.

<u>were causing</u> 9. Storms often *caused* dangerous conditions for traders.

<u>will be thanking</u> 10. We *will thank* God for all of our comforts.

Other Uses for Auxiliaries

You have seen how auxiliaries are used to form the future tense, the perfect tenses, and the progressive tenses of verbs. You can also use auxiliaries to show emphasis, to make sentences negative, and to form questions.

One way to **emphasize** a spoken statement is to stress the auxiliary.

> We *will* finish the game, even if it is raining.

If the verb has no auxiliary, use *do* to show emphasis.

> "Valerie likes skiing; she dislikes ice skating."
> "No, she *does* like ice skating, but she already has plans on Friday."

To make a sentence **negative**, add the auxiliary *do* and the adverb *not.* (If the verb is a form of *be* or already has an auxiliary, just add *not.*)

> He *did not* finish the essay.
> They are *not* here yet.
> She will *not* be running for office next year.

You can also use the auxiliary *do* to form some **questions.**

> *Did* I see you at the performance?

When forming a negative sentence, the negative *not* always follows the first auxiliary, regardless of how many auxiliaries there are in the complete verb.

We could *not* have been happier.

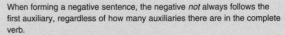 

in summary

The auxiliary *do* can be used to show emphasis, to make a sentence negative, or to form a question.

Teaching Strategy: Induction

The students have seen that auxiliaries can change the tense of a verb. Ask them to suggest other ways that an auxiliary can change or help a verb. If necessary, give the students some example sentences in which the auxiliary is being used to emphasize an idea, negate the verb, or form a question. You may wish to display the following sentences:

• You do have to finish the book.
• Reading the summary will not complete the assignment.

• Chapter 5 is not part of the assignment.
• Do you know where we are going?

ESL Strategy

See ESL Worksheet 4C (Book 2, p. 69) for practice using the auxiliary *do* correctly.

ESL Strategy

Question formation can often cause ESL students difficulty. For additional help with this skill, see ESL Worksheets 4D and 4E (Book 2, pp. 70-72).

Underline the complete verb. If the sentence contains *do* as an auxiliary, label it according to its use: *E* (emphasis), *Q* (question), or *N* (negative).

Q 1. Do you know any weather records?

N 2. I don't think so.

E 3. But I do need some for my science report.

Q 4. Do you know the location of that kind of information?

Q 5. Does the encyclopedia include weather information?

E 6. I do hope for some valuable information from the Internet.

E 7. The largest hailstone did measure 17.5 inches.

E 8. In 1924, Marble Bar, West Australia, did have the longest heat wave in the twentieth century.

N 9. Surely the city didn't have very dangerous weather.

E 10. Actually, Marble Bar did have 162 days of temperatures 100 degrees or greater!

Rewrite each sentence, using an auxiliary to create the effect indicated in parentheses. *(Answers may vary.)*

1. You know who the first Japanese adventurer was. *(question)*

   Do you know who the first Japanese adventurer was?

2. I think Yako could tell you. *(negative)*

   I don't think Yako could tell you.   OR

   I think Yako could not tell you.

3. I need to know the information for a trivia question. *(emphasis)*

   I do need to know the information for a trivia question.

4. Julia said it was Naomi Uemura. *(emphasis)*

   Julia did say it was Naomi Uemura.

Verbs   101

5. She said what his accomplishment was. *(question)*

   Did she say what his accomplishment was?
   _____

6. Naomi Uemura traveled alone to the North Pole first. *(emphasis)*

   Naomi Uemura did travel alone to the North Pole first.
   _____

7. The temperature fell very low. *(question)*

   How low did the temperature fall?   OR

   Did the temperature fall very low?

8. Actually, the temperature fell to forty below zero. *(emphasis)*

   Actually, the temperature did fall to forty below zero.
   _____

9. The weather stopped him from completing his adventure. *(negative)*

   The weather did not stop him from completing his adventure.
   _____

10. I used that information for the trivia game. *(question)*

    Did I use that information for the trivia game?
    _____

Active and Passive Voice

Sentences with intransitive verbs and linking verbs are in active voice. A sentence with a transitive verb can be in either active or passive voice. In active voice, the subject is the doer of the action. In passive voice, the subject is the receiver of the action.

> **ACTIVE** Lightning *struck* the tree.
> **PASSIVE** The tree *was struck* by lightning.

Identify a passive sentence by looking at the verb. Every passive sentence contains a form of the verb *be* followed by the past participle form of the transitive verb.

As with perfect and progressive tenses, the tense of the passive-voice verb matches the tense of the auxiliary.

Teaching Strategy: Induction

Write the following sentences for display: *Alicia's friends gave her a party. Alicia was given a party by her friends.* The message of the sentences is obviously the same. Ask the students to identify the differentiating sentence structures. *(In the first sentence, the subject performs the action. In the second sentence, the subject receives the action.)* Identify the two kinds of sentences as active and passive, respectively.

	ACTIVE	PASSIVE
PRESENT	break/breaks	am broken is broken are broken
PAST	broke	was broken were broken
FUTURE	will break	will be broken
PRESENT PERFECT	has broken have broken	has been broken have been broken
PAST PERFECT	had broken	had been broken
FUTURE PERFECT	will have broken	will have been broken

Active voice usually makes sentences more interesting and direct. To change a sentence from passive to active, make the doer of the action the subject of the sentence.

PASSIVE SENTENCES   Frankie was given two weeks by his teacher to complete a reading assignment. He was overwhelmed by the length of the book at first. Then he was interested by the story, and it was finished quickly by him.

BETTER   The teacher gave Frankie two weeks to complete a reading assignment. The length of the book overwhelmed him at first. Then the story interested him, and he finished it quickly.

in summary

In **active voice**, the subject is the doer of the action.

In **passive voice**, the subject receives the action. Every passive sentence contains a form of the verb *be* followed by the past participle form of the transitive verb.

Reinforcement

Remind the students that a passive sentence is always formed with a form of the verb *be* followed by the past participle form of a transitive verb.

Enrichment

If possible, allow the students to read over a previous writing assignment. Tell them to look for unnecessary passive sentences and change them to strong, active sentences.

Underline the complete verb and label it *active* or *passive*.

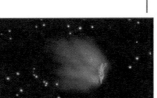

passive   1. A meteor is also called a shooting star.

active   2. *Meteor* and *meteorology* are similar terms.

passive   3. In the ancient world, meteors were mistakenly believed to be an atmospheric occurrence.

active   4. Meteors do not originate in our atmosphere.

active   5. A meteor is actually a small chunk of cosmic matter.

passive   6. Meteor showers are caused by great numbers of small pieces of matter.

active   7. A small meteorite may weigh only a fraction of an ounce.

active   8. Approximately one thousand meteorites can reach the earth in a year.

active   9. Scientists have studied many large meteorites.

passive   10. A seventy-ton meteorite has been found in Africa.

Rewrite each passive sentence, changing it to active voice. Do not change the tense of the verb. *(Answers may vary.)*

1. Lives are often endangered by severe storms.

   Severe storms often endanger lives.

2. Improving the accuracy of severe weather warnings cannot be done by one group of people alone.

   One group of people alone cannot improve the accuracy of severe weather warnings.

3. Storm chasers' information is often used by the National Weather Service.

   The National Weather Service often uses storm chasers' information.

4. Videos of severe storms are also used by the news media.

   The news media also uses videos of severe storms.

   _____

5. Supercell thunderstorms are often sought and studied by chasers.

   Chasers often seek and study supercell thunderstorms.

   _____

6. Hours and even days may be spent in the search for a storm.

   These chasers may spend hours and even days in the search for a storm.

   _____

7. Information is gathered by both amateur and professional chasers.

   Both amateur and professional chasers gather information.

   _____

8. Instruction must be received before storm chasing.

   Any chaser must receive instruction before storm chasing.

   _____

9. Some tornadoes cannot be seen with the eye alone.

   The eye alone cannot see some tornadoes.

   _____

10. Hundreds of hours are spent by chasers in the study of severe weather.

    Chasers spend hundreds of hours in the study of severe weather.

    _____

4-20 USE THE SKILL

Write an appropriate sentence to answer each question. Use the voice indicated in parentheses and underline the verb you choose. *(Answers will vary.)*

1. What do you do after a snowstorm? *(active)*

   I shovel the snow.

   _____

2. What happened when the thunderstorm came through your town? *(passive)*

   A tree was struck by lightning.

   _____

3. What happened on a sunny summer day? *(active)*

   The neighborhood children played Frisbee.
   _____

4. What activity did you do on a fall Friday evening? *(active)*

   I went to a soccer game at my school.
   _____

5. What happened when you went to the park? *(passive)*

   I was stung by a bee.
   _____

6. What happened to classes when a blizzard came? *(passive)*

   Classes were canceled because of the storm.
   _____

7. What happened on a clear, starry night? *(active)*

   Using the telescope, we gazed at the stars.
   _____

8. What did your neighbor do at the beginning of summer? *(active)*

   My neighbor planted a vegetable garden.
   _____

9. What did you do when it rained? *(active)*

   I stayed inside and read a book.
   _____

10. What did you do when the grass grew long? *(active)*

    I cut the grass.
    _____

Mood

English verbs can have different *moods*. The mood of a verb reflects the attitude of the speaker or writer. For example, a sentence may be telling someone about something or giving someone a command or request.

Indicative

The most common mood is the **indicative mood.** Sentences in the indicative mood consist mostly of factual, or declarative, sentences.

> The paper *will be* due next Thursday.
> We *read* several papers aloud in class.

Imperative

In the **imperative mood,** verbs express commands. Usually the subject *you* is understood but not expressed.

> *Put* your name and the course title on your paper.
> *Include* a bibliography with your report.

English speakers use imperatives for requests only when they want to make a strong, forceful request. Most requests are stated as polite questions, not as imperatives.

STRONG COMMAND   Close the window.

POLITE REQUEST   Would you close the window.

in summary

Use the **indicative mood** for factual, or declarative, sentences.

Use the **imperative mood** for commands.

4-21 PRACTICE THE SKILL

In the blank write the mood of the italicized verb.

indicative	1. This storm *has given* us ten inches of snow.
imperative	2. Daryl, please *shovel* the snow.
imperative	3. Sue, *do* a report on storms for your project.
indicative	4. In 1993 over 250 people *died* from a storm.
indicative	5. Two to three inches of snow *fell* per hour.
imperative	6. *Include* that information in your paper.
indicative	7. People *must listen* to weather warnings!
indicative	8. More than two hundred hikers *were rescued* from the North Carolina and Tennessee mountains during that storm.

Verbs   107

Teaching Strategy: Induction

Write the following sentences for display:

- Your pockets need to be checked before the laundry is washed.
- Empty your pockets before you put your dirty clothes in the laundry.
- Mr. Frazier has been there several times.
- Ask Mr. Frazier for directions.

The students should determine what is different about the sentences. Ask students the following question: How is the tone different? *(The first and third sentences are statements. The second and fourth sentences are commands.)* Identify the sentences that make statements as being indicative and the sentences that give commands as being imperative.

Reinforcement

Use Teaching Help 4 (Book 2, p. 41) to review the concepts learned about verbs in this chapter.

9. Wow! From now on I *will pay* attention to the weather forecast.

10. Now, *start* your paper.

4-22 REVIEW THE SKILL

Write two sentences for each verb provided: one in the indicative mood and one in the imperative mood. *(Answers will vary.)*

1. **clean**

   indicative: _I am cleaning my fish tank right now._

   imperative: _Clean your fish tank today._

2. **pour**

   indicative: _I poured out the water._

   imperative: _Pour out that stinky water!_

3. **write**

   indicative: _My grandmother writes to me weekly._

   imperative: _Write to your grandmother, please._

4. **paint**

   indicative: _I am painting my room next week._

   imperative: _Paint your room next week._

5. **open**

   indicative: _I opened the refrigerator door for too long._

   imperative: _Open the refrigerator door._

6. **ask**

   indicative: _José asked the teacher some interesting questions._

   imperative: _José, ask your question now._

7. **come**

   indicative: _Isaac is coming to the banquet._

   imperative: _Please come to the banquet with me._

8. **bring**

   indicative: _You may bring two pens and a piece of paper._

   imperative: _Bring two pens and a piece of paper._

9. **walk**

   indicative: _My friend and I are walking to the game._

   imperative: _Walk to the game._

10. **support**

    indicative: _I supported George during the difficult time._

    imperative: _Please support your sister in this difficult time._

4-23 CUMULATIVE REVIEW •

Rewrite the following paragraph, correcting the fragments, comma splices, fused sentences, incorrect plural forms, incorrect possessive noun forms, incorrect pronoun reference, incorrect pronoun case, and incorrect verb forms (e.g., *writed* or *had wrote*). There are ten errors. *(Answers may vary.)*

Weather has influenced history. For example, in 1588 heavy winds contributed to the Spanish Armadas' defeat. Afterwards, England rose to power. Which it maintained for many years. Weather also contributed to Napoleon's defeat. When the year 1812 had began, Napoleon's dominant influence shown. Him began his Russian invasion in June. The two countrys continued to battle until winter came. That winter was especially cold temperatures had went well below freezing. Only ten thousand of nearly half a million soldiers' survived. Finally, the weather aided the British evacuation at Dunkirk during World War II. A heavy blanket of fog kept Allied troops from being seen. This saved many troops' lives.

Weather has influenced history. For example, in 1588 heavy winds contributed

to the Spanish Armada's defeat. Afterwards, England rose to power, which it

maintained for many years. Weather also contributed to Napoleon's defeat.

When the year 1812 had begun, Napoleon's dominant influence showed.

He began his Russian invasion in June. The two countries continued to battle

until winter came. That winter was especially cold; temperatures had gone well

below freezing. Only ten thousand of nearly half a million soldiers survived.

Finally, the weather aided the British evacuation at Dunkirk during World War II.

A heavy blanket of fog kept Allied troops from being seen. The fog saved many

troops' lives.

Verbs   109

- action
- buzzin *(his camera)*
- *They both drop the ending g in* ing *words.*

Objectives

Students will

1. write a topic sentence that covers both subjects.
2. write a comparison and contrast paragraph using specific examples and smooth transitions.

Overview of the Writing Process

Planning—choosing a topic and method of organization and compiling similarities and differences

Drafting—writing a topic sentence and the supporting paragraph

Revising—evaluating and making changes for clarity

Publishing—handing in to the teacher

Look again at the excerpt from "Blues Ain't No Mockin' Bird."

- *Which does the author use more frequently, action or state-of-being verbs?*
- *In this excerpt find a transitive verb that is usually intransitive.*
- *How do you know that the narrator and the men speak the same dialect?*

Writing a Comparison and Contrast

How is a butterfly like a moth? How is it not? How is a toad like a frog? How is it not? Is there any similarity between a highway and an autobahn? How about a mountain and a molehill?

One way of defining something is to show how it is like, and how it is not like, something else. For example, butterflies and moths seem hardly to be any different from each other on first glance. But close observation reveals that butterflies' antennae and bodies are both more slender than moths' and that moths are nocturnal whereas butterflies are diurnal.

By *comparing*—showing the similarities between—and *contrasting*—showing the differences between—two things, we are able to see both more clearly.

How to Write a Comparison and Contrast

Step 1

Choosing your subjects well is important. Although the subjects may differ greatly, they must have something defining in common. For example, toads and frogs are often misidentified by the casual observer. They are alike enough in general appearance to make good subjects for comparison and contrast.

Step 2

Study each subject thoroughly. List the main ways they are alike and the main ways they are different. Then select from both lists points that complement each other. For example, which items would you select from the lists below to compare and contrast the appearance of moths and butterflies?

MOTHS AND BUTTERFLIES	
SIMILARITIES	**DIFFERENCES**
Both have powdery scales on wings.	Butterflies rest with wings upright; moths rest with wings out flat.
Both have six legs.	Butterflies fly in day; moths fly at night.
Both have long antennae.	Butterflies have smooth, thin bodies; moths have furry, fat bodies.
Both vary in color.	Butterfly antennae are thicker at the ends; moth antennae are feathery, tapering at the ends.

Writing a Comparison and Contrast

Lesson Support

Teacher's Edition, Book 2

Writing Worksheets—p. 136

Rubrics—p. 150

Introduction

Materials

- a moth specimen (or a picture)
- a butterfly specimen (or a picture)

Display the specimens or pictures. Ask students the following question: How can you tell these insects are of different genera? *(by their bodies and by their antennae)*

Read the introduction to the writing lesson in the student text to find more distinctions between a butterfly and a moth.

Discussion

Direct the students to read the five steps in the text about writing a comparison and contrast. Direct a discussion about the example, pointing out how the subjects in the example are supported with specific details.

Also refer students to the subsections in Chapter 15 about writing topic sentences, developing supporting sentences, and maintaining coherence. Answer any questions they may have after reading this material.

You probably would not need to include that both have six legs, as all insects have six legs. You would also not need the information about flying in day or at night. Nor would you necessarily need to use the description of how the insects hold their wings, but you might find it useful.

Step 3

Write a topic sentence that covers both subjects:

> Although butterflies and moths seem similar at first glance, they are quite distinct in appearance.

Step 4

Support the topic sentence with ideas from the lists of similarities and differences.

> Although butterflies and moths seem similar at first glance, they are quite distinct in appearance. Butterflies usually have thin, smooth bodies, but moths have plump, fuzzy bodies, making them look heavier than butterflies. Also, most butterflies have long slender antennae with knobby ends. Moths, on the other hand, have feathery antennae that taper to a point. While both have powdery scales on their wings and vary widely in color, butterflies rest with their wings up in a tent position, whereas moths rest with their wings held out flat from their sides.

Notice how the writer smoothed out the switches from one comparison or contrast to another with transitions—words or phrases such as *but, whereas, however, on the other hand.*

Step 5

If your comparison and contrast is too long for one paragraph, choose an organization that will accommodate a longer discussion. It is usually best not to divide the discussion into the two subjects, such as butterflies in one paragraph and moths in another. Such an organization taxes the reader's memory and allows the discussion to "fall in half." You should instead discuss the similarities in one paragraph and the differences in another, for example.

Your Turn

Choose topics from a list your teacher provides or choose one on your own and write a comparison and contrast.

Planning

Direct students to read the instructions in "Your Turn."

Allow time for the students to choose one of the topics you suggest or one of their own.

Distribute a copy of the Writing Worksheet (Book 2, p. 136) to each student. Direct the students to use the example as a model to help them fill out the Writing Worksheet. Make yourself available to help the students select details or examples to support their topic sentences.

Drafting

Allow time for students to write their paragraphs in class.

Revising

Direct students to re-read their paragraphs, using the revision checklist in Chapter 15 (pp. 375, 378, and 380) to evaluate their work.

Publishing

Instruct the students to hand in their paragraphs when finished.

Scriptural Application

Read Proverbs 10 to the students. Afterward, ask them to chart distinguishing characteristics of the foolish and the wise.

Evaluation

For help in grading this assignment, see "Grading Writing Assignments" (p. x) and Rubric 4 (Book 2, p. 150).

Enrichment

Encourage the students to think of real-life activities that would require them to use this skill. Discuss their responses.

5 ADJECTIVES AND ADVERBS

Objectives

Students will

1. identify adjectives and the words they modify.

2. select appropriate adjectives to answer adjective questions.

3. differentiate between proper adjectives and other adjectives.

4. identify adverbs and the words they modify.

5. select appropriate adverbs to answer adverb questions.

6. compare objects using the correct comparative forms of adjectives and adverbs.

7. distinguish adverbs from predicate adjectives.

8. use *good/well* and *bad/badly* correctly.

9. choose between words to avoid the use of double negatives.

10. revise sentences to correct modifier problems.

11. evaluate and revise a paragraph for errors.

The Most Dangerous Game

by Richard Connell

"The world is made up of two classes—the hunters and the huntees," Sanger Rainsford told his friend Whitney. "Luckily, you and I are the hunters." Soon these words came back to haunt Rainsford. After falling overboard, he would learn to his horror what it felt like to run for his life from a powerful enemy.

An abrupt sound startled him. Off to the right he heard it, and his ears, expert in such matters, could not be mistaken. Again he heard the sound, and again. Somewhere, off in the blackness, some one had fired a gun three times.

Rainsford sprang up and moved quickly to the rail, mystified. He strained his eyes in the direction from which the reports had come, but it was like trying to see through a blanket. He leaped upon the rail and balanced himself there, to get greater elevation; his pipe, striking a rope, was knocked from his mouth. He lunged for it; a short, hoarse cry came from his lips as he realized he had reached too far and had lost his balance. The cry was pinched off short as the blood-warm waters of the Caribbean Sea closed over his head.

He struggled up to the surface and tried to cry out, but the wash from the speeding yacht slapped him in the face and the salt water in his open mouth made him gag and strangle. Desperately he struck out with strong strokes after the receding lights of the yacht, but he stopped before he had swum fifty feet. A certain cool-headedness had come to him; it was not the first time he had been in a tight place. There was a chance that his cries could be heard by some one aboard the yacht, but that chance was slender, and grew more slender as the yacht raced on. He wrestled himself out of his clothes and shouted with all his power. The lights of the yacht became faint and ever-vanishing fireflies; then they were blotted out entirely by the night.

- *How does the water feel and taste to Rainsford? What words tell you this?*

- *Read the sentence in which Rainsford strikes out for the lights of the yacht. What word tells you that, despite his strong strokes, he is afraid?*

- *What word in the last sentence increases the loneliness and desperation of his situation?*

- *warm, salty;* blood-warm, salt water
- Desperately
- entirely

The words you used to answer the questions are probably modifiers: adjectives and adverbs. Even though the verbs in this story are vivid, words like *desperately* and *entirely* add more emotion and intensity. Read the sentence that begins "Desperately," leaving out all the modifiers. How do the tone and energy change?

If you think of nouns and verbs as meat and potatoes, you can think of modifiers as the salt and pepper. This chapter will help you learn to season your writing with words that give it just the right flavor.

Lesson Support

Student Text
Chapter 5 Review—pp. 411-12

Teacher's Edition, Book 1
Bulletin Boards—p. 447

Teacher's Edition, Book 2
Pretests—pp. 11-12

Teaching Helps—pp. 42-43

ESL Worksheets—pp. 73-79

Concept Reinforcements—pp. 103-6

Literature Link

Read the literature selection aloud. Discuss the questions with the class. Explain that descriptive words help make a story seem realistic. A good storyteller uses descriptive words to paint a picture in the reader's mind and to make his audience feel as though they are in the middle of the story, watching the scene unfold.

Adjectives

Modifiers of nouns and pronouns are called **adjectives.** Adjectives describe the nouns and pronouns that they modify.

The bright stars twinkled in *a dark* sky.

In the example sentence, *the* and *bright* are adjectives that modify the noun *stars; a* and *dark* are adjectives that modify the noun *sky.* The adjectives describe the nouns, telling us more about them.

Adjectives usually answer the following questions:

WHICH ONE?   The *first* man to walk on the moon was Neil Armstrong.

WHAT KIND?   The *historic* flight began July 16, 1969.

HOW MANY?   *Two* astronauts walked on the moon.

HOW MUCH?   They experienced *no* difficulty in adapting to the moon's gravity.

WHOSE?   A part of *their* walk was collecting lunar samples for testing.

To determine whether a word is an adjective, just ask yourself the adjective questions or use the adjective test frame. Any word that will fit into the test frame can be used as an adjective.

The _____ thing (or person) is very _____.
The *bright* moon is very *bright.*
The *intelligent* astronaut is very *intelligent.*

Although most adjectives will fit into the test frame, not every adjective will. For example, the words *a, an,* and *the* are called adjectives even though they do not fit the test frame. If a word modifies a noun or pronoun, it is an adjective.

Positions of Adjectives

Adjectives appear in several different sentence positions. Most adjectives come before the nouns they modify. Occasionally, adjectives will appear immediately after the nouns that they modify; these adjectives are set off from the rest of the sentence by commas. **Predicate adjectives** appear after a linking verb; a predicate adjective always describes the subject of the sentence.

BEFORE NOUN   I passed the *difficult* physical fitness test.

AFTER NOUN   The physical fitness test, *challenging* and *difficult,* was a test of endurance.

AFTER LINKING VERB   The physical fitness test was *difficult.*

Teaching Strategy: Introduction

Materials
- tennis ball or Ping-Pong ball

Bring a ball to class. Without showing it to the students, write the word *ball* for display. Tell the students you have a ball hidden in the classroom and let them ask you questions about the ball. Write their questions and your answers for display. Then reveal the ball and ask students the following questions:

- What kind of ball? *(a tennis ball)*
- Whose ball? *(my ball)*
- Which one? *(the bright yellow ball)*
- How many? *(one ball)*

Use this exercise to show that adjectives are words that describe a noun and answer certain questions about that noun.

in summary

Adjectives modify nouns and pronouns and tell *which one, what kind, how many, how much,* or *whose.*

Most adjectives will fit the adjective test frame.

Adjectives can come before or after the noun they modify. **Predicate adjectives** follow linking verbs.

5-1 PRACTICE THE SKILL

Underline the adjectives. Draw an arrow from each adjective to the noun or pronoun it modifies.

1. Different countries have always competed in various areas.

2. One area of fierce competition was the race to space.

3. Many countries have explored the universe.

4. However, the United States and the Soviet Union were in particularly intense competition.

5. In the early years, accomplishments in space determined a country's leadership in science, engineering, and national defense.

6. The Soviet Union initially launched an artificial satellite on October 4, 1957.

7. Later, the United States put the first men on the moon.

8. The United States launched the first shuttle, a reusable spaceship.

9. The programs of today have more international cooperation.

10. Many countries are working together toward common goals.

Teaching Strategy: Induction

Display a list of nouns, preferably objects in the classroom:

- eraser
- pencils
- Amanda
- *Roget's Thesaurus*
- window
- notebook

Ask students to tell you something about one of the objects and to use the object's name within the sentence. *(Amanda is tall. That is a blue eraser.)* Write their sentences for display. Underline the adjectives in each sentence. Ask the students to notice where adjectives appear in relation to the words being described. Lead them to notice the patterns. Then elicit from the students that adjectives may come before the noun or after a linking verb. (Some students may also know that adjectives occasionally appear after the noun [e.g., The window, large and grimy, overlooks the parking lot.])

Reinforcement

Using Practice the Skill 5-1 on page 115, tell the students to locate the adjectives. Ask the students the following questions:

- Where are the adjectives in each sentence? *(before the words they modify)*
- What noun is being modified by each adjective?
- What question does each adjective answer about the noun it modifies?

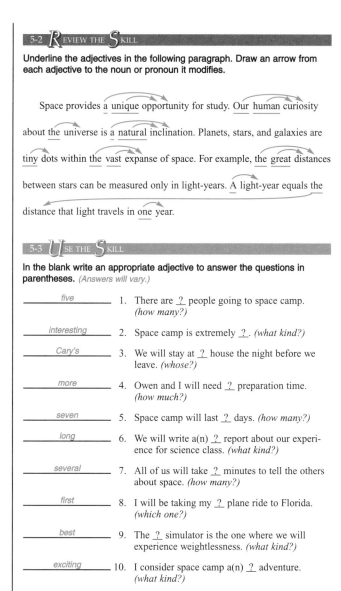

Underline the adjectives in the following paragraph. Draw an arrow from each adjective to the noun or pronoun it modifies.

Space provides a unique opportunity for study. Our human curiosity about the universe is a natural inclination. Planets, stars, and galaxies are tiny dots within the vast expanse of space. For example, the great distances between stars can be measured only in light-years. A light-year equals the distance that light travels in one year.

In the blank write an appropriate adjective to answer the questions in parentheses. *(Answers will vary.)*

five	1. There are _?_ people going to space camp. *(how many?)*
interesting	2. Space camp is extremely _?_. *(what kind?)*
Cary's	3. We will stay at _?_ house the night before we leave. *(whose?)*
more	4. Owen and I will need _?_ preparation time. *(how much?)*
seven	5. Space camp will last _?_ days. *(how many?)*
long	6. We will write a(n) _?_ report about our experience for science class. *(what kind?)*
several	7. All of us will take _?_ minutes to tell the others about space. *(how many?)*
first	8. I will be taking my _?_ plane ride to Florida. *(which one?)*
best	9. The _?_ simulator is the one where we will experience weightlessness. *(what kind?)*
exciting	10. I consider space camp a(n) _?_ adventure. *(what kind?)*

116   Chapter 5

Scriptural Application

Adjectives can answer the question "What kind" about nouns. If one has repented of his sin and asked Christ to save him, he is a *Christian*—a noun. Challenge the students to think about adjectives that would accurately describe their Christianity. Are they *sincere* Christians, striving for holiness? Or are they *hypocritical* Christians, acting one way in front of parents and teachers but acting differently when they are with their friends?

Determiners

A **determiner** is a special kind of adjective; it signals that a noun is coming in the sentence. A determiner always comes before the noun it modifies and before any descriptive adjectives (those adjectives that fit into the adjective test frame). There are several kinds of determiners.

Articles

The determiners *a, an,* and *the* are called **articles.** Articles are the most common adjectives. *A* and *an* are indefinite articles used to modify nonspecific nouns. *The* is the definite article; it modifies specific nouns.

> INDEFINITE   We live in *a* neighborhood on Peachtree Road.
> DEFINITE   We live in *the* second house on the right.

Use *a* before a word beginning with a consonant sound; use *an* before a word beginning with a vowel sound.

> While camping, the boys sleep around *a* small fire in *an* open tent.

Possessives

Most possessive nouns and possessive personal pronouns function as determiners. Possessives answer the question *whose?* about the nouns they modify.

> POSSESSIVE NOUN   *Micah's* books are on the desk.
> The *paper's* thesis should be stated at the beginning of the report.

> POSSESSIVE   May I borrow *your* gloves, please?
> PRONOUN   *His* running shoes are by the door.

If a possessive noun is modified by at least one other adjective, the possessive and its modifier form a **possessive phrase.** The entire possessive phrase shows possession.

> Has *the new teacher's* classroom been repainted?

Notice that *the* and *new* modify *teacher's,* not *classroom.* The entire possessive phrase *the new teacher's* works together to modify *classroom.*

Occasionally, a possessive noun or pronoun does not function as a determiner but like a noun instead. A possessive functioning like a noun is called an **independent possessive** because it functions alone rather than as a modifier of another noun or pronoun.

> POSSESSIVE   How are *your feet* after that long hike? *My feet* are going to
> DETERMINER   be sore for days.

> INDEPENDENT   *Mine* are going to be sore for days.
> POSSESSIVE

In the last sentence above, the possessive pronoun *mine* does not modify any noun in the sentence. Instead, the word *mine* replaces the entire noun phrase *my feet* and functions as the subject of the sentence. Independent possessives are not adjectives, because they replace nouns instead of modifying them.

Teaching Strategy: Induction

For display, write the five questions that adjectives answer about nouns:

- Which one?
- What kind?
- How many?
- How much?
- Whose?

Tell the students to think of a favorite object from home and to write the object's name on a piece of paper. Instruct the students to answer each of the above questions about their chosen objects. *(couch:* Which one? *[the blue one]* What kind? *[the soft one]*

How many? *[one]* Whose? *[my couch])* Encourage volunteers to share their objects and descriptions. Display several of their answers and, with the help of the students, find and underline each adjective. *(the blue one, the soft one, etc.)* Ask students whether they can categorize any of the adjectives. Display a list of the five kinds of determiners:

- articles
- possessives
- demonstratives
- interrogatives
- indefinites

If necessary, provide extra examples to find words to fill each category.

ESL Strategy

The use of articles can be one of the most difficult concepts for ESL students to grasp. Some languages have no articles at all, and those that do often use articles differently than English does. ESL students will have a much easier time identifying articles than they will using them. Assign ESL Worksheets 5A and 5B (Book 2, pp. 73-74) for more practice with articles.

Chapter 3: Demonstrative
Pronouns
p. 58

Chapter 3: Interrogative Pronouns
p. 60

Chapter 3: Indefinite Pronouns
p. 66

ESL: Review the formation of *wh* questions. See the section about interrogative pronouns on page 60 of Chapter 3. Refer also to ESL Worksheet 4D (Book 2, pp. 70-71).

Demonstratives

Certain words that sometimes function as pronouns can also sometimes function as determiners. The demonstrative words *this, that, these,* and *those* are determiners when they modify nouns. When a demonstrative functions as a subject, predicate noun, or object in a sentence, it is a pronoun.

> **DETERMINER** Where can I get a copy of *that* book?
> **PRONOUN** *This* is my favorite novel.

Interrogatives

The interrogative words *which, what,* and *whose* function as determiners when they modify nouns. Used alone, interrogatives are pronouns.

> **DETERMINER** *Which* story do you like best?
> **PRONOUN** *Which* do you like best?

Indefinites

Just as there are indefinite pronouns, there are also indefinite determiners. The indefinites are determiners only when they modify nouns.

> **DETERMINER** I need to get *some* warm clothing for the ski trip.
> **PRONOUN** Do you have *any?*

in summary

A **determiner** is a type of adjective that signals that a noun is coming in the sentence.

The **articles** *a, an,* and *the* are the most common adjectives.

Possessives, demonstratives, interrogatives, and **indefinites** are adjectives when they modify nouns.

5-4 PRACTICE THE SKILL

Underline the adjectives. Write *PA* over each predicate adjective. Draw an arrow from each other adjective to the noun or pronoun it modifies.

1. Some accidents of space exploration have been dangerous and deadly.

2. Which accidents have caused danger?

3. One accident was *Apollo 13's.*

4. This accident is famous for the teamwork and successful reentry to the earth's atmosphere.

5. These actions were necessary because of an oxygen tank's explosion.

6. Which accident caused many deaths?

7. On January 28, 1986, the explosion of *Challenger* killed seven people.

8. After several delays officials had ordered a liftoff.

9. That had been the coldest day ever for a shuttle launch.

10. The nation mourned the loss of the seven astronauts.

Underline the adjectives. Write *PA* over each predicate adjective. Draw an arrow from each other adjective to the noun or pronoun it modifies.

1. My report is on some strange discoveries in deep space.

2. Astronomers' studies have included many mysterious objects.

3. Several of these objects are in the deepest parts of space.

4. Which objects are particularly interesting?
   PA

5. One unusual object is a quasar.

6. Quasars are some of the brightest objects in the universe.

7. In spite of their brightness, quasars cannot be seen with
   the naked eye.

8. All quasars are a great distance from the earth.

9. Most are approximately the size of our solar system.

10. They can outshine all the other stars in a galaxy.

In the blank write an appropriate adjective as indicated in parentheses.
(Answers will vary.)

Which	1. _?_ device can I use to study the sky? *(interrogative)*
The	2. _?_ best instrument is a telescope. *(article)*
distant	3. A telescope magnifies _?_ objects. *(descriptive adjective)*

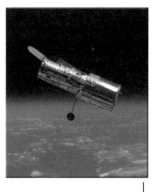

Most	4. _?_ telescopes are optical telescopes. *(indefinite)*
Whose	5. _?_ telescope is optical? *(interrogative)*
Marvin's	6. _?_ telescope is an optical telescope, and I am sure he would let you use it. *(possessive)*
these	7. Two types of _?_ telescopes are refracting and reflecting. *(demonstrative)*
One	8. _?_ famous telescope is the Hubble Space Telescope. *(indefinite)*
This	9. _?_ telescope was launched in 1990. *(demonstrative)*
many	10. The Hubble Telescope has given scientists _?_ detailed images. *(indefinite)*

Modifying Nouns

Sometimes a noun may function as an adjective in a sentence. A noun that modifies another noun is called a **modifying noun.** Modifying nouns always appear right before the nouns that they modify, after any determiners or descriptive adjectives.

NOUN	We spend a week at the *ocean* every summer.
MODIFYING NOUN	The cold *ocean* waves pounded the shoreline.

NOUN	The ornaments are made of *glass*.
MODIFYING NOUN	The *glass* ornaments are my favorite.

Chapter 11: Personal Names, Religions, Nationalities
p. 258

Proper Adjectives

Adjectives formed from proper nouns are called **proper adjectives.** Some proper nouns change form to become adjectives; other proper nouns do not change form. If a word modifies a noun, it is an adjective (even if its form does not change). Proper adjectives are capitalized, just as the original proper nouns are capitalized.

I enjoy eating *Chinese* food.
My grandparents live in a *Victorian* house.
The orchestra performed a *Beethoven* symphony.

These different kinds of adjectives have certain positions within the noun phrase; they are not randomly put together. The general order is usually close to the following:

DETERMINER	the
ADJECTIVE THAT EVALUATES	poor
ADJECTIVE THAT MEASURES	little
ADJECTIVE OF COLOR	gray
ADJECTIVE OF MATERIAL	tin
MAIN NOUN	soldier

Teaching Strategy: Induction

Display the following sentences:

- The butterfly landed on my hand.
- She wore a costume with butterfly wings.
- One day I would like to visit Italy.
- Italian food smells and tastes delicious.

Label the subjects, verbs, objects, prepositional phrases, and so forth with the students. Underline the adjectives. As a reminder, ask students what adjectives do. *(answer questions about a noun)* When the students tell you to mark *butterfly* as an adjective, ask how the word can be an adjective when *butterfly* is a noun in the first sentence. Elicit from the students that nouns can act as adjectives when they answer questions about other nouns. Nouns functioning this way are sometimes called modifying nouns. Proper nouns that function this way may be called proper adjectives.

in summary

Modifying nouns are nouns used as adjectives.

Proper adjectives are formed from proper nouns and are capitalized.

5-7 PRACTICE THE SKILL

Underline the adjectives once. Underline the proper adjectives twice.

1. American and Soviet programs have given scientists useful knowledge.

2. Planet exploration has been a valuable result of technology.

3. American probes have researched Mars, Venus, and the outer planets.

4. Many other nations have also developed space programs.

5. In 1965 France became the first European nation with a satellite launch.

6. In the 1970s two German probes flew inside Mercury's orbit.

7. The Japanese program blossomed in the 1980s.

8. Japan's two exploration probes sent back information about Halley's comet.

9. China's technological research caused the development of recoverable satellites and liquid-hydrogen engines.

10. Canadian designers built the shuttle's robot arm.

5-8 REVIEW THE SKILL

Underline the adjectives once. Underline the proper adjectives twice.

1. The auroras are beautiful light displays.

2. Particles from the sun are trapped by the earth's magnetic fields, and the energy release results in the auroras.

3. Auroras are the most visible effect of sun activity.

4. However, they are visible only in the night sky.

5. A northern display in a Canadian province would be called aurora borealis.

6. However, an Australian observer would see aurora australis.

Evaluation

If you have assigned sentence diagramming with Practice the Skill 5-7, check students' answers using pages 459-60.

Enrichment

Divide the class into teams of three to five students each. Instruct each group to write a paragraph describing an imaginary trip to the moon. Then direct one member of each team to read the team's paragraph aloud. Ask students to identify adjectives in the paragraph and then discuss how changing the adjectives would alter the meaning of the paragraph.

One on One

Ask your student whether he has ever thought about what it would be like to travel to the moon. Instruct your student to write a story about visiting the moon. After the story is finished, direct your student to underline the adjectives. Discuss how changing the adjectives would alter the meaning of the story. Allow your student to insert additional adjectives to make vague or general sentences clearer and more concrete.

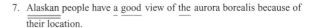

7. Alaskan people have a good view of the aurora borealis because of their location.

8. Mediterranean countries and China give us the oldest descriptions of the aurora.

9. The green aurora is common.

10. The light forms vary greatly.

Adverbs

Adverbs are modifiers primarily of verbs. Some adverbs modify adjectives and other adverbs. They describe the words they modify, giving us more information about that word.

Venus shines *brightly.*

In this sentence, *brightly* is an adverb. It modifies *shines,* describing the manner in which Venus shines. Adverbs have these main meanings:

MANNER (INCLUDING EXTENT AND NUMBER)	The astronomer peers *intently* through his telescope.
PLACE (INCLUDING DIRECTION AND ORDER)	He looks *up* at the stars.
TIME (INCLUDING FREQUENCY)	*Yesterday,* clouds obscured his view.
NEGATION	He could *not* see anything.

Unlike other adverbs, *not* can be connected to an auxiliary in a contraction. The adverb *not* can also be connected to the auxiliary *can* as a whole word *(cannot).*

An astronaut on board a space shuttle does *not* live like a person on earth.
Astronauts are*n't* able to sleep on a regular bed.
Astronauts can*not* eat the same foods in space that they eat on earth.

Positions of Adverbs

Adverbs appear in several different positions in the sentence. Often an adverb appears directly before or after the verb that it modifies. The adverb *not* appears after an auxiliary in the sentence.

BEFORE THE VERB	He *quickly* skimmed over his notes for the test.
AFTER THE VERB	He skimmed *quickly* over his notes for the test.
BETWEEN THE AUXILIARY AND THE VERB	He had *quickly* skimmed over his notes for the test. He had *not* memorized his notes.
AT THE BEGINNING OF THE SENTENCE	*Quickly,* he skimmed over his notes for the test.

Teaching Strategy: Introduction

Begin reading aloud to your students. Ask them what you are doing. *(reading)* Then read very fast. Ask them to describe how you are reading. *(quickly)* Write their responses for display. Continue reading in different ways (e.g., loudly, slowly, quietly) and display the students' responses. Underline the descriptive words. Ask the students whether the underlined terms are adjectives. *(No. They are modifying words other than nouns.)* Ask what the adverbs are doing in the sentences. *(modifying verbs)*

ESL Strategy

If your ESL students have trouble placing adverbs in normal English order, assign ESL Worksheets 5C and 5D (Book 2, pp. 75-77).

ESL Strategy

Note that different languages put the negation in different places in the sentence. For additional information and practice in making sentences negative by using *not,* assign ESL Worksheets 5E and 5F (Book 2, pp. 78-79).

Forming Adverbs

Many adverbs are made from other words. The most common way to form an adverb is to add *ly* to an adjective.

clear + ly	clearly
rapid + ly	rapidly
open + ly	openly

However, not all words ending in *ly* are adverbs. Words like *lovely* and *friendly,* which are formed from a noun plus *ly,* are adjectives. Remember that an adverb is determined by the context of the sentence: if the word modifies a verb, it is an adverb.

> Most English adverbs with the *ly* ending are adverbs expressing manner (how something was done).
>> He *eagerly* opened the letter from his grandmother.

in summary

Adverbs are modifiers of verbs, adjectives, and other adverbs; most adverbs describe manner, place, or time.

Adverbs can appear in several different positions in the sentence.

5-9 PRACTICE THE SKILL

Underline the adverbs. Draw an arrow from each adverb to the (main) verb.

1. We cannot imagine the great size of some stars.

2. Stars differ greatly in color and brightness.

3. We can usually observe the stars only at night.

4. A star consists mainly of hydrogen and helium.

5. New stars are still forming within galaxies.

6. Humans have always studied the stars with great interest.

7. Early travelers often used stars for direction.

8. Ancient peoples regularly told others stories about stars.

9. No one can possibly know the number of stars.

10. Stars are not spread evenly throughout the universe.

The adverb *only* in sentence 3 modifies the prepositional phrase *at night.* Because the students have not yet studied prepositional phrases, *only* does not appear on the diagram on page 460.

Adjectives and Adverbs   123

Evaluation

If you have assigned sentence diagramming with Practice the Skill 5-9, check students' answers using page 460.

Underline the adverbs. Draw an arrow from each adverb to the (main) verb.

1. The environment in space differs considerably from the earth's environment.

2. An astronaut's living conditions vary significantly from ours.

3. Engineers have greatly reduced the hazards of living in space.

4. Space vehicles usually have tremendous protection against radiation and foreign objects.

5. The crew members must also be protected from intense heat.

6. The astronauts' seating positions are carefully arranged for their own protection.

7. Microgravity is not true weightlessness.

8. However, microgravity often affects both the astronauts and space equipment.

9. Obviously, a spacecraft needs a source of oxygen for the crew.

10. An astronaut's muscles are used less in space than on earth. Because this inactivity can lead to atrophy, the astronaut's muscles must already be strong.

In the blank write an appropriate adverb of the category indicated in parentheses. Try to use a variety of adverbs. *(Answers will vary.)*

Today _____ 1. _?_ our Bible class studied Psalm 19. *(time)*

outside _____ 2. We went _?_ for class and looked at God's creation. *(place)*

upward _____ 3. If you look _?_ on a dark night, the number of stars will amaze you. *(place)*

Tomorrow _____ 4. _?_ our class is going to visit a planetarium. *(time)*

Reinforcement

Challenge the students to "take off" by using adverbs to add even more life to their writing. Ask whether they have ever seen a space shuttle launch. Point out the photo in the student text and encourage any students who have witnessed a launch to share the experience.

Instruct the students to write a paragraph describing a launch. Encourage them to incorporate adverbs into their work. Allow five to eight minutes for writing and then ask volunteers to share their work with the class. Select one student to record the various adverbs that the students use. Display the list and discuss the various meanings and placements of the adverbs.

<u>clearly</u> 5. The splendor of the heavens <u>?</u> displays the glory of God. *(manner)*

<u>often</u> 6. God <u>?</u> teaches lessons through His creation. *(time)*

<u>frequently</u> 7. The Bible <u>?</u> mentions the heavens. *(time)*

<u>down</u> 8. The sun stood still for Joshua; it did not go <u>?</u> for about a whole day. *(place)*

<u>sternly</u> 9. God <u>?</u> warns against worshiping the sun, moon, and stars. *(manner)*

<u>severely</u> 10. During the Tribulation, God will judge the earth <u>?</u> when He darkens the sun. *(manner)*

Qualifiers

A **qualifier** is a special kind of adverb that modifies an adjective or another adverb, either strengthening or weakening the idea of that word. Unlike other adverbs, a qualifier almost always comes directly before the adjective or other adverb that it modifies.

    Adj
That is a *very* expensive piece of art.

    PA
My new computer is *much* faster than my old one.

    Adv
His car idles *somewhat* loudly.

The qualifiers *very* and *much* strengthen the adjectives *expensive* and *faster*. The qualifier *somewhat* weakens the meaning of the adverb *loudly*.

in summary

A **qualifier** is an adverb that modifies an adjective or another adverb.

5-12 PRACTICE THE SKILL

Underline the adverbs. Draw an arrow from each adverb to the word it modifies.

1. The sun is <u>so</u> enormous!

2. However, some stars are <u>much</u> larger than the sun.

3. Nonetheless, the sun is the <u>most</u> important star to us.

Teaching Strategy: Discussion

Ask the students to identify the adverbs that could also be termed qualifiers in Practice the Skill 5-12 *(1—so, 2—much, 3—most, 4—extremely, 5—incredibly, 6—quite, 7—moderately, 9—truly, 10—rather)* and in Practice the Skill 5-13 *(1—much, 2—much, 3—more, 5—especially, 6—significantly, 7—rather, 8—extremely, 9—unusually, 10—very)* Remind them that qualifiers are a subcategory of adverbs much like articles are a subcategory of adjectives.

4. It is extremely necessary for our life.

5. The sun's incredibly extensive energy comes from nuclear reactions near its center.

6. People quite often use the sun's energy.

7. One moderately successful use has been in heating homes.

8. Direct solar energy can also be used for the creation of electricity.

9. The closeness of the sun has often given scientists a truly valuable opportunity for study.

10. Scientists rather frequently observe solar flares and their effect on Earth.

Underline the adverbs. Draw an arrow from each adverb to the word it modifies.

1. The moon is much smaller than the earth.

2. Gravity is much less on the moon.

3. For example, a ball would fall more slowly on the moon.

4. Astronomers readily recognize the unusual qualities of our moon.

5. Our moon is especially suitable for an inhabited earth.

6. The moon provides significantly more light than any other planet's moon.

7. The moon's surface is rather full of craters.

8. Because of its many craters, the moon has an extremely unusual surface.

9. Dark areas on the moon make unusually interesting shapes.

10. Can you distinguish shapes very easily?

Using Modifiers Correctly

Showing Comparison

Adjectives and adverbs can be used to show comparison. There are three levels, or degrees, of comparison.

POSITIVE	no comparison made	Jupiter is a *large* planet in our solar system.
		Scientists *often* use telescopes in their work.
COMPARATIVE	comparison of two things or groups	Jupiter is *larger* than Mars.
		Jupiter is *larger* than the other planets.
		Some scientists use telescopes *more often* than other scientists do.
SUPERLATIVE	comparison of three or more things or or groups	Jupiter is the *largest* planet in our solar system.
		Of all scientists, perhaps astronomers use telescopes *most often*.

Regular forms

One-syllable modifiers and most two-syllable modifiers show the comparative form by the addition of *er* and the superlative form by the addition of *est*.

POSITIVE	COMPARATIVE	SUPERLATIVE
tall	taller	tallest
soon	sooner	soonest
friendly	friendlier	friendliest
fast	faster	fastest

Some two-syllable modifiers sound awkward with *er* or *est* and use *more* or *most* to make comparisons. Two-syllable adverbs that end in *ly* use *more* or *most* to make comparisons.

POSITIVE	COMPARATIVE	SUPERLATIVE
joyful	more joyful	most joyful
briskly	more briskly	most briskly
famous	more famous	most famous

Adjectives and adverbs that have three or more syllables use *more* and *most* to make comparisons.

POSITIVE	COMPARATIVE	SUPERLATIVE
amazing	more amazing	most amazing
cheerfully	more cheerfully	most cheerfully
beautiful	more beautiful	most beautiful

ESL: Many ESL students have trouble choosing when to use the comparative or the superlative, since many languages do not have a superlative degree formed separately from the comparative. It may help these students to think of the comparative as functioning from a different point of view than the superlative does. The superlative looks at a group as a whole and identifies the extremes (highest v. lowest, longest v. shortest, etc.). The comparative, on the other hand, is not interested in the group but only in the relationship between two differing things within the group (A is higher than B, A is wider than B, etc.).

Teaching Strategy: Participation

Materials
- three pictures of dogs (furry, furrier, furriest)
- three photographs of a child (young, younger, youngest)
- a picture of a person walking, a picture of a person jogging, and a picture of a person running (quickly, more quickly, most quickly)

Show the sets of items to the class one set at a time. Ask the students to compare the items, labeling the positive, comparative, and superlative examples. Most students will form the comparative and superlative modifiers correctly, but they may need practice in using the terms *positive, comparative,* and *superlative* correctly.

Enrichment

Divide the class into teams with three to five students in each group. Instruct them to perform a scavenger hunt in the classroom, looking for objects to compare. Set a time limit. Once the time is up, allow each group to present its findings. Give "*Super*lative" awards for the largest number, the most creative, the most humorous, and any other category you and your students can think of.

Irregular forms

Some adjectives and adverbs have irregular comparative and superlative forms. The forms of these modifiers do not follow a regular pattern.

POSITIVE	COMPARATIVE	SUPERLATIVE
good	better	best
well	better	best
bad	worse	worst
little	less or lesser	least

Double Comparisons

Never use both *er* and *more* to form the comparative or both *est* and *most* to form the superlative. Using both creates an error called a **double comparison**.

WRONG Jupiter is the *most largest* planet in our solar system.
Blue stars shine *more brightlier* than red stars.

RIGHT Jupiter is the *largest* planet in our solar system.
Blue stars shine *more brightly* than red stars.

Adjectives cannot be made plural in English.
WRONG Some Indians chiefs were extremely brave.
RIGHT Some Indian chiefs were extremely brave.

in summary

The three degrees of comparison are **positive, comparative,** and **superlative.**

Regular adjectives and **adverbs** show comparison by the addition of *er* and *est* or *more* and *most* to the stem of the modifier.

Irregular adjectives and **adverbs** may have entirely different forms to show comparison.

Do not use *more* or *most* with a modifier that already ends in *er* or *est*.

5-14 PRACTICE THE SKILL

Underline the correct adjective or adverb from the choices in parentheses.

1. Of all the planets, Pluto was the *(more difficult, most difficult)* to find.

2. Although Percival Lowell was convinced of the existence of a ninth planet back in the 1800s, his efforts to find the planet went *(badly, more badly).*

3. Clyde Tombaugh, who discovered Pluto in 1930, was *(more successful, most successful)* than Lowell.

4. Comparing Saturn and Venus, we find that Venus is the *(brighter, brightest)* planet.

5. However, of the two, Saturn is *(more interesting, most interesting)* because of its visible rings.

6. Mars is the *(more easily, most easily)* recognized planet because of its color.

7. Mars looks *(brighter, brightest)* when it moves closer to Earth.

8. The *Viking* series of probes worked *(better, best)* than any other space probe up to its time. It provided more than fifty thousand images of Mars by 1982.

9. Compared to other planets, Venus is *(easier, easiest)* to observe.

10. Of Venus and Mars, Venus resembles Earth's size *(more closely, most closely).*

5-15 REVIEW THE SKILL

In the blank write the correct form of the modifier in parentheses.

__oldest__ 1. Astronomy is one of the _?_ sciences. *(old)*

__youngest__ 2. My sister Maria is the _?_ astronomer at her school. *(young)*

__more frequently__ 3. She studies the stars _?_ than many other astronomers. *(frequently)*

__more valuable__ 4. Maria is able to do _?_ work on clear nights than on cloudy nights. *(valuable)*

__most expensive__ 5. I think her telescope is the _?_ of all the ones at her workplace. *(expensive)*

__more slowly__ 6. However, her efforts to trace a new comet have gone _?_ than other projects. *(slowly)*

__less__ 7. Her comet project is _?_ rewarding than her other projects because of bad weather. *(little)*

__more enthusiastic__ 8. Of the two new astronomers at the university, Maria is _?_. *(enthusiastic)*

__better__ 9. Her research has been _?_ than that of the other astronomer in her department. *(good)*

__best__ 10. Astronomy is obviously Maria's _?_ subject. *(good)*

Adjectives and Adverbs   129

Distinguishing Between Adverbs and Predicate Adjectives

A linking verb is directly followed by a predicate adjective, not an adverb. Some verbs that can be linking verbs in one sentence can be transitive or intransitive in another sentence.

LINKING VERB AND PREDICATE ADJECTIVE	The sky *looks spectacular* today.
INTRANSITIVE VERB AND ADVERB	He *looks intensely* at the sky.
LINKING VERB AND PREDICATE ADJECTIVE	The cake *tasted good.*
TRANSITIVE VERB AND ADVERB	Jenna *tasted* the cake *eagerly.*

Examine your sentences to be sure that you have not placed an adverb directly after a linking verb.

WRONG	The blanket *feels* softly.
RIGHT	The blanket *feels* soft.

in summary

Use an adjective after a linking verb.

5-16 PRACTICE THE SKILL

In the blank, label each italicized word *Adv* (adverb) or *PA* (predicate adjective).

PA 1. The sky looks *clear* tonight.

Adv 2. The students look *eagerly* into the telescopes.

PA 3. After we remove our shoes, the grass feels *cool* in the late evening air.

Adv 4. Mr. Kicher feels *slowly* along the side of the telescope for the adjustment device.

Adv 5. The images of the planets grow larger *quickly* with the aid of the telescope.

PA 6. As the sky grows *dark,* the planets become brighter.

PA 7. Saturn, Mars, and Jupiter will remain *visible* together for a few more weeks.

Teaching Strategy: Induction

Write the following sentences for display:

- The school band plays loudly.
- The school band is loud.

- The sun sets quickly.
- The sunset looks lovely.

Circle the verbs and ask students to identify them as transitive, intransitive, or linking. Quickly review the linking verbs. *(am, is, are, was, were, be, being, been, appear, become, feel, grow, look, remain, seem, smell, sound, stay, taste)* Using a sentence with a linking verb, label the sentence pattern with the students' help. *(S-LV-PA)* Label all the sentences with linking verbs. Compare these sentences to those containing transitive or intransitive verbs and adverbs. Elicit from students that predicate adjectives, not adverbs, always follow linking verbs.

Adv 8. The appearance of these three planets remains _longer_ in the night sky this time of year.

_PA_ 9. The planets appear _close_ to each other.

Adv 10. The students will discover which planets will appear _later_ in the month.

5-17 REVIEW THE SKILL

Underline the correct word from the choices in parentheses.

1. Dinner for an astronaut looks _(different, differently)_ from our usual evening meal.

2. Some astronauts look _(hesitant, hesitantly)_ at their food.

3. The food is freeze-dried, which means that all the water has been removed from it, and it now appears _(dry, dryly)_ and granular.

4. This procedure helps the food stay _(fresh, freshly)_.

5. An astronaut may taste his dinner _(slow, slowly)_.

6. This kind of food may sound distasteful, but it can actually taste quite _(good, goodly)_.

7. The food feels very _(unusual, unusually)_.

8. For dessert, some crews _(eager, eagerly)_ taste their freeze-dried ice cream.

9. Even in the warm cabin, the ice cream stays _(firm, firmly)_ and does not melt.

10. Even though it looks more like a candy bar, the chocolate ice cream still smells _(delicious, deliciously)_.

Good or Well? Bad or Badly?

The words _good_ and _well_ can be confusing. Remember that _good_ is an adjective and _well_ is an adverb when it means "in a good manner."

ADJECTIVE The astronauts and engineers of _Apollo 13_ demonstrated _good_ teamwork in getting the astronauts home safely.

ADVERB The astronauts and engineers of _Apollo 13_ worked _well_ together to get the astronauts home safely.

In the first sentence, _good_ is an adjective describing the noun _teamwork_. In the second sentence, _well_ is an adverb describing the verb _worked_.

Enrichment

Divide students into groups of two or three. Instruct them to write a news release on the health condition of astronaut Stewart Nelson (fictional). After traveling to space, he contracted a rare disease and has been in the hospital. His condition has been top-secret until now. Allow students to read their stories aloud. As they read, mention their uses of the forms of _good, well, bad,_ and _badly_. Discuss whether they have used the correct forms. You may want to have a correct example to use for discussion if the students' stories fail to incorporate the terms or fail to use them correctly.

Reinforcement

Use Teaching Helps 5A and 5B (Book 2, pp. 42-43) for further practice with using adjectives and adverbs.

Bad and *badly* are two more words that are sometimes misused. *Bad* is an adjective, and *badly* is an adverb.

> **ADJECTIVE** The condition of an oxygen tank was *bad* before the *Apollo 13* launch.
> **ADVERB** Dropping the tank about two inches *badly* damaged it.

In the first sentence, *bad* is correct because it is a predicate adjective describing the oxygen tank. *Badly* is the correct choice for the second sentence because it is an adverb modifying the verb *damaged*.

Avoiding Double Negatives

In standard English we use only one negative word to make a sentence convey negative meaning. Using another negative word along with the adverb *not* is called a **double negative** and should be avoided in both speaking and writing. To correct a double negative, eliminate one of the negative words.

> **WRONG** Many times, a person does *not* need *nothing* to be able to see a meteor.
>
> **RIGHT** Many times, a person does *not* need *anything* to be able to see a meteor.

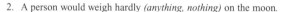

in summary

Remember that *good* and *bad* are adjectives and that *well* and *badly* are adverbs.

Use only one negative word to convey negative meaning.

5-18 PRACTICE THE SKILL

Underline the correct word from the choices in parentheses.

1. Gravity on the moon is not *(anything, nothing)* like the gravity on the earth.

2. A person would weigh hardly *(anything, nothing)* on the moon.

3. Weight actually measures the effect of gravity on a person's body. Weight will change in space without *(any, no)* change in body mass.

4. Scientists have measured *(good, well)* the amount of gravity on the moon. It is much less than the amount of gravity on the earth.

5. Astronauts must prepare *(good, well)* for a trip into space.

6. An expedition that does not accommodate for the change in gravity could go *(bad, badly)*.

7. A spaceship that weighs too little could experience a *(bad, badly)* landing on the moon.

8. Similarly, astronauts will have a difficult time walking if they have *(anything, nothing)* to give them more weight on the moon.

9. A spaceship will travel back to the earth *(good, well)* if some of the weight lost on the trip is replaced by moon rocks and other lunar findings.

10. An astronaut may feel *(bad, badly)* for a while after his return because of the drastic change in gravity.

5-19 R EVIEW THE S KILL

Underline the correct word from the choices in parentheses.

1. Several changes in our everyday lives due to space exploration have been *(good, well)*.

2. One of the advantages is hydroponically grown crops, which are crops grown without *(any, no)* soil.

3. Several experimental crops have grown *(good, well)* by having nutrients sprayed on them rather than by growing them in soil.

4. Scientists hope to develop a *(good, well)* system that will enable crops to grow in space.

5. Without hydroponics, crops would develop *(bad, badly)* in the waterless dust on the moon.

6. Another *(good, well)* advantage of space exploration is advanced technology.

7. Without space exploration, we would probably have *(any, no)* compact discs, cordless tools, or laser surgery.

8. New advances in medicine, developed as a result of space exploration, have eliminated many *(bad, badly)* physical conditions.

9. The extremely beneficial CAT scans and MRI testings would not be available without *(any, no)* research done for the purpose of space exploration.

10. These changes have not been *(bad, badly)*, but have instead increased our knowledge in science, medicine, and technology.

Adjectives and Adverbs   133

Problems with Modifier Positions

Misplaced Modifiers

A modifier needs to be reasonably close to the word it modifies. If the position of the modifier makes it seem to modify the wrong word in the sentence, it is misplaced. A **misplaced modifier** can confuse the reader.

> AMBIGUOUS   Cindy has almost learned the whole psalm.

In the example, *almost* seems to be modifying the verb *learned,* suggesting that Cindy has hesitation points throughout the psalm. But the writer may have meant for *almost* to describe *the whole psalm,* implying that she has memorized all but the last verse or two. Correct a misplaced modifier by moving it closer to what it modifies.

> CLEAR   Cindy has learned almost the whole psalm.

Some words are misplaced more frequently than others. Be especially careful with the words *only* and *not.* Notice the difference in meaning among these three sentences.

> Jeff only smiled at me.
> Jeff smiled only at me.
> Only Jeff smiled at me.

In the first sentence, Jeff only smiled (and did nothing else). In the second sentence, Jeff smiled just at me and at no one else. In the third sentence, Jeff was the only person to smile at me; no one else smiled. In the next two sentences, notice what happens when *not* is moved.

> All of the cake was not eaten.
> Not all of the cake was eaten.

The first sentence says that none of the cake was eaten. The second sentence says that some of the cake was eaten and some was left.

Two-Way Modifiers

A **two-way modifier** is unclear because it stands between two sentence elements that it might modify. If the reader cannot tell which of the two it modifies, he cannot be sure what meaning the writer intended.

> AMBIGUOUS   Scientists who study the stars constantly discover exceptions to their general theories.

Does *constantly* modify *study?* Or does it modify *discover?* Because the adverb is positioned between two verbs, the reader cannot be sure. Correct a two-way modifier by moving the modifier to a clear position in the sentence.

> CLEAR   Scientists who constantly study the stars discover exceptions to their general theories.

Depending on the meaning intended, more thorough revision may be needed.

> CLEAR   Astronomers constantly discover exceptions to their general theories.

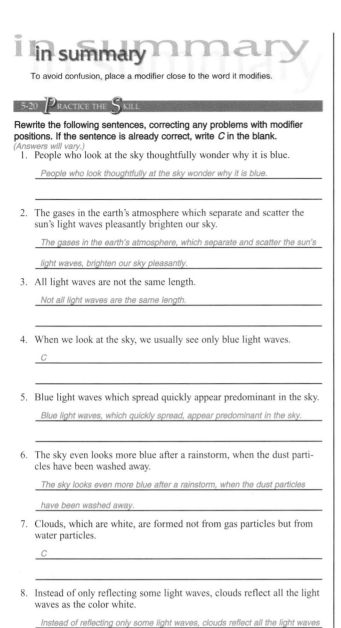

in summary

To avoid confusion, place a modifier close to the word it modifies.

5-20 PRACTICE THE SKILL

Rewrite the following sentences, correcting any problems with modifier positions. If the sentence is already correct, write *C* in the blank.
(Answers will vary.)

1. People who look at the sky thoughtfully wonder why it is blue.

   People who look thoughtfully at the sky wonder why it is blue.

2. The gases in the earth's atmosphere which separate and scatter the sun's light waves pleasantly brighten our sky.

   The gases in the earth's atmosphere, which separate and scatter the sun's light waves, brighten our sky pleasantly.

3. All light waves are not the same length.

   Not all light waves are the same length.

4. When we look at the sky, we usually see only blue light waves.

   C

5. Blue light waves which spread quickly appear predominant in the sky.

   Blue light waves, which quickly spread, appear predominant in the sky.

6. The sky even looks more blue after a rainstorm, when the dust particles have been washed away.

   The sky looks even more blue after a rainstorm, when the dust particles have been washed away.

7. Clouds, which are white, are formed not from gas particles but from water particles.

   C

8. Instead of only reflecting some light waves, clouds reflect all the light waves as the color white.

   Instead of reflecting only some light waves, clouds reflect all the light waves as the color white.

Reinforcement

After discussing the material on page 134, complete Practice the Skill 5-20 with the students. Ask volunteers to write their answers for display. Discuss the different ways to correct each sentence and the various possible meanings based on the location of the modifier.

9. At night, enough light waves from the sun are not available, and the sky is, therefore, black.

   At night, not enough light waves from the sun are available, and the sky is,

   therefore, black.

10. Without gas particles in our atmosphere, our sky would only be black all the time.

    Without gas particles in our atmosphere, our sky would be only black all

    the time.

 5-21 REVIEW THE SKILL

Rewrite the following sentences, correcting any problems with modifier positions. If the sentence is already correct, write *C* in the blank. *(Answers will vary.)*

1. You may have recently heard some scientists warning about a phenomenon called the greenhouse effect.

   C

2. In a typical greenhouse, sun rays pass through the glass easily making the inside of the greenhouse light and warm.

   In a typical greenhouse, sun rays easily pass through the glass, making the

   inside of the greenhouse light and warm.

3. After the rays are converted into heat, all of the heat cannot escape through the glass.

   After the rays are converted into heat, not all of the heat can escape

   through the glass.

4. In our atmosphere, carbon dioxide acts like glass, allowing the sun's rays to pass through easily and keeping even the converted heat from escaping.

   In our atmosphere, carbon dioxide acts like glass, allowing the sun's rays

   to pass through easily and even keeping the converted heat from escaping.

5. Some fear that carbon dioxide that is being produced excessively causes the earth's "glass" to become too thick.

   Some fear that carbon dioxide that is being excessively produced

   causes the earth's "glass" to become too thick.

6. If carbon dioxide were indeed thickening our atmosphere, the earth would be too hot soon.

   If carbon dioxide were indeed thickening our atmosphere, the earth would

   soon be too hot.

7. With increased heat, glaciers would melt, and all countries would not be able to protect their coastal towns from flooding.

   With increased heat, glaciers would melt, and not all countries would be

   able to protect their coastal towns from flooding.

8. Nature makes its own carbon dioxide, however. Cars and industries are not the sources only producing carbon dioxide.

   Nature makes its own carbon dioxide, however. Cars and industries are not

   the only sources producing carbon dioxide.

9. Not all the cars and industries in the world produce more carbon dioxide than termites do.

   All the cars and industries in the world produce less carbon dioxide

   than termites do.

10. Environmentalists only have a theory about the greenhouse effect. There is no proof that the earth's temperature is increasing.

    Environmentalists have only a theory about the "greenhouse effect."

    There is no proof that the earth's temperature is increasing.

Rewrite the paragraph, correcting any fragments, comma splices, fused sentences, incorrect plural forms, incorrect possessive noun forms, incorrect verbs or verb forms, and errors in adjective and adverb usage. There are ten errors. *(Answers will vary.)*

No life on earth would not exist without the sun. More larger than anyone can comprehend, the sun is actually ninety-three million miles from earth. The suns' intense gravity holds our planet in orbit. The sun, with a surface temperature of about 10,800°F. The sun is not even the hottest of all the stars. On the surface of the sun, you would quickly burn in the intense heat. The earth only receives heat and light energy from the sun. Many scientists who study the sun now are admitting that the energy of the sun is decreasing. The sun is becoming cooler, evidence shows that the sun will not last forever. However, the sun rises consistent each morning. The sun will raise until the Lord's appointed time.

Life on earth would not exist without the sun. Larger than anyone can comprehend, the sun is actually ninety-three million miles from earth. The sun's intense gravity holds our planet in orbit. The sun, with a surface temperature of about 10,800°F, is not even the hottest of all the stars. On the surface of the sun, a person would quickly burn in the intense heat. The earth receives heat and light energy only from the sun. Many scientists who study the sun are now admitting that the energy of the sun is decreasing. The sun is becoming cooler; evidence shows that the sun will not last forever. However, the sun rises consistently each morning. The sun will rise until the Lord's appointed time.

Look again at the excerpt from "The Most Dangerous Game." Find all the adjectives and adverbs in the selection. Try substituting other adjectives and adverbs in some sentences.
- *How does the meaning change?*
- *Do the new modifiers change the setting or the character in any way?*

Writing About a Personal Experience

Most people think nothing interesting ever happens to them. They think that because they have never been in a space shuttle, found a buried treasure, or single-handedly averted a war, they have nothing to tell that anyone would want to hear. But sometimes while looking for something monumen-

---

Objectives

Students will

1. choose a personal experience.
2. write an account of that experience.

Overview of the Writing Process

Planning—choosing an experience, reviewing the experience, and choosing a beginning point

Drafting—writing the rough draft

Revising—evaluating with a partner and making changes for clarity and tone

Publishing—reading to the class and handing in to the teacher

- *Answers will vary, but usually any change in wording affects meaning.*
- *Answers will vary, but unless the students are careful to choose synonyms, the perception of the setting or the character will probably change.*

Writing About a Personal Experience

Lesson Support

Teacher's Edition, Book 2
Writing Worksheets—p. 137
Rubrics—p. 151

Introduction

Tell the students about a personal experience that was significant to you or read an account that you have written previously. Explain why you chose to share that event.

Discussion

Direct the students to read the introduction and the text material about writing about a personal experience. Lead a discussion about the example, pointing out how the writer opened his narrative, directed the reader's attention through specific details that indicated the man's poverty, created a single impression of compassion, and concluded without telling too much.

Planning

Tell the students to read the instructions in "Your Turn."

Allow time for the students to choose an incident and to reflect on it. Distribute a copy of the Writing Worksheet (Book 2, p. 137) to each student. Instruct them to answer the questions on the Writing Worksheet and to return their worksheets to you when they have finished.

tal to write about, a person overlooks a dozen experiences that would delight, instruct, or amuse a reader.

Everyday happenings, told with expression and purpose, make good reading. This account relates an event that might have happened to anyone.

I was standing in a line at the grocery store. The line was moving slowly, so I looked past two people ahead to the person paying the bill.

He was an old man in a worn-out coat with no buttons. He pulled a knotted-up handkerchief carefully from his pocket and slowly untied it.

The people behind him frowned and huffed. He didn't seem to notice their impatience. When he had the cloth unfolded, he began to take out coins and hand them one by one to the clerk. At last he had given her all the coins he had.

The clerk still waited. It was not enough money. He started searching his pockets. While the others began looking crossly at him, I tried to get the clerk's attention, to say I would pay the rest. But she was looking at the coins in her hand.

Suddenly she said, "Oh, excuse me, sir. You have given me enough. This is enough."

The old man looked up and smiled. She put the groceries in a bag, and he took them and left.

Before she rang up the next order, however, she took fifty cents out of her own pocket and put it in the drawer.

Surely you have been in a line or a church service or a park and have seen something that touched you or amused you. It doesn't have to be earth shattering. A little human interest will suffice to make the story enjoyable.

How to Write About a Personal Experience

1. Choose an event that stands out to you—something that changed the way you think, taught you something, or made you laugh.

2. Go over the incident in your mind. Decide what information is really necessary to carry the story. In the account you read, it was not necessary for the person to say what he was buying or what day of the week it was. He gave only the information that was needed to show the most important points—the old man's problem and the clerk's kindness.

3. Decide how you will begin and end the story. Beginnings and endings are important; the beginning sets up the account, and the ending makes it sound finished and makes it memorable.

4. Write a rough draft. As in any good writing, choosing the precise words is important. The right noun, the appropriate adjective, or a strong verb can make all the difference in a piece of writing.

5. Personal experience accounts usually do not need much description. But what you do use should be vivid and appropriate. Remember, this account will be read by others. Be sure what you tell is appropriate for your audience. Don't write anything that you don't want others to read.

Your Turn

Write a personal experience, keeping in mind the main impression you want to convey and the principles of good writing.

Drafting

Return the Writing Worksheets and direct the students to read your comments. Allow time in class for students to write the rough drafts of their personal experience paragraphs.

Revising (Peer Response)

Direct each student to exchange his rough draft with a partner. Encourage each student to summarize in one word the impression that his partner's experience communicates.

Direct the students to return the papers to their authors when finished. Then assign the revision as homework.

Publishing

Ask volunteers to share their paragraphs on the next class day. Collect the paragraphs.

Scriptural Application

Read II Timothy 1:7-9. Remind the students that every Christian should be willing to share with others how his personal experience of salvation changed his life.

Evaluation

For help in grading this assignment, see "Grading Writing Assignments" (p. x) and Rubric 5 (Book 2, p. 151).

Enrichment

Encourage the students to ask their parents or grandparents to recount significant events from their own lives.

6 PREPOSITIONS, CONJUNCTIONS, AND INTERJECTIONS

Objectives

Students will

1. identify prepositions, objects of prepositions, and prepositional phrases in sentences.

2. differentiate adjectival prepositional phrases from adverbial prepositional phrases.

3. supply prepositional phrases for sentences.

4. select the correct preposition to complete a sentence.

5. distinguish between a preposition and an adverb by using the context of a sentence.

6. write sentences using prepositions correctly.

7. distinguish between coordinating conjunctions and correlative conjunctions in sentences.

8. write sentences using coordinating and correlative conjunctions correctly.

9. identify subordinating conjunctions in sentences.

10. write sentences using subordinating conjunctions correctly.

11. identify interjections in sentences.

12. write sentences using interjections correctly.

13. distinguish between prepositions, conjunctions, and interjections in sentences.

Their Finest Hour
by Winston S. Churchill

Winston S. Churchill delivered this speech on June 18, 1940, just before the Battle of Britain, in which Hitler's air force daily pounded Britain's Royal Air Force bases and civilian targets. Hitler thought it would be an easy victory, but he soon realized he could not break the English spirit. Churchill's words embody the defiance and optimism that eventually defeated Hitler.

What General Weygand called the Battle of France is over. I expect that the Battle of Britain is about to begin. Upon this battle depends the survival of Christian civilization. Upon it depends our own British life, and the long continuity of our institutions and our Empire. The whole fury and might of the enemy must very soon be turned on us. Hitler knows that he will have to break us in this Island or lose the war. If we can stand up to him, all Europe may be free and the life of the world may move forward into broad, sunlit uplands. But if we fail, then the whole world, including the United States, including all that we have known and cared for, will sink into the abyss of a new Dark Age made more sinister, and perhaps more protracted, by the light of perverted science. Let us therefore brace ourselves to our duties, and so bear ourselves that, if the British Empire and Commonwealth last for a thousand years, men will still say, "This was their finest hour."

- *Why do you think this speech became famous?*
- *How do you think such speeches helped the war effort?*
- *The first part of the speech describes a world after an Allied victory. What word signals his description of the dark turn an Axis victory would bring?*
- *What word used three times shows that the outcome of the battle is in doubt?*
- *Read the last sentence without the phrase* for a thousand years. *How is the intensity of the speech changed?*

- *Answers will vary but may include the following: It is concise, eloquent, and stirring.*
- *Answers will vary but may include the following: They inspired courage and hope and kept people focused on the goal rather than the obstacles.*
- But
- if
- *It loses some of its optimism and much of its magnitude. We do not get the sense that this battle is one of the most important in Britain's history.*

The words you probably chose are words that seem small and insignificant. However, they have much to do with the success of Churchill's speech. In this chapter, you will study many words that seem small but can carry great weight of meaning.

You have already studied five parts of speech: nouns, pronouns, verbs, adjectives, and adverbs. These words, especially verbs and nouns, often carry the major ideas of sentences. The three remaining parts of speech are prepositions, conjunctions, and interjections. Prepositions and conjunctions show how the other parts of speech fit together. Interjections provide transitions and express emotion. These words add the finishing touches to your writing.

Lesson Support

Student Text
Chapter 6 Review—pp. 413-15

Teacher's Edition, Book 1
Bulletin Boards—p. 447

Diagram Answers—pp. 460-63

Teacher's Edition, Book 2
Pretests—pp. 13-15

Teaching Helps—pp. 44-45

ESL Worksheets—pp. 80-81

Concept Reinforcements—pp. 107-9

Literature Link

Allow students enough time to read through the discussion questions that follow Winston Churchill's speech "Their Finest Hour." Read the speech aloud and discuss the questions with the students.

Prepositions

A **preposition** shows a relationship between its object and some other word in the sentence. The **object of the preposition** is a noun or pronoun that follows the preposition.

> The pie *on* the oven is a blueberry pie.
> The pie *near* the oven smells good.
> The pie *beside* the oven has not yet been baked.
> The pie *outside* the oven looks delicious.
> The pie *from* the oven is hot.
> The pie *inside* the oven is burning.

In the sentences above, different prepositions show the different relationships of the word *pie* to the word *oven*.

This list of prepositions is not exhaustive. Keep in mind the definition and function of prepositions as you look for them in sentences.

COMMONLY USED PREPOSITIONS				
aboard	at	during	off	to
about	before	except	on	toward
above	behind	for	onto	under
across	below	from	out	underneath
after	beneath	in	outside	until
against	beside	inside	over	up
along	between	into	past	upon
among	but	like	since	with
around	by	near	through	within
as	down	of	throughout	without

Many prepositions are just one word. However, some prepositions consist of more than one word. Here are just a few examples:

according to	because of	except for	in front of	instead of

Prepositional Phrases

A preposition always has an object, and so it is always part of a **prepositional phrase.** A prepositional phrase consists of the preposition, an object, and any modifiers of the object. The object and its modifiers together make up the complete object of the preposition.

> The town is building a marina *near the old mill.*

Near the old mill is the prepositional phrase. *The old mill* is the complete object of the preposition *near.*

A prepositional phrase may have a compound object.

> The new marina will be a source of *entertainment* and *education* for the *townspeople* and *visitors.*

Chapter 9: Subject-Verb Agreement with Intervening Phrases
p. 215

GRAMMAR

Chapter 5: Adjectives
p. 114

Teaching Strategy: Induction

Materials
- wooden spoon and pitcher

Place a wooden spoon in several locations in relationship to a pitcher. For example, place it inside the pitcher or beside the pitcher. Ask the students to write complete sentences that describe the spoon's location. *(The spoon is above the pitcher.)* Direct students to evaluate each of the sentences they have written. Ask them the following questions:

- Do most of your sentences begin and end the same way? *(yes)*

- Which word makes each sentence different? *(the preposition)*
- What is the significance of this word? *(It shows the relationship of the spoon to the pitcher.)*

Lead students to recognize that prepositions show the different relationships of one object to another.

ESL Strategy

Prepositions are difficult for many ESL students to learn. Some languages do not have prepositions; the prepositional function is often performed by noun case endings in such languages. Other languages that use prepositions do not necessarily have the same areas of meaning as English does for its prepositions. Some ESL students use prepositions incorrectly because they do not know the meanings. For further information, see ESL Worksheets 6A and 6B (Book 2, pp. 80-81). If you have access to *The Writer's Toolbox,* refer to pages 24-25 for the Idiomatic Use of Prepositions list.

Here the preposition *of* has two objects, *entertainment* and *education*. Likewise, *townspeople* and *visitors* are both the objects of the preposition *for.*

in summary

A **preposition** shows a relationship between its object and some other word in the sentence.

The **object of the preposition** is a noun or pronoun that follows the preposition.

A **prepositional phrase** consists of the preposition, an object, and any modifiers of the object.

If you choose to assign sentence diagramming with Practice the Skill 6-1, you may wish to wait until after the students have studied the material on pages 144-45.

6-1 PRACTICE THE SKILL

Place parentheses around the prepositional phrases. Underline the objects of the prepositions. Some sentences may contain more than one prepositional phrase.

1. Much (of Jesus' ministry) was located (in Galilee.)

2. Jesus' first disciples were fishermen (from the area.)

3. The Sea (of Galilee) was a particular focal point (during Christ's time.)

4. Jesus often taught the multitudes (from a boat.)

5. Christ performed ten miracles (beside this particular sea.)

6. Christ fed the five thousand. (After the miracle,) Christ sent His disciples (across the sea.)

7. (On the sea,) a storm caused great fear (for the disciples.)

8. Jesus walked (toward them) (on the water.)

9. Peter walked (on the water.) However, he took his eyes (off Christ) and sank (beneath the waves.)

10. Christ raised Peter (from the water) and calmed the wind.

6-2 REVIEW THE SKILL

Place parentheses around the prepositional phrases. Underline the objects of the prepositions.

1. The Jordan River flows (between the Dead Sea and Galilee.)

2. Many Bible events are associated (with the Jordan.)

3. The Israelites passed (through the Jordan.)

Teaching Strategy: Induction

Write the following sentences for display:

- Wallace sat between _____ and _____.

- An elderly gentleman sat in front of _____.

- Wallace initiated a conversation with _____.

Ask students to suggest words for each blank. Then ask them to identify each preposition in each sentence. Finally, ask students what part of speech is in each blank. *(a noun or a pronoun)* Lead students to recognize that each preposition has an object that is either a noun or a pronoun. Also point out that a preposition can have a compound object (as in the first sentence).

Evaluation

If you have assigned sentence diagramming with Practice the Skill 6-1, check students' answers using pages 460-61. Direct students to recognize that an adverbial prepositional phrase is always drawn beneath the verb and that an adjectival prepositional phrase is always drawn beneath the noun that it modifies.

4. The waters parted, and God led the Israelites (through the Jordan) (on dry land.)

5. God proved His presence (among the Israelites.)

6. God showed Himself again (to Naaman.)

7. Many (of us) know (about Naaman's leprosy.)

8. Elisha sent Naaman (to the river.)

9. Naaman was healed (after seven dips.)

10. John the Baptist baptized Jesus (in the Jordan River.)

6-3 USE THE SKILL

In the blank write an appropriate prepositional phrase to complete each sentence. Use a variety of prepositions. *(Answers will vary.)*

1. People enjoy seashores _____ *during their vacations* _____.

2. _____ *Before a swim* _____ children often look around the shore.

3. Many playful children might dig _____ *in the sand* _____.

4. They may be looking _____ *for seashells* _____.

5. High tide often brings unusual items _____ *to the shore* _____.

6. Many scientists study the plants and animals _____ *on the seashore* _____.

7. They can take pictures _____ *under the water* _____ with a waterproof camera.

8. Sometimes larger sea creatures get stranded _____ *along the shore* _____ and provide opportunity for study.

9. Some seashores have been damaged _____ *by pollution* _____.

10. We need to be good stewards _____ *of our planet's resources* _____.

Functions of Prepositional Phrases

Prepositional phrases can act as modifiers of both nouns and verbs. Prepositional phrases that modify nouns are called **adjectival prepositional phrases;** those that modify verbs are called **adverbial prepositional phrases.** Adjectival prepositional phrases modify nouns or pronouns. They answer the same questions that adjectives answer: *which one? what kind? how many? how much?* and *whose?*

> The man *with the red and black sweater* boarded the ship.
> The tapestries are silks *of blue and gold.*

G
GRAMMAR
Chapter 5: Adjectives and Adverbs
pp. 114; 122

The phrase *with the red and black sweater* modifies *man* and tells which man boarded the ship. *Of blue and gold* modifies *silks* and tells what kind of silks. These are adjectival prepositional phrases.

A prepositional phrase sometimes modifies the object of a preceding prepositional phrase.

Caren has a special album *with photos of her family.*

The prepositional phrase *of her family* modifies *photos,* which is the object of the preposition *with.* Notice that *with photos of her family* modifies *album.*

Adverbial prepositional phrases modify verbs. Like adverbs, they can express many meanings of manner, place, and time.

The ship will leave *in an hour.*
My mother is going *on a cruise.*

The phrase *in an hour* modifies *will leave* and tells when the ship will leave. *On a cruise* modifies *is going* and tells where the mother is going. These are adverbial prepositional phrases.

in summary

Prepositional phrases can act as modifiers of both nouns and verbs.

An **adjectival prepositional phrase** modifies a noun.

An **adverbial prepositional phrase** modifies a verb.

6-4 PRACTICE THE SKILL

Underline the word that each italicized prepositional phrase modifies. In the blank, label the phrase *adjectival* or *adverbial*.

Sea of Galilee

Dead Sea

_____adjectival_____   1. The seawater *of the earth* is one large body of water.

_____adjectival_____   2. The water *in the Dead Sea* is saltier than the oceans.

_____adverbial_____   3. People can float more easily *in its very salty water*.

_____adverbial_____   4. The Dead Sea is completely surrounded *by land*.

_____adverbial_____   5. A channel connects a true sea *to the ocean*.

_____adverbial_____   6. *Under the water,* there are mountains, plateaus, trenches, and plains.

_____adverbial_____   7. The center of the Arctic Ocean is covered *with ice*.

adjectival 8. The average depth *of an ocean* is twelve thousand feet.

adjectival 9. The deepest part *of the Pacific Ocean* is the Mariana Trench.

adjectival 10. The plates *on the earth's crust* often shift and move.

6-5 REVIEW THE SKILL

Underline each prepositional phrase in the following sentences. In the blank, label each phrase *adjectival* or *adverbial*.

adjectival 1. Joppa was a famous city along the Mediterranean Sea.

adjectival 2. The port for Jerusalem was Joppa.

adjectival 3. The land around the area was extremely productive.

adverbial 4. This port is mentioned in several Bible stories.

adverbial 5. Jonah ran away from God's call.

adverbial 6. He boarded a ship at Joppa.

adjectival 7. The most famous member of the Joppa congregation was Dorcas.

adjectival 8. Dorcas's good works among the people were commended.

adverbial 9. After her death, Peter raised her to life.

adverbial 10. The miracle became known throughout the city.

Using Prepositions Correctly

Some prepositions are sometimes used incorrectly. Be aware of these common preposition problems.

Troublesome Prepositions

Between/Among

Use *between* when discussing two people or things. Use *among* for more than two.

There was a lengthy correspondence *between* Josiah and his friend.
The members of the school board discussed the issue *among* themselves.

Teaching Strategy:
Discussion

Display the example sentences on pages 146-47. Read each sentence aloud and ask the students to describe the proper use of each preposition based on the examples. Discuss the differences between the two words in each set of troublesome prepositions.

In/Into

Especially in writing use *in* to show a location. Use *into* to refer to a direction.

> There are seven offices *in* the building.
> They walked *into* the building together.

Beside/Besides

Use *beside* to indicate "next to." Use *besides* to mean "in addition to" or "except for."

> Before you go to bed, place your things for tomorrow *beside* the door.
> I enjoy reading biographies of great men and women, *besides* just reading about them in my history book.
> All of the essays *besides* mine were entered in the contest.

in summary

Be aware of common preposition problems.

6-6 PRACTICE THE SKILL

Underline the correct preposition from the choices in parentheses.

1. Antoine has always enjoyed studying the various kinds of life found *(in, into)* the ocean.

2. *(Beside, Besides)* the study of underwater life, Antoine also enjoys underwater diving.

3. Antoine and Jamal especially enjoy swimming *(between, among)* several schools of fish.

4. *(Between, Among)* the two of them, they have been diving in twenty different locations.

5. One time, Antoine swam *(in, into)* the ocean near Bermuda.

6. Jamal was adventurous when he dove *(in, into)* an underwater cave.

7. Antoine and Jamal always enjoy diving *(beside, besides)* each other.

8. One time, they invited me along on a photography dive, and *(between, among)* the three of us, we took some amazing underwater pictures.

9. Last July, Antoine was able to swim *(beside, besides)* a sunken ship.

10. *(Beside, Besides)* finding a huge conch, Antoine found several sand dollars.

Underline the correct preposition from the choices in parentheses.

1. *(In, Into)* the heart of Old Testament lands lies the Fertile Crescent.

2. The Tigris River flows *(beside, besides)* the Euphrates.

3. *(Between, Among)* the two rivers is an extremely fertile area.

4. If you traveled *(in, into)* modern Iraq, you would find some of the Fertile Crescent there.

5. It also lies *(among, between)* parts of Israel, Lebanon, Jordan, Turkey, Syria, and Egypt.

6. *(Beside, Besides)* grain production, animal herding is profitable in this fertile area.

7. When Abraham's father moved his family to Haran, they moved *(in, into)* the center of the fertile area.

8. The city of Babylon is *(between, among)* many cities between the Tigris and Euphrates rivers.

9. Also, one city located *(beside, besides)* the Tigris River is Nineveh.

10. The Babylonian empire extended *(in, into)* most of the Fertile Crescent.

Chapter 5: Adverbs
p. 122

Preposition or Adverb?

Some words can function both as prepositions and adverbs. To determine whether a word in a sentence is a preposition or an adverb, look for an object of the preposition.

PREPOSITION Can you go *over* the water?
ADVERB Can you go *over?*

Over in the first sentence is a preposition because the object *water* follows it. In the second sentence, *over* is an adverb; it has no object.

PREPOSITION Please go *inside* the house.
ADVERB Please go *inside.*

In the first sentence, *inside* is a preposition with the object *house.* In the second sentence, *inside* is an adverb because it has no object. Every preposition has an object.

in summary

Some words used as prepositions can also be used as adverbs.

A preposition is followed by an object; an adverb does not have an object.

148   Chapter 6

Scriptural Application

As a springboard for discussing the difference between prepositions and adverbs, instruct students to make a list of all the prepositions found in Luke 2:4. Ask volunteers to read their lists. If some students list *up* or *out* as part of their lists, ask them to identify the objects of these prepositions. (Some translations do not include *out.*) When they cannot, explain to them that some words that appear to be prepositions are really adverbs. (If none of the students list *up* or *out* as a part of their lists, ask them why they chose not to include them.)

Emphasize to the students that a preposition will always have an object.

In the blank, label each italicized word *preposition* or *adverb*.

_____adverb_____ 1. After our trip to Greece, we went *down* to the Holy Land.

_____preposition_____ 2. The Mount of Beatitudes gave a spectacular view *over* the Sea of Galilee.

_____adverb_____ 3. We went *over* in a small boat.

_____preposition_____ 4. I was amazed as my mom and I walked *down* the streets where Christ carried the cross.

_____preposition_____ 5. Our entire group walked *up* the Mount of Olives.

_____adverb_____ 6. Jesus often went *up* and prayed with His disciples there.

_____preposition_____ 7. Tourists often go *underneath* Jerusalem.

_____adverb_____ 8. We went *below* and walked through some of the tunnels.

_____adverb_____ 9. As we walked *around,* our pastor frequently read Scripture to us.

_____preposition_____ 10. After we flew *past* Israel, I was excited to tell my friends about our visit.

In the blank, label each italicized word *preposition* or *adverb*. If the italicized word is a preposition, underline its object.

_____adverb_____ 1. Paul had been a prisoner *before* in Caesarea.

_____preposition_____ 2. There Paul exercised his rights *as* a Roman citizen.

_____adverb_____ 3. A ship was headed for Rome, and Paul was put *aboard.*

_____preposition_____ 4. The ship journeyed *across* the Mediterranean Sea.

_____adverb_____ 5. After they set *off,* a strong wind caused great danger for the ship.

_____preposition_____ 6. They were lost *amid* the storm's blackness.

_____preposition_____ 7. *After* nearly two weeks, the men feared for their lives.

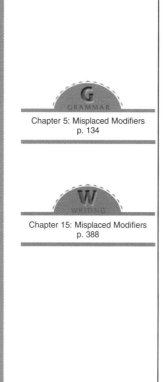

Chapter 5: Misplaced Modifiers
p. 134

Chapter 15: Misplaced Modifiers
p. 388

_____adverb_____	8.	Fear spread *throughout*.
_____preposition_____	9.	The ship ran aground *off* the <u>coast</u> of Malta.
_____preposition_____	10.	All the men jumped *into* the <u>water</u> and made it safely to shore.

Misplaced Prepositional Phrases

A prepositional phrase should be near the word that the phrase modifies. Otherwise, your sentence may be unclear.

UNCLEAR Our neighbor continuously yells at his obstinate dog *with a loud, booming voice.*

CLEAR *With a loud, booming voice,* our neighbor continuously yells at his obstinate dog.

UNCLEAR *After thirty minutes of baking,* Daniel removed the brownies from the oven.

CLEAR Daniel removed the brownies from the oven *after thirty minutes of baking.*

The phrase *with a loud, booming voice* is unclear when it comes directly after dog. Is it describing the neighbor's yell or the dog? The sentence is clarified by moving the phrase to the beginning of the sentence. In the second example, it is unclear whether the phrase *after thirty minutes of baking* modifies Daniel or the brownies. This sentence is made clear by moving the modifying phrase to the end of the sentence.

in summary

A prepositional phrase acting as a modifier should be near the word that the phrase modifies.

6-10 PRACTICE THE SKILL

Correct each misplaced prepositional phrase by rewriting the sentence correctly in the blank.

1. The little girl found a seashell with a broken leg.

   The little girl with a broken leg found a seashell.

2. The man spotted a whale aboard the ship.

   The man aboard the ship spotted a whale.

3. From the shell, Allie told how a crab molts.

   Allie told how a crab molts from the shell.

4. Like a crab, Allie reported that a lobster also molts.

   Allie reported that a lobster also molts like a crab.

Enrichment

Write the following sentence for display: *Ashton showed a rabbit to her brother under a bush.* Ask students to draw a picture of what is happening in the sentence. Allow students to share their pictures with the rest of the class. (Some students may draw Ashton's brother under a bush, and others may draw Ashton showing her brother a rabbit that is under a bush.) Use this activity to demonstrate that a misplaced prepositional phrase can cause a sentence to be unclear in its meaning. To help students avoid misplacing prepositional phrases, encourage them to picture what is being said in each sentence.

Enrichment

Assign Teaching Help 6A (Book 2, p. 44) for practice in placing prepositional phrases correctly.

5. A creature is more easily caught by a predator without a shell.

   A creature without a shell is more easily caught by a predator.

6. Fishermen in the molting process have a special name for crabs.

   Fishermen have a special name for crabs in the molting process.

7. The man over twelve feet told about some crabs with leg spans.

   The man told about some crabs with leg spans over twelve feet.

8. As a food source, we often view crabs and lobsters.

   We often view crabs and lobsters as a food source.

9. Under the sand, Jacob said that many common seashore creatures bury themselves.

   Jacob said that many common seashore creatures bury themselves

   under the sand.

10. The guide at the museum with a missing arm said that a starfish can grow a new one.

    The guide at the museum said that a starfish with a missing arm can grow a

    new one.

6-11 REVIEW THE SKILL

Correct each misplaced prepositional phrase by rewriting the sentence correctly in the blank. If the sentence is correct, write *C* in the blank.

1. From a tree my neighbor explained that he had built a canoe.

   My neighbor explained that he had built a canoe from a tree.

2. Around the state Marshall said that many canoeists enter races.

   Marshall said that many canoeists enter races around the state.

3. Last week, Marshall entered a race on the river near our house.

   C

4. The winner of the race was the man with red paint in front of the canoe.

   The winner of the race was the man in front of the canoe with red paint.

5. Marshall told us how canoes are made during supper.

   During supper, Marshall told us how canoes are made.

6. Many early Americans made canoes for food so that they could fish and hunt.

   Many early Americans made canoes so that they could fish and hunt for

   food.

7. Across land, canoes were light so that traders could carry them.

   Canoes were light so that traders could carry them across land.

8. Robert Baden-Powell, founder of the Boy Scouts, designed canoes with sails.

   C

9. Many early canoes were made from trees and were sealed with animal skins.

   C

10. The salesman at the sports store from fiberglass and plastic said that canoe makers craft canoes.

    The salesman at the sports store said that canoe makers craft canoes

    from fiberglass and plastic.

Conjunctions

A **conjunction** joins words or groups of words in a sentence. There are two kinds of conjunctions: coordinating and subordinating. Correlative conjunctions are a special type of coordinating conjunction.

Coordinating Conjunctions

Coordinating conjunctions connect two sentence parts that have the same function in the sentence. The chart below lists commonly used coordinating conjunctions.

and	or	for
but	nor	yet

A conjunction appears between the two sentence parts that the conjunction is joining. The sentence parts may be single words or entire phrases.

NOUNS *Frigates* **and** *windjammers* are two types of ships.
Giant tankers carry *cargo* **and** *supplies.*
People are fascinated by the sea's *mystery* **and** *beauty.*

VERBS The workers *clean* **and** *load* the ships.
I *have gone to Maine* **and** *have taken a lobster cruise.*

ADJECTIVES The ship was *old* **but** *seaworthy.*

PREPOSITIONS The ships went *around* **or** *through* the canal.

AUXILIARIES The ship *can* **and** *will* take the passengers to France.

Coordinating conjunctions can also connect independent or dependent clauses in a sentence. When a coordinating conjunction connects two independent clauses, a comma precedes the conjunction.

Chapter 1: Subjects and Predicates
p. 4

Reinforcement

Use the bulletin board on page 447 as an interactive teaching tool for coordinating conjunctions. Emphasize that coordinating conjunctions join two sentence parts that have the same function in the sentence.

INDEPENDENT CLAUSES	The American ship *Savannah* was the first steam-powered vessel to cross the Atlantic Ocean, **yet** it used its engines only one hundred and five hours during a twenty-nine-day journey.
DEPENDENT CLAUSES	Because a change in the wind can put a ship off course **and** because ships use complicated equipment, operating a ship takes great skill.

Chapter 12: Commas in a Series
of Independent Clauses
p. 279

Chapter 8: Independent and
Dependent Clauses
p. 192

Correlative Conjunctions

Correlative conjunctions always appear in pairs. Like other coordinating conjunctions, correlative conjunctions link sentence parts of the same function. The following chart lists the most common pairs of correlative conjunctions:

both—and
either—or
neither—nor
not only—but also

Correlative conjunctions join sentence elements of the same kind. Correlative conjunctions are used for emphasis or clarity.

> She finished **not only** today's homework **but also** tomorrow's.

Here the correlative conjunction emphasizes the fact that she finished tomorrow's homework in addition to today's. The next sentence is unclear without a correlative conjunction.

> This year he is taking algebra and French or Spanish.

A correlative conjunction would clarify one of the two possible meanings.

> This year he is taking algebra and **either** French **or** Spanish.
> This year he is taking **either** algebra and French **or** Spanish.

Various types of sentence elements can be joined by correlative conjunctions.

SUBJECTS	**Either** tankers **or** multipurpose ships can haul liquid. **Neither** dry bulk carriers **nor** traditional cargo ships are the best types to carry petroleum.
VERBS	Kendra will **both** study **and** sleep before she goes to the lake.
ADJECTIVES	The trips of an air cushion vehicle are **not only** fast **but also** short.
OBJECTS OF THE PREPOSITION	Research vessels are often distinguished externally by **not only** cranes **but also** winches.
CLAUSES	**Either** we will all travel together on the ship, **or** our father will leave a week earlier.

Prepositions, Conjunctions, and Interjections   153

Enrichment

Assign Teaching Help 6B (Book 2, p. 45) to help students practice joining sentence parts with coordinating and correlative conjunctions. Emphasize that correlative conjunctions, like coordinating conjunctions, join sentence elements of the same kind. Ask the students how their sentences joined by correlative conjunctions sound different from those that are joined by coordinating conjunctions. *(Correlative conjunctions add emphasis or clarity.)*

When *not only—but also* joins clauses, the subject of the second clause may come between the words *but* and *also*.

COMPOUND SENTENCE **Not only** did the Romans build the largest fleet of ancient times, **but** they **also** became the rulers of the Mediterranean region during the second century B.C.

in summary

A **conjunction** joins words or groups of words in a sentence.

A **coordinating conjunction** connects two sentence parts that have the same function in the sentence.

A **correlative conjunction** appears in a pair and also connects two sentence parts of the same function.

6-12 PRACTICE THE SKILL

Underline the conjunctions in the following sentences. In the blank, label the conjunctions *coordinating* or *correlative*.

coordinating 1. The ocean and its depths contain many interesting types of animals.

correlative 2. Both squid and fish swim around in schools to protect themselves.

coordinating 3. Sharks can be frightening to people, but several types of sharks are harmless.

correlative 4. Either a fish or plankton might become caught in the tentacles of a sea predator.

correlative 5. Not only do jellyfish have stinging tentacles, but a man-of-war can also have a vicious sting.

correlative 6. Neither dolphins nor porpoises grow as large as some other members of the whale family.

coordinating 7. Baleen whales are large yet gentle.

coordinating 8. The blue whale can weigh 220 tons and can be the size of a jet!

coordinating 9. Many otters are found in rivers, but two species reside in saltwater.

correlative 10. When looking casually into the water, you may not notice either a crab or a flounder; both camouflage themselves.

Underline the conjunctions in each sentence twice. Underline the main words joined by the conjunctions once. In the blank, label the conjunction *coordinating* or *correlative.*

correlative 1. Many submarines either attack enemy ships or fire missiles at enemy countries.

coordinating 2. One hundred fifty crew members can live or work on submarines.

correlative 3. Many attack submarines carry both torpedoes and missiles.

coordinating 4. Crew members locate enemy ships with periscopes and radar.

coordinating 5. Submarines are large yet swift.

coordinating 6. Submarines can be used for scientific research, but these submarines are relatively small.

correlative 7. Attack submarines attack not only enemy submarines but also surface ships.

correlative 8. Neither attack submarines nor ballistic missile submarines can work effectively from the surface.

coordinating 9. One or two propellers in the stern control the submarine.

coordinating 10. Early submarines surfaced often for their engines and crews.

Combine a word or phrase from the first sentence with a word or phrase from the second sentence to make a compound sentence joined by the type of conjunction indicated in parentheses. Try to use each correlative conjunction at least once. Use a variety of conjunctions. In the blank write the new sentence. *(Answers will vary.)*

1. *Survive the Savage Sea* is a book about a family in trouble on the sea. *The Swiss Family Robinson* is also a book about a family in trouble on the sea. *(correlative)*

   Both Survive the Savage Sea and The Swiss Family Robinson are books

   about families in trouble on the sea.

Evaluation

If you have assigned sentence diagramming with Review the Skill 6-13, check students' answers using pages 461-62.

2. The families' situations are similar. The families' situations are different. *(coordinating)*

   The families' situations are similar yet different.

3. In *The Swiss Family Robinson,* the wife trusted in God. The husband also trusted in God. *(correlative)*

   In The Swiss Family Robinson, *not only the wife but also the husband*

   trusted in God.

4. The family was frightened. The family was prayerful. *(coordinating)*

   The family was frightened but prayerful.

5. In *Survive the Savage Sea* by Dougal Robertson, the husband felt weary. He also felt hopeless. *(coordinating)*

   In Survive the Savage Sea *by Dougal Robertson, the husband felt weary*

   and hopeless.

6. However, Lyn Robertson often prayed for comfort. Lyn Robertson often sang for comfort. *(correlative)*

   However, Lyn Robertson often either prayed or sang for comfort.

7. Lyn and Dougal Robertson rarely slept on their raft. Lyn and Dougal Robertson rarely rested on their raft. *(coordinating)*

   Lyn and Dougal Robertson rarely slept or rested on their raft.

8. The Robertson family was not prepared for the wreck. The Robinson family was not prepared for the wreck. *(correlative)*

   Neither the Robertson family nor the Robinson family was prepared for

   the wreck.

9. The Robinson family lived on an island until their rescue. The Robinson family flourished on an island until their rescue. *(correlative)*

   The Robinson family not only lived but also flourished on an island until

   their rescue.

10. The Robertsons spent thirty-eight difficult days on a raft until their rescue. The Robertsons spent thirty-eight wearisome days on a raft until their rescue. *(coordinating)*

    The Robertsons spent thirty-eight difficult and wearisome days on a raft

    until their rescue.

Subordinating Conjunctions

A **subordinating conjunction** joins a dependent clause to an independent clause. A subordinating conjunction is part of the dependent clause, but its only function in that clause is to introduce it.

If everyone will work together, we will finish on time.
We will order pizza *after* we have finished painting.

In the first sentence, the word *if* introduces the dependent clause and joins it to the independent clause *we will finish on time.* In the second sentence, the two clauses are joined by the subordinating conjunction *after,* which introduces the dependent clause. Below is a list of commonly used subordinating conjunctions.

after	if	until
although	once	when
as	since	where
because	that	wherever
before	unless	while

Most subordinating conjunctions introduce adverb clauses. This means that the dependent clause modifies the verb of the independent clause.

We rode our bikes *wherever* the trail was wide enough.

Here the subordinating conjunction *wherever* introduces a dependent clause. The clause modifies the verb *rode,* and it answers the question *where?* The subordinating conjunction in an adverb clause can express several different types of meaning. Below are some common types.

TIME *When* the game was over, everyone came to our house for snacks.

PLACE People sat *wherever* they could find empty places on the floor.

CAUSE *Because* it was so late, we could not stay long.

CONTRAST Some talked in the kitchen *while* others played games in the den.

PURPOSE We moved the furniture aside *so that* there would be more room on the floor.

in summary

A **subordinating conjunction** joins a dependent clause to an independent clause.

Chapter 8: Complex Sentence
p. 197

Chapter 5: Adverbs
p. 122

Teaching Strategy: Induction

Write the word *dependent* for display. Ask students what it means to be dependent. *(to rely on someone or something else)* Then ask students how they would meet someone they didn't know. *(They would probably be introduced.)* Explain that many times we rely on others to introduce us to people whom we do not know. Use this fact as a springboard for instructing students that subordinating conjunctions "introduce" dependent clauses.

Reinforcement

Allow the students to work through the Concept Reinforcement about subordinating conjunctions (Book 2, p. 109).

Underline the subordinating conjunctions in the sentences.

1. Almost all submarines used diesel engines <u>until</u> nuclear power was developed in the 1950s.

2. <u>Before</u> nuclear-powered engines were developed, submarines were not true underwater ships.

3. Ballistic missile submarines are larger <u>than</u> attack submarines are.

4. <u>Because</u> ballistic missile submarines attack cities and bases on shore, they carry long-range missiles.

5. <u>If</u> a modern combat submarine were to dive deeper than thirteen hundred feet, it would be harmed by the water pressure.

6. <u>Although</u> the *Hunley* was the first submarine to sink a ship in war, it also sank.

7. <u>While</u> World War II raged, German U-boats sank thousands of ships.

8. German U-boats were a terror <u>when</u> they began war on Allied ships.

9. <u>After</u> a crew of an attack submarine returns from a mission, the submarine stays in port and in local operations for six months.

10. The work assignments of a crew vary <u>so that</u> all crewmen will receive days off.

Use a subordinating conjunction to combine the two sentences, making one a dependent clause. Try to find the relationship between the two ideas. Write the new sentence in the blank. *(Answers will vary.)*

1. The Arctic and Antarctic have harsh climate conditions. They are largely unexplored.

   Because the Arctic and Antarctic have harsh climate conditions, they are

   largely unexplored.

2. The Arctic is largely unexplored. The Arctic has been threatened by pollution and mining.

   Although it is largely unexplored, the Arctic has been threatened by

   pollution and mining.

3. Much of the Antarctic is frozen. Ships called icebreakers clear the ice from trade routes.

Since much of the Antarctic is frozen, ships called icebreakers clear the

ice from trade routes.

4. Arctic explorers wear heavy clothing. They can quickly get frostbite.

Unless Arctic explorers wear heavy clothing, they can quickly get frostbite.

5. Glaciers flow into the sea. Pieces of ice break off to form icebergs.

As glaciers flow into the sea, pieces of ice break off to form icebergs.

6. Many sea creatures live longer. The waters are cold.

Many sea creatures live longer where the waters are cold.

7. Deposits of minerals have been found in Antarctica. The small amounts make the minerals difficult to mine.

While deposits of minerals have been found in Antarctica, the small

amounts make the minerals difficult to mine.

8. Antarctica was discovered. Greek philosophers already believed that the continent existed.

Before Antarctica was discovered, Greek philosophers already believed

that the continent existed.

9. No one had reached the South Pole. Roald Amundsen and his men arrived there in 1911.

No one had reached the South Pole until Roald Amundsen and his men

arrived there in 1911.

10. Robert Scott and his men knew that they had not arrived at the South Pole first. They saw a tent and a Norwegian flag.

Robert Scott and his men knew that they had not arrived at the South Pole

first when they saw a tent and a Norwegian flag.

Interjections

Interjections are words that can stand alone. An interjection does not have a necessary function in the sentence. Interjections express several different meanings.

STRONG FEELING	*Amazing!* That was a flawless performance.
AGREEMENT AND DISAGREEMENT	*Sure,* I'd love to go. *No,* this issue is not resolved.
GREETING AND LEAVE-TAKING	*Goodbye.* We'll see you soon.
POLITENESS	*Sorry,* there's no extra room in our car.
HESITATION OR INTRODUCTION OF A SUBJECT	*Well,* we're not sure what the next step will be. *All right then,* let's get started.

An interjection can be a single word or a short phrase. Interjections either stand alone with separate punctuation or are set off in the sentence by a comma or a pair of commas.

Chapter 12: Exclamation Point; Commas to Separate
pp. 275; 284

in summary

An **interjection** is a word that can stand alone and does not have a necessary function in the sentence.

6-17 PRACTICE THE SKILL

Underline the interjections in the following sentences.

1. Say, have you ever heard of the Bermuda Triangle?

2. Some ships and planes have disappeared in that area, and, alas, people theorize about the disappearances.

3. Hey, what theories exist?

4. Really, some people believe in theories about creatures from other planets!

5. Oh, are any theories reasonable?

6. Sure. That area of the ocean has a unique environment.

7. See, normally a compass points toward magnetic north.

8. So, is that area different from others?

9. Yes, a compass in the Bermuda Triangle points to the true north.

10. Wow! The difference could definitely cause a ship's captain or a pilot some serious problems.

Scriptural Application

Instruct students to find the interjections in the following verses: Psalm 33:18; 35:21; Isaiah 55:1; Jeremiah 32:17; and Matthew 28:20. (To help keep students' answers consistent, have students use a King James Version of the Bible.) Remind students that not all interjections will be found at the beginning of a verse and that some verses may contain more than one interjection. Ask students to think of other verses that contain interjections. *(e.g., Psalm 23:4)*

Evaluation

If you have assigned sentence diagramming with Practice the Skill 6-17, check students' answers using pages 462-63.

Rewrite each sentence with an appropriate interjection. *(Answers will vary.)*

1. The Mediterranean Sea has many islands.

   Oh, the Mediterranean Sea has many islands.

2. Could you tell me about some of them?

   Please, could you tell me about some of them?

3. A few are significant in biblical history.

   Sure, a few are significant in biblical history.

4. Did you know about John's exile?

   Say, did you know about John's exile?

5. He was exiled on the island of Patmos.

   Yes, he was exiled on the island of Patmos.

6. Patmos was an island of banishment.

   Hey, Patmos was an island of banishment.

7. What a lonely place that must have been!

   Wow! What a lonely place that must have been!

8. How did God use that time in his life?

   Well, how did God use that time in his life?

9. He received his great visions for the Book of Revelation there.

   Why, he received his great visions for the Book of Revelation there.

10. God really did use that little island.

    Amazing! God really did use that little island.

Label each italicized word *preposition, conjunction,* **or** *interjection.*

interjection   1. *Incredible!* The ocean has such an amazing variety of animal and plant life.

preposition   2. Animals can be discovered *at* any depth in the ocean.

conjunction   3. *Because* plants need light, they are discovered in the sunlit zone.

conjunction   4. No plants live *where* there is no light.

preposition   5. *Around* 90 percent of known animal species live near the bottom of the ocean.

6. Some types of sea life, however, can be found *on* the shore.

conjunction

7. Sea life on shore must *either* take shelter *or* be able to endure the drying effects of the sun.

preposition

8. If you roam *along* a shore at low tide, you might find a starfish.

interjection

9. *Wow,* I haven't thought about sea life very much.

conjunction

10. Plants *and* animals in the ocean are unique.

6-20 CUMULATIVE REVIEW

Complete each sentence by giving a word of the part of speech indicated. *(Answers will vary.)*

_____Wow_____! Penguins are _____rather_____ interesting
(interjection)   (adverb)

_____animals_____. _____Although_____ penguins cannot fly, they
(noun)   (subordinating conjunction)

are excellent swimmers. Their feathers _____are_____ short
                                        (linking verb)

_____yet_____ thick. Because of its thick layers of fat, a penguin
(coordinating conjunction)

remains _____warm_____ even in cold water. Coming to land only
        (predicate adjective)

to breed and raise their young, penguins spend _____most_____ of
                                                (indefinite pronoun)

their time _____in_____ water. For their diet, penguins
           (preposition)

_____eat_____ fish. Interestingly, _____they_____ are found
(verb)   (personal pronoun)

only in the southern half of the world because they will _____not_____
                                                          (adverb)

cross into warm water. Finally, penguins have unusual nesting habits. A

female bird lays a single egg on _____the_____ ice and returns
                                 (article)

to the water immediately. The male keeps the egg warm by covering it with

_____his_____ belly. The male penguins huddle in groups for warmth.
(possessive adjective)

They stay there two months, and they do not eat _____during_____ this time.
                                                 (preposition)

Look again at the speech by Winston Churchill. Make a list of all the prepositional phrases he used, creating a "found poem."

- *Do you think the "found poem" of prepositional phrases carries the emotion and message of the original speech?*

Writing a Research Essay

Have you ever been asked to write a report for a class—a report that required you to look for facts or to interview other people? Maybe your science teacher asked you to write a report about your science fair project or your history teacher assigned a paper about a famous person or event. You probably had to use information from books or articles, or maybe you asked relatives to tell you about their experiences in the twentieth century. If so, then you were researching.

One common way to report the results of your research is to write an essay. An essay is a paper that consists of several paragraphs about one main idea. A typical essay has an introduction paragraph, several paragraphs of the body, and a conclusion paragraph.

Planning Your Essay

Choosing a Topic and a Purpose

One of the hardest things about writing is getting started. You need to plan what you're going to say. The planning is not easy; it takes thinking. First, you have to decide what your **topic** will be. A good topic for a short research report will be something that you can discuss thoroughly in only a few paragraphs. You also have to decide what your **purpose** for writing will be. Do you want to inform, persuade, or entertain your reader?

Researching and Taking Notes

Next, you need to gather information about your topic. The best place to start is a general reference work, such as an encyclopedia. Then go to the library catalog to search for books and perhaps other works on your topic. As you learn more about your subject, you might discover more areas to investigate. When you have located some good sources, you can begin reading and taking notes. There are two kinds of notes you will need to take: source notes and content notes.

Source notes record essential information about your sources. Write down the author or editor, title, and publication information (publisher, city of publication, and date of publication) for every source you use. Your source notes will eventually become your **bibliography,** a list of the sources you used as you wrote your essay. Follow your teacher's instructions for turning your source notes into a bibliography.

Content notes record what you learned and where you learned it. Be sure to record not only the facts about your topic but also the source and the page number where you found those facts. There are three basic methods of note taking: summary, brief phrases (to help you paraphrase), and quotation. Most notes should be in your own words—either summary or brief phrases—because you are looking for information, not someone else's wording.

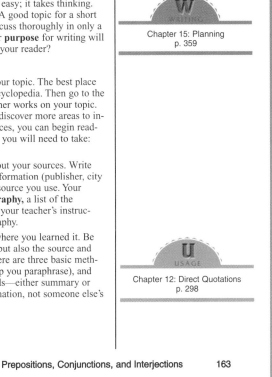

Chapter 15: Planning
p. 359

Chapter 12: Direct Quotations
p. 298

> ### Objectives
> Students will
> 1. plan, outline, and research a suggested topic.
> 2. write a research essay and a bibliography for the sources used in the essay.

> ### Overview of the Writing Process
>
> **Planning**—choosing a topic and a purpose, researching and taking notes about the topic, listing and grouping ideas about the topic, constructing an outline, and writing a thesis statement
>
> **Drafting**—writing a topic sentence for each paragraph, writing supporting sentences for each paragraph, incorporating and documenting information from outside sources, writing the introduction and the conclusion, and writing a bibliography
>
> **Revising**—proofreading for clarity, grammar, and punctuation; checking the accuracy of facts and sources for each summary, paraphrase, and quotation; and creating a clean copy
>
> **Publishing**—handing in to the teacher and presenting to another person or to a class

Writing a Research Essay

Lesson Support

Student Text
Chapter 15: Composition Skills—
pp. 373-81

Teacher's Edition, Book 2
Writing Worksheets—pp. 138-39
Rubrics—p. 152

Introduction

Introduce the topic of research by asking the students what type of professions use research to accomplish their work. *(scientists, historians, journalists, pastors)* Ask students why research would be important to these professions. *(to find a cure for a disease, to learn more about a historic event or person, etc.)*

Explain that research is important for gaining factual information that may enable a person to learn more about a topic or may verify that what a person already asserts about a particular topic is indeed accurate.

Planning

Direct the students to read the instructions in "Your Turn" on page 167. Allow time for students to choose from one of the listed topics or from additional topics that you suggest.

A **summary** is a short version of some longer work that keeps the most important facts and leaves out many of the details. If you learn to summarize well, you will save much time and get more of the information that you really need. Here are some hints for writing good summaries:

- Begin by asking significant questions. The answers to these questions will give you the main information for your summary.

- Include only the important information, not the minor details, illustrations, or examples.

- Try to use mostly your own words when writing a summary.

- If you include some of the author's words, put them in quotation marks. The quotation marks show what words were copied from the original.

Making an Outline

Now you should begin organizing your ideas. An especially useful tool is the **outline.** First, list ideas about your subject. This list does not need to be in any particular order; you can, at this point, write down ideas as they come to you. Next you should try to group the ideas from your list. Group details or instructions that have something in common. Try to arrange the details in some order inside the separate groups. Now give headings to the groups of ideas. An outline for an informative paper about the Jordan River might look like this:

I. The Israelites crossed the Jordan River.
   A. The priests and the ark of the covenant preceded the children of Israel into the Jordan.
   B. The Lord kept the river from flowing.
   C. The Israelites crossed the Jordan on dry land.
   D. God used the parting of the Jordan to show the children of Israel that He would be with Joshua.

II. Naaman was healed at the Jordan River.
   A. Naaman was an eminent military leader who had leprosy.
   B. The prophet Elisha told him to wash in the Jordan seven times.
   C. Naaman refused to dip himself in the Jordan.
   D. Naaman humbled himself by washing in the Jordan, and he was healed as a result.
   E. God changed Naaman's heart.

III. Christ was baptized in the Jordan River.
   A. John the Baptist physically baptized Jesus in the Jordan River.
   B. All three Persons of the Trinity were there.
   C. God showed the importance of the Trinity.

This is also a good time to write your **thesis statement.** The thesis statement of an essay is similar to the topic sentence in a paragraph: it states the main idea of your essay in one sentence. A good thesis statement tells the audience your topic and what you will say about that topic.

> **POOR** This essay is about the Jordan River.
> **GOOD** The Jordan River was the site of several notable biblical events in which God demonstrated His power.

When you have a satisfactory thesis, review your outline. Does everything in the outline support the thesis? If not, drop or change some points in the outline.

Discussion

Instruct students to list any ideas that could be connected with the topics they have chosen. *(differences in clothing from the Old Testament to the New Testament, cooking methods during Bible times, chariot making)* Read "Choosing a Topic and a Purpose" on page 163 with the class.

Instruct students to research and take notes on their chosen topics (and any related ideas they have come up with). Remind students to be thorough in their note taking and to keep track of the sources from which they obtain their information.

Encourage students to use their Bible concordances to look up Scripture verses that support their topics. Consider having additional concordances available for students to use.

Planning

Instruct students to begin organizing their ideas into groups by using their notes. Tell them to read "Making an Outline" on page 164 before they begin.

Direct students to assign headings to each idea group. Instruct them to create an outline from the idea groups that they have constructed.

Review the information about thesis statements and instruct students to write a thesis statement that reflects the direction in which their research has led them.

Distribute a copy of Writing Worksheet 6A (Book 2, p. 138) to each student. Instruct students to complete each part of the Writing Worksheet for homework.

Drafting Your Essay

The Body of Your Essay

Once you have completed the planning stages, you are ready to write your first draft. First, write the **supporting paragraphs**—the body of your essay. Every supporting paragraph needs a good topic sentence that tells what the paragraph will be about. The main headings in your outline will become the topic sentences of your paragraphs. After you have a good topic sentence, turn the subpoints into sentences. Make a smooth paragraph, moving from one idea to another with transitions.

- Use transitions like *however, on the other hand,* or *instead* when changing ideas.

- Use words like *also, then,* and *in addition* when continuing a thought.

- Use transitions to prepare the reader for a new paragraph.

As you write your supporting paragraphs, be sure to document the summaries, paraphrases, and quotations you use to back up your points. Follow your teacher's instructions or use **parenthetical citations** to tell your reader where you found the borrowed information.

A parenthetical citation identifies the source in the briefest possible way (usually just the author's last name) and also specifies the page or pages from which the information was taken. The bibliography at the end of your paper gives the full information about each source. A parenthetical citation appears at the end of your sentence or at a natural pause in the sentence, before the punctuation needed at that spot. Here are some other tips for using parenthetical citations:

- If you mention the author's name or other information in the sentence, do not repeat it in the parenthetical citation.

- If the authors of different sources share the same last name, include the author's first name too.

- If you use two or more works by the same author, add the title after the author's name and a comma.

- If no author or editor is named, use the title instead.

The Introduction and Conclusion of Your Essay

Just as a paragraph needs a good beginning sentence, an essay needs a good opening paragraph. In the **introduction** the writer must do three things: catch the reader's interest, introduce the topic, and draw attention to the main idea of the topic. An introduction is like a funnel: it is wide at the beginning where it introduces the broad topic, and it narrows to a specific thesis statement at the end.

An essay also needs a good **conclusion.** A conclusion sums up the main ideas of your paper. The first sentence of the conclusion is the **restatement** of the main idea: it makes a statement similar (but not identical) to the last statement of the introduction. A good conclusion usually ends with a clever or interesting sentence that makes the essay sound finished. Think of the conclusion as an inverted funnel: it begins narrowly with a restatement of the thesis and broadens to a larger view of the topic.

Chapter 15: Supporting Paragraphs
p. 373

Chapter 15: Coherence
p. 375

Chapter 15: Introduction and Conclusion
p. 374

Discussion

Review parenthetical citations with the students. Answer any questions that they may have about parenthetical citations or about drafting the paper.

Planning

Conduct individual conferences with the students to discuss Writing Worksheet 6A. Help them to troubleshoot for such problems as outline points that do not support their thesis or a thesis that does not address the assigned topic.

Drafting

While you confer with some students, allow other students time in class to write supporting paragraphs. Encourage them to incorporate transitions within and between their paragraphs.

Modeling

Review the characteristics of good introductions and conclusions. If possible, use examples found in newspapers and magazines to illustrate good introductions and conclusions. Ask students to analyze what catches their attention or sums up the main ideas of the piece.

Instruct students to write the introductions and conclusions of their reports outside of class.

A Sample Essay

Here is an example of an informative essay about the Jordan River. As you read it, look for the thesis statement, the topic sentences, the transitions, and the "funnel effect" of the introduction and conclusion. Notice too the parenthetical citations for the summaries, paraphrases, and quotations.

Today the Jordan River is considered "the only important river of Israel and Jordan" (Gubser 166). This river was also a very significant body of water in Bible times. **The Jordan River was the site of several notable biblical events in which God demonstrated His power.**

One significant incident that happened at the Jordan was the Israelites' crossing the river. This occurrence may sound ordinary, but it was quite remarkable because the children of Israel crossed the river on dry land. Furthermore, according to *Unger's Bible Dictionary,* the Israelites traversed the Jordan during the one time in the year that it was at its greatest width (605). The Lord told Joshua to send the priests and ark of the covenant into the Jordan first (Joshua 3:8, 11), and once the priests stepped into the water, the river stopped flowing (3:15-16). As soon as the priests were in the middle of the dried-up Jordan, the rest of the Israelites crossed over (3:17). God used the parting of the Jordan to show the children of Israel that He would be with their new leader Joshua just as He had been with Moses (3:7, 4:14).

Another important event that occurred at the Jordan River was the healing of Naaman. Naaman was an eminent military leader who had leprosy (II Kings 5:1); however, a little maid told his wife that the prophet Elisha could heal him of his disease (5:3). Elisha told Naaman that he would be cleansed if he would wash in the Jordan seven times (5:10), but Naaman thought that other rivers were better than the Jordan, and he refused to dip himself (5:11-12). Nevertheless, Naaman finally humbled himself by washing himself in the river, and he was healed as a result. B. K. Waltke affirms that God used this incident to change Naaman "from a proud, self-sufficient man to a believing . . . humble . . . and reverent man" (346).

In addition, the Jordan River was the site of Christ's baptism by John the Baptist. After John baptized Jesus in the Jordan River, the Holy Spirit appeared as a dove from heaven, and God's voice declared that He was "well pleased" with His Son (Mark 1:10-11). D. Edmond Hiebert states, "All three persons [of the Trinity] were involved" (34). Not only was the Jordan used as the physical means to baptize Christ, but it was also the place where God showed the importance of the Trinity.

The incidents that occurred at the Jordan River were significant because they proved God's power. God used this body of water to perform miracles as well as to baptize His own Son. God's using the Jordan River demonstrates that He often uses nature to accomplish His divine purposes.

Sidebar labels: Thesis · Summary · Topic sentences · Paraphrase · Parenthetical citations · Transitions · Quotation · Restatement

Reinforcement

Ask volunteers to read their introductions and conclusions to the class.

Drafting

Instruct students to create a bibliography page from the sources they consulted for homework. (See pp. 256-71 of *The Writer's Toolbox* for more information and for sample bibliography entries.)

Revising (Peer Response)

Distribute a copy of Writing Worksheet 6B (Book 2, p. 139) to each student. Tell students to exchange essays and bibliographies with a partner. Instruct each student to read his partner's essay and to fill out the evaluation, returning it to the writer when finished. Instruct the students to read over their own essays and bibliographies and the suggestions from their partners and to make any changes for clarity.

Assign proofreading for homework. Students should check for the accuracy of facts and for the citation of sources for each summary, paraphrase, and quotation. They should also proofread the bibliography page of their papers. Instruct students to make a clean, neat copy of their essays. If a student's bibliography needs to be revised, he should also make a clean, neat copy of it. Instruct students to proofread their revised copies before turning them in.

Here is the bibliography for the sample essay. Notice especially the formats for citing the Bible, dictionary entries, and encyclopedia entries.

Bibliography

Gubser, Peter. "Jordan, River." *The World Book Encyclopedia.* 1994 ed.

Hiebert, D. Edmond. *The Gospel of Mark: An Expositional Commentary.* Ed. Greg Kuzmic. Rev. ed. Greenville: Bob Jones UP, 1994.

Holy Bible. King James Version.

Unger, Merrill F. "Jordan, Valley of." *Unger's Bible Dictionary.* 3rd ed. rev. Chicago: Moody, 1966.

Waltke, B. K. "Naaman." *The Zondervan Pictorial Encyclopedia of the Bible.* Gen. ed. Merrill C. Tenney. Vol. 4. Grand Rapids: Zondervan, 1976. 5 vols.

Revising Your Essay

The last step is to revise your essay. When you finish your essay, read each paragraph again. Do the sentences follow one another smoothly? Are they clear? Is the grammar correct? Are the words spelled correctly? Then check your summaries, paraphrases, and quotations. Have you recorded the facts accurately? Are all quotations enclosed in quotation marks? Did you include the correct source information every time? When you have revised your rough draft, make a neat, clean copy of your essay, following your teacher's guidelines. Then proofread your work before you hand it in.

Your Turn

Now it is your turn to write an essay. Choose a topic from one of these categories or one that your teacher suggests:

- a significant event recorded in the Bible
- clothing in the Old Testament
- foods mentioned in the Bible
- education in the Roman Empire
- transportation in Bible times

Chapter 15: Revising
p. 375

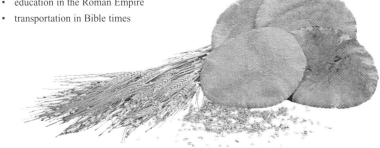

Scriptural Application

Read Acts 17:11. Share with the students that the Berean Jews "searched the scriptures daily" to discover whether what they were being taught was true. Remind students that part of writing a research essay is searching for information that is true and that supports (or disproves) what they have been told about a particular topic.

Publishing

Ask students to turn in their revised essays and bibliographies. Encourage them to share their reports with either a pastor or a youth leader in their church or to present their findings to a Sunday school class of younger students.

Evaluation

For help in grading this assignment, see "Grading Writing Assignments" (p. x) and Rubric 6 (Book 2, p. 152).

Encourage students to consult a minimum number of sources (e.g., four sources in addition to their Bibles).

Consider asking students to bring their research materials (or photocopies of relevant pages) to class with them on the day that they have conferences. This will enable you to check their work for problem areas (plagiarism, inaccuracies, inadequate research, etc.) before the paper is due.

7 VERBALS

Objectives

Students will

1. identify present participles and the nouns they modify.

2. identify past participles and the nouns they modify.

3. identify participial phrases and the nouns they modify.

4. label participial phrases *present* or *past*.

5. identify gerunds and their functions in sentences.

6. identify gerund phrases and their functions in sentences.

7. differentiate between gerunds and participles.

8. identify infinitives and their functions in sentences.

9. identify infinitive phrases and their functions in sentences.

Lesson Support

Student Text
Chapter 7 Review—pp. 417-18

Teacher's Edition, Book 1
Diagram Answers—pp. 463-66

Teacher's Edition, Book 2
Pretests—pp. 17-18

Teaching Helps—pp. 46-47

Concept Reinforcements—pp. 110-12

Come, Thou Fount

By Robert Robinson

In the first stanza of this well-known hymn, the writer asks God to tune his heart that he might always praise God.

> *Come, Thou Fount of ev'ry blessing,*
> *Tune my heart to sing Thy grace;*
> *Streams of mercy, never ceasing,*
> *Call for songs of loudest praise.*
> *Teach me some melodious sonnet*
> *Sung by flaming tongues above;*
> *Praise the mount—I'm fixed upon it—*
> *Mount of Thy redeeming love.*

- *What comparison is the songwriter making between himself and an instrument?*
- *How does the writer make God's love seem strong and everlasting?*
- *How does the writer make mercy and blessing seem abundant and free?*

- *They both need to be kept in tune.*
- *He compares it to a mountain.*
- *by comparing them to water with the terms* Fount *and* Streams

The songwriter changes verbs like *cease* and *redeem* into adjectives. Can you find them? When used in these ways, verbs become verbals. Writers use verbals to make sentences concise and elegant. For example, without verbals, the line "Mount of Thy redeeming love" would be "Mount of Thy love that redeems." That wouldn't sing very well, would it?

Literature Link

As a class, sing the first verse of Robert Robinson's "Come, Thou Fount" or listen to a recording of the song. Ask the students to answer the discussion questions and then discuss with your students how the verbals in the hymn allow the hymn to be sung more easily.

Verbals

Verbals are verb forms that function as other parts of speech in a sentence. Verbals are similar to true verbs in that they can show action and can have modifiers and objects. Verbals, however, do not function as simple predicates; they function as nouns, adjectives, and adverbs. Using verbals makes your writing more condensed and vibrant. Notice how the use of a verbal changes the following sentence.

> A society that bustles recognizes the automobile as an essential.
> A *bustling* society recognizes the automobile as an essential.

In the second example, the word *bustling* shows the action of the society and modifies the noun *society*. *Bustling* is a verbal; more specifically, it is a participle. The three kinds of verbals are participles, gerunds, and infinitives.

Participles

A **participle** is a verbal that functions as an adjective.

> *Vacationing* Americans often use cars for a more affordable vacation.
> The increase in car ownership led to the development of *improved* roads.

Vacationing is a verbal that describes *Americans*. Although it conveys action, it functions as an adjective, not a verb, in this sentence. *Improved* functions as an adjective describing *roads*. These examples demonstrate the two different kinds of participles: present participle and past participle.

Present Participle

The **present participle** consists of the first principal part of the verb plus *ing*.

> In the *growing* world, the automobile is the primary means of transportation for people around the globe.

> Even in *developing* world nations, more people own cars than ever before.

> Environmentalists fear the unhealthy air conditions caused by the *increasing* number of cars.

In these examples *growing, developing,* and *increasing* function as adjectives, not verbs. Like other adjectives, present participles usually appear before the nouns they modify. Occasionally another noun functioning as an adjective (a modifying noun) will come between the present participle and the noun they both modify.

The present participle looks exactly like part of the progressive form of the verb. To distinguish a present participle from a progressive verb, remember that the progressive verb includes a form of the auxiliary *be* and functions as the predicate in a sentence. The present participle is used as an adjective, not a verb.

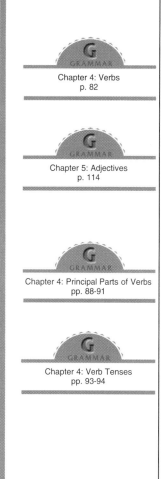

Chapter 4: Verbs
p. 82

Chapter 5: Adjectives
p. 114

Chapter 4: Principal Parts of Verbs
pp. 88-91

Chapter 4: Verb Tenses
pp. 93-94

Teaching Strategy: Induction

Write the following pairs of sentences for display:

- The book is falling from the shelf.
- The falling book landed on my foot.
- The children have been jumping on the trampoline.
- The jumping children soon became tired.

Ask students to identify the subject and the verb in each sentence. Focus the students' attention on the location of the *ing* words in each of the sentence pairs. Ask students these questions:

- What precedes the *ing* word in the first sentence of each pair? (*a form of the auxiliary* be)
- What part of speech comes after the *ing* word in the second sentence of each pair? *(a noun)*
- How does the *ing* word in the first sentence of each pair differ from the *ing* word in the second sentence? *(In the first sentence it is a progressive verb; in the second sentence it is an adjective.)*

Explain to the students that the *ing* words that appear in the second sentences of each of the sentence pairs are called participles. A participle is similar to a verb in that it shows action; however, it functions as an adjective rather than as a verb.

PRESENT PARTICIPLE	Many *developing* nations now have automotive industries.
PROGRESSIVE VERB	Many nations *are developing* automotive industries.

In the first example, the participle *developing* modifies *nations*. In the second example, *are developing* is a progressive verb conveying the action of the subject *nations*.

If you have trouble telling the difference between a participle following a linking verb and the verb in the progressive, try adding the qualifier *very* before the word that looks like a participle. If it is a verb in the progressive tense, the qualifier will not make sense.

Linking Verb Plus Participle

   RIGHT   That pianist is amazing.

   RIGHT   That pianist is very amazing.

Progressive Verb

   RIGHT   That pianist is amazing us with his talent.

   WRONG   That pianist is very amazing us with his talent.

---

in summary

Verbals are verb forms that function as nouns, adjectives, or adverbs. They can show action and can have modifiers.

A **participle** is a verbal that functions as an adjective.

The **present participle** consists of the first principal part of the verb plus *ing*.

7-1 *P*RACTICE THE *S*KILL

Underline the present participles. Draw an arrow from each underlined participle to the noun it modifies. Some sentences may not contain a present participle.

1. The automobile industry has stimulated a flourishing economy.

2. The automobile has also given people astonishing freedom.

3. Cars are essential for many traveling people.

4. People are depending on cars for everyday and long-distance travel.

5. Cars have given people increasing mobility.

6. Since its introduction into society, the automobile has been changing Americans' lifestyles.

Verbals   171

ESL Strategy

Write three pairs of sentences for display. One sentence of each pair should contain a progressive verb, and the other sentence of the pair should contain a present participle. Tell students that adding *very* before the word that looks like a participle may help them to distinguish the progressive verbs from the participles since only the participles, not the progressive verbs, will still work properly once *very* is added.

7. Before the car's arrival, people had been traveling by horse and carriage.

8. A <u>limiting</u> factor of horse and carriage was the long time of travel.

9. The invention of the automobile had an <u>improving</u> effect for the farmer.

10. Longer distances created an <u>expanding</u> market for goods.

7-2 REVIEW THE SKILL

Underline the present participles. Draw an arrow from each underlined participle to the noun it modifies. Some sentences may not contain a present participle.

1. Henry Ford introduced the Model N in 1906 for the <u>amazing</u> cost of $600.

2. Around the same time, the Oldsmobile had a <u>startling</u> price of $2,750.

3. Ford felt that <u>working</u> people should be able to afford cars.

4. Soon after, Ford was producing the popular Model T.

5. <u>Increasing</u> demand for the Model T caused a need for better production.

6. Ford was manufacturing the first Model T in six basic colors: red, black, green, blue, and light and dark gray.

7. Ford replaced the <u>existing</u> assembly line with a faster one.

8. By 1913 Model T's were being assembled in ninety-three minutes.

9. Although <u>diminishing</u> production occurred during World War I, production quickly increased afterward.

10. However, by 1926 <u>growing</u> competition between car manufacturers hurt the Model T's popularity.

Past Participle

The **past participle** is the same as the third principal part of the verb. As a verbal, the past participle appears without an auxiliary and functions as an adjective.

Operating a vehicle is a *complicated* task.

In this example we know that *complicated* is a participle, not a predicate, because it appears without an auxiliary and functions as an adjective modifying the noun *task*.

The past participle usually has a passive meaning.

Polluted air is often a result of automobile emissions.

In this example the past participle has a passive meaning: *polluted air* implies that the air was polluted by someone or something.

As the main verb in a clause, the third principal part appears with a form of *have* to produce the perfect tense. Examine the function of the word carefully before identifying the third principal part as a past participle or as a part of a predicate.

> **PAST PARTICIPLE** After the development of the gasoline engine, the use of *powered* vehicles spread quickly.
>
> **ACTIVE VERB** Steam *had powered* earlier self-propelled vehicles.
>
> **PASSIVE VERB** Earlier self-propelled vehicles *had been powered* by steam.

in summary

The **past participle** is the same as the third principal part of the verb.

7-3 PRACTICE THE SKILL

Underline the past participles. Draw an arrow from each underlined participle to the noun it modifies. Some sentences may not contain a past participle.

1. The earliest built cars were unreliable.

2. The mounted engine was located behind or under the driver.

3. Self-propelled engines first used steam.

G
GRAMMAR

Chapter 4: Principal Parts of Verbs
pp. 88-91

G
GRAMMAR

Chapter 4: Verb Tenses
pp. 93-94

Verbals   173

Teaching Strategy: Discussion

Discuss with students that there are two types of participles: present participles and past participles. Just as the present participle looks exactly like the progressive form of the verb, so the past participle looks exactly like the third principal part of the verb. Like the present participle, the past participle does not have an auxiliary. Remind students that they can distinguish a participle from a predicate by looking for an auxiliary.

4. Competition from railroad and stagecoach companies caused the continued decline of the steam car.

5. The use of steam cars resulted in damaged roads.

6. Steam cars also had other marked disadvantages.

7. The high-priced engines were a sizable disadvantage.

8. Steam cars made pronounced noise and produced smoke.

9. A person could not use a steam car immediately because of an extended warm-up time.

10. However, the steam car provided a respectable start on the path to the modern automobile.

7-4 REVIEW THE SKILL

Underline the past participles. Draw an arrow from each underlined participle to the noun it modifies.

1. Varied accessories are available for a car lover's vehicle.

2. Perhaps the chosen accessory would be a bug deflector.

3. Due to increased need for security, a car owner might buy an alarm.

4. Cellular telephones can help a motorist who finds himself in unexpected traffic.

5. Many sports teams have car flags and bumper stickers available for their most devoted fans.

6. A custom car cover might be a treasured gift for a friend.

7. A motorist can also have a covered steering wheel or seat.

8. A devoted biker can purchase a bike rack for his car.

9. With modern technology, a <u>determined</u> businessman can have a virtual office in his car.

10. For <u>increased</u> comfort, you can buy snack trays and cup holders.

Participial Phrases

Because participles retain some of their verb qualities, they can have modifiers and complements. (Complements are completers of sentence patterns, such as predicate adjectives and direct and indirect objects.) A participle and all of its modifiers and complements make up a **participial phrase.** The entire participial phrase functions as a modifier, and it can appear before or after the word it modifies. Notice that when a participial phrase comes first in the sentence, it is followed by a comma.

PARTICIPLE WITH MODIFIER — Race car drivers, *prepared for high-speed accidents,* wear safety clothing and helmets.

PARTICIPLE WITH OBJECT — *Burning methanol,* a race car engine provides maximum horsepower without too much heat.

In the first example the prepositional phrase *for high-speed accidents* modifies the past participle *prepared,* and the entire participial phrase modifies *drivers.* In the second example, *methanol* is the direct object of the participle *burning,* and the entire participial phrase modifies the noun *engine.*

G GRAMMAR
Chapter 8: Phrases and Clauses
p. 192

U USAGE
Chapter 12: Commas After Introductory Participial Phrases
p. 281

in summary

A participle and all of its modifiers and complements form a **participial phrase.**

7-5 PRACTICE THE SKILL

Underline the participles and participial phrases. Draw an arrow from each underlined participle or participial phrase to the noun it modifies. In the blank, label each underlined participle or participial phrase *present* or *past.*

_____present_____ 1. Causing thrill and adventure, automobile races fascinate man.

_____present_____ 2. Cars, racing toward a finish line, have always attracted crowds.

_____past_____ 3. The first organized races occurred in France.

Verbals   175

Teaching Strategy: Participation

Materials
- past participles written on slips of paper
- present participles written on slips of paper

Write a topic of your choice for display. Pass out slips of paper that each contain either a past or a present participle. Instruct students to write a sentence that includes a participial phrase using the participle they have been given. Remind students to write a phrase about the topic you have chosen. Collect the slips of paper and read them aloud as though they are a story. Students may find the odd juxtaposition of sentences humorous. Use the activity as a teaching opportunity to emphasize the proper and improper uses of participial phrases.

Evaluation

If you have assigned sentence diagramming with Practice the Skill 7-5, check students' answers using pages 463-64.

_____past_____ 4. Developed largely by Napoleon, France's roads were better equipped for races.

_____present_____ 5. Early races consisted of many different types of vehicles racing from one city to another.

_____past_____ 6. The winner of the first auto race in France was a steam car driven by Count De Dion.

_____past_____ 7. Whetted by the adventure, people's insatiable appetite for car races continued.

_____present_____ 8. In 1903 the Paris-Madrid race put a terrifying halt to open-road races.

_____present_____ 9. Accidents involving both drivers and pedestrians caused a number of fatalities.

_____present_____ 10. The horrifying catastrophes prompted new developments in car races.

7-6 PRACTICE THE SKILL

A. Underline the participles and place parentheses around the participial phrases.
B. Draw an arrow from each participle to the word it modifies.
C. Label the sentence patterns. Above each word of the sentence pattern, write its label.

1.   S   LV   PN
   (Forgotten by many,) Frederick Adams was a force behind one of America's first automobile races.

2.   S   InV
   (Sponsored by the *Chicago-Times Herald*,) the race ran from Chicago to Evanston.

3.   S   InV
   Frederick Adams was traveling across the country (looking for public support.)

4.   S   LV   PA
   However, waning interest in auto races was evident.

5. Thanksgiving Day of 1895 was the day for the scheduled race.
   (S) (LV) (PN)

6. (Faced with harsh weather conditions,) only six contestants appeared.
   (S) (InV)

7. (Bogged down in the snow,) the cars often needed a push by the crowds.
   (S) (TrV) (DO)

8. Accidents and breakdowns plagued the progress of the competing drivers.
   (S) (S) (TrV) (DO)

9. The winning driver finished the fifty-five mile course in ten and one-half hours.
   (S) (TrV) (DO)

10. (Hindered by the cold and mechanical problems,) only one competitor finished the race.
    (S) (TrV) (DO)

Gerunds

A **gerund** is a verbal with *ing* that functions as a noun.

    S   TrV   DO
Good *driving* requires concentration.

  S TrV DO
I enjoy *driving.*

In both sentences *driving* functions as a noun, not a verb. In the first sentence, *driving* is the subject of the verb *requires.* In the second sentence, *driving* is the direct object of the transitive verb *enjoy.*

The most common gerund form consists of the first principal part of the verb plus *ing.* Notice that this is the same verb form as the present participle. The two verbals are distinguished by their function: a present participle functions as an adjective, and a gerund functions as a noun. As a noun, the gerund can function as a subject, a predicate noun, a direct object, an indirect object, an object of the preposition, or an appositive.

SUBJECT   *Traveling* is difficult without a car.

PREDICATE NOUN   My uncle's favorite sport is *racing.*

DIRECT OBJECT   Computers greatly aid the *manufacturing* of cars.

INDIRECT OBJECT   Before the release of a vehicle, engineers and automakers gave *testing* their full attention.

OBJECT OF THE PREPOSITION   Many drivers cause accidents by *speeding.*

APPOSITIVE   Another common maneuver, *passing,* can be dangerous.

GRAMMAR

Chapter 2: Uses of Nouns
p. 38

Teaching Strategy: Induction

Write the following sentence for display: *The spinning spider fascinated us by spinning an intricate web.* Then ask students these questions: What do the two *spinning*s have in common? *(They both have* ing *in their endings.)* How do they differ, and how do they function in the sentence? *(The first acts as an adjective; the second acts as a noun, specifically as the object of the preposition.)*

Direct the students' attention to the function of gerunds described on page 177. Then ask students the following question:

What is the part of speech for each of the functions listed? *(noun)*

Emphasize to students that participles always function as adjectives, and gerunds always function as nouns.

Enrichment

Assign Teaching Help 7A (Book 2, p. 46) to help students distinguish between present participles and gerunds.

A **gerund** is a verbal that functions as a noun.

7-7 $\mathcal{P}$RACTICE THE $\mathcal{S}$KILL

Underline the gerunds.

1. One of Ransom Olds's first ventures was the <u>manufacturing</u> of the steam engine.

2. When various companies heard of the engine, they began <u>buying</u>.

3. Were there other uses for his engine? Olds started <u>exploring</u>.

4. Olds gave the <u>developing</u> of his engine his attention.

5. Upon <u>riding</u> in a gas-powered car, Olds saw its potential.

6. The <u>designing</u> of his own gas engine soon interested Olds.

7. Olds began <u>producing</u> gas engines in 1896.

8. Then Olds focused his attention on <u>engineering</u>.

9. <u>Attaching</u> the engine to a carriage fulfilled Olds's dream of a horseless carriage.

10. Ransom Olds's developments provided a basis for the <u>making</u> of modern automobiles.

7-8 $\mathcal{R}$EVIEW THE $\mathcal{S}$KILL

Underline the gerunds. In the blank, label each underlined gerund *S* (subject), *DO* (direct object), *IO* (indirect object), *PN* (predicate noun), or *OP* (object of the preposition).

___PN___ 1. One of William K. Vanderbilt Jr.'s greatest passions was <u>racing</u>.

___IO___ 2. Because of his love for the automobile, Vanderbilt also gave <u>manufacturing</u> much of his attention.

___OP___ 3. Vanderbilt felt that American automakers were slow in <u>producing</u>.

___OP___ 4. Vanderbilt established races so that America's auto makers would advance in <u>engineering</u>.

___S___ 5. The <u>improving</u> of American cars was a result of Vanderbilt's races.

_S_ 6. The <u>running</u> of the races was on local roads.

_OP_ 7. Because of the danger, Vanderbilt's love for <u>racing</u> could not be satisfied by the use of ordinary roads.

_DO_ 8. He wanted a road only for races, so he began <u>building</u>.

_S_ 9. His <u>completing</u> of the project aided the Vanderbilt Cup race.

_PN_ 10. A great success of Vanderbilt was the <u>designing</u> of the American highway.

Gerund Phrases

Like a participle, a gerund can have modifiers and complements, such as direct and indirect objects. Because the gerund retains some of its verb qualities, it can be followed by complements and modified by adverbs. Because it functions as a noun, it can be modified by adjectives. A **gerund phrase** consists of a gerund and all of its modifiers and complements. The entire gerund phrase functions as a noun.

Chapter 5: Adjectives and Adverbs
pp. 114; 122

GERUND WITH ADVERB	One concern of automobile manufacturers is *driving safely.*
GERUND WITH ADJECTIVES	*The requiring of shoulder seat belts* began in 1968.
GERUND WITH OBJECT	*Selling cars* often requires a strong personality.

In the first example the adverb *safely* modifies the gerund *driving,* and the entire phrase functions as the predicate noun in the sentence. In the second example the gerund *requiring* is modified by the adjective *the* and the adjectival prepositional phrase *of shoulder seat belts.* The entire gerund phrase is the subject of the sentence. In the third example *cars* is the direct object of the gerund *selling,* and the gerund phrase functions as the subject of the sentence.

in summary

A **gerund phrase** consists of a gerund and all of its modifiers and complements.

7-9 PRACTICE THE SKILL

Underline the gerunds. Place parentheses around the gerund phrases.

1. (<u>Repairing</u> automobiles) can be extremely expensive.

2. You can avoid some costly repairs by (<u>knowing</u> your vehicle.)

3. Another safeguard is (<u>asking</u> knowledgeable questions.)

Verbals   179

Teaching Strategy: Discussion

Display questions 11-15 from the Concept Reinforcement about gerunds (Book 2, p. 111). Instruct students to identify the gerund in each sentence and then ask them to find the complete gerund phrase. Explain how each gerund functions in the sentence and discuss the gerund's modifiers and complements.

Evaluation

If you have assigned sentence diagramming with Practice the Skill 7-9, check students' answers using pages 464-65.

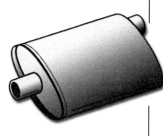

4. One helpful routine maintenance is (changing the oil.)

5. You can detect common problems by (using your common sense.)

6. Brake problems often produce (a high-pitched squeaking.)

7. (Listening for squeals, clicks, and other noises) can give a car owner clues about problems.

8. A defective muffler can cause (a low-pitched rumbling.)

9. (Ignoring ordinary maintenance) causes more costly repairs.

10. You can find a good mechanic by (doing some research.)

7-10 REVIEW THE SKILL

Place parentheses around the gerunds or gerund phrases. In the blank, label the gerund or gerund phrase *S* (subject), *DO* (direct object), *IO* (indirect object), *PN* (predicate noun), or *OP* (object of the preposition).

_OP_ 1. Many people are concerned about (polluting the environment.)

_PN_ 2. Their goal is (finding helpful methods of pollution reduction.)

_DO_ 3. Many enjoy (owning electric vehicles.)

_PN_ 4. One pollution problem caused by a motor vehicle is (discharging pollutants through exhaust.)

_OP_ 5. Electric cars operate by (running on rechargeable batteries.)

_S_ 6. (Riding in an electric car) is a unique experience.

_S_ 7. (Buying an electric car) benefits the environment.

_OP_ 8. However, electric cars have an extremely short range of (operating.)

_DO_ 9. Also, many people cannot afford (buying an electric car.)

_S_ 10. (Choosing between motor and electric vehicles) can be a difficult decision.

7-11 REVIEW THE SKILL

Label each italicized word *G* (gerund) or *P* (participle).

_P_ 1. People *buying* a car have various tastes and desires.

_G_ 2. A minivan is good for *traveling* with a family.

_G_ 3. *Riding* in comfort is also a benefit of a van.

_P_ 4. People may want a sport utility vehicle for the *thrilling* experience of mountain travel.

_G_ 5. Some people's difficulty is *living* in areas with harsh winters.

_G_ 6. *Driving* through snow with a four-wheel drive is easy.

_P_ 7. A man *working* in construction may want a truck.

_G_ 8. A truck is useful for *hauling*.

_G_ 9. Some people may want a small car for *moving* around town more easily.

_G_ 10. *Dealing* with traffic will always be a problem.

Infinitives

An **infinitive** is a verbal that can function as a noun, an adjective, or an adverb.

	S TrV DO
NOUN	My brother likes *to race.*
ADJECTIVE	The pit crew is the group *to ask.*
ADVERB	We are going to the concession stand *to eat.*

A simple infinitive consists of the word *to* followed by the first principal part of the verb. Since *to* often functions as a preposition, an infinitive may look like a prepositional phrase. In a prepositional phrase, however, the word *to* is followed by a noun or pronoun. In an infinitive, the word *to* is followed by the first principal part of the verb.

INFINITIVE	My family likes *to travel.*
PREPOSITIONAL PHRASE	This summer we are traveling *to Mexico.*

> Be careful not to make the common mistake of using the *to* of the infinitive when you use a modal auxiliary.
>
> **WRONG** He can to go in an hour.
> **RIGHT** He can go in an hour.
>
> **WRONG** She might to paint the fence.
> **RIGHT** She might paint the fence.

Chapter 6: Prepositional Phrases
pp. 142-43

in summary

An **infinitive** is a verbal that functions as a noun, an adjective, or an adverb.

An infinitive consists of the word *to* and the first principal part of the verb.

Infinitives tend to follow verbs of belief, advice, attempt, desire, or permission.

Belief: *believe, imagine* (mental cognition verbs like *find, know, show, think,* and *understand*)

Catholics believe the pope to be the head of the church.

Advice: *advise, order* (verbs that express an attempt to affect someone physically/mentally, such as *force* and *persuade*)

I advise you to consult a professional banker.

Attempt: *try, attempt, promise*

He tried to fix the leak, but the pipe broke.

Desire: *want, intend, hope* (verbs oriented toward future plans)

I want to go to China someday.

Permission: *permit, allow, let*

He allowed me to use his phone to call my parents.

(*Note: Let* is also a verb of permission, but it occurs with a *bare-stem infinitive*—an infinitive without the *to.* This text does not cover bare-stem infinitives. Example: *He let me use his phone.*)

Scriptural Application

Instruct students to find all of the infinitives in Philippians 1. However, caution them to distinguish between infinitives and prepositional phrases. Remind them that each infinitive will be directly followed by a verb. (Students should find eleven infinitives in the King James Version.)

Underline the infinitives. Some sentences may not contain an infinitive.

1. People have a need <u>to drive</u> for many different reasons.

2. In the days before the automobile, people had many difficulties <u>to overcome</u>.

3. What if you had a serious illness <u>to cure</u>?

4. <u>To ride</u> by horse was a necessity for doctors.

5. The people <u>to see</u> in an emergency were often miles away.

6. Because of great distances, families were often unable <u>to visit</u>.

7. Also, mail was slow <u>to arrive</u>.

8. If a person needed <u>to move</u>, the process was long and difficult.

9. We depend on automobiles <u>to travel</u>.

10. The automobile has become a great boon to society.

Underline the infinitives. Label the function of each infinitive _noun_ (noun), _adj_ (adjective), or _adv_ (adverb).

adv	1. Roads are especially interesting <u>to study</u>.
adj	2. The need <u>to build</u> has become greater.
noun	3. People like <u>to drive</u> for many reasons.
adj	4. Engineers have challenges <u>to overcome</u>.
noun	5. One of engineering's accomplishments has been <u>to build</u>.
adv	6. <u>To succeed</u>, engineers have built bridges over rather large spans of water.
adj	7. Sometimes, another way <u>to travel</u> is possible.
adj	8. Engineers may form plans <u>to dig</u>.
noun	9. <u>To tunnel</u> is their goal.
adv	10. <u>To travel</u>, we often use these bridges and tunnels.

Infinitive Phrases

Like participles and gerunds, infinitives may have modifiers and complements. The infinitive and its modifiers and complements make up an **infinitive phrase.** The entire phrase functions like a noun, an adjective, or an adverb.

	S	LV	PN
NOUN	*To build a popular, inexpensive car*	was Henry Ford's dream.	

ADJECTIVE   In England, attempts *to promote the use of steam cars* failed because of pressure from railroad and stagecoach companies.

ADVERB   Soon after, companies experimented *to provide even better methods of transportation.*

In the first example *a popular, inexpensive car* is the direct object of the infinitive *to build.* The entire infinitive phrase functions as the subject of the sentence. In the second example *the use of steam cars* is the direct object of the infinitive *to promote.* The entire infinitive phrase functions like an adjective, modifying the noun *attempts.* In the third example *even better methods of transportation* is the direct object of the infinitive *to provide.* The entire infinitive phrase modifies *experimented.*

Some experts teach that a modifier should not come between the word *to* and the verb of an infinitive. This kind of problem is called a **split infinitive.** Sometimes there is no good alternative to a split infinitive, but usually it can be avoided.

SPLIT INFINITIVE   Manufacturers failed at several attempts *to hurriedly produce* an auto car.

BETTER   Manufacturers failed at several attempts *to produce* an auto car *hurriedly.*

in summary

The infinitive with its modifiers and complements make up an **infinitive phrase.**

Avoid using a modifier between the word *to* and the verb of an infinitive.

7-14 PRACTICE THE SKILL

Underline the infinitive phrases. Some sentences may not contain an infinitive phrase.

1. In 1909 Alice Huyler Ramsey's goal was <u>to drive from coast to coast in the United States.</u>

2. She would become the first woman <u>to accomplish this task.</u>

3. Alice Ramsey did not have any maps <u>to point her in the right direction.</u>

Teaching Strategy: Discussion

Explain to students that, like participles and gerunds, infinitives may have modifiers and complements. The infinitive and its modifiers and complements make up an infinitive phrase. Point out to students that the infinitive can function as a noun, as an adjective, or as an adverb.

Reinforcement

For practice in finding infinitive phrases, ask students to complete questions 11-15 of Chapter 7 Review on pages 417-18 of the student text. Once students have answered these questions, allow them to discuss their answers with another student. Ask the students for their answers. Encourage them to be prepared to defend their answers if called upon.

Evaluation

If you have assigned sentence diagramming with Practice the Skill 7-14, check students' answers using pages 465-66.

4. Sometimes, Ramsey and her companions became lost and looked for telephone lines <u>to find the transcontinental railroad</u>.

5. Her attempt <u>to drive the car for a long distance</u> had many troubles.

6. A sheriff in Nebraska stopped the car <u>to search for escaped murderers</u>.

7. In the western part of the United States, the roads began <u>to become worse</u>.

8. The road conditions produced the need <u>to repair the car often</u>.

9. Tourists did not have many paved roads <u>to use</u>.

10. <u>To drive from Manhattan to San Francisco</u> took Ramsey fifty-nine days.

7-15 REVIEW THE SKILL

Underline the infinitive phrases. In the blank, label the function of each infinitive phrase *noun* (noun), *adj* (adjective), or *adv* (adverb).

noun 1. <u>To ride in comfort</u> is a daily experience for us; however, early travelers did not have such comfort.

adj 2. Early cars had interesting devices <u>to operate the car</u>.

noun 3. Travelers needed <u>to wear protective clothing</u>.

adv 4. Drivers often wore a helmet and goggles <u>to protect them from dust and dirt</u>.

noun 5. <u>To drive at night</u> was difficult because of poor lights.

adv 6. <u>To light the way</u>, early cars had actual candle lamps.

adj 7. However, the efforts <u>to keep the candles lit on a windy night</u> proved difficult.

adv 8. A good tire is necessary <u>to hold a car's weight</u>.

adv 9. Early tires came from bicycles or horse carts, and they were unable <u>to support the car adequately</u>.

adv 10. Early cars did not have electric starters <u>to start the car</u>; people cranked the car by hand.

Reinforcement

Display Teaching Help 7B (Book 2, p. 47). Ask the students to identify the infinitives. Sometimes the word *to* appears with a phrase that is not an infinitive. Ask the students to explain why those phrases are not infinitives. *(They are followed by objects; they are prepositional phrases.)*

Underline the verbals (not the entire phrases). In the blank, label each verbal *P* (participle), *G* (gerund), or *I* (infinitive). If the verbal is a modifier, draw an arrow from the verbal to the word it modifies.

   G   1. Using special equipment is necessary for the military.

   I   2. To aid the military, vehicles must be reliable.

   P   3. Military vehicles might be used in many threatening situations.

   I   4. The ability to drive in rough terrain is a necessity for the driver of a military vehicle.

   G   5. Another requirement for a good military vehicle is lasting a long time.

   P   6. Companies have designed enduring military vehicles.

   I   7. To help it maneuver, one modern military vehicle has a large ground clearance of sixteen inches.

Verbals   185

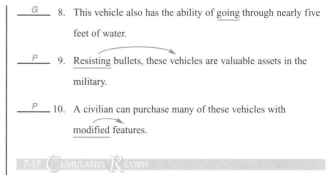

___G___ 8. This vehicle also has the ability of <u>going</u> through nearly five feet of water.

___P___ 9. <u>Resisting</u> bullets, these vehicles are valuable assets in the military.

___P___ 10. A civilian can purchase many of these vehicles with <u>modified features.</u>

7-17 CUMULATIVE REVIEW

A. Rewrite the following paragraph, correcting any fragments, comma splices, fused sentences, incorrect noun forms, incorrect verb forms, errors in adjective or adverb usage, and preposition errors. There are five errors. *(Answers will vary.)*

Building roads and highways takes planning, an engineer in highway construction must first research. Then he can begin to build. Once the engineer has gathered the needed information, he can begin to analyze the different materials. John L. McAdam was a Scottish engineer. He developed macadam, a road surface. Asphalt, another road covering, is a cementlike substance found in most crude petroleum. Used for street's and coatings. Asphalt is versatile. Gravel is more common than asphalt or macadam on low-traffic roads. Throughout the planning process, engineers consider this factors real carefully.

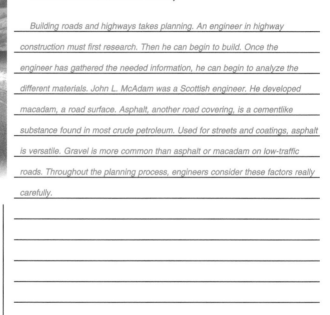

Building roads and highways takes planning. An engineer in highway

construction must first research. Then he can begin to build. Once the

engineer has gathered the needed information, he can begin to analyze the

different materials. John L. McAdam was a Scottish engineer. He developed

macadam, a road surface. Asphalt, another road covering, is a cementlike

substance found in most crude petroleum. Used for streets and coatings, asphalt

is versatile. Gravel is more common than asphalt or macadam on low-traffic

roads. Throughout the planning process, engineers consider these factors really

carefully.

_____

_____

_____

_____

_____

Objectives

Students will

1. write a quatrain.
2. write a diamante.

Overview of the Writing Process

Planning—choosing a topic as well as a tune for writing a quatrain and choosing a topic for writing a diamante

Drafting—writing the quatrain and writing the diamante

Revising—evaluating with a partner and making changes for rhythm, rhyme, or form

Publishing—copying poems onto the form and handing in to the teacher

Reinforcement

Assign Chapter 7 Review on pages 417-18 of the student text to review the types and functions of verbals. (If you have already assigned questions 11-15, allow the students to complete the remaining questions.)

Literature Link

Direct students to identify any participles, gerunds, or infinitives in "Come, Thou Fount."

Writing Poetry

Lesson Support

Teacher's Edition, Book 1
Bulletin Boards—p. 448

Teacher's Edition, Book 2
Writing Worksheets—p. 140
Rubrics—pp. 153-54

Introduction

How are diamonds formed? *(Carbon under extreme pressure forms the gem we call a diamond.)* Another useful product—coal—is produced when carbon is put under less intense pressure.

B. From your rewritten paragraph, find an example of each of the following.
(Answers will vary.)

1. An adjectival prepositional phrase ___*in highway construction*___

2. An adverbial prepositional phrase ___*on low-traffic roads*___

3. A coordinating conjunction ___*and*___

4. A subordinating conjunction ___*Once*___

5. A gerund (not in a phrase) ___*planning*___

6. A gerund phrase ___*Building roads and highways*___

7. An infinitive (not in a phrase) ___*to build*___

8. An infinitive phrase ___*to analyze the different materials*___

9. A participle (not in a phrase) ___*needed*___

10. A participial phrase ___*Used for streets and coatings*___

Look again at the hymn "Come, Thou Fount."
- *Can you find any participles, gerunds, or infinitives in the poem? If so, identify those that you find.*

Writing Poetry

Poems can appear in as many different forms as there are colors on an artist's palette. Here are two forms for you to practice—one that rhymes and one that does not.

Quatrain

If you have studied Latin, French, or Spanish, you probably recognize the prefix *quatr-* as meaning "four." A quatrain is simply a poem containing four lines. Sometimes quatrains stand alone; other times they occur as stanzas, or verses, in a long poem such as a ballad. Quatrains usually contain rhyme at the ends of lines. Many quatrains have a rhyme scheme of *abcb*, as in the following hymn stanza:

> O soul, are you weary and troubled?
> No light in the darkness you see?
> There's light for a look at the Saviour,
> And life more abundant and free!

Others have a rhyme scheme of *abab:*

> Amazing grace! How sweet the sound,
> That saved a wretch like me!
> I once was lost, but now am found,
> Was blind, but now I see.

- *participals—ceasing, sung, flaming, redeeming*

  gerunds—blessing

  infinitives—to sing

Discussion

Direct a discussion about how carbon, an element, under great pressure becomes either coal or a diamond. Both coal and diamonds are useful: one warms the body and the other warms the eye.

Explain that words are like carbon: they are the element from which prose and poetry are formed. Good prose has been under the pressure of logic, mechanics, conciseness, and so on. Good poetry has been under the added pressures of brevity and economy.

Planning

Materials
- a hymnal for every two students

Direct the students to read about quatrains. Then ask them to work in pairs to find other hymns with the rhyme schemes discussed.

Discuss how the stanza from "Amazing Grace" reprinted in the text represents compressed language. *(The first lines of the song convey not only the subject of salvation but also the emotion the speaker feels at hearing the word* grace. *The writer uses metaphors from the physical realm to represent his spiritual condition.)*

Direct the students to read "Your Turn."

Allow time for the students to choose a hymn tune to which to write a quatrain.

Drafting

Allow time for students to write their quatrains in class.

The rhyme scheme *aabb* is also common:

> My Father is rich in houses and lands,
> He holdeth the wealth of the world in His hands!
> Of rubies and diamonds, of silver and gold,
> His coffers are full, He has riches untold.

Your Turn

Choose one of the rhyme schemes given above and write a quatrain that could be used in a hymn. You might want to choose a common hymn tune first and then fit your poem to it.

Diamante

How would you describe a diamond? If you are thinking of the gem, you might use adjectives like *sparkly*, *multifaceted*, or *crystalline*. You might even say *expensive* or *valuable*. But if you are thinking of the shape, you would probably say something like "a shape that can be divided into two identical triangles," or as the dictionary states it: "a figure with four equal sides forming two inner obtuse angles and two inner acute angles."

The word *diamante* means "diamond." It is a form of poetry that is written in the shape of a diamond. Since it contrasts two opposing ideas, it could also be called "multifaceted." But whether it is "sparkly" depends upon the poet's choice of words, and whether it is "valuable" depends upon the worth of the idea he leaves with the reader.

A diamante has no rhyme or meter. It goes from one idea to an opposite or contrasting idea in a series of seven lines. Here is an example:

> Winter
> Barren, leafless
> Snowing, drifting, dripping
> Icicles, slush, puddles, rivulets
> Blowing, budding, blooming
> Warm, colorful
> Summer

Notice the pattern in each line. Lines 1-4 contain the same number of words as their line numbers. (Line 1 contains one word; line 2 contains two words, and so on.) After line four, the number of words decreases by one with each new line (line 5 contains three words; line 6 contains two words), bringing the count back down to one word in line 7. The word counts in each line give the poem its shape.

But there is an additional pattern to this poem. Notice that all of the words in each line are a particular part of speech.

1. noun
2. adjective, adjective
3. participle, participle, participle
4. noun, noun, noun, noun
5. participle, participle, participle
6. adjective, adjective
7. noun

Planning

Direct the students to read about diamantes. Then direct a discussion about opposites, letting students brainstorm as many pairs of contrasting ideas as they can.

Discuss the form of the diamante. Compare the shape of the poem to a baseball diamond. Explain that the first word in the poem is second base and the last is home plate as you look to the field from the umpire's perspective. Call attention to the place in the poem where the change to the opposite begins. *(Line 4 is transitional; the middle of that line marks the change in topic.)* Students may refer to this position as "the pitcher's mound."

Be sure that the students know all the parts of speech required in the lines. If necessary, refer them to Chapter 2 (Nouns), Chapter 5 (Adjectives and Adverbs), and Chapter 7 (Verbals) where the parts of speech are defined.

Direct the students to read "Your Turn."

Allow time for students to choose a set of contrasting ideas about which to write a diamante.

Drafting

Allow time for students to write their diamantes in class.

Revising (Peer Response)

Direct students to choose one of their rough drafts to exchange with a partner. Instruct each student to evaluate his partner's quatrain or diamante. If the poem is a quatrain, encourage the evaluator to "sing" the poem in his mind to the tune it was written for and to point out any flaws in the rhythm. If the poem is a diamante, encourage the evaluator to check the poem for adherence to

The words in lines 2 and 3 describe winter, the opening idea presented in line 1. The words in lines 5 and 6 describe summer, the closing idea in line 7. Notice how line 4 makes a transition between the two ideas with the words *icicles, slush, puddles, rivulets*. The sequence of these nouns pictures the ice and snow of winter melting—the first step in the transition to a new season, and eventually, to summer.

Your Turn

Using the structure given above, write your own diamante. Before beginning, choose the two words you want to contrast and make a list of the supporting words you could use for each one. (Remember you will need nouns, adjectives, and participles.) Develop your words into a poem.

form and for success in changing to the opposite idea within the poem.

Distribute a copy of the Writing Worksheet (Book 2, p. 140) to each student. Direct students to revise their poems and to copy each final draft onto the appropriate part of the worksheet.

Publishing

Collect the Writing Worksheets with the finished poems. Assemble them in a notebook as a book of poetry or display them as directed on page 448.

Scriptural Application

The Bible contains many poems. In fact, six books of the Old Testament are written in the Hebrew poetic style: Job, Psalms, Proverbs, Ecclesiastes, Song of Solomon, and Lamentations. The psalms, of course, are not only poems but also songs. Encourage your students to examine the psalms for these characteristics of Hebrew poetry: figures of speech (metaphor, simile, etc.) and parallelism (the repetition of ideas in successive lines).

Evaluation

For help in grading this assignment, see "Grading Writing Assignments" (p. x) and Rubrics 7A and 7B (Book 2, pp. 153-54).

Enrichment

Direct the students to name their favorite hymns. Ask them to determine the rhyme scheme and to explain why the hymn is special to them.

8 CLAUSES

Objectives

Students will

1. differentiate between phrases, clauses, independent clauses, and dependent clauses.

2. differentiate between simple, compound, complex, and compound-complex sentences.

3. compose simple, compound, complex, and compound-complex sentences.

4. identify adjective clauses, relative pronouns, and relative adverbs in sentences.

5. determine what an adjective clause modifies in a sentence.

6. label the function of a relative pronoun in a sentence.

7. identify adverb clauses and differentiate between relative pronouns and relative adverbs.

8. determine what an adverb clause modifies in a sentence.

9. identify the modifying words of adverb clauses.

10. identify subordinating conjunctions in adverb clauses.

11. differentiate between adjective clauses and adverb clauses.

12. evaluate and revise a paragraph for errors.

Men of Iron
by Howard Pyle

Myles Falworth, just a boy when Henry IV took the throne of England
from Richard II, wins a reputation for courage and independence. The following excerpt recounts the beginning of his adventure.

In the anteroom was the knight in black
armor whom Myles had seen from the window.
He was sitting at the table, his great helmet lying
upon the bench beside him. A clerk sat at the
other end of the table with inkhorn in one hand
and pen in the other and a parchment spread in
front of him.

Master Robert, the castle steward, stood before the knight. Every now and then the knight
asked him a question, and as he answered, the
clerk wrote it down upon the parchment.

Myles's father stood with his back to the fireplace, looking down upon the floor with his blind
eyes, his brows drawn moodily together. The scar
of the great wound that he had received at the
tournament at York—the wound that had made
him blind—showed red across his forehead, as it
always did when he was angered or troubled.

There was something about it all that frightened Myles. He crept to his father's side and slid
his little hand into the palm that hung limp and
inert. In answer to his touch, his father grasped
the hand tightly, but he did not seem otherwise to
notice that he was there. Neither did the black
knight pay any attention to Myles but continued
putting his questions to Master Robert.

- *What in the passage makes you like or dislike the knight? Myles's
  father?*
- *What do you think makes Myles uneasy?*
- *Read the sentence that describes Myles's father's scar. How does the
  author use the scar to help develop the character?*

The sentence describing Myles's father's scar is a complex sentence. It
contains one independent clause and four dependent clauses. Using the
clauses helps the author get all the necessary information about the scar
smoothly in one place.

- *Answers may vary but may include the following: the knight
  wears black armor and is completely focused on his work;
  Myles's father has a scar, he is
  blind, and Myles goes to him
  for comfort.*
- *He sees that his father is wor-
  ried or angry.*
- *He uses it to tell that Myles's
  father was in a tournament,
  that he was blinded there, and
  that the scar now sometimes
  indicates his state of mind.*

Lesson Support

Student Text
Chapter 8 Review—pp. 419-20

Teacher's Edition, Book 1
Bulletin Boards—p. 448

Diagram Answers—pp. 466-68

Teacher's Edition, Book 2
Pretests—pp. 19-20

Teaching Helps—p. 48

ESL Worksheets—pp. 82-84

Concept Reinforcements—pp. 113-15

Literature Link

Ask for four volunteers to read the excerpt
from Howard Pyle's *Men of Iron* aloud.
Direct each student to read one paragraph
of the excerpt. Allow students time to write
their answers to the discussion questions on
a piece of paper. Then allow students to
share their answers with the class.

Chapter 1: Subjects and
Predicates
p. 4

Phrases and Clauses

A **clause** is a group of words containing both a subject and a predicate (verb). A **phrase** may have a subject or a verb, but not both.

CLAUSE   Logan frequently visits used bookstores on weekends.

PHRASE   Frequently visits used bookstores

PHRASE   Logan, collecting old books

PHRASE   On weekends

The first phrase contains a verb but not its subject. The second phrase contains both a noun, *Logan,* and a word that looks like a verb, *collecting.* The word *collecting,* however, is not a verb; it is a participle describing *Logan.* The last phrase, a prepositional phrase, contains neither a subject nor a verb. A clause must have both a subject and a predicate.

Independent and Dependent Clauses

There are two kinds of clauses: independent clauses (sometimes called main clauses) and dependent clauses (often called subordinate clauses). An **independent clause** can stand alone as a sentence. A **dependent clause** cannot stand alone. A dependent clause is often an important part of the sentence, but it depends on the independent clause for its complete meaning. When a dependent clause is written as if it were a sentence, it is a fragment.

INDEPENDENT   Dominick enjoys collecting stamps from all over the world.
DEPENDENT   Because he enjoys different cultures
INDEPENDENT   Harriet enjoys creating new computer programs.
DEPENDENT   Since she majored in computers in college

All of the clauses in the examples have both a subject and a predicate, but only the independent clauses can stand alone as sentences. Each of the dependent clauses is introduced by a word that makes it incomplete; the dependent clause depends on the independent clause for its complete meaning.

When identifying dependent clauses, look for subject and predicate pairs introduced with words such as relative pronouns *(who, which, that)* and subordinating conjunctions *(if, since, because).* (See Chapter 3 to review relative pronouns and Chapter 6 to review subordinating conjunctions.)

in summary

A **phrase** is a group of words that does not contain both a subject and a predicate.

A **clause** is a group of words that contains both a subject and a predicate.

An **independent clause** can stand alone as a complete sentence.

A **dependent clause** cannot stand alone as a complete sentence.

Teaching Strategy: Induction

Instruct students to copy each of the following groups of words onto a piece of paper:

- the father, talking to his son
- to his son
- The father was talking to his son.
- talks to his son

Instruct students to underline each subject once and each verb twice. Ask students how each group of words differs from the others. Then ask the students the following question: How does the third group of words differ from the other groups? *(It has both a subject and a verb.)* Point out to students that the other groups are phrases. Lead students to recognize that a phrase may have either a subject or a verb (or neither if it is a prepositional phrase) but that a clause always has both a subject and a verb.

Teaching Strategy: Induction

Instruct students to write each of the following clauses on a piece of paper:

- Henry lives in Cameroon.
- If you visit him
- He will show you many interesting sites.
- Because he is proud of his country

Instruct students to underline each subject once and each verb twice. Ask students how they can know that these groups of words are clauses. *(Each has a subject and a verb.)* Ask students how the clauses differ from one another and then lead students to recognize that the second and fourth clauses are preceded by a subordinating conjunction. A clause that is preceded by a subordinating conjunction is a dependent clause.

Label each italicized group of words *P* (phrase), *IC* (independent clause), or *DC* (dependent clause).

  P 1. Archaeologists enjoy *studying the remains of human cultures.*

  IC 2. *Archaeologists study objects.*

  P 3. Some of their discoveries have revealed information *about early civilizations.*

  DC 4. *Since archaeologists dig in many interesting places,* they have uncovered magnificent ruins.

  DC 5. *Because early civilizations did not keep written records,* archaeology provides one of the only sources of information about those societies.

  IC 6. Because they need precise evidence, *archaeologists use specialized techniques and equipment.*

  P 7. Even a few tools or grains of corn can be valuable discoveries *for an archaeologist.*

  IC 8. Some archaeologists may be professional; *others enjoy archaeology as a hobby.*

  P 9. One of the first jobs of an archaeologist is *to locate a site.*

  DC 10. *Whereas some sites may be easy to find,* other sites may be underwater.

8-2 REVIEW THE SKILL

Place parentheses around each dependent clause.

1. (Although a person may not be a pilot by profession,)he may want a pilot's license.

2. Some people own small planes(because they enjoy flying just for recreation.)

3. (Even though many people would like a pilot's license,)pilot school takes time and money.

4. A person must enroll in flight school(before he can get a license.)

5. (If you are interested,)the basic pilot license is the private pilot's license.

6. (After you get a physical exam,)you can enroll in flight school.

Teaching Strategy: Discussion

Write the word *independent* for display. Ask students to define this word. *(standing alone, not relying on anyone else, not needing support)* Explain that an independent clause can stand alone as a sentence. Then remove the *in* from *independent*. Ask students to define this word. *(not being able to stand alone, relying on someone, needing support)* Explain that, like its definition, a dependent clause cannot stand alone as a sentence.

7. (While a student is in flight school,)he must complete a minimum of forty flying hours.

8. (As soon as the necessary skills are demonstrated,)the student will take a flight test and a written test.

9. (When a person has received a license,)he may find it difficult to locate an airplane to rent.

10. (Since this license is private,)a pilot may not charge for his services.

Using Independent and Dependent Clauses

Every sentence has at least one independent clause. However, sentences may contain any number of independent and dependent clauses. All sentences can be placed into one of four categories based on the structure of the sentence. These categories describe the number of independent and dependent clauses in the sentence.

> If you often use many short simple sentences in your writing assignments, try to vary your sentence structure by combining several of your simple sentences into longer compound, complex, or compound-complex sentences, using the sentence combining techniques explained in this chapter.

Simple Sentence

A **simple sentence** consists of only one independent clause. There are no dependent clauses in a simple sentence. A simple sentence can, however, have compound parts, such as compound subjects or compound predicates.

SIMPLE SENTENCE   People have many different types of hobbies.

COMPOUND
SUBJECT   Both *men* and *women* enjoy gardening.

COMPOUND
PREDICATE   Some people *collect* and *fix* broken electronic items.

COMPOUND
SUBJECT AND
PREDICATE   *Plants* and *flowers grow* and *flourish* with proper care.

Compound Sentence

A **compound sentence** has two or more independent clauses. The two clauses are normally joined by a semicolon or by a comma and a coordinating conjunction. There are no dependent clauses in a compound sentence; but as in a simple sentence, each independent clause may contain compound parts.

COMPOUND
SENTENCE   Heather enjoys juggling, but she has difficulty juggling more than three objects.

COMPOUND
SENTENCE   Danielle loves fishing, but her mother must skin the fish.

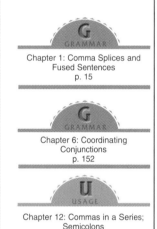

Chapter 1: Comma Splices and
Fused Sentences
p. 15

Chapter 6: Coordinating
Conjunctions
p. 152

Chapter 12: Commas in a Series;
Semicolons
p. 279; 294

194   Chapter 8

Teaching Strategy: Participation

Materials
- several slips of paper
- several envelopes

Write each word from each of the following sentences on a different slip of paper:

- Sherri and Rosemary invited their neighbor to church.
- We picked and ate strawberries.
- Brendan and Sabrina rode their bikes and hiked in the woods.

Place all of the slips from one sentence into an envelope, producing a set of three envelopes. Divide the class into groups of three or four students each and have a set of the three envelopes prepared for each group in the class. Label the three envelopes in each set *1, 2,* and *3*. Instruct each group to open their *1* envelope and tell them to place the slips in order so that they form a sentence. Once students have constructed the first sentence, they may open their *2* envelope. (Follow the same process for opening the last envelope.) When students have all three of their sentences laid out, focus their attention on the placement of *and* in each sentence. Point out that each sentence contains a compound element; however, each sentence is a simple sentence.

One on One
Prepare the same activity for your student. After he has constructed all three sentences, discuss the placement of *and* and point out that the sentences are simple sentences despite their compound parts.

WITH COMPOUND PARTS	Chaim and Kim enjoy painting in their spare time; last week, they painted and refurbished their dining room.
WITH COMPOUND PARTS	Shelby and her brothers play the violin, and they perform and sing as a group.

Because a compound sentence consists of two or more independent clauses, two simple sentences can be combined into a compound sentence. Also, a compound sentence can be split into simple sentences.

TWO SIMPLE SENTENCES	Ashleigh and Stella make their own cards and stationery. Their friends sometimes buy notepaper from them.
ONE COMPOUND SENTENCE	Ashleigh and Stella make their own cards and stationery, and their friends sometimes buy notepaper from them.

in summary

A **simple sentence** consists of only one independent clause.

A **compound sentence** consists of two or more independent clauses. Usually two independent clauses are joined by a semicolon or by a comma and a coordinating conjunction.

8-3 PRACTICE THE SKILL

Underline the coordinating conjunctions. Label each sentence *S* (simple) or *Cd* (compound).

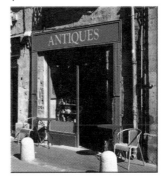

_S_ 1. Many people enjoy collecting antiques.

_Cd_ 2. There are different opinions about judging an antique's value, but experts judge an antique's value on its age, its artistic value, and its historical importance.

_S_ 3. According to many collectors and the United States government, an antique must be over one hundred years old.

_S_ 4. Collectors obtain antiques for delight, investment, or money.

_Cd_ 5. The variety of antiques is great, but the four main categories are ceramics, furniture, glass, and metalwork.

_S_ 6. Ceramics can be divided into the categories of pottery and porcelain.

_Cd_ 7. Porcelain is commonly called china, and pottery is made from baked clay.

_Cd_ 8. Antique gold is rare, but antique silver is relatively common.

Teaching Strategy: Participation

Instruct each student to write a simple sentence on a sheet of paper. Then tell students to exchange their sentences with another person. Instruct the students to turn the simple sentences into compound sentences and then ask them to read their sentences aloud. Finally, ask students to analyze their rewritten sentences and to describe what they did to their original sentence to make it compound.

<u>S</u> 9. Furniture from the Victorian age has become especially valuable to antique dealers.

<u>Cd</u> 10. Antique markets are common, <u>and</u> people often find valuables at ordinary sales.

8-4 REVIEW THE SKILL

In the blank, label each sentence *S* (simple) or *Cd* (compound). Label the sentence patterns. Above each word of the sentence pattern, write its label.

<u>S</u> 1.
            S   LV   PN
A hobby for many people is photography.

<u>Cd</u> 2.
        S   TrV   DO   S   LV
A person may take pictures for fun, or he may be a profes-
           PN
sional photographer.

<u>Cd</u> 3.
          S   TrV IO DO   S
Photographs give us pictures of unknown lands, and we can
    InV
learn about other people in the world.

<u>S</u> 4.
         S   LV
A picture by a well-known photographer may seem rather
     PA
expensive.

<u>S</u> 5.
               S   LV
A great achievement in photography has been the instant
     PN
processing of film.

<u>Cd</u> 6.
         S   TrV   DO   S
Many universities offer courses in photography, and some
    TrV   IO   DO
even offer students photography degrees.

<u>Cd</u> 7.
         S   TrV   DO
Many families record important events with pictures, and
         S   TrV   DO
some parents make albums for their children.

<u>Cd</u> 8.
         S   LV   PN   S
Photography is an interesting hobby, yet the equipment
    LV   PA
can be expensive.

<u>S</u> 9.
         S   TrV   DO   DO
Taking professional pictures requires skill and knowledge.

<u>S</u> 10.
                 S   TrV   DO
A professional photographer takes pictures for weddings and
other special events.

Complex Sentence

A **complex sentence** has one independent clause and one or more dependent clauses. A dependent clause may appear before the independent clause, within the independent clause, or after the independent clause.

COMPLEX SENTENCE	*While she was visiting Mexico,* my mom found several interesting coins for my coin collection.
COMPLEX SENTENCE	*When the windows were clean,* Sarah started on the floors.
WITH TWO DEPENDENT CLAUSES	*While she was visiting Mexico,* my mom found several interesting coins, *which I added to my coin collection.*
WITH TWO DEPENDENT CLAUSES	*After the opera ended,* my brother picked up the program *that had fallen under the chair in front of him* and took it home.

Chapter 12: Commas After Introductory Adverb Clauses p. 282

Compound-Complex Sentence

A **compound-complex sentence** has two or more independent clauses and one or more dependent clauses. A compound-complex sentence is compound because it contains at least two independent clauses; it is complex because it also contains at least one dependent clause.

COMPOUND-COMPLEX SENTENCE	*Because he enjoys writing,* Ryan adds to his journal every day, and he has written several poems and short stories.
COMPOUND-COMPLEX SENTENCE	*As soon as the race was over,* Stephen watered his horse, and he checked the horse's hooves for any rocks *that might have lodged themselves in the horseshoe.*

in summary

A **complex sentence** consists of one independent clause and one or more dependent clauses.

A **compound-complex sentence** consists of two or more independent clauses and one or more dependent clauses.

Writing Link

Display the following three sentences:

- My uncle owns many pets.
- The class wants to go on another field trip.
- Owen likes to play racquetball.

Instruct the students to make each sentence complex by adding a dependent clause. Allow volunteers to share their sentences with the rest of the class.

Teaching Strategy: Participation

Group students into pairs. Allow the students several minutes to interview one another. They can ask each other questions such as "What's your favorite sports team?" or "How many cousins do you have?" Instruct students to use the answers to construct a compound-complex sentence describing the classmates they interviewed.

One on One

Follow the same activity listed above. Allow your student to interview you.

8-5 PRACTICE THE SKILL

Label each sentence *S* (simple), *Cd* (compound), or *Cx* (complex).

<u>Cx</u> 1. Potters have shaped and baked clay since civilization began several thousand years ago.

<u>Cx</u> 2. Although a potter may be an amateur, he can often sell his pottery at shows and exhibitions.

<u>S</u> 3. Pottery can be classified by clay mixtures and baking temperatures.

<u>Cd</u> 4. Potters must prepare the clay, for any bubbles may cause cracks in the clay.

<u>Cd</u> 5. Pottery can include valuable works of art, or the pieces may be simple household items.

<u>Cx</u> 6. Pottery can be very valuable because many potters make the pieces individually.

<u>S</u> 7. From early times, people have made vessels on a potter's wheel.

<u>S</u> 8. Many potters also shape the clay by hand.

<u>Cd</u> 9. Potters often decorate their pottery; many simply scratch designs into the clay.

<u>Cx</u> 10. If you enjoy art, you may enjoy pottery.

8-6 REVIEW THE SKILL

Label each sentence *S* (simple), *Cd* (compound), *Cx* (complex), or *Cd-Cx* (compound-complex).

<u>Cx</u> 1. If you do not enjoy pottery, you might enjoy origami.

<u>S</u> 2. Origami is the art of folding paper into various shapes.

<u>Cx</u> 3. Although with origami the artist uses paper for various shapes, he does not cut, paste, or decorate the paper.

<u>Cd</u> 4. This art is popular in Japan; the country has much literature on the subject.

<u>Cd-Cx</u> 5. Because many people work on origami, the shapes can be very complex, and they often include many types of animals, flowers, and even humans.

<u>Cd</u> 6. Many types of paper are used in origami, but the preferred type of paper is a thin Japanese paper called *washi*.

Reinforcement

Use the bulletin board on page 448 as an interactive teaching tool. Explain to the students that the numbers on the scoreboard represent the number of dependent and independent clauses found in each sentence type. Emphasize that complex and compound-complex sentences have *at least* one dependent clause. Encourage students to memorize this chart to help them remember how many dependent and independent clauses are found in each sentence type.

Evaluation

If you have assigned sentence diagramming with Practice the Skill 8-5, check students' answers using pages 466-67.

Enrichment

Assign Teaching Help 8 (Book 2, p. 48). Encourage the students to identify each independent and dependent clause before they choose their answers.

Cd-Cx 7. Origami can be difficult, but if a person will learn the basic symbols and directions, he will have an easier time.

S 8. The purchase of a beginner's book on origami may be the first step for an interested person.

Cx 9. As practice makes perfect in many other areas, a person interested in origami also needs practice.

Cd-Cx 10. Since paper is the only item needed, origami can be done anywhere; thus many people enjoy this particular hobby.

Kinds of Dependent Clauses

In a complex or compound-complex sentence, the entire dependent clause functions like one part of speech. In this section, we will study two kinds of dependent clauses: adjective clauses and adverb clauses.

Adjective Clauses

An **adjective clause** is a dependent clause functioning like an adjective in the sentence. An adjective clause modifies a noun or a pronoun. Like all clauses, an adjective clause must have both a subject and a predicate.

> The poems *that Ryan wrote* were entered in the school poetry contest.
> The winning poem will be announced in the paper *that the students publish each week.*

Chapter 5: Adjectives
p. 114

Relative Pronouns

Most adjective clauses begin with **relative pronouns.** A relative pronoun relates an adjective clause to a noun or pronoun that the clause modifies. The noun or pronoun that the adjective clause modifies is the antecedent of the relative pronoun. The relative pronouns are the words *who, whom, whose, which,* and *that.* A relative pronoun functions as a subject, an object, or an adjective in the dependent clause.

>   S   InV
> The winner of the poetry contest, *whose name will be posted in the paper,* will receive a new book of poetry.

In this example the relative pronoun *whose* does several things. First, it modifies the noun *name* within the adjective clause itself. Second, *whose* replaces the word *winner* in the adjective clause *(whose name* instead of *winner's name).* Third, it relates the adjective clause to the word *winner* in the independent clause (in other words, it shows the connection between the two clauses). The entire dependent clause is an adjective clause, because it modifies the noun *winner.*

>   S   TrV   DO
> Haley, *who practices gymnastics every day,* is also an excellent runner.

In this example the relative pronoun *who* functions as the subject of the adjective clause, which modifies *Haley* in the independent clause.

Teaching Strategy: Induction and Discussion

Remind the students that a word, a phrase, or a clause may function as one part of speech even if it is (or contains) a different part of speech. Ask the students for examples of one part of speech functioning as another. *(Both nouns and verbs may function as adjectives.)* Write the following sentence for display: *The person who submits the best photo will win a new camera.* Ask the students to identify the dependent clause. *(who submits the best photo)* Then ask the students to identify the function of this clause. *(It describes the word* person *and functions as an adjective.)* You may want to write other sentences for display and ask the students to identify each adjective clause.

Teaching Strategy: Induction and Discussion

With the class, examine the sentence or sentences that contain adjective clauses again. This time underline any relative pronouns. Ask the students to identify the part of speech of each underlined word. *(pronoun)* Elicit from the students the purpose of these pronouns. *(They relate the adjective clause to the word being modified.)* Explain that these words are called relative pronouns. You may want to write the complete list of relative pronouns for display.

Scriptural Application

Instruct students to find the relative pronouns in the following verses: Colossians 3:4, I Thessalonians 1:10, Hebrews 11:8-10, and I John 2:16. Some passages will contain more than one relative pronoun. Encourage students to find additional relative pronouns in other verses.

Sometimes the relative pronoun *that* is omitted (simply "understood") when it is the direct object or the object of a preposition in the dependent clause.

DO   S   TrV
Leslie has several books (that) I have not read.

OP S   InV
He has the book (that) I have been looking for.

Both of these sentences are clear and understandable even without the relative pronoun.

> Although relative pronouns look like interrogative pronouns, there is no subject and verb inversion in clauses introduced by relative pronouns. The relative pronoun always comes at the beginning of the clause and is followed by the subject and verb in normal order.

Relative Adverbs

Most adjective clauses begin with a relative pronoun. Some, however, begin with the words *when, where,* and *why.* These words are called **relative adverbs.** A relative adverb modifies the verb in the adjective clause, introducing the clause and relating the clause to the rest of the sentence.

> I exercise early in the morning *when the air is coolest outside.*
> We are going to a park *where we can play tennis.*

In each example, the italicized adjective clause modifies the word immediately preceding it. The relative adverbs modify the verbs in the adjective clauses (not the verbs in the independent clauses). To understand why the words *when, where,* and *why* are adverbs in these sentences, think of the entire sentence as a combination of two separate simple sentences.

> We are going to the park.
> We can play tennis *in the park. or* We can play tennis *there.*

Combine the two sentences by making the second sentence an adverb clause. The word *where* substitutes for *in the park* or for *there.* Because the phrase *in the park* or the word *there* functions as an adverb, *where* is an adverb; it modifies the verb *play.* *Where* is a relative adverb because it relates the entire adjective clause to the word *park.* Remember that an adjective clause may have several parts: it has a subject and a verb and may include modifiers and complements. Although an adjective clause may begin with a relative adverb, it always functions like an adjective.

in summary

An **adjective clause** is a dependent clause that functions as an adjective in a sentence.

A **relative pronoun** relates an adjective clause to a noun or pronoun in an independent clause; it functions like a subject, an object, or an adjective in the adjective clause.

A **relative adverb** relates an adjective clause to a noun or pronoun in an independent clause; it functions as an adverb in the adjective clause.

Teaching Strategy: Induction

After the students have learned that relative pronouns introduce adjective clauses, explain that another kind of word can also introduce an adjective clause. Write the following sentences for display: *I study in my room. It is quiet there.* Ask the students to combine the two sentences by making the second sentence an adjective clause. Answers may vary, but elicit from the students the following sentence: *I study in my room where it is quiet.* Identify the word *where* as an adverb. The students may not understand how an adverb can introduce an adjective clause. Explain that the word *where* modifies the verb in the adjective clause. Look again at the sentences. Explain that the word *where* replaces the word *there.* Relative adverbs function as adverbs within adjective clauses, but they also introduce adjective clauses.

In the blank write the word modified by the italicized adjective clause.

fishermen 1. In Bible times, many men were fishermen *who caught fish for a living.*

fishermen 2. Jesus' first disciples were fishermen *whom He called.*

skill 3. For many people fishing was a skill *that provided basic food.*

recreation 4. For many people today, fishing is recreation *that relaxes them.*

friends 5. Some learn helpful tips from friends *with whom they fish.*

times 6. Mornings and evenings are times *when fish are more active.*

equipment 7. Fishing equipment, *which is of a wide variety,* can include rods, reels, lines, leaders, sinkers, floats, hooks, and bait.

tools 8. The rod, reel, and line are three fishing tools *that are basic.*

states 9. Colorado and Alaska are states *where people might enjoy ice fishing.*

sport 10. People must use caution in ice fishing, a sport *that can be dangerous.*

Place parentheses around each adjective clause. Underline each relative pronoun once. Underline each relative adverb twice.

1. Many people play sports, (which help them relax.)

2. There are many sports (that have excellent health benefits.)

3. I like a gym (where I can play racquetball.)

4. My friend and I need a time (when we can play.)

5. Racquetball is a sport (that uses all the surfaces of an indoor court.)

6. Joseph George Sobek is the man (who invented racquetball.)

7. Another sport (that I enjoy) is tennis.

Clauses   **201**

8. The gym near my house is a place(where Paul and I can play either tennis or racquetball.)

9. Paul is a person(with whom I have played tennis before.)

10. Many people enjoy a tennis game(where they can relax.)

Place parentheses around each adjective clause. Underline each relative pronoun once. Underline each relative adverb twice. In the blank, write the function of each relative pronoun within the clause: *S, DO, OP, PN, or Adj.* Write *Adv* as the function of each relative adverb.

PN 1. I do not know(what a philatelist is.)

S 2. A philatelist is someone(who enjoys collecting stamps.)

DO 3. Stamp collecting is a hobby(that many people enjoy.)

Adj 4. Famous people(whose hobbies have involved philately)have been Franklin D. Roosevelt and King George V of England.

Adv 5. There are many reasons(why people collect stamps.)

S 6. Commemorative stamps are stamps(that honor important events.)

DO 7. People may collect stamps based on a theme(that they enjoy.)

Adv 8. Stamp shows and auctions are two events(where a person can buy stamps.)

S 9. Philatelists look for any unusual or unique characteristics (that increase a stamp's value.)

Adj 10. Large amounts of money have been raised by the estates of famous people(whose collections have been auctioned.)

Adverb Clauses

An **adverb clause** is a dependent clause functioning like an adverb in the sentence. An adverb clause usually modifies the verb in the independent clause, although it sometimes modifies the entire independent clause. Remember that an adverb clause, like all other clauses, must have both a subject and a verb.

> He practiced *as if each rehearsal were the real performance.*
> *As soon as the play began,* everyone stopped talking.

The adverb clauses in both of these examples modify the verbs in the independent clauses. They describe the action of the verbs, telling the manner of the verb in the first example and the time of the verb in the second example.

Reinforcement

Review the definitions of adjective clauses, relative pronouns, and relative adverbs. Ask the students to identify the similarities and differences between a relative pronoun and a relative adverb. *(Both relate a dependent clause to an independent clause. The word being modified in the independent clause is the antecedent of the relative pronoun. A relative adverb modifies the verb in the dependent clause.)*

Teaching Strategy: Introduction

The students have already learned that an adjective clause is a dependent clause that modifies a noun or a pronoun in the independent clause. Now explain that an adverb clause is a dependent clause that functions as an adverb for the independent clause. An adverb clause may modify either the verb of the independent clause or the entire independent clause.

Subordinating Conjunctions

Adverb clauses begin with **subordinating conjunctions.** A subordinating conjunction is a conjunction that joins a dependent clause to an independent clause. Because it is a conjunction, the subordinating conjunction does not have a separate function in the dependent clause (unlike relative pronouns and relative adverbs). Subordinating conjunctions describe meanings such as time, place, condition, and cause.

TIME   They will study *before they go to the game.*

PLACE   They prefer to study *where there are few disturbances.*

CONDITION   We will go out onto the lake *if everyone in the boat is wearing a life jacket.*

CAUSE   *Because the meeting begins at seven o'clock,* I should leave here at half past six.

after	in order that	until
although	provided	whenever
as	since	where
as soon as	so	whereas
as though	so that	when
because	than	wherever
before	unless	while

in summary

An **adverb clause** is a dependent clause that usually modifies a verb in the independent clause.

A **subordinating conjunction** joins an adverb clause to the word modified in the independent clause; it has no other function in the dependent clause.

8-10 PRACTICE THE SKILL

In the blank, write the word modified by the italicized adverb clause.

    read   1. *When I want to relax,* I read a good book.

    go   2. I go *where I can read without interruption.*

    find   3. I find a place without people *so that I can concentrate on my book.*

    focus   4. *Whenever I am by myself,* I focus much better.

    read   5. I also read *when I have homework assignments or research projects.*

    read   6. I read *so that I can learn.*

Teaching Strategy: Induction

Display a few sentences with adverb clauses. Ask the students to name the words that introduce adjective clauses. *(relative pronouns and relative adverbs)* Now identify the introductory word of an adverb clause as a special kind of conjunction called a subordinating conjunction. Ask the students to list other subordinating conjunctions and write their suggestions for display.

ESL Strategy

For a further explanation of connecting words used to combine sentences, use ESL Worksheets 8A and 8B (Book 2, pp. 82-84).

Literature Link

Instruct students to find the four dependent clauses in the sentence that describes Myles's father's scar in *Men of Iron.* Direct students to determine which clauses are adjective clauses and which are adverb clauses. Ask students to find other adjective and adverb clauses in the excerpt.

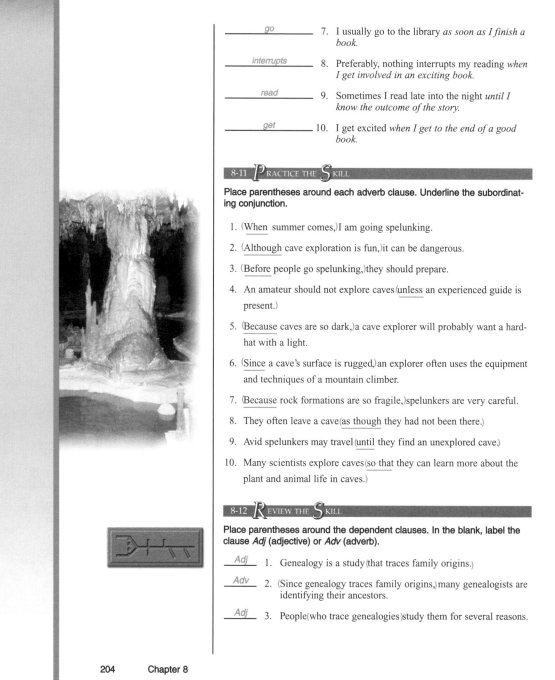

_____go_____ 7. I usually go to the library *as soon as I finish a book.*

_____interrupts_____ 8. Preferably, nothing interrupts my reading *when I get involved in an exciting book.*

_____read_____ 9. Sometimes I read late into the night *until I know the outcome of the story.*

_____get_____ 10. I get excited *when I get to the end of a good book.*

8-11 PRACTICE THE SKILL

Place parentheses around each adverb clause. Underline the subordinating conjunction.

1. (When summer comes,) I am going spelunking.

2. (Although cave exploration is fun,) it can be dangerous.

3. (Before people go spelunking,) they should prepare.

4. An amateur should not explore caves (unless an experienced guide is present.)

5. (Because caves are so dark,) a cave explorer will probably want a hard-hat with a light.

6. (Since a cave's surface is rugged,) an explorer often uses the equipment and techniques of a mountain climber.

7. (Because rock formations are so fragile,) spelunkers are very careful.

8. They often leave a cave (as though they had not been there.)

9. Avid spelunkers may travel (until they find an unexplored cave.)

10. Many scientists explore caves (so that they can learn more about the plant and animal life in caves.)

8-12 REVIEW THE SKILL

Place parentheses around the dependent clauses. In the blank, label the clause *Adj* (adjective) or *Adv* (adverb).

_____Adj_____ 1. Genealogy is a study (that traces family origins.)

_____Adv_____ 2. (Since genealogy traces family origins,) many genealogists are identifying their ancestors.

_____Adj_____ 3. People (who trace genealogies) study them for several reasons.

Evaluation

If you have assigned sentence diagramming with Review the Skill 8-12, check students' answers using pages 467-68.

Adv   4. Some individuals search for parents or children (whose identity has been lost.)

Adv   5. (Although some people know about their immediate family,) they may need past medical history.

Adv   6. Many people enjoy genealogical research (because it is interesting.)

Adv   7. (Before a person begins research,) he records his family tree.

Adv   8. (As he finds information about new family members,) he adds those to his tree.

Adj   9. Birth certificates, marriage licenses, and death certificates are important records (that establish family members.)

Adj 10. Computers are a helpful place (where a searcher can find information.)

8-13 CUMULATIVE REVIEW

A. Rewrite the following paragraph, correcting the fragments, comma splices, fused sentences, incorrect noun forms, incorrect verb forms, errors in adjective or adverb usage, preposition errors, and dangling or misplaced modifiers. There are ten errors. *(Answers will vary.)*

Skiing, a popular hobby throughout the world. Thousands of ski areas exist all over the world that people enjoy, they are concentrated in Europe, the United States, and Canada. Before the invention of artificial snow, people had went to resorts almost located exclusively in cold mountain regiones. However, many ski resorts now produce artificial snow that makes skiing possible for longer periods of time many of these ski areas also provide instruction and equipment. Between the many styles of skiing, downhill and cross-country are the most popularest for recreation. For a real exciting vacation, a ski resort is a great place to start.

Skiing is a popular hobby throughout the world. Thousands of ski areas that people enjoy exist all over the world, but they are concentrated in Europe, the United States, and Canada. Before the invention of artificial snow, people had gone to resorts located almost exclusively in cold mountain regions. However, many ski resorts now produce artificial snow that makes skiing possible for longer periods of time. Many of these ski areas also provide instruction and equipment. Among the many styles of skiing, downhill and cross-country are the most popular for recreation. For a really exciting vacation, a ski resort is a great place to start.

B. From your rewritten paragraph, find an example of each of the following:

Participle _located_

Gerund _Skiing_

Infinitive _to start_

Complex sentence _However, many ski resorts now produce artificial snow that makes skiing possible for longer periods of time._

Compound-complex sentence _Thousands of ski areas that people enjoy exist all over the world, but they are concentrated in Europe, the United States, and Canada._

Adjective dependent clause _that people enjoy_

Look again at the excerpt from _Men of Iron._
• _Read the last paragraph. What crucial information do the dependent clauses supply?_

Writing a Devotional

Tamika sat with her pencil and a blank sheet of paper, thumbing through the pages of her Bible. Her sixth-grade brother Jerome came into the kitchen, opened the refrigerator, and poured himself a glass of milk.

Tamika frowned. "Since when have you started drinking milk?" she asked. "I thought you liked it only in the form of chocolate milkshakes."

Jerome took a long drink, set his glass down, and licked a milk mustache off his lips. "We talked about milk in health class today," he said. "Mrs. Jeffson said that kids my age need three servings of milk a day to help us get the calcium our bones need to grow." He faked a slam-dunk with an invisible basketball. "I had milk with my breakfast cereal and ice cream for lunch, so there are two. Now I need one more." He spun the unseen ball on his fingertip.

"That's it!" said Tamika. She began rustling through the pages of her Bible as fast as her fingers could move. "Now if only I can find the verse!"

"Huh?" Jerome took another gulp of milk and stood frowning with a fresh milk mustache on his upper lip.

Have you ever heard someone tell a story or an interesting fact that reminded you of a biblical truth? Perhaps that story is something you could use in writing a devotional. A devotional is a short essay drawing a biblical application from an anecdote or a striking fact.

Here is Tamika's devotional about the importance of desiring God's Word.

Did you know that children need three servings of milk a day to get the calcium they need? Even adults should have two or more servings of milk daily. Without calcium, our bones would not be strong and healthy. And yet, do you know many people who desire to drink milk at every opportunity?

Sidebar (left margin)

• _that Myles was frightened and that his father is so concerned about what is happening that he seems oblivious not only to Myles but also to everything except the conversation_

Objectives

Students will

1. select a Scripture text.
2. make an application.
3. write a devotional.

Overview of the Writing Process

Planning—choosing a text and making an application

Drafting—writing the devotional

Revising—evaluating with a partner and making changes for clarity

Publishing—reading to the class and handing in to the teacher

---

Writing a Devotional

Lesson Support

Teacher's Edition, Book 2
Writing Worksheets—p. 141
Rubrics—p.155

Introduction

Direct the students to read the story and the sample devotional at the beginning of the section. Ask the students the following question: What experiences have made you see a biblical truth in a fresh way?

Discussion

Direct a discussion about the example in the text, pointing out that the opening must gain attention immediately because it is brief.

Discuss how the application makes its point without explaining too much.

Ask the students why the writer begins and ends her devotional with questions. _(The opening question gains attention and provokes thought; the closing questions reinforce the need to act.)_

Refer students to the sections "A Few Points About Style" and "And Most Importantly." Answer any questions they may have after reading this material.

Planning

Direct the students to read the instructions in "Your Turn."

Distribute a copy of the Writing Worksheet (Book 2, p. 141) to each student. Allow time for the students to fill out their worksheets, choosing a Scripture text and an appropriate application.

Most people do not crave a glass of milk the way they do a soda. Milk-flavored bubble gum is not a popular item. Even though milk is so important, most people just do not have much of a taste for it.

First Peter 2:2 compares God's Word to milk that helps us grow as Christians. "As newborn babes, desire the sincere milk of the word, that ye may grow thereby." Daily servings of God's Word are absolutely necessary if we are to become mature Christians. Most of us read the Bible, hear sermons about it, and even quote from it occasionally. But do we really desire it as I Peter 2:2 commands? Does it affect every decision? How greatly do we crave its taste?

Opening

Since Tamika wanted to gain her reader's attention quickly, she put her interesting fact at the beginning of the devotional.

Keep opening stories or facts brief, and tell them in a way that will keep your readers reading. You want to draw them toward the biblical truth, the part of the devotional they should focus on and remember.

Application

Tamika used the end to give the Scripture and draw the application.
- Before including your Scripture verse, read the context (the surrounding verses) to make sure that you know what the verse is saying.
- After quoting the Scripture, make your point in a sentence or two. Your readers do not need to be told the same thing twice.
- If you use a verse that is fairly familiar to your readers, try to comment on it in a fresh way.

A Few Points About Style

- Remember your audience. Who will be reading it: your friends? your parents? your teachers? Just as your style of speaking varies, your writing style will change slightly, depending on your reader.
- For adult readers, use a somewhat formal style, without slang or contractions; but keep it natural enough to avoid sounding stuffy.
- For younger children, use a less formal style and familiar words.

And Most Importantly . . .

Before you start writing, pray about your devotional. Ask God first what He wants you to say, and then ask His help to say it in the most effective way.

Your Turn

Write a devotional. Include an anecdote or an interesting fact to illustrate your point. It might help you to recall a verse that is especially striking to you or an event from which you learned an important lesson.

Drafting

Remind the students to consider their audience as they draft their openings.

Allow time for students to write their devotionals in class.

Revising

Direct students to take their devotionals home and to evaluate them, making revisions according to "A Few Points About Style."

Publishing

Ask volunteers to share their devotionals the following day. Collect the assignments.

Scriptural Application

Read Ephesians 4:29 aloud. Explain that Christian writers must always have the spiritual benefit of their audiences in mind.

Evaluation

For help in grading this assignment, see "Grading Writing Assignments" (p. x) and Rubric 8 (Book 2, p. 155).

Enrichment

Supply the students with devotionals that you can recommend.

9 AGREEMENT

sandlotscience.com

Objectives

Students will

1. choose the verb forms that agree in number with the subject.

2. use auxiliaries that agree with the subject.

3. choose the correct verb in sentences containing compound subjects, intervening phrases, or predicate nouns.

4. choose the correct verb in sentences with inverted order.

5. choose verbs that agree with indefinite pronouns in sentences.

6. choose and supply the correct verb form for subjects that appear in a plural form; as a collective noun; or as a title, a quotation, or an amount.

7. select a pronoun that agrees with the antecedent in a sentence.

8. supply pronouns that agree in gender and number with their antecedents.

9. evaluate and revise a paragraph for agreement errors.

Lesson Support

Student Text
Chapter 9 Review—pp. 421-22

Teacher's Edition, Book 1
Bulletin Boards—p. 449

Teacher's Edition, Book 2
Pretests—pp. 21-23
Teaching Helps—p. 49
Concept Reinforcements—pp. 116-20

An optical illusion is a visually perceived image that is deceptive. Some optical illusions, like this one, refuse to let you make complete sense of what you're seeing. Do you think it is really possible to see nine cubes floating in this formation? Which sides of the cubes would you probably not be able to see if this picture were reality?

A writer sometimes wants to create a difference between illusion and reality, but he always does so intentionally. He never wants to confuse the reader by his careless mistakes. Mistakes in agreement keep a reader from making complete sense of what he is reading. A good writer avoids such optical confusions.

Subject-Verb Agreement

Subjects and Predicates

In order to communicate clearly and effectively, you must make every verb agree with its subject. In other words, a singular subject takes a singular verb, and a plural subject takes a plural verb. When the number of the subject and the verb are the same, the sentence has correct **subject-verb agreement.**

Most nouns make the plural form by adding the suffix *s* or *es.* Verbs, however, form the plural in just the opposite way. Singular present-tense verbs end in *s* or *es,* and plural verbs do not. A good rule to remember is that if your subject ends in a suffix *s,* your verb usually should not.

Chapter 2: Plural Forms of Nouns
p. 24

SINGULAR   A cowboy sleeps on the ground by the campfire.

PLURAL   Cowboys sleep on the ground by the campfire.

This form change in verbs occurs only in present tense with subjects in third person. For example, *the horse ran* and *the horses ran* use the same past-tense verb form for singular and plural subjects. With the exception of the verb *be,* verbs in past tense and future tense stay the same, whether singular or plural.

Chapter 4: Simple Tenses
pp. 93-94

in summary

Every verb must agree with its subject in number.

A singular subject takes a singular verb, and a plural subject takes a plural verb.

Teaching Strategy: Introduction and Scriptural Application

Lead the class in a discussion about the importance of unity and agreement. Ask them to identify several objects or organizations for which unity is a necessity. *(automobiles, factories, computer systems, sports teams, committees, families, and classrooms)* Ask students what happens if there is disharmony in a mechanical system or disagreement in an organization. *(The whole system or organization suffers.)* You may wish to bring to class an interesting gadget that can be taken apart and put back together in order to emphasize the importance of all the parts' working together. You may also want to read selections from Ephesians 4:1-16. Verse 3 states the necessity of working to maintain the unity of the Spirit. Verse 16 explains the worth of the individual parts and the beautiful results of their harmony. Relate these concepts to a study of subject-verb and pronoun-antecedent agreement by emphasizing the beauty and effectiveness of harmony in language.

Underline the simple subject in each sentence. Then underline the correct verb from the choices in parentheses.

1. Sculpture *(interests, interest)* many types of people.

2. Often, sculptured pieces *(shows, show)* the history of a people.

3. A monument *(lasts, last)* for a significant time.

4. Memorials *(commemorates, commemorate)* historical people or events.

5. Many artists *(creates, create)* sculptures as a form of expression.

6. Many times, architecture *(contains, contain)* sculpture.

7. A building's features *(displays, display)* the intricate designs of sculpture.

8. Many cathedrals *(includes, include)* beautiful artwork and sculpture.

9. A sculptor *(uses, use)* many of the techniques of other artists.

10. A sculptured form *(embodies, embody)* three dimensions.

Underline the simple subject in each sentence. Then underline the correct verb from the choices in parentheses.

1. Architecture *(involves, involve)* the enclosing of space for human use.

2. Good plans *(uses, use)* space wisely for the purpose of the building.

3. A structure *(needs, need)* permanence.

4. The raw materials *(influences, influence)* the form of a building.

5. Stone *(resists, resist)* compression.

6. Wooden beams *(withstands, withstand)* tension and compression.

7. Past construction *(includes, include)* much decoration.

8. For the most part, modern architects *(rejects, reject)* ornate decoration.

9. All societies *(possesses, possess)* methods of building.

10. Every person *(requires, require)* shelter from the weather.

Auxiliaries

If a complete verb contains one or more auxiliaries, then the first auxiliary must agree with the subject. The only auxiliaries that change form to agree with a singular or plural subject are *be, have,* and *do.* (Remember

---

ESL: Be sure to emphasize this information with your ESL students: among auxiliaries, only *be, have,* and *do* change form. Auxiliaries such as *can, should, might, would, could, shall,* and *will* never change form. Non-native English speakers often take a while to get used to this in common speech and writing, even after learning the rule. Consequently, this is something they should carefully proofread their own writing for.

Teaching Strategy: Induction

Ask the students to identify what distinguishes a subject as plural. (*the fact that it identifies more than one person, place, thing, or idea and usually ends in an* s) Next, ask them to describe a plural verb. You may want to write the following example sentences for display in addition to a few of your own:

• The investigator studies the case.

• The witnesses tell what happened.

• Their stories contradict each other.

Ask the students to identify the plural verbs. *(tell, contradict)* How do these verbs differ from the singular verbs? (*The plural verbs do not end in* s.)

Reinforcement

Remind the students that the only verbs (other than *be, have,* and *do*) that change to plural forms are singular, present-tense verbs.

Teaching Strategy: Induction

Write the following list of auxiliaries for display: *be, can, could, do, have, should, may,* and *will*

Allow the students to construct several sentences using these auxiliaries. You may want to write the sentences for display. Ask students to identify which auxiliaries change form between singular and plural. *(be, have,* and *do)* You may want to divide the class into teams. Ask one team member to record and then to read his team's answers aloud. Observe which teams found the three correct auxiliaries.

that *have* and *do* change form only in the present tense.) Other auxiliaries do not change form between singular and plural.

	Singular	**Plural**
be	He *is sleeping* under a tent.	They *are sleeping* under a tent.
do	He *does sleep* under a tent.	They *do sleep* under a tent.
have	He *has slept* under a tent.	They *have slept* under a tent.

Auxiliaries do not change form when they come later in the complete verb. Only the first auxiliary in the complete verb shows agreement.

> **SINGULAR** He *has been sleeping* under a tent.
> **PLURAL** They *have been sleeping* under a tent.

Proofread your writing carefully for these errors in subject-verb agreement. Remember, auxiliaries like *can, could, shall, should, may, might, will,* and others do not change form; only *be, have,* and *do* change form to agree with the subject.

Special Rules for *Be*

Whether it is functioning as a main verb or as an auxiliary, the verb *be* is different from all other verbs in its form. Other verbs, including *do* and *have,* change form for singular or plural only in present tense with a third-person subject. The verb *be,* however, changes in form with first-, second-, and third-person singular subjects. It also changes form for singular and plural in past tense as well as present tense. To make *be* agree in number with its subject, you must know all its forms.

	Present		**Past**	
	Singular	Plural	Singular	Plural
FIRST PERSON	I am	we are	I was	we were
SECOND PERSON	you are	you are	you were	you were
THIRD PERSON	he is	they are	he was	they were

The first-person singular pronoun *I* takes *am* for the present tense and *was* for past tense.

> **PRESENT** I *am* surprised by the speed of that horse.
> **PAST** I *was* tired after the game.

All plural nouns and pronouns and the second-person singular pronoun *you* take *are* for present tense and *were* for past tense.

> **PRESENT** The horses *are* friendly.
> They *are* well trained.
> You *are* welcome to pet them.

> **PAST** We *were* glad to see you.
> You *were* so kind to come.
> The children *were* excited about petting the horses.
> They *were* afraid of them at first.

Enrichment

Some students may have trouble using all the forms of *be* correctly. Play a game of fast answers with the students to review these verb forms. Give the person and number (e.g., second person, singular) and instruct the students to say the correct subject and form of *be.* *(you are)*

All singular nouns and third-person singular pronouns *(it, he, she)* take *is* for the present tense and *was* for the past tense.

PRESENT   The pony *is* a family pet.
Sharon *is* an experienced rider.

PAST   The horse *was* strong and powerful.
Her brother *was* a horse trainer.

in summary

The only auxiliaries that change form to agree with singular and plural subjects are *be, have,* and *do.*

The verb *be* has special singular and plural forms.

9-3 PRACTICE THE SKILL

Underline the simple subject in each sentence. Then underline the correct verb from the choices in parentheses. In the blank, label the verb you choose *V* (main verb) or *Aux* (auxiliary).

Aux   1. Since ancient times, man *(has, have)* created visual art.

_V_   2. The images here *(is, are)* examples of early art.

_V_   3. The oldest examples *(is, are)* paintings on the walls of caves.

Aux   4. Modern historians *(does, do)* not know much about these painters.

_V_   5. The bull *(was, were)* a common subject of those paintings.

Aux   6. Along with cave paintings, some people *(was, were)* carving goddesses.

Aux   7. Often, a mask *(was, were)* made for ritual dances.

Aux   8. Natural forces *(has, have)* been the subjects of art from early times on.

Aux   9. Also, pictures *(has, have)* often represented religious beliefs.

Aux 10. Art *(does, do)* represent various aspects of the daily life and customs of a society.

In the blank write the correct form of *be, have,* or *do* to complete the sentence.

___is___	1. Painting _?_ one of the oldest arts.
___Do___	2. _?_ people enjoy paintings?
___have___	3. Many artists _?_ expressed various emotions in their art.
___have___	4. Many artists' creations _?_ great value for humanity.
___does___	5. What _?_ an artist paint?
___are___	6. Often, their subjects _?_ the everyday things around them.
___was___	7. Religion _?_ a major subject of paintings in Europe during the Middle Ages.
___has___	8. Most Asian artwork _?_ depicted religious subjects.
___was___	9. Art _?_ a major form of preserving history in ancient times.
___does___	10. Artwork _?_ tell us much about a particular time period.

Compound Subjects

Sentences often have compound subjects. If the compound subject is joined by the conjunction *and* or by *both—and,* the verb should be plural. If the compound subject is joined by *or, nor, either—or,* or *neither—nor,* the verb must agree with the subject that is closer to it.

> **PLURAL** She *and* her sister *appear* on stage in Act III.
> Costumes *and* lighting *are* part of the effect on the audience.

In both examples above, the parts of the compound subject are joined by the conjunction *and* and take a plural verb.

> **PLURAL** *Neither* the director *nor* the actors *realize* how many people are coming this evening.

> **SINGULAR** *Neither* the actors *nor* the director *realizes* how many people are coming this evening.

In these sentences, the two parts of the subject are joined by *neither—nor.* The verb is plural in the first sentence because it is closer to the plural subject *actors.* In the second sentence, the verb is singular because it is closer to *director,* which is singular.

Chapter 1: Subjects and Predicates
p. 4

Chapter 6: Conjunctions
p. 152

ESL: You may need to caution ESL students that native speakers do not always follow these rules on proper subject-verb and pronoun-antecedent agreement. Sentences with compound subjects joined by *either . . . or* and *neither . . . nor* and sentences with indefinite pronouns are common areas of error for native English speakers.

Agreement   213

Teaching Strategy: Participation

Allow the students to demonstrate their understanding by using *or, nor, either . . . or,* and *neither . . . nor* with compound subjects. Read the following sentence aloud: *Neither the policeman nor the witnesses know who broke into the building.* Choose one student to be the policeman (one subject) and two students to be the witnesses (additional subjects). Then choose one student to be the verb. Place the students in a row with the witnesses closer to the verb. Say aloud with the students, "Neither the policeman nor the witnesses know who broke into the building." Now switch the policeman and the witnesses and replace the verb. Say aloud with the students, "Neither the witnesses nor the policeman knows who broke into the building." You may want to use other sentences with other conjunctions to involve more students.

One on One
To adapt the preceding activity, write the subjects and the two forms of the verb on strips of paper. Move the subjects to demonstrate how the verb changes depending on the number of the subject closer to it.

in summary

When compound subjects are joined by *and* or *both—and*, the verb is plural.

When compound subjects are joined by *or, nor, either—or,* or *neither—nor*, the verb agrees with the subject closer to the verb.

9-5 PRACTICE THE SKILL

Underline the simple subject(s) in each sentence. Then underline the correct verb from the choices in parentheses.

1. Isabel and Owen *(wants, want)* to hear some unusual instruments in the recital at the arts festival.

2. Either Lola or Roger *(plays, play)* the lute, I believe.

3. Pedro or Khan *(likes, like)* the vibraphone.

4. Neither the school nor the church *(has, have)* a gong.

5. Both Roger's uncle and his aunt *(enjoys, enjoy)* the glockenspiel.

6. Either a sitar or a celesta *(is, are)* going to be displayed in the music room at school.

7. Olly's mother and her sisters *(comes, come)* from Scotland and *(plays, play)* the bagpipes.

8. Neither Roberto nor his parents *(has, have)* a flageolet.

9. Well, the choir and the instrumental ensemble *(creates, create)* unusual sounds.

10. The festival and the recital *(is, are)* certainly unique.

9-6 REVIEW THE SKILL

Underline the simple subject(s) in each sentence. Then underline the correct verb from the choices in parentheses.

1. The Louvre and the Metropolitan Museum of Art *(is, are)* famous art museums.

2. Both famous paintings and various sculptures *(is, are)* found in many art museums.

3. Often, libraries and churches *(has, have)* beautiful art.

4. Either Lesli or Kayla *(is, are)* going with me to Williamsburg.

5. Both Williamsburg in Virginia and Old Sturbridge Village in Massachusetts *(is, are)* living history museums.

6. Neither Jason nor Thomas *(is, are)* able to go to Williamsburg.

7. Neither my uncles nor my father *(is, are)* interested in museums.

8. Both my mother and my aunt *(enjoys, enjoy)* the museums in town.

9. New York and Washington, D.C., *(has, have)* wonderful museums.

10. Either a corporation or the government *(sponsors, sponsor)* many museums.

Finding the Subject

Intervening Phrases

The verb does not always appear directly after the subject in a sentence. Often **intervening phrases** appear between the subject and verb, and these phrases can be distracting. Always locate the true subject and check that the verb agrees with it.

One common interrupter is the **negative phrase.** Be sure that the verb agrees with the true subject, not a word in the negative phrase.

> His *speeches and lectures,* but not his book, *are* still studied today.
> *Jared,* but not his brothers and sisters, *is* going to visit his grandparents.

In the first example, the negative phrase is singular, but the subject is plural and takes a plural verb. In the next example, the negative phrase is plural, but the subject is singular and takes a singular verb. When determining whether to choose a singular or plural verb, ignore the intervening negative phrase.

Another common interrupter is the **prepositional phrase.** Like the negative phrase, an intervening prepositional phrase does not affect the agreement of the subject and verb. The true subject of the sentence can never be the object of the preposition. The verb must agree in number with the subject, not the object of the preposition.

> An *anthology* of works by those authors *is* a good place to start.
> The *benefits* of regular exercise *are* increased energy and better health.
> The *fence* around the flower gardens *needs* to be repaired.

In the first example, the subject *anthology* is singular and takes the singular verb *is*. The word *authors* cannot be the subject because it is the object of the preposition *by.* Ignore the intervening prepositional phrase when determining agreement of subject and verb.

Agreement 215

Enrichment

Direct a contest using a detective theme. Divide the class into groups and ask them to investigate each sentence, finding the true subject and identifying the correct verb. Create your own story or use the story found in the Concept Reinforcement on pages 116-17 of Book 2.

Predicate Nouns of a Different Number

In sentences containing a linking verb, the subject and the predicate noun might not have the same number. If the predicate noun does not have the same number as the subject, the verb must agree with the subject and not the predicate noun.

> S LV   PN
> The *prize is* two plane tickets to Hawaii.

> S   LV   PN
> The *books are* a favorite family collection.

> S   LV   PN
> The *problem* in the parking lot *is* several large trucks blocking the entrance.

In each example, the predicate noun and the subject differ in number. The verb, however, agrees with the subject, not with the predicate noun.

Inverted Order

Although the verb usually follows the subject, that order is sometimes reversed, or inverted. In many inverted sentences, the word *there* or *here* introduces the sentence and comes before the verb. Be sure that the verb agrees with the delayed subject, not with the word *there* or *here.*

>   LV   S
> **SINGULAR**   There *is something* heavy in this box.

>   LV   S
>   Here *is* a *list* of items needed from the grocery store.

>   LV   S
> **PLURAL**   There *are stacks* of old books in the attic.

>   LV   S
>   Here *are* the *coupons* that you will need.

Notice in the examples that the words *there* or *here* do not affect the number of the verb. In each example, the verb agrees with the subject, which follows the verb.

The subject appears after the verb in some other declarative sentences and many interrogative sentences. In some interrogative sentences, the subject comes between the first auxiliary and the main verb.

>   LV   S
> **SINGULAR**   Inside the buckets *is* enough *paint* for the room.

>   LV   S
>   Where *is* the *meeting?*

>   Aux S   InV
>   *Are you coming* to the meeting?

>   LV   S
> **PLURAL**   With the paint *are* several *brushes.*

>   LV   S
>   Where *are* the other *brushes?*

>   Aux S   InV
>   *Will I be going* with you to the meeting?

Always find the true subject of the sentence so that you can make the subject and verb agree.

Chapter 4: Linking Verbs
p. 84

Chapter 1: Position of Subjects and Predicates in Inverted Order
p. 5

in summary

A verb agrees with the subject, not an intervening phrase.

A verb agrees with the subject, not the predicate noun.

There and *here* usually introduce a sentence in which the subject follows the verb.

Inverted sentence order does not affect subject-verb agreement.

9-7 PRACTICE THE SKILL

Underline the simple subject in each sentence. Then underline the correct verb from the choices in parentheses.

1. What *(is, are)* the five basic elements of music?

2. At the beginning of the list of elements *(is, are)* tone.

3. The list of elements *(is, are)* tone, rhythm, melody, harmony, and pitch.

4. Tone, not rhythm, *(is, are)* any musical sound of definite pitch.

5. A scale *(consists, consist)* of arranged tones.

6. There *(is, are)* eight notes in a scale.

7. The distance between a note and the next note of the same name *(is, are)* an octave.

8. The rhythm of pieces of music *(is, are)* the way a composer arranges notes in time.

9. The combination of pitches and rhythms *(creates, create)* melody.

10. Tone colors *(refers, refer)* to the quality of musical sounds.

9-8 REVIEW THE SKILL

Underline the simple subject in each sentence. Then underline the correct verb from the choices in parentheses.

1. What *(was, were)* the various keyboard instruments before the piano?

2. The dulcimer and the harpsichord *(is, are)* forerunners of the piano.

3. A piano, unlike many instruments, *(produces, produce)* a large range of musical sounds.

4. A pianist, not a trumpeter, usually *(plays, play)* melody and harmony at the same time.

5. On a piano *(is, are)* eighty-eight <u>keys</u>.

6. One important piano <u>part</u> *(is, are)* the pedals.

7. The <u>length</u> of the piano's strings *(<u>determines</u>, determine)* the pitch of a tone.

8. A particular <u>type</u> of piano *(is, are)* the grand piano.

9. Grand <u>pianos</u>, but not an upright piano, *(has, have)* strings parallel to the floor.

10. On Saturday *(is, are)* my piano <u>recital</u>.

Chapter 3: Indefinite Pronouns
p. 66

Indefinite Pronouns as Subjects

Indefinite pronouns can produce difficulties for subject-verb agreement. Most indefinite pronouns are singular; some are plural; and some can be either singular or plural, depending upon the meaning of the sentence.

SINGULAR *One* of the building project phases *begins* next week.
PLURAL *Many have helped* with this project.

ALWAYS SINGULAR				
another	each	everything	neither	one
anybody	either	less	nobody	somebody
anyone	everybody	little	no one	someone
anything	everyone	much	nothing	something

ALWAYS PLURAL				
both	few	fewer	many	several

SINGULAR OR PLURAL		
all	any	more
most	none	some

If an indefinite pronoun can be either singular or plural, determine its number by its meaning in the sentence. Often a prepositional phrase will give a clue to the indefinite pronoun's meaning and number.

SINGULAR *Most* of the report *focuses* on the advantages of parental involvement in school.

PLURAL *Most* of the students *agree* that parents should be significantly involved in their child's education.

In the first sentence, the prepositional phrase *of the report* indicates that the indefinite pronoun *most* refers to a part of the report, which is singular. In the second sentence, the word *students* in the prepositional phrase indicates that *most* is plural, referring to a number of students.

Evaluation

Students must know which indefinite pronouns are singular, which are plural, and which can be both. Give the students a quiz asking them to identify the indefinite pronouns as "singular," "plural," or "both." You may also play a game of fast answers, asking them to quickly identify the number of each indefinite pronoun you say aloud.

Enrichment

Use Teaching Help 9 (Book 2, p. 49) for more practice with indefinite pronouns as subjects.

in summary

Some **indefinite pronouns** are singular, some are plural, and some can be either singular or plural.

A verb must agree in number with an indefinite pronoun used as its subject.

Underline the simple subject in each sentence. Then underline the correct verb from the choices in parentheses.

1. Many of us *(enjoys, enjoy)* music.

2. Most of the musical instruments *(makes, make)* characteristic sounds.

3. Anyone in an orchestra *(recognizes, recognize)* a drum.

4. Everyone in my music class *(has, have)* tried to play the drum.

5. Every year each of the students *(makes, make)* his own musical instrument.

6. Nobody in any of the classes *(is, are)* making a wind instrument.

7. Someone *(was, were)* making a harp.

8. Several of my classmates *(plays, play)* wind instruments.

9. One *(works, work)* in a music store.

10. No one in my class *(is, are)* a member of the orchestra.

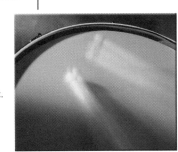

Underline the simple subject in each sentence. Then underline the correct verb from the choices in parentheses.

1. Everybody *(knows, know)* something about musical instruments.

2. *(Does, Do)* anybody play an instrument?

3. Most of the musical instruments *(has, have)* a string, a reed, or another device that creates sound waves.

4. Some of the stringed instruments *(is, are)* plucked.

5. One of that type *(is, are)* the mandolin.

6. Except for the saxophone, all of the wind instruments *(was, were)* once made of wood.

7. Today, a <u>few</u> *(is, are)* made of metal or other materials.

8. <u>Each</u> of the percussion instruments *(is, are)* struck or shaken.

9. <u>Neither</u> of the percussion players *(comes, come)* to every rehearsal.

10. <u>Nothing</u> *(sounds, sound)* as great as a well-written piece of music!

Problem Nouns as Subjects

Nouns of Plural Form

Certain nouns have only one form, a form that appears to be plural. Many of these words are used in only one way, either as singular or as plural nouns.

> **SINGULAR**   *Checkers is* a game of mental skill.
> **PLURAL**   My gym *clothes are* dirty.

Below are some common plural-form nouns. Some require a singular verb; some require a plural verb. (Check other words in your dictionary.)

SINGULAR	PLURAL
billiards	clothes
checkers	eyeglasses
measles	goggles
molasses	pants
news	riches
Niagara Falls	scissors
United States	tweezers

The plural-sounding names of teams and organizations, such as the Cubs and the Girl Scouts, usually require a plural verb.

> The Chicago Cubs *are* my favorite baseball team.
> The Girl Scouts *train* girls to be good citizens.

Many plural-form nouns end in *ics,* such as *athletics, ceramics, electronics, ethics,* and *mathematics.* Many of these words can be used as singular or plural, depending on the meaning of the sentence.

> **SINGULAR**   *Ethics is* the study of moral philosophy.
> **PLURAL**   That man's business *ethics are* honest and benevolent.

The context of the first sentence indicates that *ethics* is a singular field of study and takes a singular verb. In the second sentence, *ethics* stands for a man's various business principles and takes a plural verb.

Reinforcement

Students need to be familiar with these problem nouns and to be able to identify them accurately as singular or plural. If a student has trouble with a particular word, encourage him to add that word to his list of troublesome words in his spelling notebook. The student should review these words daily or weekly until he has mastered them.

Collective Nouns

Collective nouns are nouns that refer to groups. These nouns, such as *team* or *committee,* usually take singular verbs.

> The team *is* hoping to win this season's championship game.
> The committee *needs* more time to plan the awards banquet.

A collective noun can take a plural verb, however, when the sentence focuses specifically on the individual members of the group.

> The team *are* getting their speeches ready for the awards banquet.
> The crowd *are* fighting among themselves for seats.

In the first sentence, the phrase *their speeches* indicates that the sentence is focusing on each team member's speech. The second sentence focuses on the individual members of the crowd: they are fighting *among themselves.*

in summary

Certain nouns have only one form, a form that appears to be plural. Many of these nouns are only singular or plural.

Collective nouns refer to groups. A singular collective noun usually takes a singular verb; however, it can take a plural verb if the sentence focuses on the individual members.

9-11 PRACTICE THE SKILL

Underline the simple subject in each sentence. Then underline the correct verb from the choices in parentheses.

1. The <u>orchestra</u> *(is, <u>are</u>)* going to different places for their vacations.

2. A large <u>group</u> *(<u>is</u>, are)* taking advanced professional training during that time.

3. <u>Acoustics</u> *(is, <u>are</u>)* a good study for them.

4. The <u>United States</u> *(<u>is</u>, are)* a popular destination for many musicians from other countries.

5. The <u>National Endowment for the Arts</u> *(<u>distributes</u>, distribute)* funds to the orchestra for their needs.

6. The leadership <u>committee</u> *(<u>meets</u>, meet)* during vacation to see what changes need to be made.

7. The orchestra's <u>clothes</u> *(is, <u>are</u>)* changing in design.

8. The <u>team</u> *(<u>has</u>, have)* conflicting opinions regarding the change.

Agreement   221

9. The <u>news</u> of the orchestra's schedule for the new season *(causes,* <u>*cause)*</u> excitement every year.

10. The orchestra's <u>performances</u> *(has,* <u>*have)*</u> drawn worldwide attention.

Underline the simple subject in each sentence. Then underline the correct verb from the choices in parentheses.

1. <u>Ceramics</u> <u>*(is,*</u> *are)* an art form that my cousin enjoys.

2. <u>Plastics</u> <u>*(is,*</u> *are)* a class that Jerome has already taken.

3. His <u>trousers</u> always *(becomes,* <u>*become)*</u> dirty after a ceramics class.

4. His <u>class</u> <u>*(is,*</u> *are)* preparing works for several different art shows.

5. <u>Measles</u> <u>*(was,*</u> *were)* the reason that Jerome didn't go to the last art show.

6. The <u>news</u> often <u>*(gives,*</u> *give)* Jerome information on art shows.

7. At the art shows, a <u>crowd</u> often <u>*(gathers,*</u> *gather)* around Jerome's ceramics display.

8. The art <u>committee</u> <u>*(interviews,*</u> *interview)* people to see whether they like the art.

9. The <u>group</u> then <u>*(decides,*</u> *decide)* whose art is to be placed in the local museum.

10. The <u>politics</u> of the decisions *(is,* <u>*are)*</u> often difficult to understand.

Titles, Quotations, and Amounts

A **title** is always singular. Words in the title may be plural, but the title refers to only one work.

> *Little Women is* a classic story of four sisters growing up during the Civil War era.

> "Wynken, Blynken, and Nod" *is* a favorite children's poem by Eugene Field.

> *Riders to the Sea,* by J. M. Synge, *is* considered the first great modern tragedy.

Each of these titles contains key plural or compound words, but each title refers to a singular work.

Like titles, a **quoted word or phrase** may contain plural words, but it is a single item and takes a singular verb.

> *Aesthetics is* a difficult word to spell.
> "The lights along the waters" *is* the opening phrase of the second act.

In the first example, *aesthetics* is a singular item. In the second example, the quoted phrase is treated as singular.

An **amount** is also treated as a singular item, although the items that make up the amount may be plural. Singular amounts include measured amounts, amounts of money, and periods of time.

> Two cups of chocolate chips *is* needed for the cookies.
> Thirty dollars and seventy-five cents *was* the price of the shoes.
> Two dollars *is* the cost of each ticket.
> Three months *seems* a long time to me.

Each of the amounts contains plural words and items, but each is treated as one singular amount.

in summary

A **title** is always singular.

A **quoted word or phrase** takes a singular verb.

An **amount** is also a singular item. Singular amounts include measured amounts, amounts of money, and periods of time.

9-13 PRACTICE THE SKILL

Underline the correct verb from the choices in parentheses.

1. "No furniture is so charming as books" *(is, are)* an interesting notation by Sydney Smith, implying that printing is an art.

2. Two thousand feet of paper *(is, are)* printed in one minute by some web presses.

3. The *New York Times (is, are)* an example of an everyday item from a printing press.

4. Four plates *(is, are)* needed to make a color printing.

5. The word *copies (was, were)* probably frightening to an early scribe because he copied everything by hand.

6. "Words are loaded pistols" *(is, are)* a quotation from Jean Paul Sartre.

7. *The Times* of London *(was, were)* the first newspaper to use a steam-powered press.

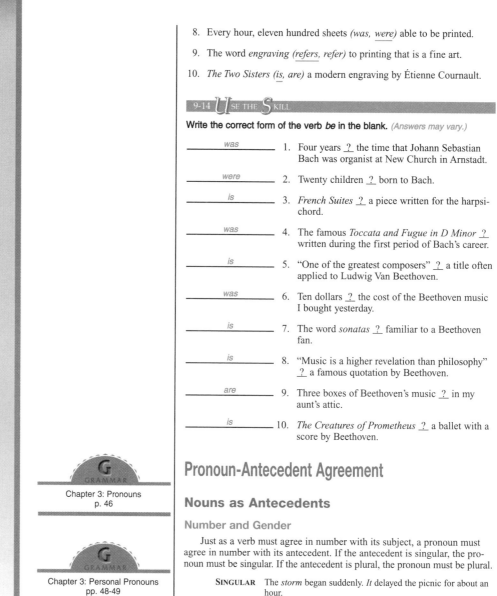

8. Every hour, eleven hundred sheets *(was, were)* able to be printed.

9. The word *engraving (refers, refer)* to printing that is a fine art.

10. *The Two Sisters (is, are)* a modern engraving by Étienne Cournault.

9-14 USE THE SKILL

Write the correct form of the verb *be* in the blank. *(Answers may vary.)*

was	1. Four years *?* the time that Johann Sebastian Bach was organist at New Church in Arnstadt.
were	2. Twenty children *?* born to Bach.
is	3. *French Suites ?* a piece written for the harpsichord.
was	4. The famous *Toccata and Fugue in D Minor ?* written during the first period of Bach's career.
is	5. "One of the greatest composers" *?* a title often applied to Ludwig Van Beethoven.
was	6. Ten dollars *?* the cost of the Beethoven music I bought yesterday.
is	7. The word *sonatas ?* familiar to a Beethoven fan.
is	8. "Music is a higher revelation than philosophy" *?* a famous quotation by Beethoven.
are	9. Three boxes of Beethoven's music *?* in my aunt's attic.
is	10. *The Creatures of Prometheus ?* a ballet with a score by Beethoven.

Pronoun-Antecedent Agreement

Nouns as Antecedents

Number and Gender

Just as a verb must agree in number with its subject, a pronoun must agree in number with its antecedent. If the antecedent is singular, the pronoun must be singular. If the antecedent is plural, the pronoun must be plural.

SINGULAR   The *storm* began suddenly. *It* delayed the picnic for about an hour.

PLURAL   The *children* enjoyed playing in the rain. *They* were not reluctant to get wet.

Chapter 3: Pronouns
p. 46

Chapter 3: Personal Pronouns
pp. 48-49

Teaching Strategy: Induction

Ask the students to identify the four characteristics of pronouns. *(number, gender, case, and person)* For display, write the following sentences that illustrate pronoun-antecedent agreement:

* The police officers used their logic and intuition to track down several suspects.

* Each of the four suspects had his alibi ready.

* Investigator Young knew that he would need more evidence.

* Neither the police officers nor the investigator could rest until he had the case solved.

Ask the students to identify which characteristics of a pronoun need to be considered in pronoun-antecedent agreement. *(gender and number)* Ask them to use the sentences written for display to point out potential problems with agreement.

Unlike verbs, pronouns often show gender as well as number. A pronoun can be masculine, feminine, or neuter. A pronoun must agree with the gender of its antecedent.

MASCULINE *Thomas Gage,* a British general, became governor of Massachusetts in 1774. *His* restrictions on the American colonists were largely responsible for the start of the opening battle of the Revolutionary War.

FEMININE *Florence Kelly* was an American social reformer. *She* fought for the abolition of child labor.

NEUTER The new *bookshelf* is much taller and wider. *It* will have enough room to hold all of my books.

If an antecedent referring to a person does not specify a gender, use a singular masculine pronoun.

Please share with *anyone* who has forgotten *his* book.

Use a neuter pronoun when referring to animals unless the context of the sentence implies that the animal is masculine or feminine.

NEUTER The *kangaroo* maintains balance with *its* large tail.

FEMININE The *mother kangaroo* keeps *her* newborn safely in *her* pouch.

The hopping marsupial in the first sentence could be either male or female. In the second sentence, however, the "mother kangaroo" is clearly a female. Always consider the meaning of your sentence when choosing a pronoun to replace an antecedent.

in summary

A pronoun must agree with its antecedent in number and gender.

9-15 PRACTICE THE SKILL

Write an appropriate personal pronoun in the blank.

_____*he*_____ 1. Miss Landry told us that German artist Albrecht Dürer's engravings demonstrate that _?_ was interested in Christian themes.

_____*her*_____ 2. At which gallery in New York did Wanda Gág, an illustrator of children's books, first display _?_ woodcuts and lithographs?

_____*she*_____ 3. Early in her life, Gág drew for a newspaper so that _?_ could support her family.

_____*it*_____ 4. Engravers cut into a flat metal plate and then use _?_ to print the design.

Agreement   225

his   5. An artist's slow movements dictate how good ? cutting will be.

them   6. Ink, paper, and a press are vital tools for the artist because he uses ? to pull the impression.

she   7. My aunt who is an engraver started taking art classes when ? was a small child.

him   8. My father enjoys my aunt's art; in fact, she gave ? one of her best pieces.

they   9. Aunt Sheila gave Grandma two of her engravings; ? will hang in Grandma's living room.

her   10. One particular engraving showed a lioness and ? cubs.

9-16 REVIEW THE SKILL

Write an appropriate personal pronoun in the blank.

_It_   1. Landscape architecture involves designing land. ? can affect human enjoyment of land.

their   2. Early Romans had elaborate courtyards with ? homes.

its   3. In the 1600s and 1700s, France was famous for ? city gardens.

they   4. Frederick Law Olmsted and Calvert Vaux were landscape architects; ? designed New York City's Central Park.

him   5. Olmsted was head of the design of the park; his success earned ? the opportunity to design a number of other famous parks.

_he_   6. Later, as head of the Yosemite commission, ? had success in helping to preserve that area.

His   7. ? followers formed the American Society of Landscape Architects.

She   8. My cousin Sarah is a landscape architecture major. ? really enjoys her classes.

her   9. Sarah helped design and plant the gardens outside ? apartment building.

them   10. Butchart Gardens in British Columbia and the International Peace Garden on the border of North Dakota and Manitoba are famous. My family visited ? last year.

Compound Antecedents

If the antecedent of a pronoun is compound, look at the conjunction joining the parts of the antecedent. If the nouns are joined by *and* or *both—and,* the pronoun must be plural. If the nouns are joined by *or, nor, either—or,* or *neither—nor,* the number of the pronoun is determined by the noun closer to it.

Chapter 6: Conjunctions
p. 153

PLURAL   *Damon and Curtis* will give *their* reports on the same day.

SINGULAR   *Either the boys or Mr. Wetterlund* will bring *his* slide projector for the presentation.

PLURAL   *Neither Justin nor the girls* were planning to give *their* presentations on Friday.

In the first example, the compound subject is joined by the conjunction *and,* which requires a plural pronoun. In the second example, the compound subject is joined by *either—or.* The pronoun is singular because it is closer to *Mr. Wetterlund,* which is singular. Likewise, the pronoun in the third example is plural since it is closer to *the girls.*

in summary

Use the conjunction with compound antecedents to determine the number of the pronoun. If the parts of the antecedent are joined by *and,* the pronoun must be plural. If the nouns are joined by *or* or *nor,* the number of the pronoun is determined by the noun closer to it.

9-17 PRACTICE THE SKILL

Underline the correct pronoun from the choices in parentheses.

1. Both ancient philosophers and modern writers have used drama to express *(his, their)* philosophical ideas.

2. Either a tragedy or a serious drama explores questions about the meaning of life in *(its, their)* theme.

3. Often a nobleman or an admirable person comes to disaster through *(his, their)* tragic flaw.

4. Usually neither the tragic hero nor his loved ones can escape *(his, their)* fate in the play.

5. In many tragedies, one or more characters are faced with dilemmas, and *(he, they)* must make difficult moral decisions.

Reinforcement

Remind the students that the rule for pronoun-antecedent agreement with a compound antecedent is similar to the corresponding rule for subject-verb agreement. The noun closest to the pronoun determines the number of the pronoun.

6. Either the hero of the play or several characters in the play usually experience disproportionate suffering for *(his, their)* sin or wrong decisions.

7. Both Aeschylus' *Orestia* and Sophocles' *Oedipus Rex* are considered great Greek tragedies because of *(its, their)* masterfully constructed plots and characters.

8. Neither modern writers nor the modern critic can define exactly what *(he, they)* will call true modern tragedy.

9. Some critics and literary authorities say that *(he, they)* would prefer modern tragedy to be called serious drama.

10. Whether you are reading ancient tragedies or modern serious drama, you should be able to determine how *(it, they)* might evoke pity and fear in the reader.

9-18 REVIEW THE SKILL

Underline the correct pronoun from the choices in parentheses.

1. Both the stage manager and the scenic designer consider the dramatic genre when drawing *(his, their)* floor plans for a play.

2. Either the open stage or the theater-in-the-round allows a closer interaction between *(it, them)* and the audience.

3. Either an individual or a group of individuals can raise the amount of money that *(he, they)* will need for a successful performance.

4. Many professional productions make extensive use of scenery changes and lighting because *(it, they)* can drastically alter the mood and atmosphere of a play.

5. Neither the lighting nor the scenery by *(itself, themselves)* guarantees the success of a play.

6. A designer and the set builders must work together so *(he, they)* can build the best possible scene.

7. Either the director or the performers might give the costume director *(his, their)* suggestions for the design of the costumes.

8. A makeup artist uses either makeup or plastic pieces to alter appearance by carefully applying *(it, them)* to a character's face.

9. Both community theaters and professional theaters pay *(its, their)* director and stage manager.

10. A high school or a college usually gets *(its, their)* director and cast from the faculty and student body.

Indefinite Pronouns as Antecedents

Number

The antecedent of a personal pronoun may be an indefinite pronoun instead of a noun. The pronoun must agree in number with the indefinite pronoun.

> **SINGULAR** *Each* will provide *his* own transportation.
> **PLURAL** *Many* still need to secure *their* visas.

> **SINGULAR** *One* of the pieces of luggage lost *its* identification tag.
> **PLURAL** *Several* of the tourists still need *their* luggage.

Some indefinite pronouns can be either singular or plural. Consider the meaning of the sentence to determine the number of an indefinite pronoun. If the indefinite pronoun refers to only one thing, the personal pronoun should be singular. If the indefinite pronoun refers to more than one thing, the personal pronoun should be plural. Often a prepositional phrase gives a clue to the number of the indefinite pronoun.

> **SINGULAR** *All* of the birthday cake had chocolate icing on *it*.
> **PLURAL** *All* of the girls took their umbrellas with *them*.

> **SINGULAR** *None* of the house has siding on *it*.
> **PLURAL** *None* of the teachers have *their* grades posted yet.

In the first two sentences, the word *all* is the indefinite pronoun. In the first sentence, *all* is singular because it refers to one thing, the birthday cake. In the second sentence, *all* is plural because it refers to more than one girl.

Gender

An indefinite pronoun does not show gender, but sometimes the context of the sentence may indicate a specific gender. If so, the pronoun should agree in gender with the meaning of the indefinite pronoun.

> **MASCULINE** *Each* of the boys volunteered *his* help for the building project.

> **FEMININE** *One* of the girls might be late; I will wait for *her*.

> **NEUTER** *Another* of the tiles has slipped out of *its* place in the bathroom.

If the indefinite pronoun is singular and clearly refers to people without indicating a specific gender, use a singular masculine pronoun. Do not use a plural personal pronoun to refer to a singular indefinite pronoun.

> **WRONG** *Everyone* in the class wanted *their* own copy of the book.
> **RIGHT** *Everyone* in the class wanted *his* own copy of the book.

G
GRAMMAR
Chapter 3: Indefinite Pronouns
p. 66

Reinforcement

The rule for indefinite pronouns as antecedents is also similar to the corresponding rule for subject-verb agreement. Unlike the subject-verb agreement rule, however, the pronoun sometimes shows gender if gender is indicated by the context of the sentence.

in summary

A personal pronoun must agree in number with the indefinite pronoun.

The personal pronoun should agree in gender with the indefinite pronoun if the context indicates the gender.

If the indefinite pronoun is singular and clearly refers to a person without indicating specific gender, use a singular masculine pronoun.

9-19 PRACTICE THE SKILL

In the blank write an appropriate possessive pronoun that agrees with its antecedent.

his	1. Each of the art students enjoyed working on _?_ drawing project.
his	2. Everyone in art class was given _?_ own subject.
their	3. Several of the girls drew _?_ pictures to use in a later painting.
her	4. One of the girls used chalk for _?_ drawing.
her	5. Another used pencil for _?_ entry.
his	6. Somebody in the class drew _?_ project in charcoal.
their	7. A few of the instructors drew _?_ own pictures.
their	8. Some used pen and ink for _?_ drawings.
its	9. Each of the drawings had _?_ own individuality.
their	10. Many of the drawing masters of the past were also famous for _?_ paintings.

9-20 REVIEW THE SKILL

If the italicized pronoun does not agree with its antecedent, write the correct pronoun in the blank. If the sentence does not contain an agreement error, write *C* in the blank.

_C_	1. Most of my classmates enjoyed *their* decoupage assignment.
his	2. However, not everybody enjoyed *their* task of cutting out paper to decorate items.
their	3. All of the girls disliked taking *her* time to cut out the intricate designs.
_C_	4. Neither of the boys enjoyed decorating *his* box.

	5.	However, both of them enjoyed sanding and staining *his* boxes.
their		

	6.	A few of the students put *his* effort into helping others with their boxes.
their		

	7.	Anybody can enjoy *their* finished product.
his		

	8.	No one is keeping *their* box. Each artist is giving the box as a present for Mother's Day.
his		

	9.	Several in the class are excited about *their* chance to make pottery.
_C_		

	10.	One of the instructors sells *his* pottery around the world.
_C_		

9-21 USE THE SKILL

Rewrite the paragraph, correcting the five errors in subject-verb agreement or pronoun-antecedent agreement.

Many kinds of poetry has developed over the years. One of the most common types are lyric poems. Many poems are written to commemorate important events. Often, these poems are an ode. Either an ode or an elegy can take their rightful place among lyric poems. Another of the types is narrative poetry. Many times, lyric poetry, dramatic poetry, and narrative poetry overlaps. During the romantic period, William Wordsworth and Samuel Taylor Coleridge wrote *Lyrical Ballads.* Each of these men had their own important place in the history of poetry. Many poets write poems that are skillful blendings of the different types of poetry.

Many kinds of poetry have developed over the years. One of the most

common types is lyric poems. Many poems are written to commemorate

important events. Often, these poems are an ode. Either an ode or an elegy

can take its rightful place among lyric poems. Another of the types is narra-

tive poetry. Many times, lyric poetry, dramatic poetry, and narrative

poetry overlap. During the romantic period, William Wordsworth and Samuel

Taylor Coleridge wrote Lyrical Ballads. Each of these men had his own

important place in the history of poetry. Many poets write poems that are

skillful blendings of the different types of poetry.

Objectives
Students will

1. choose a favorite piece of literature.

2. write a paragraph that relates that piece of literature to their own experiences.

Overview of the Writing Process

Planning—choosing a piece of literature and formulating a response based on personal experience

Drafting—writing a paragraph of response to the piece of literature

Revising—evaluating with a partner and making changes for clarity

Publishing—reading to the class and handing in to the teacher

Writing a Personal Response to Literature

Lesson Support

Teacher's Edition, Book 2
Writing Worksheets—p. 142
Rubrics—p. 156

Introduction

Materials
• literature anthologies (optional)

Read one of your favorite poems or short stories to the students, explaining briefly that work's significance to you.

Ask students to list the poems or stories that they have enjoyed reading. If time allows, let them browse through some literature anthologies for ideas. As they work, write these questions for display: *In what way could you relate to the feelings of the narrator or of a character in this piece?*

What experiences in your own life made that story or poem come alive for you?

Writing a Personal Response to Literature

"Hey, Miin, do you think we'll have a quiz over that reading we had for English?" asked Joel. Miin's seat jolted as Joel plopped down in the desk behind her. He flung open his book and riffled through the pages. "What was it about?"

Miin smiled and looked over her shoulder at him. "You mean you didn't read it? It was really good."

"I read it really fast." He stopped and gazed at a page. "'The Foundling'—it was about a foundling."

"Right. Did you like it?"

"It was okay." He pushed his book away, folded his arms behind his head, and leaned back in his chair. "What did you think was so great about it?"

Miin glanced away and said, "I don't know. I guess I understood how Willy felt."

"So you're a foundling? You never told me."

She laughed and pulled her long braid over her shoulder. "No, it's just that I stayed with my aunt one summer and she threw out my sketches because she thought they were scrap paper."

"So what does that have to do with the story?"

She cocked her head at him. "Maybe you should read it."

Discussion

Direct the students to read the introduction and the text material about writing a personal response to literature. Direct a discussion about the example, pointing out how the writer's thesis, the opening sentence, is supported by a specific incident from her personal life. Point out that the concluding sentence reinforces the writer's ideas.

Also refer students to the subsection in Chapter 15 about writing paragraphs (pp. 367-73). Answer any questions they may have after reading this material.

Planning

Direct the students to read the instructions in "Your Turn."

Allow time for the students to choose one of the literature pieces from their lists and to write out answers to the two questions that you have written for display. Encourage them to be as specific as possible in their responses to the questions, using concrete details rather than general, abstract expressions such as "I liked it" or "I felt bad for the character."

Drafting

Allow time for students to write their paragraphs in class.

Revising

Distribute a copy of the Writing Worksheet (Book 2, p. 142) to each student. After students have composed their paragraphs, direct each student to exchange paragraphs with a partner and to fill out the evaluation, returning it to the writer when finished.

Instruct the students to read over their paragraphs and the suggestions from their partners and to make any changes for clarity or concreteness.

Every person has a unique set of experiences. Whenever we read stories, we think about those stories in light of our own personal experiences, looking for ways we can relate to the characters. In the excerpt from *The Foundling*, Willy reacts with violent indignation when the maids burn his clothes, the only items of value he can call his own. When Miin read this excerpt, she remembered her own childhood experience of losing something she treasured because an adult underestimated its value. We remember better those stories and poems that call to mind emotions we have felt.

When Miin and Joel's teacher asked them to write a personal response to the excerpt from *The Foundling*, Miin wrote:

> I really could understand Willy's unhappiness at having his clothes tossed in the fire. They might have been dirty, but they were his. When I was eleven, I spent part of the summer at my aunt's house. I would sit outside for hours and draw. One day my aunt found some of my sketches on the desk when she was cleaning and threw them out, thinking they were scrap paper. I cried, and my aunt felt really bad, but she had already burned the trash. When I read *The Foundling*, I felt the same way I had that day.

Your Turn

Choose a piece of literature that you really like and ask yourself what makes you like it. Then write a paragraph explaining how some experience of yours makes the story or poem more real to you.

Publishing

Ask volunteers to read their paragraphs aloud.

Scriptural Application

Read Hebrews 4:12. Remind the students that, above all other books, God's Word has the power to reach the hidden thoughts and motives of our hearts. Encourage the students to read God's Word daily, maintaining a teachable spirit and relying on the Holy Spirit's help to respond obediently to God's teaching.

Evaluation

For help in grading this assignment, see "Grading Writing Assignments" (p. x) and Rubric 9 (Book 2, p. 156).

Enrichment

Explain to the students that sometimes an author's response to a piece of literature becomes literature itself. Share examples of such works with the students. For some examples, see John Keats's "On Sitting Down to Read *King Lear* Again" or Sir Walter Raleigh's "The Nymph's Reply to the Shepherd" and William Carlos Williams's "Raleigh Was Right"; these works can be found in many literary anthologies.

10 SPELLING AND TROUBLESOME WORDS

Objectives

Students will

1. spell singular present tense verbs and plural nouns correctly.

2. spell words containing *ie* or *ei* correctly.

3. spell words containing suffixes correctly.

4. identify misspelled words in a sentence.

5. choose correctly between *lie/lay, rise/raise, sit/set, may/can,* and *shall/will* in sentences.

6. write sentences using troublesome words correctly.

7. write sentences using homonyms correctly.

8. write sentences using possessive pronouns and contractions correctly.

9. evaluate and revise a paragraph for errors.

Lesson Support

Student Text
Chapter 10 Review—pp. 423-24

Teacher's Edition, Book 1
Bulletin Boards—p. 449

Teacher's Edition, Book 2
Pretests—pp. 25-27

Teaching Helps—pp. 50-51

Concept Reinforcements—pp. 121-23

ESL: ESL students' problems with spelling often arise from the students' transferring of spelling procedures in their native languages to English or from a misunderstanding of English rules. When correcting spelling problems, try to point the students to an English spelling rule and then encourage them to memorize and review it.

When something looks very much like its surroundings, we say it is camouflaged. Can you see what is camouflaged in this picture? (Hint: He might have escaped from a zoo.)

Sometimes misspelled words can blend in with their surroundings too. In this chapter, you'll find some tips for "spotting" spelling errors in your writing.

Spelling

Good spelling is an essential writing skill. Whether you are writing a research paper or a personal letter, your message is communicated most clearly by using the right words and spelling them correctly. Use these spelling hints and master these rules so that you will be a better writer.

Spelling Hints

Spell by syllables.

Dividing a word into its individual syllables will help you to spell it correctly. Think about prefixes, suffixes, and other word parts as you are spelling words by syllables.

personal + ly	personally
green + ness	greenness
mis + spell	misspell

Use a dictionary.

Look up the spelling of words when you are unsure of the correct spelling. Keep a good dictionary available at all times when you are writing. Although you might be unsure of a word's exact spelling, you probably know enough of the word to find it in the dictionary.

Chapter 13: Dictionaries (Library Skills)
pp. 332-33

Keep a list of words that are problems for you.

Whenever you misspell a word and locate the correct spelling of a word, put it on your list of problem words. Study your list systematically. Begin by writing a word several times, concentrating on its appearance and pronunciation. Repeat this procedure three or four different days of the next week. Then have someone quiz you on that word. If you can write the word correctly without hesitation, transfer it to your "learned" list. If a problem remains, keep working on the word.

Look for possible groupings among your problem words.

If you find a group of similar words, try to formulate or find a rule for that group. For example, you may find that several of your

Teaching Strategy: Introduction

Materials
- a typed business letter with spelling errors

Pass out a copy of a typed, formal business letter containing many spelling errors. Ask the students to read the letter as if it were addressed to them and to give their responses to the writer of the letter. Discuss the responses. Elicit the following points from the students:

- The letter appears hastily written.
- This haste communicates that the writer did not care much about what he was doing.
- Poor spelling takes away from the quality of the work and makes the reader question the intelligence of the writer and the significance of his message.

problem words contain *ie* and *ei*. Learning the rules for *ie* and *ei* will allow you to spell an entire group of words correctly.

An important step to becoming a good speller is mastering the following basic spelling rules.

Rules for Spelling Singular Present-Tense Verbs and Plural Nouns

If the word ends in *ch, sh, s, x,* or *z,* add *es.*

church	churches
brush	brushes
glass	glasses
fox	foxes
buzz	buzzes

If the word ends in *y* preceded by a consonant, change the final *y* to *i* and add *es.*

strawberry	strawberries
city	cities
folly	follies

If the word ends in *y* preceded by a vowel, add *s.*

say	says
monkey	monkeys
play	plays

If the word ends in *f* or *fe,* consult your dictionary. For most, add *s;* for others, change the *f* to *v* and add *s* or *es.*

bailiff	bailiffs
safe	safes
leaf	leaves
life	lives

If the word ends in *o,* consult your dictionary. For most, add *es;* for others, add *s.*

do	does
tomato	tomatoes
piano	pianos
tuxedo	tuxedos

Musical terms are more likely to require *s* than *es.*

soprano	sopranos
trio	trios
solo	solos

Add *s* to most other words.

flower	flowers
income	incomes

Some nouns have irregular plural forms. Consult your dictionary for the spelling of nouns with irregular plurals.

sheep	sheep
alumnus	alumni
child	children

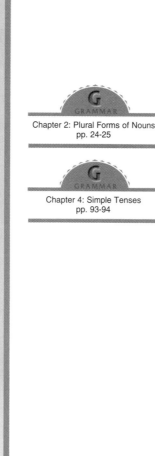

Chapter 2: Plural Forms of Nouns
pp. 24-25

Chapter 4: Simple Tenses
pp. 93-94

Teaching Strategy: Induction

Instruct students to list some singular nouns and then display the words they give you. If necessary, add a few words of your own that form unusual or troublesome plurals. *(birch, fly, donkey, 1920)* With the students' help, make each noun plural. Ask the students whether they notice any patterns. Then group the words into categories based on their ending patterns. Based on the patterns recognized in each group, ask the students to formulate rules for making singular nouns plural.

Plurals of Numbers

Use *s* alone for the plural of a number that is expressed in figures.

The **1700s** were the years of American freedom.
Among the scores on the tests were two **100s.**

Compounds

Attach *s* or *es* to the end of most compounds.

baseball	baseballs
cupful	cupfuls
baby-sit	baby-sits
brainwash	brainwashes

Pluralize the first element of certain compound nouns—those in which the first element is felt to be the most important part of the compound. When in doubt, consult your dictionary.

brother-in-law	brothers-in-law
master of ceremonies	masters of ceremonies

10-1 PRACTICE THE SKILL

In the blank write the correct plural form of each italicized word.

__bodies__ 1. A lizard's *body* can resemble a salamander's.

__areas__ 2. Lizards thrive when they have access to a warm *area.*

__leaves__ 3. You may find a chameleon in a tree under a *leaf.*

__feet__ 4. Chameleons have unusual toes so that the *foot* can grasp branches.

__geckos or geckoes__ 5. A *gecko* is a type of lizard.

__panes__ 6. A gecko can cling to a *pane* of glass.

__days__ 7. If a *day* becomes too hot, a lizard may find shelter.

__catches__ 8. A spiky moloch is not a good *catch* for a predator because of its spikes.

__species__ 9. An iguana is another *species* of lizard.

__women__ 10. Ugly lizards getting into houses have caused strife for many a *woman* or man.

Underline any misspelled word and write the correction in the blank. If the sentence is correct, write *C* in the blank.

_____ *C* _____ 1. Cattle, hogs, poultry, sheep, and horses are the main examples of livestock.

_____ *C* _____ 2. However, in some places, farmers raise buffaloes, deer, llamas, and yaks.

_____ *oxen* _____ 3. A team of <u>oxes</u> may be used for plowing.

_____ *autos* _____ 4. In some countries where <u>autoes</u> are scarce or roads are poor, people still use horses for transportation.

_____ *centuries* _____ 5. Throughout the <u>centurys</u>, farmers improved livestock by changing breeding procedures.

_____ *methods* _____ 6. Farmers have developed <u>methodes</u> to increase meat production.

_____ *C* _____ 7. Manufacturers use the hoofs of livestock to make various items.

_____ *Bacteria* _____ 8. <u>Bacteriums</u>, parasites, and viruses often cause diseases in livestock.

_____ *ranches* _____ 9. Most livestock is raised on farms and <u>ranchs</u>.

_____ *C* _____ 10. Many farmers store livestock feed in silos.

Rules for Spelling with *ie* and *ei*

When the sound is "long e," put *i* before *e* except after *c*.

i before e	**except after c**
niece	deceit
brief	misconceive
headpiece	deceive

Exceptions: *caffeine, leisure, either, neither, protein, seize, sheik, weird.*

When the sound is "long a," put *e* before *i*.

neighbor	weigh
reign	vein

When the two vowels are pronounced separately, spell according to the pronunciation of the first vowel.

quiet	variety
science	atheist

Exceptions: *alien, alienate.*

Complete the word correctly. Write either *ie* or *ei* in the blank.

1. ch__*ie*__f

2. retr__*ie*__ve

3. b__*ei*__ge

4. gr__*ie*__vous

5. v__*ei*__l

6. inconc__*ei*__vable

7. sh__*ie*__ld

8. ath__*ei*__st

9. heavyw__*ei*__ght

10. rec__*ei*__pt

In the blank write the letter that corresponds to the correctly spelled word.

1. __*B*__ A. fiegn
          B. feign

2. __*A*__ A. frontier
          B. fronteir

3. __*A*__ A. alien
          B. alein

4. __*A*__ A. premiere
          B. premeire

5. __*B*__ A. cieling
          B. ceiling

6. __*B*__ A. frieght
          B. freight

7. __*A*__ A. cashier
          B. casheir

8. __*A*__ A. patience
          B. pateince

9. __*A*__ A. priest
          B. preist

10. __*A*__ A. convenient
          B. conveneint

Reinforcement

Assign Teaching Help 10A (Book 2, p. 50)
as practice in spelling *ie* and *ei* words.

Underline the five misspelled words. Write the corrections in the blank.

Today's generation often cannot <u>conceive</u> of life in the 1800s. If people were able to be <u>passerbys</u> and see back in time, they would perceive great differences. The term *streetes* often referred to muddy <u>pathsway</u>. For a significant portion of the century, cars were nonexistent. By the end of the century, many new modes of transportation existed. Also, electricity was not discovered until the end of the century. Great <u>acheivements</u> have been made in technology.

conceive, passersby, streets, pathways, achievements

Rules for Adding Suffixes

Doubling a Final Consonant

If a one-syllable word ends with a single consonant preceded by a single vowel, double the final consonant before adding a suffix.

plan	planning
wrap	wrapper
fit	fitted

If a multisyllable word with its main accent on the final syllable ends with a single consonant preceded by a single vowel, double the final consonant before adding a suffix.

commit	committed
begin	beginning
occur	occurrence

If a word ends with a single consonant preceded by two vowels, do not double the final consonant before adding a suffix.

creep	creeping
shoot	shooting
fool	foolish

Changing the Final *y* to *i*

If a word ends with a consonant and *y,* change the final *y* to *i* before adding a suffix.

accompany	accompanied
bossy	bossiness
plenty	plentiful

However, if the suffix itself begins with *i,* do not change the final *y* to *i.*

accompany	accompanying
identify	identifying

Reinforcement

To help students practice adding suffixes, assign Teaching Help 10B (Book 2, p. 51).

Evaluation

To determine whether the students thoroughly understand the rules for spelling, display a list of incorrectly spelled words and ask the students to identify which rule each misspelled word violates. For example, write the word *jumpping* for display. The students should respond by explaining that when a suffix follows a word ending in a consonant, the final consonant should not be doubled.

Dropping the Final Silent *e*

Drop the final silent *e* that is preceded by a consonant before adding a suffix beginning with a vowel.

atone	atoning
move	movable
accommodate	accommodating

Exceptions: *noticeable, courageous.*

Keep the final silent *e* before adding a suffix beginning with a consonant.

absolute	absolutely
involve	involvement
hate	hateful

Exceptions: *truly, argument, judgment, acknowledgment.*

10-6 PRACTICE THE SKILL

Add the suffix to the word. Write the new word in the blank.

bitten	1.	bit + en
complying	2.	comply + ing
abhorred	3.	abhor + ed
fanciful	4.	fancy + ful
definable	5.	define + able
adventurous	6.	adventure + ous
conciseness	7.	concise + ness
meeting	8.	meet + ing
courageous	9.	courage + ous
alienation	10.	alienate + ion

10-7 REVIEW THE SKILL

In the blank write the letter that corresponds to the correctly spelled word.

1. __B__   A. skined
         B. skinned

2. __B__   A. rotteness
         B. rottenness

3. __A__   A. fortunate
         B. fortuneate

4. __B__   A. leviing
         B. levying

Enrichment

Materials

- list of words for a spelling bee

Announce an upcoming spelling bee and encourage the students to study in preparation for the event. Complete a list of words that conform to the spelling rules in this chapter. Students should stand in order and take turns spelling the given words. A student may ask questions about pronunciation, but once he begins spelling, he must finish. One misspelling disqualifies a participant, and he must return to his seat.

5. _A_ A. flooding
   B. floodding

6. _B_ A. identifyable
   B. identifiable

7. _A_ A. argument
   B. arguement

8. _B_ A. integratetion
   B. integration

9. _B_ A. forbiden
   B. forbidden

10. _B_ A. crazyness
    B. craziness

10-8 Use the Skill

Underline the ten misspelled words. Write the corrections in the blanks.

Lions are interesting animals. Most lions live in the African plaines. Also, many live in woodsland. Lions can wiegh up to five hundred pounds. Life within a lion's pride is peacful. Prides stay together like familys. However, lionesses will not always sheild their cubs; if she is hungry a lioness will leave the cubs helpless while she hunts. About half the cubs survive. A male lion has a mane, which can provide pading if he is attacked. People often percieve lions as attacking humans. However, that anxiety is often unfounded; lions rarely kill people. Lions will prey on a vareity of animals. A person's journies to Africa may enable him to spot a pride of lions.

plains, woodlands, weigh, peaceful, families, shield, padding,

perceive, variety, journeys

Troublesome Words

Troublesome Verbs

Lie/Lay

The verb *lie* means "to recline." When *lie* in any of its forms is used, the verb never has a direct object. It is intransitive and is used only in the S-InV sentence pattern. The principal parts are *lie, lay,* and *lain;* and the present participle is spelled *lying.*

GRAMMAR
Chapter 4: Transitive and Intransitive Verbs
p. 86

Teaching Strategy: Participation and Discussion

Display a list of the troublesome verbs. Then ask the students to choose three pairs and to write one sentence for each word in the three pairs. After the students are finished writing, read through the original list of words, allowing one student to read his sentence for each of the words from the list. The student should provide an informal definition of the word and explain why he used it in that particular sentence.

LIE	Opossums often **lie** down and pretend to be dead.
LYING	An opossum might be **lying** very still because of a nearby predator.
LAY	Just yesterday, an opossum **lay** down in the woods behind my house.
LAIN	He has **lain** there for several hours.

Chapter 4: Principal Parts of Verbs
pp. 88-91

The verb *lay* means "to put or place." *Lay* is a transitive verb and must have a direct object. The principal parts are *lay, laid,* and *laid;* and the present participle is spelled *laying.*

LAY	Every afternoon I **lay** the saddle on my pony.
LAYING	I am **laying** the saddle on her to help her get used to it.
LAID	Yesterday, when I **laid** it on her, she seemed more comfortable.
LAID	I had **laid** it on her several times before I took her for a ride.

The confusion between *lie* and *lay* is probably due to the fact that the past tense of *lie* sounds the same as the present tense of *lay.* Always think carefully about your meaning and the principal parts before choosing which verb to use.

Rise/Raise

Rise means "to go up." The verb *rise* is intransitive. The principal parts are *rise, rose,* and *risen;* and the present participle is spelled *rising.*

RISE	Many birds, including gulls, **rise** using currents of air.
RISING	A gull's narrow wings help it when it is **rising** into the air.
ROSE	Yesterday I watched a gull as it **rose** into the air.
RISEN	It had **risen** quickly before it flew away.

Raise means "to make something go up." It is a transitive verb needing a direct object. The principal parts are *raise, raised,* and *raised;* and the present participle is spelled *raising.*

RAISE	My aunt and uncle **raise** their American flag to show their patriotism.
RAISING	They have been **raising** their flag for the past twenty years.
RAISED	Last week they **raised** their flag for Memorial Day.
RAISED	They have **raised** their flag for other holidays as well.

As with *lie* and *lay,* be sure of your meaning and of the principal parts before you decide which form of *rise* or *raise* to use in speaking or writing.

Sit/Set

The verb *sit* means "to be in a seated position." *Sit* is an intransitive verb. The principal parts are *sit, sat,* and *sat;* and the present participle is spelled *sitting.*

SIT	I often **sit** with my cat and listen to music.
SITTING	My cat, Ollie, is **sitting** on my bed right now.
SAT	Yesterday he actually **sat** and listened to me playing the piano!
SAT	He has also **sat** down and listened to a recording.

The verb *set* means "to put or place." It is transitive and requires a direct object. The principal parts are *set, set,* and *set;* and the present participle is spelled *setting.*

SET	We often **set** traps for mice in our farmhouse.
SETTING	My dad is **setting** five traps right now.
SET	Yesterday he **set** three traps and caught three mice!
SET	He has **set** so many traps that I have lost count!

May/Can

The auxiliaries *may* and *can* are often used interchangeably to express uncertainty. *May* also means "to be allowed or permitted to," and *can* also means "to have the capacity to do something."

MAY	You **may** get closer to look at the elephant.
CAN	The height of an Asian elephant **can** be ten and one-half feet.

Shall/Will

Shall and *will* are two more auxiliary verbs that sometimes cause trouble. In older styles of English, *shall* and *will* often had different meanings. Today *will* is the normal sign of the future. *Shall* has two main uses, both with the first person pronouns *I* and *we* in a question of preference or in a formal statement.

SHALL	**Shall** we get in the car now? I **shall** try to assist you in any way possible.
WILL	**Will** we be going to the zoo, Mother? Yes, but we **will** eat first.

10-9 PRACTICE THE SKILL

Underline the correct verb from the choices in parentheses.

1. *(Shall, Will)* I tell you more about poisonous and nonpoisonous snakes?

2. Most snakes *(shall, will)* not harm people.

Scriptural Application

Choosing the correct word is important in order for a speaker to communicate his message accurately and clearly. In addition, word choice reveals much about a man's inner character.

God communicates who He is through His Word, the Bible. From the beginning, He proves His power by speaking the universe into existence (Ps. 33:6; Heb. 11:3). In His power and sovereignty, He commands and directs His people and the events on the earth (Dan. 2:21). In addition, He demonstrates His faithfulness by always keeping His word (Num. 11:23; Ps. 105:8). In His infinite love for man, He gave His Son as the only way of salvation (I John 4:9-11). Throughout the Old Testament, God promised the Messiah's coming to die as the perfect sacrifice (Isa. 7:14; 9:6-7; 52:13–53:12; Mic. 5:2). Every word of the Spirit-led prophecy concerning Christ's birth and death has been fulfilled (Luke 2:7-16; 23:1–24:27). God's Word holds true, and what He promises He will provide.

Challenge the students to search the Bible to find promises God makes to Christians. Remind them that each promise reveals something about God's character. Encourage them to ask themselves what each promise teaches them about the Lord.

3. *(May, Can)* I look at the snake you are holding?

4. It is *(lying, laying)* very still right now.

5. Watch as it *(raises, rises)* its head.

6. How can you *(sit, set)* there and hold a snake?

7. Some snakes give birth to live young, and some *(lie, lay)* eggs.

8. A snake's head *(rises, raises)* when the snake is ready to strike.

9. *(May, Can)* you tell me how a snake captures its prey?

10. *(Sit, Set)* down that snake now and show me another one.

Underline the correct verb from the choices in parentheses.

1. I *(will, shall)* endeavor to help you answer any questions you have as you walk through the seal exhibit.

2. Seals enjoy water, but they *(lie, lay)* on land to give birth.

3. You *(can, may)* step closer to the exhibit.

4. A Weddell seal of the Antarctic *(can, may)* dive as deep as 2,360 feet.

5. A seal *(rises, raises)* to the surface to breathe.

6. Watch as we *(sit, set)* a ball on Barko's nose.

7. Sea lions learn tricks easily. When Martha *(lies, lays)* a ball on Barko's nose, he will shoot a basket.

8. How high can Barko *(rise, raise)* the ball?

9. Barko *(will, shall)* learn a new trick tomorrow.

10. Many northern fur seals will *(sit, set)* on the islands in the summer and then travel south for winter.

Other Troublesome Words

Some words cause confusion because they are similar to other words in pronunciation, spelling, or meaning. Other troublesome words are nonstandard forms or misspellings of other words. Be sure to use the correct word.

accept/except: *Accept* is a verb that means "to receive"; it is never a preposition. *Except* is a preposition that means "not including."

> I **accepted** the gift of a new horse.
> Everyone **except** my younger brother is going to the horse show.

Reinforcement

Once students learn the proper use of these troublesome words, they will become more conscious of their own correct or incorrect use of them. Encourage students to think carefully about their word choices.

affect/effect: *Affect* is usually a verb meaning "to influence." *Effect* is usually a noun meaning "the result of some action." *Effect* can also be a verb meaning "to cause or bring about."

> A class pet would **affect** the atmosphere of the classroom.
> What **effects** would it have?
> Perhaps it would **effect** changes in the students' behavior.

borrow/lend/loan: *Borrow* is a verb meaning "to receive something on loan." *Lend* is a verb meaning "to provide something temporarily." *Loan* is a noun meaning "something lent temporarily." Some dictionaries list *loan* also as a verb, a synonym for *lend*. However, in formal writing *loan* should be used only as a noun.

> I need to **borrow** some money.
> Would you **lend** it to me?
> I promise to repay your **loan** tomorrow.

etc.: *Etc.* is the abbreviation of *et cetera,* meaning "and others." Because *etc.* includes the meaning "and," it is never correct to use *and etc. Etc.* (and *et cetera*) should not be used in formal writing; they are generally appropriate in informal writing or in technical or business writing. Substitute an English phrase such as *and others* when needed or else introduce the list with *such as.*

> My aunt raises breeds **such as** Dalmatians, schnauzers, and German shepherds.

fewer/less: *Fewer* is used with plural count nouns (items that can be counted), such as *fewer coins. Less* is properly used with noncount nouns, such as *less rain.*

> **Fewer** cheetahs exist today than years ago.
> A sand cat consumes **less** water than many other wild cats do.

hisself/theirself/theirselves: Do not use *hisself, theirself,* or *theirselves* for the correct pronouns *himself* and *themselves.*

> **WRONG** Mr. Lapazor owns twenty horses hisself.
> **RIGHT** Mr. Lapazor owns twenty horses himself.

prophecy/prophesy: *Prophecy* is a noun referring to a revelation or prediction. *Prophesy* is a verb meaning "to reveal by divine revelation" or "to predict."

> Isaiah's **prophecy** described Christ's birth.
> Many of the prophets **prophesied** about His resurrection.

real/really: *Real* is an adjective. *Really* is an adverb.

> Rover has been a **real** friend to my family.
> I had a **really** difficult time training my dog.

than/then: *Than* is a conjunction meaning "in comparison with." *Then* is an adverb meaning "at that time" or "next."

> My cat won more awards **than** hers.
> **Then** we took our awards home.

Underline the correct word from the choices in parentheses.

1. Will you *(lend, loan)* me your Bible for the report I am writing?

2. The Bible mentions dogs, horses, donkeys, *(etc., and others)*.

3. In Zechariah 9:9, Zechariah's *(prophecy, prophesy)* was that Christ would ride on a donkey.

4. According to Proverbs 26:11, a fool will not *(accept, except)* instruction; he returns to his foolishness "as a dog returneth to his vomit."

5. A great fish swallowed Jonah. This event was an *(affect, effect)* of his wrong choice.

6. I am sure that the Egyptians cried for *(fewer, less)* flies during the plagues.

7. Christ cast out demons *(Hisself, Himself)*.

8. According to Proverbs, an ant is often more industrious *(than, then)* a person is.

9. We need to be *(real, really)* careful because the Devil is like a roaring lion.

10. Studying biblical comparisons of animals to humans can *(affect, effect)* great changes in our Christian life.

On the blanks below, rewrite the incorrect sentences according to formal usage. If the sentence is correct, write *C* in the blank.

1. I have asked Renee to loan me her saddle for the horse show.

   I have asked Renee to lend me her saddle for the horse show.

2. The saddle is made from real leather.

   C

3. I hope the new saddle will affect how I ride Tucker.

   C

4. Tucker needs a bridle, a saddle, etc.

   Tucker needs items such as a bridle and a saddle.

5. My cousin is training Tucker by hisself.

   My cousin is training Tucker by himself.

6. Roger has less time for training then he had last year.

   Roger has less time for training than he had last year.

7. However, there are less contestants in the show this year.

   However, there are fewer contestants in the show this year.

8. My sister Megan and her friends prophesy that Tucker will win the jumping competition.

   C

9. All of my family will be there accept my brother.

   All of my family will be there except my brother.

10. A trophy for Roger and Tucker would effect great joy in our family.

    C

Homonyms

Homonyms are words that sound alike but differ in meaning and often in spelling. They can be troublesome because of the similar pronunciations.

capital/capitol/Capitol: The noun *capital* refers to the city that is the seat of government in a state. The noun *capitol* refers to a legislative building. The proper noun *Capitol* refers to the structure in Washington, D.C., where the United States Congress convenes.

> The **capital** of Pennsylvania is Harrisburg.
> You can visit the state senate at the **capitol** while you are there.
> Have you ever seen the **Capitol** in Washington, D.C.?

council/counsel: *Council* is a noun referring to a governing body or an assembly. *Counsel* is a noun meaning "advice" or a verb meaning "to give advice."

> The **council** met to determine what **counsel** they would give the mayor.

desert/dessert: When pronounced with the accent on the first syllable, *desert* is a noun meaning "a wasteland." When pronounced with the accent on the second syllable, *desert* is a verb meaning "abandon." *Dessert* is a noun indicating a dish, usually sweet, served as the last course of a meal.

> Sand cats, which dwell in the **desert,** are rarely seen.
> A security guard should never **desert** his post.
> I enjoy eating ice cream for **dessert.**

pray/prey: *Pray* is a verb that means "to make an earnest request." *Prey* can be used as a verb to mean "to hunt" or "to victimize" or as a noun to mean "an animal that is hunted" or "a victim."

> Christians who **pray** for others are a blessing to those around them.
> Birds that **prey** on other animals have long talons.
> Their **prey** might include small mammals or other birds.

principal/principle: *Principal* can be used as a noun to mean "a person who holds the highest rank" or as an adjective to mean "main or most important." *Principle* is a noun that means "a basic truth or guiding policy."

> Our high school **principal,** Mr. Owens, founded our school ten years ago.
> He always teaches us that our **principal** desire should be to be like Christ.
> Our school is run on biblical **principles.**

stationary/stationery: *Stationary* is an adjective that means "unmoving." *Stationery* is a noun that means "writing paper."

> You can sign the guest book on the **stationary** stand next to the door.
> Your guest book pages are similar to some **stationery** I have.

In addition to homonyms (words that sound alike but have different meanings and often different spellings), English also has words in these two other categories:

- words that sound and are spelled alike but have different meanings

  The *bear* got into our food supply.

  We shall *bear* this trial without complaining.

- words that are spelled alike but sound different and have different meanings

  The *wind* blew softly through the trees.

  Please remember to *wind* the clock each night.

10-13 Practice the Skill

Underline the correct word from the choices in parentheses.

1. The *(capital, capitol, Capitol)* of the United States is Washington, D.C.

2. In the *(capital, capitol, Capitol),* the Senate and the House pass laws.

3. I wonder whether they have various *(councils, counsels)* that recommend which laws to pass?

4. They have passed laws about humans unnecessarily *(praying, preying)* on animals.

5. A *(principal, principle)* behind these laws is that animals should receive humane treatment.

6. The *(principal, principle)* theme of my paper is that people need a scriptural approach to the treatment of animals.

7. I recently wrote a letter to Congress on company *(stationery, stationary)* inquiring about other animal laws.

8. I took my father's *(council, counsel)* and proofread my letter several times.

9. Many animals, from those in the forests to those in the *(deserts, desserts),* have become extinct.

10. After I write my paper, I will eat *(desert, dessert).*

10-14 REVIEW THE SKILL

On the blanks below, rewrite the incorrect sentences according to formal usage. If a sentence is correct, write *C* in the blank.

1. Our family council decided that we should buy a dog.

   C

2. However, Dad is the principle decision maker in our house, so we had to ask him.

   However, Dad is the principal decision maker in our house, so we had to ask him.

3. After getting much family council, he agreed to buy a dog.

   After getting much family counsel, he agreed to buy a dog.

4. My family lives in a city near Richmond, the capitol of Virginia.

   My family lives in a city near Richmond, the capital of Virginia.

5. We drove into Richmond to buy a dog, but Mom decided that an educational trip to the capitol was needed first.

   C

6. After we bought the dog, I bought some stationery with dogs on it.

   _C_

7. Dad actually took our family and our new dog out for desert.

   Dad actually took our family and our new dog out for dessert.

8. We later found out that my little sister had preyed for a new puppy, so the family decided that she could pick the name.

   We later found out that my little sister had prayed for a new puppy, so the

   family decided that she could pick the name.

9. We decided that the new puppy could sleep in our basement next to the stationary bicycle.

   _C_

10. Now, we can all hope that our cat does not become prey to our dog.

    _C_

Possessive Pronouns vs. Contractions

Some contractions and possessive pronouns are homonym pairs. These words also sound the same (and may or may not have the same spelling) but mean different things. Be careful to spell the possessive personal pronouns correctly—without apostrophes.

Its is a possessive pronoun.	*Its* jaws can crush extremely large bones.
It's is a contraction of *it is*.	*It's* a hyena.
Your is a possessive pronoun.	*Your* zoology book has an excerpt on hyenas.
You're is a contraction of *you are*.	I noticed that *you're* going on an African safari.
Whose is a possessive pronoun.	*Whose* travel company is in charge of the safari?
Who's is a contraction of *who is*.	*Who's* your guide?
Theirs is a possessive pronoun.	*Theirs* is a good safari.
There's is a contraction of *here is*.	*There's* a good chance you will see hyenas on your safari.
Their is a possessive pronoun.	*Their* meals often consist of dead animal carcasses.
They're is a contraction of *they are*.	*They're* more similar to cats than to dogs.
There is an adverb.	*There* are three species of hyena.

Reinforcement

Apostrophes in contractions signal that at least one letter has been taken out. Tell the students that to test whether they should use a contraction or a possessive pronoun, they should read the sentence as if no letters have been taken out of the contraction. *("It's hot today" becomes "It is hot today," and "She brought you're coat" becomes "She brought you are coat.")* Use Practice the Skill 10-15 on page 252 to reinforce this concept. Ask the students to read each sentence aloud. If they choose a contraction as the answer, instruct them to read the contraction as the two words it represents.

Underline the correct word from the choices in parentheses.

1. A flamingo is a bird known for *(its, it's)* long legs.

2. *(Its, It's)* pink color is distinctive.

3. *(Their, They're, There)* are flamingos in Africa.

4. I heard that *(your, you're)* interested in seeing some flamingos.

5. *(Who's, Whose)* going to the flamingo exhibit?

6. I do not know *(who's, whose)* camera this is.

7. *(Your, You're)* report was about flamingos, wasn't it?

8. They live *(their, they're, there)* lives near lakes, marshes, and seas.

9. Most flamingos eat shellfish and algae. *(Theirs, There's)* is an interesting diet.

10. *(Their, They're, There)* fairly noisy birds.

10-16 REVIEW THE SKILL

Underline the correct word from the choices in parentheses.

1. Falcons are a type of bird; *(their, they're, there)* similar to hawks.

2. Grasslands, forests, deserts, and Arctic tundras are often *(their, they're, there)* habitats.

3. A falconer is a person *(whose, who's)* sport uses birds of prey to hunt.

4. A falconer *(whose, who's)* avid about his sport will buy special equipment.

5. I know that *(you're, your)* grandfather was a falconer.

6. *(You're, Your)* fascinated by different types of hunting, aren't you?

7. *(Theirs, There's)* a falconer living in our neighborhood.

8. In ancient falconry, different falcons were given to different social classes. *(Theirs, There's)* was a symbol of importance.

9. The gyrfalcon grows to a length of two feet. *(It's, Its)* the largest species of falcon.

10. *(It's, Its)* coloring is usually gray or white.

Writing for the Media

Lesson Support

Teacher's Edition, Book 2
Writing Worksheets—p. 143
Rubrics—p. 157

Rewrite the paragraph on the blanks below, correcting the ten errors in subject-verb agreement, pronoun-antecedent agreement, spelling, and troublesome words.

This week my uncle and my dad is taking my brothers and me on a camping trip. Each of my brothers are really excited. Mom says that our excursion is a feild trip. She is haveing us study animal life in the woods. We are going to lie very still and observe the animals. Last year, after I had laid around for a while, I was able to observe some mallard ducks. Interestingly, the male mallard, not the females, raise the young. My brothers and I were also able to see some moose calfs. Everyone was fascinated by what they saw; it was a new experience to see those moose. Later, we sat out some food and watched as deer came to eat it. Either my uncle or my dad is going to give their help to my younger brother. Mom is nervous because this trip is Dylan's first camping trip. We will make sure that he enjoys himself.

This week my uncle and my dad are taking my brothers and me on a camping trip. Each of my brothers is really excited. Mom says that our excursion is a field trip. She is having us study animal life in the woods. We are going to lie very still and observe the animals. Last year, after I had lain around for a while, I was able to observe some mallard ducks. Interestingly, the male mallard, not the females, raises the young. My brothers and I were also able to see some moose calves. Everyone was fascinated by what he saw; it was a new experience to see those moose. Later, we set out some food and watched as deer came to eat it. Either my uncle or my dad is going to give his help to my younger brother. Mom is nervous because this trip is Dylan's first camping trip. We will make sure that he enjoys himself.

Writing for the Media

When you see a televised public service announcement that whips by in fifteen or thirty seconds, it's hard to realize that it may have taken seventy-five people six months or more to produce it. And that it probably cost far more than a million dollars, not counting the price of airing it.

Although many of the announcements look effortless, you can be sure that they were carefully planned and meticulously carried out. Just the right actors have to be chosen and a set either found or built. Then the clothes and the props have to be selected or made. There are rehearsals to run, equipment to rent or purchase, shoots to schedule, takes to review.

Introduction

Materials

- a video recording of a public service announcement (*Note:* Federal copyright laws govern educational use of video recordings. Before recording and playing any video for classroom use, check that you are complying with all applicable copyright laws.)

Ask students to describe some public service announcements that impressed them. Show and discuss the public service announcement if you have recorded one.

Discussion

Direct a discussion about how public service announcements and other short media events influence the viewer. *(They can change his thinking, his emotions, or even his way of doing things. They are meant to inspire action or to stop certain actions.)*

Direct the students to read the introduction on pages 253-54. Point out the great expense of time and effort even very short pieces require. Remind the students that creativity and efficiency are two tools a media writer must have. Emphasize that a media writer must also consider budget constraints when writing a script.

Direct the students to read the subsections about summarizing strategy, brainstorming, revising, storyboarding, and writing a treatment. Discuss the storyboard in the text, pointing out how it shows only the main action, not every nuance that film would show.

Discuss that every step in the creation of a good public service announcement is important and not to be overlooked.

But before all of that work can even begin, writers have to create the blueprint for the whole endeavor. When a team of creative people is assigned to write a public service announcement, the job is to take the message that the producer wants to tell and to make it an attention-getting blend of images and words that fits in the number of seconds allotted. Easy, right?

Summarizing the Strategy

The creative team reviews the points that the announcement must present and the audience that it is meant to reach. Usually a marketing research team has studied these elements and has determined the plan.

For example, if the American Medical Association has come out with a new study showing that walking is better than jogging for keeping fit, the American Heart Association may want to promote walking as a way of preventing heart attacks in middle-aged people. The marketing department will tell the creative team that the points to cover are general health and heart health. And the target audience will be nonactive people in their late forties and early fifties. The announcement will be thirty seconds long.

Brainstorming

The creative team then starts suggesting ideas for the announcement that will accomplish those goals. During brainstorming, no idea is critiqued—everything is recorded (preferably in a way that allows all in the group to see it simultaneously) for discussion later.

At the end of the brainstorming session, the team sorts the ideas into categories. Every team has its own methods of sorting, but all eventually get the list down to a few ideas that might work.

For the American Heart Association announcement, the final list might include these options:

- A tired business man is standing in his driveway waiting for a ride and using a cell phone. His wife comes out of the house, takes him by the hand, and leads him to walk with her. He is puzzled, but she keeps leading him; then he starts to keep up with her, smiling. He puts away his cell phone.

- A businessman is trying to find a place to park close to a building. He looks rather frustrated. Another businessman drives deliberately to the far end of the lot and gets out whistling. He starts his hike toward the building.

- A cartoon of two hearts—one in good shape and another all tired out. One belongs to a "hard-driving" businessman who never walks anywhere. The other is the heart of someone who walks.

Revising and Refining

The team then details the ideas that make the final list. For example, the team decides that in the second scenario, the first businessman will drive a black sports car. The second man will drive a white sports car. The frustrated driver will arrive in the building later than the man who walked. Both men will be dressed well, although in different colors. The slogan "A little walk can be heartening" will appear at the end.

Planning and Drafting

Direct the students to read the instructions in "Your Turn."

Present a list of topics for public service announcements that the students may choose from. Offer the following topics or provide some of immediate interest to your school or region:

- putting up smoke detectors in the home
- maintaining crosswalk protocol
- driving responsibly in school zones
- developing healthful backpack habits

Ask students to work in groups of three or four as a creative team. Allow time for the students to choose a topic.

Distribute a copy of the Writing Worksheet (Book 2, p. 143) to each student. Allow time for students to plan a strategy, to brainstorm, and to make rough drafts of their storyboards and treatments.

Discussion

Direct students to read "Trying It Out." Tell them that the creative teams will soon be presenting their work to their "clients." Assign one team to play the client role first.

Revising

Direct the students to revise their storyboards and treatments, remembering that they must persuade a client to let them do the work.

Then direct the students to prepare a presentation for prospective clients, including the storyboard and the treatment.

Storyboarding

Once the ideas have been detailed, each gets a storyboard. The storyboards roughly illustrate with sketches how the scripted announcement will look on screen. The sketches are intended to make some concepts visible, not to be great works of art. And not every moment in the spot is represented. In this example, only the five high points make the board: the close-up of the first driver; the second driver pulling in after the black sports car goes by; the second car parking far away; the second driver walking to the building as the black sports car circles again; and the last shot of the walking man ready for the meeting—first.

Writing a Treatment

With the storyboards completed, writers compose a *treatment*—a thorough, written description of the announcement. For example, here's a treatment for the second idea.

> The public service announcement begins as a late-model black sports car passes the camera. A close-up shows the driver to be about fifty years old, in a hurry and frustrated. He drives up a row, but no spaces close to the building are open. As the sports car makes another round, a white sports car pulls in. It goes without hesitation to the far end of the lot. A long shot shows the car pulling into the last space in the row, far from the building. The black sports car passes again in the foreground, still looking for a close parking space. A close-up of the second driver shows him locking his car and walking away whistling. He is the same age as the first driver, but more trim. He has to wait for the black sports car to go by and then he goes on toward the building. Inside the building, we see the second driver come up to the receptionist's desk from her point of view. He is smiling and chatting with her. She gives him a visitor's pass, and he goes down a hall. Then the first sports car driver bustles in, still annoyed and now late. He does not smile but checks his watch. The last shot shows the second driver happy and ready for his meeting. Over the visual the slogan "A little walk can be heartening" and the words "Paid for by the American Heart Association" appear.

The treatment describes the announcement from beginning to end. It gives the effect of watching moving pictures. Its main goal is to help the president of the American Heart Association imagine what the spot will look like and be willing to pay for the commercial to be shot. It is, in short, an announcement of the announcement.

Trying It Out

The team then shows the storyboards to the representatives of the American Heart Association, along with the treatments for each. The representatives will chose one of the ideas, and then the creative team will write a final script for the announcement.

Your Turn

Create a storyboard and a treatment for a public service announcement your teacher assigns.

A little walk can be ♡HEARTENING

Publishing

Allow the creative teams to present their work to their clients, getting feedback from the clients during and after their presentations. Allow the clients to tell whether they will accept each proposal and to explain the reasons for their decision. Collect the assignments.

Scriptural Application

Just as each creative team tailored its message to the client, so Paul tailored his message to his audience. Encourage your students to read Acts 13:14-41 and Acts 17:16-31. How does Paul adapt his message to two very different audiences: the Israelites in the synagogue and the Athenians on Mars' Hill?

Evaluation

For help in grading this assignment, see "Grading Writing Assignments" (p. x) and Rubric 10 (Book 2, p. 157).

Enrichment

Direct the students to read passages from Proverbs, watching for truths that could be presented in video form.

11 CAPITALIZATION

Objectives

Students will

1. correctly capitalize personal names, religions, and nationalities.

2. correctly capitalize proper adjectives.

3. correctly capitalize place names, transportation terms, and astronomical terms.

4. correctly capitalize businesses and organizations as well as cultural and historical terms.

5. correctly capitalize titles and first words.

6. identify capitalization errors within sentences.

7. evaluate and revise a paragraph containing capitalization errors.

8. identify proper capitalization.

Lesson Support

Student Text
Chapter 11 Review—pp. 425-26

Teacher's Edition, Book 1
Bulletin Boards—p. 450

Teacher's Edition, Book 2
Pretests—pp. 29-32
Teaching Helps—pp. 52-53
Concept Reinforcements—pp. 124-27

Is the center figure a number or a capital letter? Its identity depends on its context. If you read it in its vertical context, it's a number. But if you look at its horizontal context, it's a letter. When the figure is with letters, the eye automatically closes the gap between the *1* and the *3,* reading the letter *B.*

In writing, capital letters help to define the context of certain nouns (common or proper) and introduce the sentences in paragraphs. When the eye sees a capital letter at the beginning of a sentence, the mind automatically registers a new thought. Without capitals, writing would be as tricky to interpret as this illusion.

Personal Names, Religions, Nationalities

Names and initials	Kai Mueller L. H. Soltau
Titles used with a name	President Ron Schaffner Colonel Marion Chalker Dr. Darla Klingen Pastor Phillip McShane
Do not capitalize titles used in place of a person's name.	The president will introduce the special speaker.
Family words used as proper nouns	I may be late, Mom, because we will have to take several people home. Do you know what time Uncle Blake is coming?
If a word for a family relationship is modified by an adjective, it is not being used as a proper noun.	My aunt and uncle are going to England for a vacation with my mom and dad.
Terms used as descriptive substitutes for proper nouns	the Morning Star of the Reformation (John Wycliffe) Silent Cal (Calvin Coolidge)
Personifications	"And death shall be no more; Death, thou shalt die." ("Holy Sonnet 10" by John Donne)

Teaching Strategy: Introduction

Review nouns briefly with the students. Ask the students to define a noun and then to list different kinds of nouns. *(count, non-count, common, proper, collective, and compound)* Next, ask the students how they differentiate between common and proper nouns. *(Proper nouns are always capitalized.)* Proper nouns always name a specific person, place, thing, or idea. Such words must always be capitalized.

Scriptural Application

A capital letter sends different signals than a lowercase letter does because it has a different appearance. Likewise, the physical appearance and the behavior of Christians send signals to people around them. (I Pet. 1:15; 2:9-12) Encourage the students to think about the signals that their behavior and choice of clothing send.

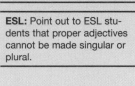

ESL: Point out that often an *s* is added when the word is used as a proper noun but that the *s* is removed when the word is used as a proper adjective.

ESL: Point out to ESL students that proper adjectives cannot be made singular or plural.

Names of religions and denominations	Judaism Methodism
All nouns and personal pronouns referring to the one true God	God is our Father, and He is more powerful than all other gods.
Do not capitalize common nouns or pronouns referring to mythological gods.	Poseidon is the Greek god of the ocean.
The words *Holy Bible* or *Bible* and the parts of the Bible as well as the names of sacred writings of other religions	Old Testament Psalms Torah
Nationalities Races Languages	Brazilian, British Asian, Hispanic Flemish, Swahili
Proper adjectives	German aircraft Shakespearean sonnet
Do not capitalize a word modified by a proper adjective unless the two together form a proper name.	That style of furniture is from the Victorian era. He lives in Dade County.

11-1 PRACTICE THE SKILL

Underline each capitalization error.

1. I was telling mother about Samuel Langhorne Clemens.

2. Samuel Clemens denied God's revelation to man through scripture.

3. Clemens did not want any responsibility to his creator.

4. Clemens spent much time with Orion, his brother. Orion received a special appointment from president Lincoln.

5. The President appointed Orion as Secretary of the Nevada territory.

6. Clemens's Father died when Samuel was only eight.

7. Samuel Clemens later took the name mark twain.

8. "The marvel of nature shaking off sleep and going to work unfolded itself to the musing boy." (from *Tom Sawyer*)

9. Many note Twain's importance in american literary history.

10. *The Innocents Abroad* is a book that exaggerates certain features of european culture.

Teaching Strategy: Demonstration

America is called a melting pot because of the great diversity of ethnic backgrounds found among the American people. Tell the students about your own background (e.g., the ethnic or national background of your parents and grandparents). As you name a nationality, write it for display. Then ask volunteers to share their national backgrounds. Write each new nationality for display. Afterward, show the students that each example is capitalized because it refers to people from a specific nation.

Underline each capitalization error and write the correction in the blank. If the sentence is correct, write *C* in the blank.

_____*C*_____ 1. We learned about William Tyndale from Pastor Kissinger.

_____*Rising Sun*_____ 2. William Tyndale was called the <u>rising sun</u> of the Reformation.

_____*chaplain*_____ 3. At the age of twenty-six, William Tyndale became a <u>Chaplain</u> and a tutor.

_____*Latin*_____ 4. Tyndale knew eight languages, including <u>latin</u>.

_____*Protestant*_____ 5. The prefaces to his books contain clear and forceful expositions of major <u>protestant</u> doctrines.

_____*Word*_____ 6. Tyndale had a zeal to make the <u>word</u> of God easily understandable and accessible to everyone.

_____*His*_____ 7. The understandable language in Tyndale's translation is illustrated in the Lord's conversations with <u>his</u> disciples in Tyndale's Bible.

_____*Gospels*_____ 8. Much of the King James New Testament is drawn from Tyndale's translation; the proportion is especially high in the <u>gospels</u> and Acts.

_____*C*_____ 9. George's aunt has a book on William Tyndale.

_____*M.*_____ 10. Dr. Thomas <u>m.</u> Underwood is a local expert on Tyndale.

In the following paragraph, underline the five capitalization errors.

Edgar <u>a.</u> Poe's writings have intrigued many readers. Poe wrote on morbid themes. The following quotation from "The Masque of the Red Death" illustrates his fascination with death: "And <u>darkness</u> and <u>decay</u> and the Red Death held illimitable dominion over all." His works are ethically deficient, especially for the <u>christian</u> reader. The death of a beautiful woman was a common theme in Poe's writings. The fact that both his mother and his wife had died contributed to this theme. Alcohol, which could have contributed to Poe's strange state of mind, was a god in his life. In spite of his problems, Poe remains a dominant figure in american literature.

Place Names, Transportation, Astronomical Terms

Countries Continents	Japan South America
Flag names	the Star-Spangled Banner the Union Jack
Cities States	St. Louis Minnesota
Sections of a country or the world	Highlands the North
Do not capitalize compass words when they indicate direction.	The town is four hours northeast of the state border.
Geographic features and recreational areas	Pikes Peak Death Valley Hawaii Volcanoes National Park
Streets and roads	7000 Collegiate Drive
Bodies of Water	the Great Lakes Mediterranean Sea
Do not capitalize a geographic noun unless it is part of a proper noun.	Did you know that there are mountains in the ocean?
Aircraft Spacecraft Ships Trains	*Polar Star* *Gemini* *Merrimac* *Tom Thumb*
Planets Stars Other heavenly bodies	Venus Betelgeuse Orion, Ganymede (Jupiter's largest moon)
Capitalize the words earth, sun, *and* moon *only when they are listed with another specific heavenly body.*	The planets Mercury, Jupiter, and Earth are closest to the Sun.
Never capitalize earth *when it is preceded by* the.	The earth receives heat and light from the sun.

Teaching Strategy: Induction

Instruct the students to write the following sentences as you read them aloud:

- Have you ever lived in the West?
- Kendall's new house is located one mile west of town.
- He worked as a news correspondent in the Middle East.
- The highway forms the southern border of the county.

Next, ask volunteers to write their sentences for display and to explain why they capitalized some words but not others.

Lead the students to understand that only the first word of each sentence and the proper nouns (those that name a specific person, place, or thing) should be capitalized.

Teaching Strategy: Demonstration

Some students may have trouble distinguishing a direction word that functions as a proper noun from one that merely indicates direction. Encourage those students to substitute a word they know to be a proper noun for the direction word in question.

- Have you ever lived in the West?
- Have you ever lived in Colorado?
- Kendall's new house is located one mile west of town.
- Kendall's new house is located one mile Colorado of town.

If the test sentence using the substituted proper noun sounds natural and logical, then students will know the direction word in question should likewise be capitalized as a proper noun in the original sentence. If the test sentence does not make sense, the direction word should not be capitalized.

Underline each capitalization error. Some sentences may be correct.

1. My cousin from the Black <u>forest</u> writes about the geography of <u>north</u> America.

2. Aba really enjoyed her trip on the *<u>concorde</u>,* the world's first commercial supersonic jet.

3. We took a lengthy trip through many <u>States</u>.

4. Aba and I started by driving <u>East</u> toward the coast.

5. We took the ferry from Manhattan to Staten Island.

6. We drove in the tunnel beneath the <u>chesapeake bay</u>.

7. I remembered our country's fight in the Revolutionary War as I saw the <u>stars</u> and <u>stripes</u> flying at Ft. McHenry in Maryland.

8. When we visited Michigan, we went to Mackinac <u>island</u>.

9. We saw mountains, valleys, lakes, and rivers.

10. Our trip ended at my house, which is located at 800 <u>valley</u> <u>drive</u>, <u>bellefonte</u>, <u>pennsylvania</u>.

Underline each capitalization error. Some sentences may be correct.

1. Dr. James Spalding, a notable historian, lives at 3 Bryce <u>court</u>.

2. He will be lecturing and selling his new book in Jefferson <u>city</u> next week.

3. He will be driving east through Kansas.

4. Dr. Spalding's best works are on the history of the <u>west</u>.

5. Dr. Spalding is originally from the Black <u>hills</u> of South Dakota.

6. Dr. Maria Gomez, a colleague of Dr. Spalding, is a scientist from <u>costa rica</u> in <u>central</u> America.

7. Her writings have included information on <u>venus</u> and <u>saturn</u>.

8. She took some information from the data of *<u>pioneer</u>,* which mapped the surface of these <u>Planets</u>.

9. She has written on the relationship between <u>earth</u> and Mars.

10. The moon's effect on the earth is amazing.

Enrichment

Divide the class into teams with three to four students in each group. Instruct the teams to write a short advertisement for a vacation spot or for a historical site that someone in the group has visited. Encourage students to include written directions for driving to that place. Remind the teams of the capitalization charts in this chapter. Allow students to use a dictionary if they are unsure of the capitalization of a particular word. When the teams are finished writing, remind them to proofread their work carefully for capitalization and spelling errors. Collect the papers and redistribute them to different teams who will then proofread the papers. Instruct the groups to return the papers to the proper teams once the errors have been marked.

One on One

With your student, write a brief advertisement for a vacation spot or for a historical site that he has visited. Include directions for driving to that place. If the student has questions about capitalization, instruct him to look up the problem word in a dictionary.

Businesses and Organizations, Cultural and Historical Terms

Businesses	Uptown Bakery M&M Mars, Inc.	
Do not capitalize the common noun for a business.	Do you need anything at the grocery store?	
Brand names of business products	Tylenol Jell-O	
Do not capitalize the product name unless it is part of the brand name.	Xerox machine	
Government departments	**FBI** Internal Revenue Service	
Programs	New Deal Food Stamp Program	
Political parties	Labor Party	
Organizations	Mothers Against Drunk Driving	
Do not capitalize the common noun for a team or club.	My son's baseball team is traveling this weekend.	
Members of most organizations	Democrat	
Do not capitalize members of an academic class.	We are responsible for next week's freshmen class meeting.	
Schools	United States Naval Academy	
Do not capitalize the common name for a school.	Her high school is one of the best in the county.	
Buildings Structures Monuments	Sears Tower Golden Gate Bridge Lincoln Memorial	
Months Days	June Saturday	
Do not capitalize the name of a season unless it is personified.	We are going to Hawaii this summer.	

Holidays	Memorial Day
	New Year's Day

The abbreviations B.C. and A.D. *Notice that B.C. ("before Christ") is correctly placed after the year and that A.D. (anno Domini, "in the year of the Lord") is correctly placed before the year.*	The prosperous city of Pompeii became a community of Rome in 91 B.C. The eruption of Mount Vesuvius destroyed Pompeii in A.D. 79.

The abbreviations A.M. and P.M. may be either capitalized or not. (Whichever you choose, be consistent in your writing.)	Class begins at 9:00 A.M. I have to be home by 10:00 p.m.

Historical events and periods	French Revolution
	the Renaissance
Historic documents	Magna Carta

Special events and awards	Cherry Blossom Festival
	Teacher of the Year
	President's Award

11-6 PRACTICE THE SKILL

In the blank write the letter of the choice that is capitalized correctly.

___B___ 1. A. Buick century
  B. the gas station
  C. the local Elementary School

___C___ 2. A. shopping on saturday
  B. party for the Sophomores
  C. the Middle Ages

___B___ 3. A. at the Courthouse
  B. National Book Award
  C. the Atlantic charter

___C___ 4. A. the Populist party
  B. Faith Christian junior high
  C. the Rose Parade

___C___ 5. A. the local Book Club
  B. the seven years' war
  C. Bayer aspirin

___B___ 6. A. faith Bible academy
  B. fast food restaurant
  C. Chicago cultural center

<u>C</u> 7. A. visit Greenwich palace
       B. eat at Lilly's sub shop
       C. go to the supermarket

<u>B</u> 8. A. a Revolution
       B. the Great Awakening
       C. national security council

<u>B</u> 9. A. drive over Hawthorne bridge
       B. celebrate Arbor Day
       C. bought an IBM Computer

<u>A</u> 10. A. an editor for the school's newspaper
       B. Penn State university
       C. better business bureau

11-7 REVIEW THE SKILL

Underline each capitalization error and write the correction in the blank. If the sentence is correct, write *C* in the blank.

library	1. I really enjoy reading at my local <u>Library</u>.
high school	2. Last Tuesday there were some <u>High School</u> students there doing research.
C	3. They were researching the Cold War era for their senior papers.
Prize	4. Books by winners of the Nobel <u>prize</u> are sometimes good to read.
A.D.	5. Bede, an outstanding scholar of his age, wrote around <u>a.d.</u> 700.
C	6. My brother is a member of the Bluemont Reading Club.
Center	7. The club members recently read a book on famous New York landmarks, including Rockefeller <u>center</u>.
summer	8. For a week next <u>Summer</u>, my brother is going with a group to Europe to study literature.
Day	9. His group will be leaving on Independence <u>day</u>.
college	10. His <u>College</u> will give him credit for the time spent there.

Titles and First Words

Chapter 12: Quotation Marks and Underlining for Italics pp. 298; 303

Newspapers and magazines	*New York Times* *Reader's Digest*
Do not capitalize the word the when referring to a newspaper.	Did you read the cover story of the *Atlanta Journal and Constitution?*
Literary compositions (including books, essays, poems, and plays)	*The Institutes of the Christian Religion* "A Modest Proposal" *Paradise Lost* *Pygmalion*
Sections of a book or play *(Some authorities do not capitalize the parts of a book or play unless they appear as a title.)*	Chapter 5 Prologue Act VII
Musical compositions (including songs, operas, and instrumental music)	"All Creatures of Our God and King" *Lohengrin* *Water Music*
Works of art	*Sunday Afternoon on the Island of La Grande Jatte*
Television and radio programs	*Larry King Live* *Gangbusters*
Specific courses of study	Language Arts Algebra 1
Do not capitalize the common noun for a course.	We have a test in math tomorrow.
The first word in a sentence	Always do your best.
First word in a line of dialogue	After the lawn was mowed, Dad said, "Now we can play basketball."
Do not capitalize the second part of a divided quotation unless the second part is the beginning of a new sentence.	"Let's play until dark," I suggested, "and then grill some hotdogs."
The first word in a line of poetry	Sweet day, so cool, so calm, so bright, The bridal of the earth and sky: (from "Virtue" by George Herbert)

Capitalization   265

Enrichment

Materials
- list of titles corresponding to the categories on page 265 (have at least one title for each student)

Divide the class into two teams: A and B. Read the first title aloud and direct a member of team A to write the title for display, capitalizing it correctly. Team B will judge whether the title is correctly capitalized. If a member of team A writes the title correctly, his team earns one point. If team A writes the word incorrectly, team A does not earn a point. If B makes the correct call, B earns one point. However, if B makes the wrong judgment, B loses one point.

Only the first word (and any proper nouns or proper adjectives) in each item of a formal outline	Anne Bradstreet
	  I. Early life
	  II. Journey to America
	  III. Poetry and prose

The first word and all nouns in the greeting of a letter	Dear Mr. and Mrs. Domnitz and Family,
The first word in the closing of a letter	Respectfully yours,
Personal pronoun *I*	He does not know whether **I** am going.
Archaic interjection *O*	What shall I do, **O** king?
Single letters used as words (including academic grades, vitamins, musical notes and major keys)	The book will be level **H** in the reading series. Carrots are a good source of vitamin **A**. The song begins with middle **C** in the key of **F**.
Letters used to clarify a following word	The summer staff will be staying in the **A**-frame houses.

11-8 PRACTICE THE SKILL

In the blank write the letter of the choice that is capitalized correctly.

_C_ 1. A. I am taking Science.
  B. I am taking science 101.
  C. I am taking Science 101.

_A_ 2. A. the *New York Times*
  B. The *New York Times*
  C. The *New York times*

_B_ 3. A. *to the Golden Shore*
  B. *To the Golden Shore*
  C. *To The Golden Shore*

_A_ 4. A. "Are you coming to the meeting?" asked Caleb.
    "Yes," replied Ken.
  B. "Are you coming to the meeting?" asked Caleb.
    "yes," replied Ken.
  C. "Are you coming to the meeting?" Asked Caleb.
    "Yes," replied Ken.

_A_ 5. A. "That's wonderful," said Caleb, "because we're
    discussing a new book."
  B. "That's wonderful," said Caleb, "Because we're
    discussing a new book."
  C. "that's wonderful," said Caleb, "because we're
    discussing a new book."

Evaluation

To evaluate the students' ability to proofread a text to find and correct capitalization errors, assign Teaching Help 11A (Book 2, p. 52).

Reinforcement

For additional practice in determining the correct capitalization of a phrase, assign Teaching Help 11B (Book 2, p. 53).

<u>C</u> 6. A. "Shall I compare thee to a summer's day?
            Thou art more lovely and more temperate:
            rough winds do shake the darling buds of May,
            and summer's lease hath all too short a date."
        B. "Shall I compare thee to a summer's day?
            Thou art more lovely and more temperate:
            Rough winds do shake the darling buds of May
            and summer's lease hath all too short a date."
        C. "Shall I compare thee to a summer's day?
            Thou art more lovely and more temperate:
            Rough winds do shake the darling buds of May,
            And summer's lease hath all too short a date."
            (from "Sonnet 18" by Shakespeare)

<u>A</u> 7. A.   I. Prewriting
                II. Writing the first rough draft
               III. Revising
        B.   I. Prewriting
                II. Writing the First Rough Draft
               III. Revising
        C.   I. prewriting
                II. writing the first rough draft
               III. revising

<u>B</u> 8. A. Dear Dr. Polson and associates:
        B. Dear Dr. Polson and Associates:
        C. Dear Dr. Polson And Associates:

<u>A</u> 9. A. Yours truly,
        B. Yours Truly,
        C. yours truly,

<u>B</u> 10. A. That report earned Luis an a.
        B. That report earned Luis an A.
        C. That Report earned Luis an a.

11-9 REVIEW THE SKILL

Underline each capitalization error. If the sentence is correct, write *C* in the blank.

_____ 1. Did you remember to bring your <u>Government</u> book to class?

_____ 2. Let's look at the headlines of <u>The</u> *Detroit Daily.*

_____ 3. Many current events are discussed on <u>*the today show*</u>.

<u>C</u> 4. You may write about a current event for your Composition
            100 class.

_____ 5. Yes, you may also write about a novel like *Alice's Adventures
            <u>In</u> Wonderland.*

<u>C</u> 6. Perhaps you could research a famous painting such as *The Adoration of the Magi.*

_____ 7. If you meet just the basic requirements, you will get a <u>c</u>.

_____ 8. Writing is a process. <u>you</u> need to make certain that you give yourself enough time.

_____ 9. Please read <u>chapter</u> 10 in your book by tomorrow.

<u>C</u> 10. You are dismissed to your calculus class.

11-10 CUMULATIVE REVIEW

Rewrite the letter on the blanks below, correcting the ten errors in subject-verb agreement, pronoun-antecedent agreement, spelling, troublesome words, and capitalization.

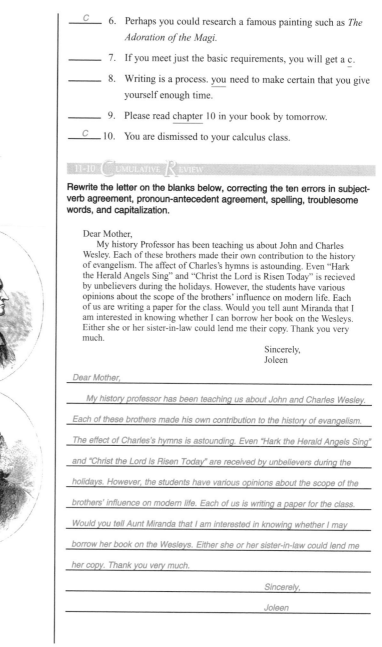

Dear Mother,

My history Professor has been teaching us about John and Charles Wesley. Each of these brothers made their own contribution to the history of evangelism. The affect of Charles's hymns is astounding. Even "Hark the Herald Angels Sing" and "Christ the Lord is Risen Today" is recieved by unbelievers during the holidays. However, the students have various opinions about the scope of the brothers' influence on modern life. Each of us are writing a paper for the class. Would you tell aunt Miranda that I am interested in knowing whether I can borrow her book on the Wesleys. Either she or her sister-in-law could lend me their copy. Thank you very much.

Sincerely,
Joleen

Dear Mother,

My history professor has been teaching us about John and Charles Wesley.

Each of these brothers made his own contribution to the history of evangelism.

The effect of Charles's hymns is astounding. Even "Hark the Herald Angels Sing"

and "Christ the Lord Is Risen Today" are received by unbelievers during the

holidays. However, the students have various opinions about the scope of the

brothers' influence on modern life. Each of us is writing a paper for the class.

Would you tell Aunt Miranda that I am interested in knowing whether I may

borrow her book on the Wesleys. Either she or her sister-in-law could lend me

her copy. Thank you very much.

Sincerely,

Joleen

_____

_____

_____

_____

_____

Recording an Oral History

Have you ever seen someone standing before a mirror, carefully plucking a gray hair from his head? Most people dread the day when their hair will turn gray. But what does God think of a gray head? According to Proverbs 16:31, "The hoary head is a crown of glory, if it be found in the way of righteousness." Proverbs 20:29 says that "the beauty of old men is the gray head." In Leviticus 19:32 the Israelites were instructed to "rise up before the hoary head, and honour the face of the old man." Why does the Bible place such an emphasis on valuing the elderly?

Perhaps one reason is found in Job 12:12, which tells us that "with the ancient is wisdom; and in length of days understanding." We may learn much from the practical wisdom and experience elderly people have gained through living. We can learn what kinds of choices and mistakes brought them to the place they are today. We can learn what experiences and difficulties have shaped their character. But in order to learn, we have to listen.

When someone gives an oral account of his background and experiences, we call it an *oral history.* Listening to oral histories and recording them for others to read are the best ways to pass along the wisdom and the beauty of "the gray head."

Choosing a Subject for Your Oral History

Think about the elderly people you know. Which of them has had a significant influence on your life? Whom do you especially admire? Whose life would you be interested in learning more about?

Call your subject on the telephone or write him a letter, explaining that you would like to talk with him about his life and background. Explain that you are doing this for a class project and mention how long the interview will last and some specific things you would like to know. Offer him some choices of times and places for the interview and let him choose which is most convenient for him. Remember to treat your interviewee with honor and respect; go out of your way to accommodate his schedule or physical limitations.

Objectives

Students will

1. interview a subject about his history.
2. record their subject's oral history.

Overview of the Writing Process

Planning—choosing a subject, writing questions, and conducting the interview

Drafting—organizing and formatting the interview

Revising—reviewing with the subject and making any changes for clarity

Publishing—presenting the oral history to an audience

Recording an Oral History

Lesson Support

Teacher's Edition, Book 2
Writing Worksheets—p. 144
Rubrics—p. 158

Introduction

If possible, invite someone who you know has an interesting background to visit your class. Allow the person ten or fifteen minutes to tell his story and another ten minutes or so to field questions.

Discussion

Direct the students to read the introduction and first three sections of "Recording an Oral History."

Direct a discussion about what the students might be most interested in hearing from an older person. If you have had a guest speaker, ask the students what parts of his presentation were the most memorable.

Emphasize to them that points of interest in an interview are good indications of what to include in a history.

Getting the Facts for Your Oral History

In order to listen to your subject, you must first get him or her talking. Write down a list of questions you would like to ask when you interview your subject. Be sure to ask open-ended questions that leave him free to include as much or as little information as he wishes in his responses.

Here is a list of topics you might want to cover in the interview:

- religious background

- upbringing and family life

- education

- special moments in his life: happiest, saddest, most frightening, most embarrassing

- important historical events that took place in his lifetime

- types of transportation he has used

- inventions developed during his lifetime; his feelings about various modern conveniences

- personal choices that changed his life

- mistakes he learned from

If you plan to record or videotape the interview, be sure to ask your friend's permission ahead of time. If he prefers that the interview not be recorded, respect his privacy and be prepared to take notes as he speaks.

Presenting Your Oral History

Order

After you have interviewed your subject, look over the information you have gained from him. Which information is most important, and which could be left out? Make an outline that sorts the most important facts into the order you would like to present them. It would be a good idea to put the most important thing your subject said last in your presentation, since endings are often what readers remember best.

Format

What would be the best format for presenting this oral history?

Interview

You may choose to write out your questions and your friend's answers in dialogue form, introducing each new speaker with his name and a colon.

Essay

You may choose to write an essay, either in first or third person, presenting the subject's life in an autobiographical or biographical sketch.

Planning

Direct the students to read the instructions in "Your Turn."

Distribute a copy of the Writing Worksheet (Book 2, p. 144) to each student, directing the students to consider possible subjects for an interview.

Encourage them to fill out their worksheets before going to interview their subjects. Assign the interview as homework to be completed within one week.

ESL Strategy

ESL students need to learn how to conduct a standard interview. If your ESL students are new and still in their silent phase (that is, mostly listening to English and not yet speaking much) they will have great difficulty conducting an interview. You could direct them to write interview questions and conduct a written interview, or you could arrange for them to interview someone with whom they feel comfortable (perhaps you).

Discussion

Ask students to share their experiences from interviewing and allow time for students to tell about their subjects and the interview process.

Photo Essay

If your subject is willing to lend you photos, you can arrange them as a photo essay and present your information through captions.

Your Turn

Interview an elderly person and record the oral history, using one of the formats given above. Show your appreciation to the interviewee after you have finished the project by sending him a thank-you note and a copy of the history you have written.

Drafting

Direct the students to re-read the section "Presenting Your Oral History." Remind them to make an outline of the most important facts in the order of presentation.

Allow time in class for students to work in groups or in pairs to help each other select the best formats.

Allow the rest of the time for students to write rough drafts of their oral histories.

Revising

Direct the students to read their rough drafts to their subjects if possible, getting suggestions for revision. Assign the revision as homework.

Publishing

When the students have completed their oral histories, schedule times convenient for parents and for students' subjects so that these guests may attend students' presentations.

Scriptural Application

Instruct the students to read Joshua 4. Point out that the Lord commands us to remember His works from generation to generation (Josh. 4:21-24).

Evaluation

For help in grading this assignment, see "Grading Writing Assignments" (p. x) and Rubric 11 (Book 2, p. 158).

Enrichment

Encourage students to create a class magazine (perhaps called *Crown of Glory*), using their recorded oral histories as feature articles.

12 PUNCTUATION

Objectives

Students will

1. choose the correct marks of punctuation for a sentence.
2. identify and correct any incorrect punctuation.
3. write sentences using punctuation correctly.
4. evaluate and revise a paragraph for punctuation errors.

Lesson Support

Student Text
Chapter 12 Review—pp. 427-29

Teacher's Edition, Book 1
Bulletin Boards—p. 450

Teacher's Edition, Book 2
Pretests—pp. 33-35

Teaching Helps—pp. 54-55

ESL Worksheets—p. 85

Concept Reinforcements—pp. 128-32

What do you see in this picture? A snow scene or an animal? Using just one or two black marks as reference points, you can transform the snow scene into a cow. (The large black area in the center is its left eye.)

Writing also must have reference points if it is to be interpreted clearly. Punctuation marks indicate pauses, changes of tone, relationships between ideas, and much more. Without such reference points, a reader may be "cowed" by the confusing arrangement of words on the page.

When you communicate through speech, you use intonation patterns and pauses to clarify exactly what you want to communicate. In writing, you have to rely on punctuation to communicate effectively and to avoid misreading. Do not let these punctuation guidelines be a hindrance to you; instead learn them well and allow them to be a great help to you in your writing.

End Marks

Sentences end with periods, question marks, and exclamation points. These end-punctuation marks depend almost completely on the type of sentence: declarative, imperative, interrogative, or exclamatory.

Period

Most sentences end with a period. A period signals the end of all declarative sentences and most imperative sentences.

Chapter 1: Four Kinds of Sentences
p. 2

> I am preparing for a trip to China next summer.
> Tell me about your visit to China.

Question Mark

A question mark comes at the end of a direct question (an interrogative sentence).

> Have you ever needed a passport?

Indirect questions do not end with a question mark.

> I asked Courtney where she was going this summer.

A question mark follows interrogatives that end a sentence.

> That's a good plan, isn't it?

Chapter 6: Interjections
p. 160

A request courteously stated like a question does not end with a question mark.

> Would you please help me with this luggage.

Exclamation Point

An exclamation point shows strong feeling. It ends brief exclamations, exclamatory sentences, and some imperative sentences.

> Stop! Watch out!
> I'm going to Europe!

The exclamation point should be used mainly in quoting spoken exclamations and should be used sparingly. The overuse of exclamation points usually seems overly emotional and may weaken the effectiveness of writing.

12-1 PRACTICE THE SKILL

Insert the correct end mark(s) for each sentence.

1. What country is the United States's nearest neighbor?

2. Tell me about Canada.

3. Is Canada a good place to visit?

4. Absolutely! Parts of Canada are completely breathtaking! or .

5. Come to Toronto with me.

6. I thought that parts of Canada were cold, but thirty degrees below zero is unbelievable! or .

7. Canada has ten provinces.

8. Where is Alberta?

9. Canada has land profitable for farming, and Canadians mine gold, zinc, lead, silver, uranium, nickel, titanium, and copper.

10. Amazing! Canada has a wealth of natural resources! or .

ESL Strategy

Be aware that some ESL students may have difficulty with punctuation. Some languages use different punctuation marks from those used in English, and other languages use very little punctuation at all.

For an overview of the most common punctuation marks in English, see ESL Worksheet 12 (Book 2, p. 85).

Writing Link

Remind the students that using too many exclamation points can weaken the effectiveness of their writing. Write several example sentences such as the following for display:

- I'm going to Hawaii!
- I can't believe it!
- It's so beautiful there!

Now rewrite these sentences:

- I am thrilled to be going to Hawaii!
- I never dreamed that I would have the privilege of such a trip.
- I long to see the unimaginable beauty of vast sky and ocean.

In the first set of sentences, exclamation points were poor substitutes for creative expression. In the second set, an exclamation point follows only the truly exclamatory sentence. Ask the students to bring a letter (or a printed e-mail message) they have written or received that has an excessive number of exclamation points. The students should rewrite the letters, substituting descriptive writing for unnecessary exclamation points. If a student cannot locate a letter, he may create his own fictional letter.

Insert the correct end mark(s) for each sentence.

1. What is unique about Australia?

2. Australia is the only country that is also a continent.

3. A tourist can see some amazing things in Australia.

4. Wow! That camel race was great!

5. Why is the Great Barrier Reef such a popular Australian attraction?

6. Many divers come from around the world to explore its wonders.

7. No kidding! It is an extensive chain of more than 2,500 reefs.

8. Do you know any of Australia's unusual animals?

9. Kangaroos, wombats, and emus are pretty unusual.

10. Have you ever heard of an echidna, a skink, or a bandicoot?

Other Uses of the Period

Initials and Abbreviations

Periods follow most abbreviations and initials.

Names and titles	Dwight Rupert Jr.
	Iris Huffstetler, Ph.D.
Periods may be omitted after most abbreviations of the names of government agencies and international organizations, including well-known businesses.	CIA (Central Intelligence Agency)
	NCR (National Cash Register)
Terms in addresses	12 Peachtree Rd.
	P.O. Box 42311
	Sacramento, CA 43256
Periods do not follow state or province postal abbreviations.	MA (Massachusetts)
	BC (British Columbia)
Times and dates	2:00 P.M.
	A.D. 350
Measurements	6 ft. 1 in.
	210 lb.
Periods should not be used with metric measurements.	25 cm
	500 mg

Teaching Strategy: Induction and Participation

After studying end marks, introduce other uses for the period. Divide the class into two or more teams and hold a contest to determine which team can list the most uses for the period. The team members can work together, listing their answers on paper; or you can conduct the contest orally, writing for display one answer from each team until one team can no longer give an answer. After the game, review the listed rules and discuss rules not given by the students.

One on One

Give your student a number (e.g., five) and challenge him to list that many additional uses for the period.

Enrichment

Remind the students that postal abbreviations are not the same as traditional abbreviations. Postal abbreviations always consist of two capital letters that are not followed by periods. Use a map of the United States or Canada and help the class recognize the postal abbreviations for all the states or provinces.

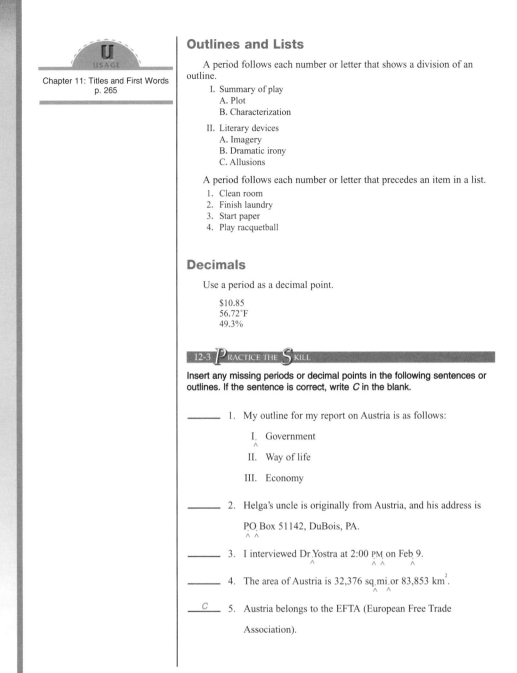

Outlines and Lists

A period follows each number or letter that shows a division of an outline.

    I. Summary of play
       A. Plot
       B. Characterization

   II. Literary devices
       A. Imagery
       B. Dramatic irony
       C. Allusions

A period follows each number or letter that precedes an item in a list.

1. Clean room
2. Finish laundry
3. Start paper
4. Play racquetball

Decimals

Use a period as a decimal point.

$10.85
56.72°F
49.3%

12-3 PRACTICE THE SKILL

Insert any missing periods or decimal points in the following sentences or outlines. If the sentence is correct, write *C* in the blank.

_____ 1. My outline for my report on Austria is as follows:

      I. Government

     II. Way of life

    III. Economy

_____ 2. Helga's uncle is originally from Austria, and his address is

    PO Box 51142, DuBois, PA.

_____ 3. I interviewed Dr Yostra at 2:00 PM on Feb 9.

_____ 4. The area of Austria is 32,376 sq mi or 83,853 km^2.

___C___ 5. Austria belongs to the EFTA (European Free Trade

    Association).

Teaching Strategy: Induction

Display an outline with at least three levels. Ask the students to supply the periods for the outline. Make sure the students know that a period follows the headings of outline divisions only if the heading is a complete sentence.

_____ 6. Austria has six main land regions:

1. the Granite Plateau

2. the Eastern Forelands

3. the Alpine Forelands

4. the Northern Limestone Alps

5. the Central Alps

6. the Southern Limestone Alps

_____ 7. In the lowlands and eastern sections, the temperatures range from 304°F in January to 686°F in July.

_____ 8. By 15 BC. the Romans controlled Austria.

_____ 9. At the end of World War I, Austria signed an armistice on Nov. 3, 1918.

_____ 10. Thank you, Mrs. Fielding, for allowing me to present this report about Austria.

12-4 REVIEW THE SKILL

Insert any missing periods and decimal points in the following sentences. If the sentence is correct, write *C* in the blank.

_____ 1. The width of the Atlantic Ocean grows by about $^1/_2$ in (15 cm) each year.

_____ 2. My dad's friend J. R. Wilkinson visits the Atlantic Ocean several times a year.

__C__ 3. In 1982, the UN adopted a law to limit ocean pollution.

_____ 4. You can get information about the Atlantic Ocean by writing to Stuart Troyka, PhD, 9 Constitution Ave, Washington, DC 20230.

_____ 5. There are three marginal seas on the western side of the Atlantic:

    1. the Gulf of St. Lawrence
    ^

    2. the Gulf of Mexico
    ^

    3. the Caribbean Sea
    ^

__C__ 6. NOAA is the National Oceanic and Atmospheric Administration.

_____ 7. The Bay of Fundy in Canada has the highest tides, some reaching 50 ft. (15 m).
                                      ^

_____ 8. The Atlantic Intracoastal Waterway is 12,000 miles long with a depth of 12 feet (3.7 meters) or more.
                                      ^

_____ 9. A three-hour whale-watching cruise in New England might cost $24.99.
                    ^

_____ 10. We are leaving at 9:00 A.M. for our vacation at the ocean.
                      ^ ^

Commas

The comma is probably the most important mark of punctuation used inside the sentence. It is certainly the one used most often.

Commas in a Series

Commas are used to separate items in a series.

In a Series of Equal Elements

A series of three or more words or groups of words of the same type, joined with a conjunction, should be punctuated as follows:

> _first item_, _second item_, conjunction _third item_
> _first item_, _second item_, _third item_, conjunction _fourth item_

The items joined might be single words or groups of words.

> _British Columbia_, _Alberta_, and _Ontario_ are all provinces of Canada.

> In Nova Scotia one can _see the towering lighthouses_, _visit the fishing villages_, and _learn about celebrating Celtic culture_.

Reinforcement

Many students tend to think that commas go wherever one would take a breath while reading. Remind them that there are definite rules for comma placement. Commas are the most frequently used marks of punctuation and can, therefore, be the most misused.

Writing Link

Use page 278 to demonstrate parallel sentence structure. Examine the example sentences for "In a Series of Equal Elements." Point out the parallel structure of the words or groups of words separated by commas. You may want the students to revise a recent writing assignment. In their revisions the students should focus on two things: rewriting sentences with series so that the individual elements are parallel or combining sentences to create a parallel series.

In some informal writing, the comma before the conjunction is omitted. However, you would be wise to make a habit of always using that comma; it is often needed and is never wrong.

With Coordinate Adjectives in a Series

Groups of adjectives can modify nouns in two different ways. One adjective may build on another.

> her heavy black coat
> the square chocolate bars

Here *heavy* tells us what kind of black coat it is, and *square* tells us which chocolate bars are meant. Both adjectives are needed to identify the object. This situation does not call for any commas.

However, sometimes two adjectives have independent meanings, so that both would not really be necessary to identify the thing described. These adjectives, called **coordinate adjectives,** modify the noun separately; we put a comma between them.

> She has a *reserved, quiet* personality.

Participles can be coordinate in the same way:

> He is a *stirring, challenging* speaker.

There is a test that can help you identify coordinate adjectives: coordinate adjectives can usually have *and* put between them and still sound correct.

> stirring **and** challenging speaker = a stirring, challenging speaker
> (but not "her heavy and black coat")

In a Series of Independent Clauses

A comma is used to separate the first independent clause from the conjunction in a compound sentence. (Do not use a comma before a conjunction that joins the parts of a compound predicate.)

> The Strait of Gibraltar opens the Mediterranean Sea to the Atlantic Ocean, and the Suez Canal opens the Mediterranean Sea to the Red Sea. (*But:* The Suez Canal connects Europe with South Asia and opens the Mediterranean Sea to the Red Sea.)

When two independent clauses are very short, the comma may be omitted before the conjunction.

> The wind is strong and the waves are dangerous.

If a compound sentence contains three or more independent clauses, a comma is used after all except the last.

> The air is warm, the sky is clear, and the water is calm.

Chapter 5: Adjectives
p. 114

Chapter 1: Comma Splices and Fused Sentences
p. 15

Chapter 6: Conjunctions
p. 152

Chapter 8: Compound Sentence
p. 194

Punctuation   279

Teaching Strategy: Participation

Write several nouns for display and ask the students to supply two adjectives for each noun. Then lead the class to apply the test using the word *and* to determine whether the adjectives are coordinate adjectives or cumulative adjectives, which build on one another.

Insert any missing commas in the following sentences. If a sentence is correct, write _C_ in the blank.

———— 1. Venice is an unusual‚interesting city.

——_C_—— 2. Venice lies on about 120 islands and has canals instead of streets.

———— 3. The people of Venice use boats instead of automobiles‚buses‚ taxis‚and trucks.

——_C_—— 4. Venice is a popular tourist attraction.

——_C_—— 5. The location of Venice gives the city its fame but also causes problems.

———— 6. During a storm, waters can flood streets‚cover walkways‚and damage buildings.

———— 7. The Grand Canal is a large‚important waterway.

———— 8. Palaces stand on both sides of the Grand Canal‚and the Rialto Bridge crosses the canal.

———— 9. My family flew to Italy‚visited Rome‚and then went to Venice.

——_C_—— 10. I rode a gondola but Mom walked.

Insert any missing commas in the following sentences. If a sentence is correct, write _C_ in the blank.

———— 1. The Bahamas are a chain of about seven hundred islands‚and together they form a nation.

———— 2. The mild‚beautiful climate of the Bahamas has drawn a number of tourists.

_C_ 3. Most of the native island people live on New Providence and Grand Bahama.

_____ 4. Andros,Bimini,and Cat Island are some of the more popular Bahamian Islands.

_____ 5. Marlin,sailfish,and tuna are just a few types of fish found off the coast of Bimini.

_____ 6. A profitable,busy city on New Providence is Nassau.

_C_ 7. Many large cruise ships dock at Nassau.

_____ 8. Uncle Finley and Aunt Nadine left their home on Tuesday, drove to Florida,and flew to the Bahamas.

_C_ 9. On Thursday my aunt swam and my uncle fished.

_C_ 10. Tourists can buy many colorful straw items from Bahamian craftworkers.

Commas After Introductory Elements

Use a comma to set off or separate certain kinds of elements when they come first in the sentence.

Introductory Participial Phrases

An introductory participle or participial phrase should be set off by a comma.

> *Holding allegiance to no particular nation*, pirates generally attack ships from any country.

Long Introductory Prepositional Phrases

A long prepositional phrase (generally, five words or more) or multiple prepositional phrases at the beginning of a sentence should be set off by a comma.

> *In the Battle of New Orleans*, notorious pirate Jean Laffite aided the United States against the British.

Introductory Numbering Words

Commas are often used after numbering words like *first* and *second* and are sometimes used after *next, finally,* and *last.*

G
GRAMMAR
Chapter 6: Prepositional Phrases
p. 142

First, decide on a topic.
Second, research your topic.
Finally, create a detailed outline.

Introductory Adverb Clauses

An introductory adverb clause always requires a comma.

> *Before they were defeated in the Tripolitan War*, the Barbary pirates attacked and raided ships in the Mediterranean Sea and the Atlantic Ocean.

Other Introductory Elements

Other introductory elements that may require commas include modifiers of the sentence as a whole.

> *Although we consider it a part of the past*, the frequency of piracy has actually increased in recent years.

When an introductory phrase contains a verbal, a comma is often needed.

> *After attacking*, the pirates often set fire to a ship.

Chapter 8: Adverb Clauses
p. 202

12-7 PRACTICE THE SKILL

Insert any missing commas in the following sentences. If a sentence is correct, write *C* in the blank.

_____ 1. Before a trip to Germany, you should consider including in your visit a trip to the Bavarian Alps.

___C___ 2. In the Bavarian Alps one can visit several famous castles.

_____ 3. First, a traveler can visit the famous Neuschwanstein Castle.

_____ 4. Visiting this castle, a tourist must walk one mile into the Bavarian Alps near Füssen, Germany.

_____ 5. After studying a castle in Germany, King Ludwig II of Bavaria made plans to build his own.

_____ 6. Although Neuschwanstein resembles a medieval castle, it was actually built in the nineteenth century.

___C___ 7. Today Neuschwanstein is one of Germany's most visited attractions.

___C___ 8. Then you can visit Linderhof.

_C_   9. In 1864 King Ludwig began the building of Linderhof.

_____ 10. If you visit Linderhof, you will notice the splendor of the gar-

dens.

Insert any missing commas in the following sentences. If a sentence is correct, write _C_ in the blank.

_C_   1. In North America one famous vacation spot is Niagara Falls.

_C_   2. Often vacationers will choose to camp near Niagara Falls.

_____ 3. Located on the Niagara River, the falls are part of the bound-

ary between the United States and Canada.

_C_   4. The great Niagara Falls is really a combination of two falls.

_____ 5. On the United States side of Goat Island, the American

Falls is more than one thousand feet long.

_____ 6. When you visit the Canadian side, you are visiting

Horseshoe Falls.

_C_   7. We learned that Niagara Falls is the most powerful falls

in North America.

_C_   8. At night the waterfall is especially beautiful.

_____ 9. Unbelievably, 73,000 metric tons of rock fell from the

American Falls in 1931.

_C_ 10. Then about 167,800 metric tons fell in 1954.

Commas to Set Off Certain Sentence Elements

Commas often set off a word or a group of words from the rest of the sentence. The number of commas needed depends on where the word or word group is—at the beginning, in the middle, or at the end of the sentence. At the beginning and at the end, just one comma is needed. In the middle, two commas are needed—regardless of whether or not you can "hear" them both. The following sentence elements are set off by commas wherever they come in the sentence.

Interjections

Most interjections are set off from the rest of the sentence by commas.

> *Well,* I have studied the history of the Vikings.
> I can tell you about them, *yes.*

Nouns of Direct Address

Sometimes we call a person by his name or courtesy title when we speak to him. That name or title, called a **noun of direct address,** should be set off by commas.

> *Mr. President,* do you plan to take immediate action to solve this problem?
> May I ask, *sir,* what is your opinion about the current project?

Parenthetical Expressions

Use commas to set off a phrase that could be left out of the sentence.

> Mr. Stephens, *as you may already know,* will be leaving us next year.
> *As you may already know,* Mr. Stephens will be leaving us next year.
> Mr. Stephens will be leaving us next year, *as you may already know.*

Phrases That Show Contrast

A phrase that shows contrast should be set off by commas, particularly when the phrase begins with a negative word like *not* or *never.*

> Mrs. Wells, *not Mr. Stephens,* will be teaching geometry next year.
> Always see that your appearance is clean and orderly, *never sloppy or unkempt.*

Chapter 6: Interjections
p. 160

Chapter 2: Functions of Nouns in the Sentence
p. 38

12-9 PRACTICE THE SKILL

Insert any missing commas in the following sentences. If a sentence is correct, write *C* in the blank.

_____ 1. My parents visited London, not Paris, last year.

_____ 2. Generally speaking, they had a nice vacation.

___C___ 3. Did they have any problems, Peter?

_____ 4. Well, they were amazed at the cost of everything.

_____ 5. They were always with a group, never alone.

_____ 6. They did, of course, enjoy visiting historic places.

___C___ 7. Oh, where did they visit?

_____ 8. Some of the places they visited, Jacob, were the Tower of London, Westminster Abbey, and Buckingham Palace.

_____ 9. Westminster Abbey, not Buckingham Palace, was one of their favorite places.

_____ 10. Westminster Abbey, as you know, is the scene of many important events.

12-10 ## R EVIEW THE S KILL

Insert any missing commas in the following sentences. If a sentence is correct, write _C_ in the blank.

_____ 1. Hey, you should visit the South Pacific for a tropical island vacation.

_____ 2. You could, for example, visit Fiji.

_____ 3. Do you know where Fiji is, class?

_____ 4. Well, Mrs. McCaffey, Fiji is a country in the South Pacific.

_____ 5. Yes, Fiji is in the South Pacific and is made up of more than eight hundred islands.

_____ 6. Suva, not Nadi, is Fiji's capital city.

_____ 7. Most of the Fiji islands were formed by volcanoes, Stephen.

_____ 8. Larger islands have high volcanic peaks, as a matter of fact.

___C___ 9. Visitors are always welcome, never shunned.

_____ 10. The people of Fiji, in fact, are known for their friendliness.

Appositives

Most appositives are set off by commas.

> The school newspaper, _the Eagle_, circulates every other Friday.

The exception is that no comma is used with a "close appositive"—a short appositive that is more important than the noun before it.

> The famous explorer _Balboa_ discovered the Pacific Ocean.

G
GRAMMAR

Chapter 2: Functions of Nouns in the Sentence
p. 38

Restrictive and Nonrestrictive Elements

A **restrictive** element is one that is necessary to identify (restrict the possibilities to) the particular thing that is meant. Restrictive elements use no commas.

A **nonrestrictive** element gives extra information but is not necessary for identification of the thing modified. Nonrestrictive elements are set off by commas.

The examples below include nonrestrictive and restrictive elements of various types. Since appositives follow the same punctuation rule, they are included as well.

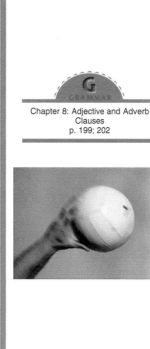

G
GRAMMAR

Chapter 8: Adjective and Adverb Clauses
p. 199; 202

NONRESTRICTIVE ADJECTIVE CLAUSE	Volleyball, *which is an intense sport,* is played with a white leather or synthetic ball.
RESTRICTIVE ADJECTIVE CLAUSE	The kind of volleyball *that is played at the beach* has different rules from regulation volleyball.
NONRESTRICTIVE PHRASE	Our team captain, *showing a lot of spirit,* led us on to our first victory.
RESTRICTIVE PHRASE	A team captain *with a lot of spirit* is a great encouragement to the team.
NONRESTRICTIVE APPOSITIVE	The team that we played last night, *the Crusaders,* is from Mentor.
RESTRICTIVE APPOSITIVE ("CLOSE APPOSITIVE")	My friend *Brenda* is our team captain.
NONRESTRICTIVE ADVERB CLAUSE	The close score and the cheering fans heightened the excitement in the gym, *even though all of the players were calmly focused on the game.*
RESTRICTIVE ADVERB CLAUSE	We won *because we worked together well.*

12-11 PRACTICE THE SKILL

Insert any missing commas in the following sentences. If a sentence is correct, write *C* in the blank.

__*C*__ 1. A tourist who wants to visit Africa may wish to start in Morocco.

_____ 2. Morocco‚ because of its culture‚ is a popular vacation destination.

Teaching Strategy: Participation

To help the students understand which elements are restrictive and which are nonrestrictive, ask them to read the example sentences on page 286 aloud, leaving out the element in question. If the sentence meaning is not altered, then the element is nonrestrictive.

_____ 3. The Strait of Gibraltar, which connects the Mediterranean and the Atlantic, separates Morocco from Spain by only about eight miles.

_C_ 4. The city Chechaouene is a beautiful place to visit.

_____ 5. Rabat, Morocco's capital, lies on the Atlantic Ocean.

_C_ 6. A visitor may want to study the architecture of Rabat after he strolls along the ocean.

_____ 7. Casablanca, with over 2.5 million people, is the largest North African city outside Egypt.

_C_ 8. Troops from the United States landed in Casablanca during World War II.

_C_ 9. Some Roman sites that a tourist may enjoy are the ruins at Lixus.

_____ 10. The Roman ruins at Volubilis are more popular, whereas the ruins at Lixus are less visited.

12-12 REVIEW THE SKILL

Insert any missing commas in the following sentences. If a sentence is correct, write *C* in the blank.

_C_ 1. Another African country that attracts many visitors is Egypt.

_____ 2. A small part of Egypt, the Sinai Peninsula, is in Asia.

_____ 3. Giza, near Cairo, is the site of the Great Sphinx and the Great Pyramids.

_____ 4. Many archaeologists, with their love of history, enjoy excavating near the sites of the pyramids of Egypt.

_C_ 5. The great architect and statesman Imhotep built the first known pyramid around 2650 B.C.

<u> *C* </u> 6. The largest pyramid was built for the Egyptian pharaoh Khufu.

<u> *C* </u> 7. When pharaohs died, they were often buried with great treasures.

<u>   </u> 8. The Great Sphinx, which is a huge limestone statue, stretches 240 feet long and rises about 66 feet high.

<u> *C* </u> 9. The pyramid near the Great Sphinx was King Khufu's. Many believe Khufu built the Great Sphinx as well.

<u>   </u> 10. Weather forces, including sandstorms and wind, have caused some deterioration of the Great Sphinx.

Commas with Quotations, Dates, and Addresses; and Commas in Letters

With Direct Quotations

A "quotation tag" (*John said, said she,* and so on) is joined to the quoted sentence with one or two commas. One comma is used if the quotation tag comes at the beginning or at the end, and two are used if it comes in the middle of the quoted sentence.

> *Olivia asked,* "Where was the first permanent settlement in America?"

> "The first settlement," *replied Jason,* "was Jamestown, which was located near the Chesapeake Bay."

> "Captain John Smith was the famous leader of the colony," *added Jason.*

No comma is used at the end of a quotation if a question mark or an exclamation point is needed there instead.

> "Did the colony survive?" asked Olivia.

Commas always go before quotation marks.

> "The colony had almost given up," explained Jason, "but new settlers and supplies came at a sorely needed time in 1607."

See page 292 for special uses of quotations when commas should not be used.

With the Parts of a Date

When using the normal order of month-day-year, put a comma between the day and the year.

> The USS *Maine* sank in Havana harbor on February 15, 1898.

If the date does not end the sentence, put a comma also after the year.

> On February 15, 1898, the USS *Maine* sank in Havana harbor.

With the Parts of an Address

Use a comma between the parts of an address. Also use a comma after the last word in the address if the sentence is not yet finished.

> He was born in Oak Brook, Illinois, and lived there until his family moved to Madrid, Spain.

Do not use a comma between the state and the ZIP code.

> Please forward our mail to 17 Hammond Avenue, Brookpark, Ohio 44142.

After Certain Parts of a Letter

A comma is used after the salutation in a friendly letter.

> Dear Sarah,
> Dear Miss Ames,

In either a business letter or a friendly letter, a comma is used after the complimentary closing.

> Your friend,   Sincerely,
>
> Frankie   Tom Baker
>
>   Tom Baker

Chapter 11: Titles and First Words
p. 265

12-13 PRACTICE THE SKILL

Insert any missing commas in the following items. If an item is correct, write *C* in the blank.

_____ 1. Dear Juro,

__C__ 2. My family moved to Martha's Vineyard in May of 1998 because my father got a new job.

_____ 3. My mother owns an antique shop located at 2 Staton Avenue, Chilmark, MA 02535.

_____ 4. In a recent letter your mother asked, "What are people's opinions about Martha's Vineyard?"

_____ 5. "Maybe," my mother said, "we can send them a magazine about the island."

_____ 6. A popular magazine recently stated, "The island of Martha's
          ^
          Vineyard is breathtaking."

_____ 7. In Vineyard Haven, Massachusetts, you can rent a sailboat.
                             ^   ^

_____ 8. We recently went to a restaurant in Edgartown, Massachusetts,
                                                        ^   ^
          for a seafood dinner.

_____ 9. On June 4, 2001, we were able to take a small plane to see the
                    ^   ^
          entire island; I am sure you will enjoy your vacation here.

_____ 10. Your friend, Jacob
                       ^

In the blank write the letter of the item that is punctuated correctly.

1. ___*A*___ A. Dear Mr. Frederick,

                    Please excuse Diana from classes next week. She
               will be with us in Maryland.

                                              Sincerely,
                                              Marta Patton
           B. Dear Mr. Frederick,

                    Please excuse Diana from classes next week. She
               will be with us in Maryland.

                                              Sincerely
                                              Marta Patton

2. ___*B*___ A. The address of the Office of Tourism Development is
                  217 East Redwood Street, Baltimore, MD, 21202.
           B. The address of the Office of Tourism Development is
                  217 East Redwood Street, Baltimore, MD 21202.

3. ___*B*___ A. "Are the historical sites in Maryland impressive?",
                  asked Diana.
           B. "Are the historical sites in Maryland impressive?"
                  asked Diana.

4. ___*A*___ A. My mother always said, "A historical vacation is a
                  learning experience."
           B. My mother always said "A historical vacation is a
                  learning experience."

5. ___*B*___ A. The capital has been Annapolis, Maryland since 1694.
           B. The capital has been Annapolis, Maryland, since 1694.

6. ___*A*___ A. On April 28, 1778, Maryland became a state.
           B. On April 28, 1778 Maryland became a state.

7. ___*A*___ A. "If you visit Fort McHenry," Mr. Frederick said, "you
                  need to remember our national anthem."
           B. "If you visit Fort McHenry", Mr. Frederick said, "you
                  need to remember our national anthem."

8. ___B___ A. Mother replied "I have been there before."
        B. Mother replied, "I have been there before."

9. ___B___ A. The famous Battle of Antietam took place near
        Sharpsburg, Maryland, on September 17 1862.
        B. The famous Battle of Antietam took place near
        Sharpsburg, Maryland, on September 17, 1862.

10. ___B___ A. "I am looking forward to seeing the places I have
        learned about in history class." said Diana.
        B. "I am looking forward to seeing the places I have
        learned about in history class," said Diana.

Incorrect Commas

Commas in the wrong places can be distracting and even confusing.

Before a Conjunction That Joins Only Two Elements

Normally no comma should be used when only two words, phrases, or dependent clauses are joined by a conjunction.

> **WRONG** The Boers founded the republics of Transvaal, and the Orange Free State.

> **RIGHT** The Boers founded the republics of Transvaal and the Orange Free State.

Between a Subject and a Verb

Do not put a comma between a subject and a verb.

> **WRONG** In the 1850s the government of Great Britain, gave the Dutch republics their independence.

> **RIGHT** In the 1850s the government of Great Britain gave the Dutch republics their independence.

However, a pair of commas (not just one) may set off a nonrestrictive item between the subject and the verb.

> Diamonds and gold, which were discovered in the region in the 1890s, caused thousands of British to flood the area.

Do not try to use a comma to salvage a sentence that has an awkwardly long subject. Revise the sentence instead.

> **AWKWARD** Your taking dinner to the family whose father has been ill, was very kind.

> **BETTER** It was very kind of you to take dinner to the family whose father has been ill.

After a Conjunction

A comma should not ordinarily follow a conjunction.

> **WRONG** We had a lot of things left to do, and, we did not have much time to finish.

> **RIGHT** We had a lot of things left to do, and we did not have much time to finish.

Chapter 6: Conjunctions
p. 152

Of course, a pair of commas may set off an item after a conjunction as well as anywhere else.

> We asked for help, and, fortunately, many people volunteered.

With Quotations Used in Certain Ways

When a quotation functions as either the subject or the predicate noun of the sentence, it should not be set off by commas.

> **SUBJECT** "Failing to plan is planning to fail" was my dad's favorite admonishment.

> **PREDICATE NOUN** My dad's favorite motto was "Failing to plan is planning to fail."

Like other restrictive appositives, a quoted restrictive appositive is not set off by commas. (See p. 286 for restrictive appositives.)

> My dad's admonishment "Failing to plan is planning to fail" still encourages me to be diligent and organized.

In Certain Places in a Date

A comma should not come between a month and a year.

> **WRONG** Please come to the reception scheduled for June, 24.
> The new building will be ready by March, 2008.

> **RIGHT** Please come to the reception scheduled for June 24.
> The new building will be ready by March 2008.

12-15 ℙRACTICE THE 𝕊KILL

Insert any missing commas in the following sentences. If a sentence is correct, write *C* in the blank.

_____*C*_____ 1. Visiting the Statue of Liberty in Upper New York Bay is common for a tourist in New York.

_____ 2. French citizens donated the money to build the statue, and citizens of the United States raised the money for the base.

_____*C*_____ 3. The Statue of Liberty and the immigration station at Ellis Island form the Statue of Liberty National Monument.

_____ 4. The dedication of the statue on October 28, 1886, was celebrated on land and sea.

_____ 5. A crown, a torch, and a tablet are part of the statue.

_C_ 6. Lady Liberty proudly holds a glowing torch.

_C_ 7. The statue was first called "Mother of Exiles" in a poem by Emma Lazarus.

_C_ 8. Frédéric Auguste Bartholdi designed the statue and supervised its construction in Paris.

_____ 9. The statue was later restored, and, interestingly, an entirely new torch was created.

_C_ 10. Official celebrations for the newly restored statue were held in July 1986.

12-16 USE THE SKILL

Rewrite the following paragraph, correcting the ten errors in incorrect comma usage.

Ranking among the four most spectacular waterfalls in the world Victoria Falls lies between Zambia, and Zimbabwe. The falls, dramatically drops 355 feet over a crest, that spans one mile. Actually, the height of the falls is 256 feet at the right bank, and, it rises to 355 feet in the center. The discoverer of the falls David Livingstone, visited the site on November 16, 1855 while on a trek down the Zambezi River. He said, "Scenes so lovely must have been gazed on by angels in their flight." He later stated that the falls was, "the most wonderful sight I had witnessed in Africa." The native name of the falls means, "the smoke that thunders," but, honoring Queen Victoria, was Livingstone's goal in naming the falls.

Ranking among the four most spectacular waterfalls in the world, Victoria Falls lies between Zambia and Zimbabwe. The falls dramatically drops 355 feet over a crest that spans one mile. Actually, the height of the falls is 256 feet at the right bank, and it rises to 355 feet in the center. The discoverer of the falls, David Livingstone, visited the site on November 16, 1855, while on a trek down the Zambezi River. He said, "Scenes so lovely must have been gazed on by angels in their flight." He later stated that the falls was "the most wonderful sight I had witnessed in Africa." The native name of the falls means "the smoke that thunders," but honoring Queen Victoria was Livingstone's goal in naming the falls.

Evaluation

Materials

- a paragraph with several commas

To determine whether the students understand the rules about commas, give them a sample paragraph that incorporates several commas. (Be sure to choose a paragraph with commas that follow the rules in this chapter; other comma rules will be introduced in later grades.) The students should locate and number the commas. On their own paper, they should write the purpose for each comma. _(separates two independent clauses, sets off an introductory phrase, separates coordinate adjectives, etc.)_

Semicolons

The semicolon signals a stronger break in the sentence than does the comma. The semicolon always joins equal elements. A fairly strong mark of punctuation, the semicolon should not be overused.

Between Two Independent Clauses

A semicolon may connect two closely related independent clauses. Often the second independent clause reinforces the first, and there may or may not be a transitional word within the second independent clause.

> As a young boy William Carey possessed a gift for learning languages; Carey used his gift by translating the Scriptures into several Asian languages.

Colons

The colon is a strong mark of punctuation, separating elements almost as definitely as the period. The colon often points up what follows it, marking it as being important, explanatory, or more specific.

In Bible References and Expressions of Time

An unspaced colon separates the chapter and the verse in Bible references.

> Romans 6:10
> John 14:1-3

An unspaced colon also separates the hour and the minute in expressions of time.

> 2:00 P.M.
> 10:05 a.m.

After the Salutation of a Business Letter

A colon follows the salutation of a business letter.

> Dear Mr. President:
> Dear Representative Estes:

Before a Series at the End of a Sentence

A colon can introduce a series that comes at the end of a sentence. Often *the following* or *as follows* appears somewhere before the colon, as in the second and third examples below.

> The Yalta Conference was a summit of the three great leaders during World War II: Churchill, Roosevelt, and Stalin.

> During World War II, the Japanese invaded the following British colonies: Hong Kong, Malaya, Singapore, Burma, and Indonesia.

> The awards are as follows: first place, second place, and honorable mention.

GRAMMAR

Chapter 8: Compound Sentence
p. 194

USAGE

Chapter 11: Titles and First Words
p. 265

Reinforcement

Students should remember that semicolons join equal elements. If a semicolon joins two independent clauses, the second clause should be closely related to the first clause. Remind students not to combine sentences with a semicolon if the two sentences are unrelated.

For emphasis, a colon can introduce a single appositive at the end of a sentence.

My brother wants only one gift for his birthday: a basketball.

A colon can introduce such a series *only* if the series is not part of the basic structure of the sentence. That is, we do not put a colon before a direct object, an object of a preposition, a predicate adjective, or a predicate noun.

WRONG The campers took: tents, sleeping bags, and flashlights.

RIGHT The campers took the following items: tents, sleeping bags, and flashlights.

WRONG Our camp counselor is: enthusiastic, athletic, and friendly.

RIGHT Our camp counselor is enthusiastic, athletic, and friendly.

Do not use a colon after *such as* or *including.*

WRONG Several extracurricular activities are available, including: chorus, debate, and volleyball.

RIGHT Several extracurricular activities are available, including chorus, debate, and volleyball.

Before a Long or Formal Direct Quotation

A colon is often used before a long or formal direct quotation, especially if the introduction to it is rather formal.

President Luttmann commended the student body with the following statement in yesterday's speech: "We are deeply appreciative of all your support. We could not have withstood the opposition without the loving loyalty of the students."

The quotation after the colon must be the last element in the sentence, as it is in the example.

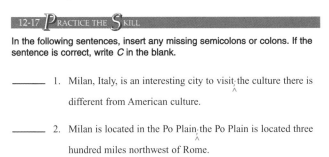

In the following sentences, insert any missing semicolons or colons. If the sentence is correct, write *C* in the blank.

———— 1. Milan, Italy, is an interesting city to visit; the culture there is

different from American culture.

———— 2. Milan is located in the Po Plain; the Po Plain is located three

hundred miles northwest of Rome.

Writing Link

Many students may not be comfortable with using colons in their writing. Colons can add special emphasis and create a variety in sentence structure. Encourage students to use colons when appropriate in their writing.

_____ 3. Milan's ancient culture originated with the Celts;Milan later became a pawn between France and Spain.

_____ 4. Milan houses many famous art museums and exhibitions:the Luigi Bocconi School of Commerce, Brera Academy of Fine Arts, and Giuseppe Verdi Conservatory of Music.

_____ 5. *The Last Supper* is in the refectory adjacent to the Church of Santa Maria delle Grazie;the fresco was restored in the twentieth century.

__C__ 6. I recently e-mailed the museum curator and asked for a museum schedule.

_____ 7. Dear Sir:Please send me information concerning the hours and admission prices for the museum.

__C__ 8. My family and I are leaving for Milan on May 17.

_____ 9. I will need to bring the following items on my trip:clothes, an umbrella, and an Italian pocket dictionary.

_____ 10. Our plane leaves for Italy at 5:26 in the afternoon.

12-18 REVIEW THE SKILL

In the following sentences, insert any missing semicolons or colons. If the sentence is correct, write *C* in the blank.

_____ 1. The Grand Canyon is one of the scenic wonders of the world; because of the changing light, the view from the rim never appears exactly the same.

_____ 2. The Grand Canyon extends 217 miles from east to west;the width of the Grand Canyon ranges from four to eighteen miles.

_____ 3. Some of the rock formations are named for ancient pagan gods Diana's Temple and Wotan's Throne.

_____ 4. Some other names are from Indian sources Pima Point and Shinumo Amphitheater.

_____ 5. In 1908 President Theodore Roosevelt designated most of the canyon as a national monument Congress voted for it to become a national park in 1919.

_____ 6. Ronald Ives from Northern Arizona University wrote the following about the Grand Canyon "The national park is noted for its scenic beauty and abundant wildlife. More than 200 species of birds, resident and migratory, 60 species of mammals, and 15 species of reptiles and amphibians have been reported."

_____ 7. Because of heavy snowfall, the north rim is closed in winter the north rim has extensive forests as a result of the large amount of rain it receives.

_____ 8. We went to the Grand Canyon when I was in sixth grade that trip was one of my favorite vacations.

_____ 9. At 627 this morning, the sun came up over the rim and gave the whole canyon a rainbowlike appearance.

__C__ 10. Tourists began coming to see the canyon in 1890; now there are over two million visitors every year.

Chapter 11: Titles and First Words
p. 265

Quotation Marks

Quotation marks have two main uses: to enclose direct quotations and to indicate the titles of shorter works. Quotation marks are always used in pairs.

Direct Quotations

Quotation marks indicate that the exact words of a writer or speaker are being reported.

> In her closing remarks, Sarah Taman acknowledged that "many critics do not agree on what is the central theme of the story."

> "Several different conclusions are based on good arguments," she added.

Sometimes the quotation tag (such as *he said*) comes in the middle of the quoted sentence. In that case commas surround the quotation tag, and both halves of the divided quotation are enclosed in quotation marks.

> "If you're ready," said Brock, "I'll start loading your things in the car."

(In American usage, commas and periods always come before quotation marks.)

There are two common exceptions to the usual need for quotation marks around someone's exact words.

- Quotation marks are not used within a play for the speeches of the dramatic characters.

- They are often not used for well-known proverbs (including certain biblical sayings).

> After his summer job expired, Tim learned not to count chickens before they hatch.

Dialogue

In reported dialogue, a new paragraph should begin whenever there is a change in speaker.

> "There's no way I can finish all this work," said Jeff, as he surveyed the stacks of research books on the table.

> "Don't worry," said Ron. "Just start doing a little bit at a time."

In this example, a period is used after the quotation tag because the preceding quotation is a complete sentence.

Teaching Strategy: Discussion

Some students may be confused about when commas appear before quotations. Remind them that if a quotation tag (e.g., *Sarah replied,*) comes before a quotation, then a comma must follow the tag. If the quotation is integrated into the sentence, then no comma is necessary. For example, the sentence *The book says that "organization is necessary for success"* does not require a comma.

Reinforcement

Remind students that a quotation tag is not a conjunction. A tag cannot join two independent clauses. Write the following sentence for display: *I think I will be able to come," replied Theo, "I just need to check with my parents first."* This sentence is incorrect. Students can correct the sentence by placing a period after *Theo* or by inserting a semicolon after *come* and then moving the quotation tag to the end of the sentence. If the student chooses the second correction, he should also delete the quotation marks after *come* and before *I*.

Writing Link

Materials
- pictures of individuals (two for each student)

Give each student two pictures of individuals. Each student should write a realistic dialogue between those two characters. You may want to provide another picture as a setting or give students a short introductory situation with which to begin their dialogues. Check the papers for correct use of quotation marks and commas. Read several of the dialogues to the class.

Indirect Quotations

An indirect quotation gives the idea but not the exact words of the speaker or writer. Indirect quotations should not have quotation marks.

DIRECT QUOTATION   Mark said, "**I** have several books you will need for that project."

INDIRECT QUOTATION   Mark said **that he** has several books you will need for that project.

Titles of Short Works

Titles of short works are normally enclosed in quotation marks. A piece of writing is considered a short work if it is part of a larger work or is too short to be a book by itself. Short works include articles, chapters of a book, short stories, essays, songs, and most poems.

Tonight's assignment is to read Chapter 7, "Free Verse in Modern Poetry."

Wallace Stevens uses free verse in his poem "Thirteen Ways of Looking at a Blackbird."

An exception is that we use only capitalization—no quotation marks—with the major subdivisions of the Bible.

That passage is found in Philippians, which is one of the prison Epistles in the New Testament.

Another exception is that no quotation marks are used with a title when it stands as the heading of the work itself. For example, do not use quotation marks with the title of a report you write for class.

Single Quotation Marks

Single quotation marks should be used whenever quotation marks are needed within quotation marks.

Bryan asked, "Do you know where I can find a copy of the song 'Jesu, Joy of Man's Desiring'?"

"Mrs. Johnson said, 'Be sure your presentation is at least twenty minutes long,'" Carmen explained to Steve.

Quotation Marks and Other Punctuation

In American usage, commas and periods always go before adjacent quotation marks, regardless of what may seem logical.

Martin Luther proclaimed that "salvation is through faith alone," and he received much persecution from religious leaders.

Scriptural Application

In modern narrative and drama, authors sometimes reveal character traits by describing a person's physical features. A dishonest man may be tight lipped with small, shifty eyes. The Bible reveals a person's character most often by what he does and by what he says. Give students a list of prominent individuals from the Bible and challenge them to find one statement that is representative of each person's character. The students' completed lists might include the following:

- Joshua: "As for me and my house, we will serve the Lord." (Josh. 24:15)
- David: "This day will the Lord deliver thee into mine hand . . . that all the earth may know that there is a God in Israel." (I Sam. 17:46)
- Esther: "If I perish, I perish." (Esther 4:16)
- Satan: "I will ascend into heaven, I will exalt my throne above the stars of God." (Isa. 14:13)
- Thomas: "Except I shall see in his hands the print of the nails, and put my finger into the print of the nails, and thrust my hand into his side, I will not believe." (John 20:25)
- Paul: "This one thing I do, forgetting those things which are behind, and reaching forth unto those things which are before, I press toward the mark for the prize of the high calling of God in Christ Jesus." (Phil. 3:13-14)

Now challenge the students to consider their own speech. If their dialogue were recorded for a day, what would a reader assume to be true about them?

Colons and semicolons always go after closing quotation marks. (Because the colon or semicolon is punctuation for the whole sentence, it stays outside the quoted item.)

> One of Isaac Watts's most famous hymns is "When I Survey the Wondrous Cross"; some of his other hymns include "O God, Our Help in Ages Past" and "I Sing the Mighty Power of God."

Question marks and exclamation marks go inside the quotation marks unless the entire sentence is meant to be exclamatory or interrogative.

> Patrick Henry exclaimed, "Give me liberty or give me death!"

> Can you determine the theme of Hawthorne's short story "The Birthmark"?

The concluding period of a sentence should be omitted if the sentence ends with an interrogative or exclamatory quotation.

> The lawyer asked, "What were you doing when the accident occurred?"

Ellipses

Ellipses (or "ellipsis marks") are three spaced dots that most often indicate the omission of something in quoted matter. The dots look like periods, but there should be a space before and after each one.

Omission of Words in a Quotation

Whenever words are omitted within a sentence, a set of three spaced dots should appear wherever the word or words would have been.

ORIGINAL	"True Christianity, the religion that holds the Bible as the sole and sufficient Word of God, is a unique religion. Only Bible-believing Christians teach that man is completely powerless to save himself but that God has taken the initiative and done all the work necessary to save man." (Coart Ramey, Why the Bible Matters)
WITH OMISSIONS	"True Christianity . . . is a unique religion. Only Bible-believing Christians teach that man is completely powerless to save himself but that God has . . . done all the work necessary to save man."

Of course, honesty requires that the omissions not distort the meaning of the original.

Within a quoted passage of two or more sentences, use a period followed by three spaced dots to show the omission of (1) the end of the preceding sentence or (2) the beginning of the following sentence. What precedes the four dots must be a grammatically complete sentence and what follows them must be too.

> "True Christianity, the religion that holds the Bible as the sole and sufficient Word of God, is a unique religion. . . . Man is completely powerless to save himself."

Teaching Strategy: Participation

Ask students to name their favorite books, magazines, poems, stories, and songs. List these titles for display and then ask the class to identify whether each title should appear in quotation marks or in italics.

Enrichment

Point out that American usage dictates that periods and commas usually appear inside quotation marks. In usual British style, however, periods and commas appear inside quotation marks only if they are part of the quoted material.

Reinforcement

If four dots appear within a quotation of two or more sentences, what precedes the four dots must be a grammatically complete sentence and what follows them must be too. This does not mean, however, that the entire sentence from the original passage must appear; it means only that the quoted portions must be grammatically complete sentences.

Notice that the first letter of the sentence following the ellipsis may be capitalized, just as it would be at the beginning of any other sentence, even if the word was not capitalized in the original.

In addition, a full line of spaced dots may be used to indicate the omission of one or more lines of poetry.

Ellipses are not needed at the beginning or end of a quoted passage.

> The paragraph states that "God has taken the initiative and done all the work necessary to save man."

Halting or Unfinished Speech

Ellipses may be used to indicate hesitant pauses in speech, and they may also show that a sentence has just slowly trailed off before completion. Inside a sentence three spaced dots are used, but at the end of the sentence a period precedes the three spaced dots.

> Evan tried to break the news gently: "I need to tell you . . . um, well, I'm not sure how to say this, but. . . ."

12-19 PRACTICE THE SKILL

Insert any missing quotation marks in the following sentences. Circle any unnecessary quotation marks. If the sentence is correct, write *C* in the blank.

_____ 1. My mom asked me, "Alexandra, would you like to go camping with us next week?"

___C___ 2. I told her, "That idea sounds like fun."

_____ 3. I stated, "Before I leave, I am going to read the short story 'The Masque of the Red Death.' "

___C___ 4. My mom said, "Be sure you bring the rest of your homework along with you."

_____ 5. My father asked, "Have you already read 'Young Goodman Brown,' or will you need to read that over vacation too?"

___C___ 6. Our campsite was at the bottom of a steep mountain, and I asked my father, "Dad, do you think we will be able to hike up the whole mountain today?"

_____ 7. My dad warned me that⌣I needed to be careful on our hike☺

_____ 8. "Dad," I exclaimed, "this is the biggest waterfall I have ever

seen!"
      ∧

_____ 9. "This is the largest waterfall in North Carolina!"my father
                                                            ∧
said.

___C___ 10. My teacher told me that hiking is one of the best exercises

we can do.

12-20 REVIEW THE SKILL

Read the paragraph and determine whether the quotations following the paragraph are correct. In each blank write the letter of the quotation that does not contain a usage error with either quotation marks or ellipses.

Passage from "Sailing Across Oceans" in *Great Adventurers of the Twentieth Century* by Ron Tagliapietra:

Heyerdahl visited forty-five-square-mile Easter Island for more evidence. Europeans named the island in 1722 because they sighted its coast lined with the great heads on Easter Sunday, but the natives call it *Rapa Nui* or *Te Pito o Te Henua,* "The Navel of the World," a fitting name for the most isolated island in the world. The nearest lands are the Pitcairn Islands, twelve hundred miles west, and Chile, twenty-six hundred miles east. No wonder the natives think of the heavens before they think of other earthly lands. They say that "Easter Island lies east of the sun and west of the moon."

1. ___B___ A. "Heyerdahl visited Easter Island . . . for more
            evidence."
         B. "Heyerdahl visited . . . Easter Island for more
            evidence."

2. ___A___ A. "The nearest lands are the Pitcairn Islands . . . and
            Chile."
         B. "The nearest lands are the Pitcairn Islands…and
            Chile."

3. ___A___ A. "Europeans named the island . . . because they sighted
            its coast lined with the great heads on Easter Sunday."
         B. "Europeans named the island . . . . because they
            sighted its coast lined with the great heads on Easter
            Sunday."

4. ___A___ A. "Heyerdahl visited forty-five-square-mile Easter
            Island for more evidence. . . . They sighted its
            coast lined with the great heads on Easter Sunday."
         B. "Heyerdahl visited forty-five-square-mile Easter
            Island for. . . . Its coast lined with the great heads
            on Easter Sunday."

5. __A__ A. "Heyerdahl visited forty-five-square-mile Easter Island for more evidence. . . . The nearest lands are the Pitcairn Islands, twelve hundred miles west, and Chile, twenty-six hundred miles east."
    B. "Heyerdahl visited forty-five-square-mile Easter Island for more evidence. . . The nearest lands are the Pitcairn Islands, twelve hundred miles west, and Chile, twenty-six hundred miles east."

6. __A__ A. "They say that 'Easter Island lies east of the sun and west of the moon.'"
    B. "They say that 'Easter Island lies east of the sun and west of the moon'."

7. __B__ A. "Europeans named the island in 1722 . . .'The Navel of the World,' a fitting name for the most isolated island in the world."
    B. "Europeans named the island in 1722 because they sighted its coast lined with the great heads on Easter Sunday, but the natives call it . . . 'The Navel of the World.'"

8. __B__ A. "Europeans named the island in 1722 because they sighted its coast lined with the great heads on Easter Sunday. . . ."
    B. "Europeans named the island in 1722 because they sighted its coast lined with the great heads on Easter Sunday."

9. __A__ A. "Heyerdahl visited . . . Easter Island. . . . The natives call it *Rapa Nui* or *Te Pito o Te Henua,* 'The Navel of the World.'"
    B. "Heyerdahl visited. . . . *Rapa Nui* or *Te Pito o Te Henua,* 'The Navel of the World.'

10. __B__ A. ". . . They say that 'Easter Island lies east of the sun and west of the moon.'"
    B. "They say that 'Easter Island lies east of the sun and west of the moon.'"

Underlining for Italics

Italic print is used mainly to indicate titles of books and other long works. In handwritten papers, underlining is used instead of italics.

HANDWRITTEN VERSION   People still enjoy reading the exciting ancient tales of Homer's <u>Iliad</u> and <u>Odyssey</u>.

WORD PROCESSED OR PUBLISHED VERSION   People still enjoy reading the exciting ancient tales of Homer's *Iliad* and *Odyssey.*

Titles of Long Works

Italicize or underline the title of any work that is long enough to be published by itself.

BOOKS	*Jane Eyre* by Charlotte Brontë (Exception: the Bible)
PERIODICALS	*Science News*
NEWSPAPERS	*Chicago Tribune*
EPIC POEMS	Homer's *Iliad*
MUSICAL COMPOSITIONS	Vivaldi's *The Four Seasons*
PLAYS	*Pygmalion*

Italicize or underline the names of works of art.

MOTION PICTURES	*Swiss Family Robinson*
WORKS OF VISUAL ART	*Pietà* *Horatio's Oath*

Large Transport Vehicles

The names of specific ships, aircraft, trains, and spacecraft should appear in italics.

SHIPS	*Monitor*
AIRCRAFT	*Spirit of St. Louis*
TRAINS	*Tom Thumb*
SPACECRAFT	*Gemini*

Words, Letters, and Numerals Being Discussed

Italicize words, letters, and numerals that are referred to as words.

The word *parallel* has one *r* and three *l*'s.
Write a *C* next to the sentences that are correct.
Some people draw a horizontal line through their *7*s.

Notice that the plural *s* is not italicized in the first or last sentence.

Insert any missing quotation marks or underlining for italics. If a sentence is correct, write C in the blank.

———— 1. London brings to mind the words history and literature.

———— 2. A visit to Shakespeare's Globe Theatre may help you understand how a play like Julius Caesar would have been performed.

———— 3. Isaac Watts, who wrote "O God, Our Help in Ages Past" and other hymns, studied in London.

———— 4. "London" is a short poem by William Blake that shows his opinion of eighteenth-century London.

———— 5. A Tale of Two Cities by Charles Dickens is a novel about Paris and London.

———— 6. Chapter 1, called "The Period," begins with the famous line, "It was the best of times, it was the worst of times."

———— 7. Perhaps you could watch a drama of one of Dickens's novels on Masterpiece Theatre.

———— 8. A music lover may be able to hear Beethoven's Ninth Symphony performed by the London Symphony.

———— 9. Near London Bridge, you may want to visit the Belfast, a large cruiser with a distinguished war record.

———— 10. Maybe you can get some information about London by reading a newspaper such as the London Daily.

Insert any missing quotation marks or underlining for italics. If a sentence is correct, write C in the blank.

_____ 1. I am writing an essay called "Interesting Museums."

_____ 2. Jane Austen's house in England, where she wrote and revised <u>Pride and Prejudice</u>, has become a museum.

_____ 3. In Baltimore you can visit the Poe House and Museum, where Poe presumably wrote his story "MS. Found in a Bottle."

_____ 4. The British Library has an exhibit on John Keats. The exhibit includes a copy of his poem "Ode to a Nightingale."

___C___ 5. Many museums contain rare copies of the Holy Bible.

_____ 6. The Special Collections Library at Duke University has fragments of Homer's great epic poem <u>The Odyssey</u>.

_____ 7. An art lover would enjoy getting a glimpse of the <u>Mona Lisa</u> at the Louvre.

_____ 8. The Mid America Air Museum displays the <u>Mustang II</u>, a homebuilt glider.

_____ 9. At the National Air and Space Museum, a student can learn more about <u>Apollo 11</u>.

_____ 10. Another museum in Washington, D.C., is Explorer's Hall, sponsored by the magazine <u>National Geographic</u>.

Apostrophes

Apostrophes were once used in English only to indicate that one or more letters had been omitted from a word. Today they are used mainly with contractions and possessives.

G
GRAMMAR
Chapter 5: Adverbs
p. 122

Omission of Letters and Numbers

In a contraction, an apostrophe indicates that letters have been omitted. It appears at the spot where the missing letter or letters would have been.

> wouldn't
> we're
> can't

Some contractions with *not* change the spelling of the main word slightly.

will + not = won't

Some words, such as *may* and *ought*, are rarely contracted with *not*. The contractions would be understood by a native English speaker, but they would sound very formal or old-fashioned. Avoid *mayn't* and *oughtn't*.

Any noun or pronoun subject can form a contraction with an appropriate form of *be, have, will,* or *would.*

> John's coming and he'll know how to fix the leak.
> They've been informed of who'll be available on that day.

The contraction *it's* (for *it is* or *it has*) should not be confused with the possessive *its.*

In informal writing, an apostrophe may be used to replace the first two figures for a year.

> the '04 graduation
> class of '99

Chapter 3: Personal Pronouns
pp. 48-49

Special Plurals

Regular common and proper nouns do not use apostrophes to create plurals; however, some special plural forms do need apostrophes. An apostrophe is used to form the plurals of letters or words being discussed. An apostrophe is not necessary to form the plurals of numbers, symbols, and dates.

> Bennie wants to visit the Smiths on Saturday morning.

> Try to avoid overusing *um*'s and *uh*'s in your speech. These oral pauses can be distracting.

> Mandy's computer does not print any *&*s or *#*s. She has to draw them in herself.

> Ronald Reagan was president during the great economic boost of the 1980s.

Reinforcement

Students often confuse the contraction *it's* with the possessive pronoun *its.* Because so many possessives end with *'s,* students may assume that the *'s* always indicates a possessive pronoun. Remind them that *it's* is a contraction for *it is. Its* is the possessive pronoun.

Chapter 2: Possessive Forms of
Nouns
pp. 27-28

Possessives

Nouns and many indefinite pronouns can be made possessive by the addition of *'s* or sometimes just the apostrophe.

For most singular nouns and indefinite pronouns, add *'s.*

> Brannon's artwork
> somebody's coat
> the bass's solo

The *s* after the apostrophe may be omitted for the traditional exceptions *Jesus* and *Moses.*

> Jesus' teachings fill the New Testament.
> Miriam was Moses' sister.

Add only an apostrophe to a regular plural noun ending in *s* or *es.*

> the members' club
> the classes' room assignments

If a plural noun does not end with an *s,* add *'s* to form the possessive.

> the women's meeting

Individual or Joint Ownership

When two or more persons possess something together, the possession is expressed just once, at the end of the series.

> Bruce is Connie and Nancy's brother.

When the possession is separate, each noun or pronoun should be possessive.

> Dave's and Lane's projects are both very good.

12-23 PRACTICE THE SKILL

Insert any missing apostrophes in the following sentences. If a sentence is correct, write *C* in the blank.

_____ 1. You need to spell *Massachusetts* with four *s*'s and two *t*'s.

___C___ 2. Its nickname is "The Bay State."

_____ 3. Our students' favorite field trip was the trip to Old Sturbridge Village, a re-creation of a nineteenth-century town.

_____ 4. The state's beauty and historic landmarks make it popular.

308   Chapter 12

308   Chapter 12

_____ 5. Massachusetts's capital is Boston.

_____ 6. I'm sure you'll enjoy Boston.

_____ 7. It's full of fun and exciting things to do.

__C___ 8. The Pilgrims landed in Massachusetts in the 1600s.

__C___ 9. The Kennedys have been a powerful political family from

Massachusetts, especially in the mid to late 1900s.

_____ 10. John F. Kennedy became president in '61.

12-24 REVIEW THE SKILL

Insert any missing apostrophes in the following sentences. If a sentence is correct, write *C* in the blank.

_____ 1. I'm writing a paper on Switzerland.

_____ 2. I have received A's on my last two papers.

_____ 3. Grandma and Grandpa's vacation was to Switzerland.

_____ 4. Switzerland's area in square miles is in the 15,000s.

_____ 5. People's visits in Switzerland often involve skiing.

__C___ 6. Switzerland is famous for its spectacular mountain views.

_____ 7. The Alps' popularity never wanes.

__C___ 8. Since the early 1800s, large numbers of tourists have visited
Switzerland.

__C___ 9. The countries that border
Switzerland are France, Germany,
Austria, and Italy.

_____ 10. Those countries' wars have not changed
Switzerland's neutrality.

Hyphens

The hyphen, about half as long as the dash, is used to join the parts of words or sometimes to join separate words. (Compare with the dash, p. 311.)

Omission of Connecting Word

A hyphen can be used in place of a single connecting word, especially between figures.

> Chapters 12-16
> We're open 8:00-10:00.
> We offer classes for grades 7-12.

A hyphen can replace a single connecting word, but it cannot be used when there is a pair of connecting words, such as *from* and *to* or *between* and *and.*

> His report traces church history from Luther to Wesley.

Word Division at the End of a Line

When necessary, use a hyphen to divide a word at the end of a line. The hyphen goes at the end of a line, not at the beginning of the next line.

A word to be divided must contain at least two actual (pronounced) syllables, but the accepted places for dividing the written word may not exactly follow the division between pronounced syllables. Consult a dictionary to see the places where any specific word can be divided. You may divide the word at any of those spots as long as the following two rules are not violated: (1) At least two letters and the hyphen must remain on the first line. (2) At least three letters must appear on the second line.

If you cannot satisfy these requirements, do not divide the word. For example, *asleep* should be carried entirely to the next line.

> Mrs. Unruh requested that our history reports be completed by Friday.

Numbers and Fractions

When you spell out the multiword numbers from twenty-one through ninety-nine, use a hyphen between the parts. Also hyphenate these numbers when they are part of larger numbers spelled out, as on a check.

> thirty-seven book orders
> *two hundred fifty-two and 00/100* dollars

Use a hyphen between the numerator and the denominator of a spelled-out fraction, unless either of these already contains a hyphen.

> one-half
> forty-seven hundredths

Compounds

Hyphens are used to create some compound words.

> sister-in-law
> court-martial

Multiword Modifiers

When two or more words function as a single unit to modify a following noun, this "temporary compound" should be hyphenated.

> third-floor offices
> long-haired dachshund

Dashes

The dash—a rather informal mark—is used mainly for interrupting elements, for emphasis, and for abrupt changes in thought. It should be used sparingly. In appearance a dash is at least twice as long as a hyphen. Most word processing programs automatically convert two consecutive hyphens into a dash. Otherwise two unspaced hyphens are the standard typed substitute for a dash.

Interrupting Phrase and Clause

An interrupting phrase or clause is commonly set off by a pair of dashes.

> Jonathan Edwards was one of the intellectual leaders—some may believe him to be the most intellectual leader—in church history.

However, interrupting elements of this type should not be overused. Use dashes primarily for the following kinds of interruptions:

FALTERING SPEECH	"But you were going to—what did you say?" "I just thought—um—that it would work out."
ABRUPT BREAKING OFF OF A SENTENCE	"But" Chad exclaimed, "the reports proved—"
ABRUPT CHANGE IN THOUGHT	"The answer can be found in Chapter 7 of— have you read this book?"

Parentheses

Parentheses, as well as commas and dashes, are used to enclose extra information within the rest of the sentence. Parentheses (singular, *parenthesis*) are always used in pairs, regardless of whether the extra information comes in the middle or at the end of the sentence.

Reinforcement

Just as the students were reminded not to use too many exclamation points, they should also be cautioned not to use too many dashes. Students should use descriptive words and purposeful sentence structure for emphasis, not an excessive number of dashes.

Supplementary Elements

Parentheses are most often used to enclose words, phrases, or clauses that give additional, often explanatory information.

> The deadline for paper submissions is June 15 (must be postmarked on or before this day).

> The presiding officer (Mr. Daley) will present the information.

Sometimes an entire sentence appears within parentheses.

> You are required to submit a short summary of your paper. (The deadline for this summary will be announced next week.)

Placement of Other Punctuation with Parentheses

Notice the examples just above. When an entire sentence is enclosed in parentheses, the end punctuation comes before the final parenthesis. Otherwise, sentence punctuation stays on the outside of the parentheses.

The only exception is that a question mark or an exclamation point would go inside if the parenthetical material itself is a question or an exclamation.

> The announcement about the new building (have you heard?) was made yesterday.

Because a parenthesized Bible reference in a paragraph is considered part of the sentence to which it refers, it follows the general rule.

> The verse admonishes the reader to "incline thine ear unto wisdom, and apply thine heart to understanding" (Prov. 2:2).

The appropriate sentence punctuation goes after the final parenthesis, not at the end of the quotation. Of course, if the quotation is itself a question or an exclamation, it is punctuated appropriately.

> Paul asks, "How shall we, that are dead to sin, live any longer therein?" (Rom. 6:2).

Numbers or Letters That Identify Divisions Within a Sentence

Parentheses enclose numbers or letters used as in the following sentence:

> Your paper must include the following: (1) a thesis statement, (2) five references to outside sources, and (3) a bibliography page.

Enrichment

Use Teaching Helps 12A and 12B (Book 2, pp. 54-55) for extra practice in using punctuation marks correctly.

Insert any missing hyphens, dashes, or parentheses in the following sentences.

1. Vacation Bible School was July 16-20.

2. There were two hundred and forty-three students signed up to attend.

3. In VBS, we studied Philippians 2:5-10 during our Bible time.

4. After the teams were assigned, my sister and I were on the Gold Knights team, and that week each of us girls on the team mem-orized over thirty verses.

5. My six-year-old sister was in the Happy Hearts class.

6. Their class met in the third-grade room.

7. We are all looking forward to tomorrow's final meeting (the victory announcement).

8. Our class verses were "Who, being in the form of God, thought it not robbery to be equal with God: But made himself of no reputation, and took upon him the form of a servant, and was made in the likeness of men" (Phil. 2:6-7).

9. For the final day, we brought (1) a notebook, (2) a Bible, and (3) our workbooks.

10. My sister brought her crafts to show-and-tell.

Insert any missing hyphens, dashes, or parentheses in the following sentences.

1. My church is taking its teens to camp August 13-18 (can you come?).

2. The camp was very beautiful with modern facilities for the sponsors, but the campers had to stay in the cabins.

3. Twenty-six girls came from our teen group.

4. Two-thirds of us stayed together in one cabin.

5. Our counselor was an eighteen-year-old college student.

6. I brought (1) my shampoo, (2) my toothbrush, and (3) my sunscreen.

7. I memorized Romans 6:1-16.

8. Part of that passage says, "Neither yield ye your members as instruments of unrighteousness unto sin: but yield yourselves unto God" (Rom. 6:13).

9. We sent our counselor a thank-you note when we got home.

10. Our next camp (which will be a school camp) will have a completely different emphasis.

12-27 USE THE SKILL

Add any missing punctuation marks to the following sentences.

1. Sweden is extremely prosperous because of the country's three most important natural resources—timber, iron ore, and water power.

2. Sweden's mountains are good places for skiing, hiking, and other outdoor activities.

3. Do many Swedes celebrate St. Lucia Day on December 13?

4. More than three-fourths of the population lives in urban areas.

5. Selma Lagerlöf is a famous Swedish author who wrote the novel The Wonderful Adventures of Nil and the short story "The Silver Mine."

6. The story is set in Dalecarlia, a region of west central Sweden, during the reign of Gustaf III (1791-92).

7. My mother asked, "When did Selma Lagerlöf write 'The Silver Mine'?"

8. Sweden's highest mountain is 6,926 ft.(2,111m).

9. Most tourists' destinations are the mountains or the sea.

10. The northern part of Sweden is often called the "Land of the Midnight

Sun."

12-28 CUMULATIVE REVIEW

**Rewrite the paragraph on the lines below, correcting the ten errors in sub-
ject-verb agreement, pronoun-antecedent agreement, troublesome words,
spelling, capitalization, or punctuation.** *(Answers may vary.)*

For Christmas vacation either Aunt Helga or Aunt Isabel invites us to
their house. We stay near Washington, D.C., when we go to Aunt Helga's.
Her nieghbor is a Senator and we often celebrate Christ's birth with his
family. Each of our families enjoy reading the Christmas story. Luke 211
says, "For unto you is born this day in the city of David a Saviour, which
is Christ the Lord". Mom thinks that learning to give has a great affect on
us children. There is a children's Hospital near Aunt Isabel's. Last year,
we laid presents under the tree for some children in the hospital. During
Christmas we also have many enjoyable interesting times. The ski slopes
near Aunt Isabel's house are great. Overall, I love Christmas vacation.

For Christmas vacation either Aunt Helga or Aunt Isabel invites us to

her house. We stay near Washington, D.C., when we go to Aunt Helga's. Her

neighbor is a senator, and we often celebrate Christ's birth with his

family. Each of our families enjoys reading the Christmas story. Luke 2:11

says, "For unto you is born this day in the city of David a Saviour, which is

Christ the Lord." Mom thinks that learning to give has a great effect on us

children. There is a children's hospital near Aunt Isabel's. Last year, we laid

presents under the tree for some children in the hospital. During Christmas

we also have many enjoyable, interesting times. The ski slopes near Aunt

Isabel's house are great. Overall, I love Christmas vacation.

Objectives

Students will

1. write a letter of gratitude.

2. send a letter of gratitude.

Overview of the Writing Process

Planning—choosing a recipient for a letter of gratitude

Drafting—selecting details to include in the letter and writing a rough draft

Revising—rewriting the letter and preparing the envelope

Publishing—mailing the letter

Letter Writing

Writing a Letter of Gratitude

"I'm not sure it's even worth getting birthday presents, since you have to write all these thank-you notes." Michael glanced over the list of names of the people who had given him gifts. "This is gonna take the whole morning!"

"You're making it too hard," said his brother Randy. "Just borrow my computer program."

"Your computer program?"

"Sure. I designed it for a class project. It's kind of like a form letter. All you do is plug in the names of the people you need to write to, and the presents they gave you, and hit enter! The program does the rest." He propped up his feet on the coffee table and opened a computer magazine.

"So this letter—what does it say?"

"Oh, you know—the basic stuff. 'Dear *Blank:* The *blank* that you gave me for my birthday is really neat. I have always wanted a *blank*. I will really enjoy it. Thanks—it really made my birthday fun to get a *blank* from you." He smiled and then fell silent, intent on reading an article.

Michael watched him for a moment. "Hey, uh, Randy?" he asked after a while. "What kind of grade did you get on this project?"

Randy looked up. "Grade? Oh—I got a C. Mr. Matthews thought it was kind of—well, lame, I guess. He said the thank-you notes were too generic—whatever that means. But it sure saves time. Want to use it?"

Michael shook his head. "No, thanks. Generic is okay for some things—like paper towels and potato chips. But for letters, generic is just *cheap.*"

Michael is right; no one enjoys receiving a generic letter, a letter so general that it could have been written to anyone. When you are writing to thank someone, it is doubly important that you show your appreciation by taking time to write a thoughtful, specific letter.

What kinds of things should you write a thank-you note for?

- a gift you received

- a service someone performed for you

- a visit in someone's home

After a few moments of thought, Michael wrote the following letter to his Aunt Valerie:

Dear Aunt Valerie,

Thank you very much for the Thermos bottle you gave me for my birthday. It has already come in handy on those cold mornings when I ride the

---

Writing a Letter of Gratitude

Lesson Support

Teacher's Edition, Book 2
Rubrics—p. 159

Introduction

Materials

- a copy of a famous letter of gratitude, such as Abraham Lincoln's letter to Mrs. Bixby (available in many anthologies of American literature and on some government websites), or a letter you have received and have kept for its importance to you

Read the letter (or letters) you have brought to the students.

Discussion

Ask students how they feel when they receive a thank-you letter and direct a discussion about the importance of showing appropriate gratitude.

Direct the students to read the narrative on page 316 and the sample letter on pages 316-17. Discuss the story of Michael and Randy, pointing out the attitudes underlying Michael's desire to hurry and Randy's shortcut letter form. *(selfishness, self-absorption, and possibly pride)* Emphasize that the humility arising from gratitude is the opposite of pride.

bus to school. We have about a forty-minute ride, and I've really enjoyed drinking hot chocolate to keep me warm on the way.

I'm planning to go camping with a couple of my friends and our dads next weekend. We're planning to take the tent and spend the night up on Mount Peregrine. I know I'll be taking the Thermos bottle along for our hike up the mountain. It fits perfectly in my backpack.

Thank you for remembering my birthday and sending such a great gift—I know I'll enjoy it for a long time to come.

Sincerely,
Michael

Here are some points to remember when writing a letter of gratitude:

- Be prompt in expressing your gratitude. If you put off writing your letter, you might forget about it altogether.

- Think of the person you are writing to. How would you speak to him? Write to him in the same way. You would probably address your youth pastor's wife or an older relative in a more respectful tone than you would a friend or a classmate.

- Be specific in the way you word your letter.

For a gift: Avoid writing simply, "Thank you for the _____. I liked it." Mention a specific way you plan to use the gift the person gave you or one of its specific features that you like.

For a service: Give a specific detail telling how the service the person did for you has helped you or saved you time.

For a visit: Write your letter to the hostess, thanking her for her hospitality. You might mention a specific dish she prepared that you especially enjoyed, or tell her how comfortable she made you feel in her home.

- Add some other news besides just saying thank you for the gift. Share something interesting that you have done recently or plan to do in the future. An extra touch of friendliness rounds out the letter and gives it a more gracious tone.

- It's all right to keep the letter brief; but be careful not to sound hurried or unfriendly. Make sure you say enough to let your reader know you have spent some time thinking about what he has done for you or given you.

Your Turn

Write a letter of gratitude to someone for a gift, a service, or a visit. Before you begin, look over the points above one more time. Try to make your letter as gracious and sincere as possible—a letter that will make your reader glad to have done something for you.

Writing E-mail

Once upon a time (and not so *very* long ago) a person could write a letter only by hand or by typewriter. And he could send it only by post. Then along came the Internet. Ray Tomlinson sent out an e-mail message in 1972, the first of billions now flying through cyberspace.

Planning

Direct the students to read the information on page 317 about writing letters of gratitude. Answer any questions they may have after reading this material.

Direct the students to read the instructions in "Your Turn." Allow time for students to think of gifts, services, or visits that they need to acknowledge.

Drafting

Direct each student to write a rough draft of his letter. Encourage each student to think of his letter's recipient and to choose details that will make the letter special to that person.

Revising

Assign the revision as homework, directing the students to re-read their letters and to make any additions or deletions for warmth and clarity. Instruct them to copy their letters onto nice paper and to prepare envelopes for mailing.

Publishing

Collect the letters in class. When you have evaluated them, return them for mailing. Encourage those students with errors in their letters to recopy their letters before mailing them.

Scriptural Application

Read Hebrews 13:15, pointing out that the Bible calls praise and thanksgiving a "sacrifice." Offering a sacrifice requires humility. Encourage the students to remember the importance of including praise and thanksgiving in their worship of the Lord.

Overview of the Writing Process

Planning—choosing a subject and a recipient

Drafting—writing the first version of the e-mail message

Revising—evaluating the message with the Writing Worksheet

Publishing—posting the message in the classroom

E-mail has many benefits, the most significant of which is speed—faster than a telephone call in some cases. Another advantage is cost. For the most part, e-mail is less expensive than regular mail.

But for all its convenience and efficiency, e-mail does have a couple of drawbacks. It tends to be rather informal. People say things in e-mail in ways they probably never would in handwritten letters or in person.

Another disadvantage is closely related to the advantage of speed. An e-mail message can be forwarded to thousands of people in a moment—something that can be very damaging and embarrassing to the original sender. And one slip of a finger can transmit an e-mail message before the sender is actually ready to send it.

A good writer controls his prose no matter what medium he uses. E-mail is far from an exception to his goal of writing clearly and well. It may be the best arena in which to learn control, style, and etiquette.

E-mail *Don't*s

In Form

- Don't type in all CAPS. Your writing will look like shouting.
- Don't send jokes. Many jokes floating around on the Internet often are copyrighted and used without permission.
- Don't attach large files without asking the recipient.
- Don't put *Important* in the subject line unless the message really is important.

In Content

- Don't consider e-mail private. Write only what you would want read in public.
- Don't be sarcastic or flippant. (This rule is good advice no matter what medium you use.)
- Don't send a message you wrote in anger.
- Don't send chain letters. By doing so, you may violate federal law.

E-mail *Do*s

In Form

- Do use a spelling checker.
- Do begin messages with a friendly greeting and end them on a positive note.
- Do check the address. Twice. Once you send an e-mail message, you cannot retract it. Check the *CC:* and *BC:* boxes as well as the *To:* box.
- Do put your answer to e-mail at the top of the original message or highlight the answers you put among the lines of the original.

Evaluation

For help in grading this assignment, see "Grading Writing Assignments" (p. x) and Rubric 12 (Book 2, p. 159).

Enrichment

Encourage students to write letters of gratitude to the subjects of their oral history assignments. (See Chapter 11.)

Writing E-mail

Lesson Support

Teacher's Edition, Book 2
Writing Worksheets—p. 145

Introduction

Direct the students to read the information about the advantages and disadvantages of e-mail.

Discussion

Direct a discussion about whether the students have experienced these or other advantages and disadvantages.

Planning

Instruct the students to read the *do*s and *don't*s of writing e-mail. Answer any questions they may have after reading this material. Allow students to add items to the *do*s and *don't*s based on their own experiences.

In Content

- Do keep the message short. Although most e-mail is inexpensive, sometimes cost is involved.

- Do create a good subject line, one that sums up the content or gets interest.

- Do sign your name.

- Do read your e-mail before you send it, checking the spelling, tone, and accuracy of the message.

What is wrong with this e-mail message?

To: jadams@badwriter.oops

CC: jsmom@home.yikes

From: insulted@worsewriter.sorry

Subject: CRUCIAL ERROR

WHAT WERE YOU THINKING? How could you ask Jack to be on the debate team when he is flunking history? See if you can change things, will you??? I DON'T WANT TO LOSE AGAIN THIS YEAR!! We can't afford to have him mess up.

No one would write such an e-mail, you say. Sadly, people do. Don't be one of them.

Here's an e-mail message written on the same topic in a much more proper way:

To: jadams@writer.pen

From: polite@goodwriter.ok

Subject: Considerate Suggestion

Dear Jeff,

I just heard from Mr. Applegate that you asked Jack to be on the debate team. I know he has a quick wit and would be a lot of fun to work with. I am just concerned because I know he is trying to keep his grades up in history. Do you think having him on the team will be okay? Let's talk.

Thanks,
Peter

Your Turn

Write a message, pretending it will be sent via e-mail. Check it against the *Do*s and *Don't*s above.

Drafting

Direct the students to read the instructions in "Your Turn" on page 319.

Allow time for students to choose subjects and recipients. Remind them that e-mail is a more public medium than handwritten letters are. Encourage them to avoid writing a message that they would not want anyone else to read.

Revising

Distribute a copy of the Writing Worksheet (Book 2, p. 145) to each student. Direct the students to read the rough drafts of their messages as though they themselves were the recipients. After they have answered the questions on the worksheet, encourage them to make any necessary changes for correctness or clarity.

Publishing

Direct the students to print their e-mail messages. Display the messages in the classroom.

13 LIBRARY SKILLS

Lesson Support

Teacher's Edition, Book 1
Bulletin Boards—p. 451

Teacher's Edition, Book 2
Teaching Helps—pp. 56-58

Libraries today contain much more than books; they often contain magazines, newspapers, and audio-visual materials too. At many libraries you can attend classes, listen to lectures, or view displays on a variety of topics. Some libraries even offer free access to the Internet. Today's libraries provide a broad selection of information and tools for you to use. Before you can use these tools, however, you need to know where to find them.

The Organization of the Library

Libraries are usually organized into several sections. Some libraries have a separate room for each section; other libraries designate separate areas of shelves for each section. Each section contains a different kind of library material. (The main section of shelves is often called the **stacks.**) Many of these materials carry a special label that indicates the library section to which they belong.

KIND OF MATERIAL	EXAMPLES	LABEL
Books	fiction and nonfiction books, both hardcover and paperback	
Periodicals	newspapers and magazines	PER
Audio-visual Materials	audiocassettes, CDs, videocassettes, works of art, puppets, and games	AV
Reference	encyclopedias and other noncirculating materials that must be used in the library	R or REF
Children/Young Adult	books, periodicals, and audio-visual materials designed especially for children or teens	J or JUV (juvenile) or YA

Teaching Strategy: Introduction

If possible, visit your local library or school library at some point during your presentation of this chapter. Take your class on a tour and show them the location and organization of the books, the catalog, the *Readers' Guide to Periodical Literature,* and any other useful resources your library has.

The Arrangement of Books

Fiction

A **fiction** book, regardless of its topic, is shelved alphabetically according to the author's last name. If two or more authors share the same last name, their books are arranged alphabetically by the authors' first names. If a library has more than one book by the same author, that author's books are arranged alphabetically according to the first words of the titles (not including *A, An,* or *The*). The list below shows the order in which these books would appear on a library shelf.

> Sir Walter Scott, *The Antiquary*
> Sir Walter Scott, *Ivanhoe*
> D. E. Stevenson, *The English Air*
> Robert Louis Stevenson, *Kidnapped*
> Robert Louis Stevenson, *Treasure Island*

Some libraries separate certain kinds of fiction books from the rest of the fiction collection. For example, a library may have separate shelves for mystery fiction, science fiction, or westerns. In addition, the book spines are usually marked with letters that indicate that special section, such as *MYS* for mystery fiction. Many libraries separate the paperback fiction books from the hardcover books. Paperback books are usually marked with the letters *PB.*

Nonfiction

Nonfiction books are arranged by topic. Almost all libraries organize nonfiction books according to one of two classification systems: the Dewey decimal system and the Library of Congress system.

Dewey Decimal

The **Dewey decimal system** is named for its creator, American librarian Melvil Dewey (1851-1931). This system gives every nonfiction book a number according to its subject matter. This number appears on the spine of the book and in the library catalog. Here are the ten major classifications in the Dewey decimal system.

NUMBER	CATEGORY	EXAMPLES
000-099	Generalities	encyclopedias, general reference works, computing, journalism
100-199	Philosophy and psychology	logic, ethics
200-299	Religion	mythology
300-399	Social sciences	government, education, etiquette

Reinforcement

Materials
- envelopes (one for each team of two or three students)
- sets of fifteen slips of paper, each slip containing the name of an author and the title of one of his works of fiction (one set of fifteen slips for each team)

Each envelope should contain fifteen slips of paper. Each slip should have on it the name of an author and the title of a work of fiction he has written. Divide the class into teams of two or three students each. Before distributing the envelopes, instruct the teams to keep the envelopes closed until you say to begin. Instruct the teams to arrange the slips in the same order in which the books would appear on a library shelf. The first team to arrange the papers correctly will be declared the winner.

Reinforcement

With students' input, make a list of all their textbooks. Display the list and direct the students to categorize each book and to assign it an appropriate number based on the Dewey decimal system. Then instruct students to use their own paper to arrange and classify the books according to the Library of Congress system. Discuss the results, comparing and contrasting the two lists.

400-499	Language	linguistics
500-599	Natural sciences and mathematics	physics, chemistry, biology
600-699	Technology (Applied sciences)	medicine, engineering, manufacturing
700-799	The arts	painting, music, sports
800-899	Literature and rhetoric	novels, short stories, plays
900-999	Geography and history	travel, biography

The Dewey system is called a decimal system because it is based on divisions of ten. Each division can be divided by ten as many times as necessary. For instance, here are the ten divisions within the 300 division.

300-309	Social sciences	350-359	Public administration
310-319	General statistics	360-369	Social services; association
320-329	Political science	370-379	Education
330-339	Economics	380-389	Commerce, communications, transport
340-349	Law	390-399	Customs, etiquette, folklore

Each subdivision can be further divided. The number 324, the political process, is a subdivision of 320, political science. Further levels of subdivision use a decimal point. For example, 324.7 indicates the conduct of election campaigns (a subdivision of 324), and 324.73 indicates the use and effect of the media in an election campaign (a subdivision of 324.7).

Did you notice that the 900s division includes **biography?** Some libraries separate the biographies and autobiographies from the other nonfiction books and shelve them in a separate area. A capital letter *B* or the Dewey decimal number *920* on the spine of a book indicates that the book is a biography or an autobiography. These books are arranged alphabetically by the last name of the subject, not the author. For example, Carl Sandburg's biography of Abraham Lincoln would be shelved under *L,* not *S.*

Other libraries shelve biographies with the appropriate subject area. For example, a biography of a philosopher would be shelved with the other books about philosophy in the 100s.

Under a book's Dewey decimal number is a number that identifies the book by its author or perhaps by one or more letters of its title. The **Dewey decimal number** and the **author number** (also known as the Cutter number) together make up the **call number** of the book.

Library of Congress

Some large libraries use the **Library of Congress system** instead of the Dewey decimal system. The Library of Congress system uses a combination of letters and numbers to classify books. There are twenty-one basic categories in the Library of Congress system.

A	General works	M	Music and books on music
B	Philosophy, psychology, religion	N	Fine Arts
C	Auxiliary sciences of history (such as archaeology, genealogy, biography)	P	Language and literature
D	History: general and old world	Q	Science
E	History: America	R	Medicine
F	History: America (local)	S	Agriculture
G	Geography, anthropology, recreation	T	Technology
H	Social sciences	U	Military science
J	Political science	V	Naval science
K	Law	Z	Library science
L	Education		

Number the titles and authors of the following fiction books in the order in which they would appear on the fiction shelves of a library.

_2_	1.	Alexander Dumas, *The Count of Monte Cristo*
_3_	2.	Arthur Ransome, *Winter Holiday*
_1_	3.	Samuel Clemens, *Huckleberry Finn*
_4_	4.	Cecil Roberts, *One Small Candle*
_5_	5.	Elise Sanguinetti, *The Dowager*
_6_	6.	Mabel Seeley, *The Whistling Shadow*
_8_	7.	Anya Seton, *Avalon*
_7_	8.	Shirley Seifert, *Farewell, My General*
_10_	9.	Johanna Spyri, *Heidi*
_9_	10.	Anya Seton, *Foxfire*

Using the Dewey decimal chart on pages 322-23, write the number range of the correct category for each of the following books.

800-899	1.	*Cambridge History of American Literature*
200-299	2.	*Lands and Peoples of the Bible*
000-099	3.	*World Book Encyclopedia*
800-899	4.	*Epic and Romance*
100-199	5.	*The Ethics of Aristotle*
300-399	6.	*Concentration of Control in American Industry*
900-999	7.	*Amish People*
400-499	8.	*501 Spanish Verbs*
300-399	9.	*Equal Justice for the Accused*
700-799	10.	*The Art of Mime*
700-799	11.	*Cubism*
900-999	12.	*The New England Leaders*
400-499	13.	*The Greek Particles*
600-699	14.	*Soil Analysis*
500-599	15.	*Catastrophes in Earth's History*

Catalog

Computer Catalog

Most libraries today have a **computer catalog,** sometimes called **OPAC** (online public access computer). A computer catalog contains electronic records for each book. Each record includes the same information you would find on a catalog card: the title, the author, the place of publication, the date of publication, the publisher, the number of pages, and the call number (for a nonfiction book). In fact, a computer catalog may contain even more information. Many electronic records include a summary of the book, and almost all computer catalogs include each book's status. The status information will tell you whether the book is currently available, reserved for another patron, or already checked out ("charged"). It may even tell you when the book is due to be returned to the library.

To use the computer catalog, you must know the author, title, or subject of the book you want to find. Type the information you know into the computer according to the instructions on the screen. The computer will begin to search for the book you want by comparing the words you typed to the information in its database. When it finds a match, the screen will display the record for that book. If the information you typed was not specific enough, the screen will display a list of authors, titles, or subjects. To see the record for an individual book, simply type the number displayed next to that entry on the list or click on it. If you want more information about the book, you may need to type or click on an additional command, such as *F* for *full title record.*

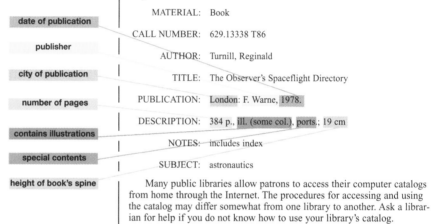

Many public libraries allow patrons to access their computer catalogs from home through the Internet. The procedures for accessing and using the catalog may differ somewhat from one library to another. Ask a librarian for help if you do not know how to use your library's catalog.

Card Catalog

A **card catalog** is a cabinet with small drawers filled with cards containing information on each book in the library. There are three kinds of cards: the author card, the title card, and the subject card. These cards are usually alphabetized together. Each kind of card has a different top line: the author card starts with the author, the title card starts with the title, and the subject card starts with the subject. Each card includes the title, the author, the place of publication, the date of publication, the publisher, the number of pages, and the call number (for a nonfiction book).

To use the card catalog, you need to know the author or the title or the subject of the book you want. Perhaps you want a book by a particular author, but you are not sure of the title. Find the author card, which is filed alphabetically according to the author's last name. Title cards are arranged alphabetically according to the first word in the title (not including *A, An,* and *The*). If you do not know the titles or authors of nonfiction books on a subject that interests you, look for subject cards. There may be more than one subject card for some books.

When you find the card for the book you want, write down the call number from the upper left-hand corner of the card and copy the name of the author and the title of the book. With this information you can ask for the book or go to the shelf and get it yourself.

13-3 PRACTICE THE SKILL

Using the catalog entry below, answer the following questions.

MATERIAL: Book

CALL NUMBER: J 629.45 R433

AUTHOR: Ride, Sally.

TITLE: To Space and Back.

EDITION: 1st ed.

PUBLICATION: New York: Lothrop, Lee and Shepard, c1986.

DESCRIPTION: 96 p.: col. ill.; 29cm.

NOTES: Describes in texts and photographs what it is like to be an astronaut on a space shuttle. Includes a glossary of terms.

NOTES: Includes index.

SUBJECT: Space flight—Juvenile literature.

SUBJECT: Space shuttle—Juvenile literature.

1. What is the complete title of the book?

   To Space and Back

2. What company published the book?

   Lothrop, Lee and Shepard

3. What is the book's call number?

   J 629.45 R433

4. Where was the book published?

   New York

5. What year was the book published?

   1986

6. Does the book contain illustrations? How do you know?

   Yes. The description includes the abbreviation ill.

7. How would you find other books by the same author?

   Use the computer author search.

8. How would you type the author's name in the computer?

   Ride, Sally

9. Under what subject headings would you find other books on the same topic?

   space flight or space shuttle

10. What extra information is given about the book?

   There is a glossary of terms and an index.

Choose five topics from the list below. Use your library's card catalog or computer catalog to find one book on each topic. List the title, author, and call number for each book you choose. *(Answers will vary.)*

1. Scottish folklore

   _____

2. Adolescent psychology

   _____

3. Commentary on Ecclesiastes

   _____

4. The Supreme Court

   _____

5. Computer analysts

   _____

6. Basketball champions in 1946

   _____

7. British literature

   _____

8. Greek grammar

   _____

9. Building machinery

   _____

10. Map of South America

   _____

Periodical Indexes

The library catalogs will help you find books and audio-visual materials, but they will probably not help you find specific articles in magazines or newspapers. To find these articles, you need to consult a **periodical index.**

Readers' Guide to Periodical Literature

The most generally useful periodical index is the *Readers' Guide to Periodical Literature.* It lists articles from over two hundred magazines by subject and by author. The *Readers' Guide* is available in both printed and electronic formats. Most libraries have the print version, and many also offer the electronic version online or in CD-ROM. All of the versions are

Reinforcement

Assign Teaching Help 13B (Book 2, p. 57) for more practice in using the *Readers' Guide to Periodical Literature.*

updated regularly throughout the year. Soon after publication, articles are listed in one of the paperback volumes issued during the year. At the end of each year, these volumes are combined and reissued in a single large volume.

To find an article about a particular subject, look up the keyword. Under the subject heading, you may find "see also" entries that suggest related subject headings. Each individual entry includes the article's subject, its title, its author, the magazine in which it appears, the volume number or date of the magazine, and the page numbers of the article. If the article has illustrations, the entry will include that information too. The listings use several abbreviations, explained in the front of each volume.

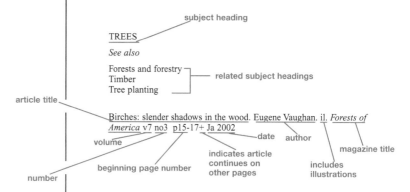

New York Times Index

Most public libraries subscribe to several newspapers. In addition to local newspapers, many libraries also carry the *New York Times* and its index, both of which are available in print and electronic versions. The *New York Times Index* lists articles that have appeared in that newspaper only. However, it can help you find information in back issues of other newspapers as well as the *New York Times,* since it will help you discover the dates of newsworthy events.

Subject Indexes

If you need detailed information about a particular subject, you may want to check other periodical indexes. Examples of other indexes include the *Social Sciences Index* and the *Humanities Index,* both of which cover scholarly journals in certain fields of study. Ask the librarian about the subject indexes available in your library.

Chapter 13

Special Reference Tools

Almanacs and Yearbooks

Both almanacs and yearbooks supplement encyclopedias by giving current information about statistics and recent events. Most almanacs and all yearbooks are published every year.

Almanacs include tables of weights and measures, lists of sports statistics, names of award winners, information about government agencies and programs, summaries of recent events, and other facts. You can find the information you need by looking in the index, which may appear at the front of the book like a table of contents.

Yearbooks tend to concentrate on special subjects. For instance, the *Year Book of Sports Medicine* includes information on topics such as treating athletic injuries, and the *Supreme Court Yearbook* has summaries of every decision made by the Supreme Court that year.

Atlases and Gazetteers

Atlases are books of collected maps. Most atlases also contain information about weather, geography, population, and other statistics. The index lists the page number for each map in the collection. **Gazetteers** are indexes of place names. Some gazetteers include additional information, such as elevation or population, for each place listed.

Bible Commentaries and Concordances

Bible commentaries are explanations of the Bible, going through part or all of the Bible, verse by verse or section by section. Some commentaries cover individual books of the Bible; longer works cover the entire Bible.

Bible concordances are alphabetical indexes to the words of the Bible. They are helpful for locating a passage and sometimes for studying a subject through the Bible. Some concordances include the Hebrew or Greek word from which the English word was translated. When you can remember only part of a verse, look up an important word from the verse in the alphabetical list. If the particular passage you want is not listed, try another keyword. Not all keywords or passages will appear in every concordance.

Some commentaries and concordances are available in electronic versions, which make searching the Scriptures even easier. Finding all the occurrences of a particular word or phrase in a printed concordance would be time consuming, and error is possible. But with an electronic version, your search would be reliable and take only a few seconds.

Biographical Sources

In addition to book-length biographies of particular people, the library contains a number of sources for more concise biographical information. Prominent people living today appear in **biographical dictionaries,** such as

Current Biography, Contemporary Authors, and the various *Who's Who* publications. Persons no longer living may be described in older editions of these works and in sources such as the *Dictionary of American Biography* and the British *Dictionary of National Biography.* Most of these sources are arranged alphabetically by the subject's last name; some of the multivolume works may be arranged alphabetically within chronologically arranged sections. Check the index to find the pages that discuss the person you are researching.

Dictionaries

Dictionaries contain a wealth of helpful information about words and languages. Large **unabridged dictionaries** contain several hundred thousand words. Abridged dictionaries, or **desk dictionaries,** are much shorter, but even they contain thousands of words, usually all the words we use on a regular basis. **Special-purpose dictionaries** include dictionaries of synonyms, Bible dictionaries, foreign language dictionaries, and dictionaries of subjects like sports or the sciences. Some dictionaries are available in both printed and electronic versions.

Finding the Word

The **entry words** are arranged alphabetically according to each letter in the entry, whether the entry is one or more words. **Guide words** at the top of each page indicate the first and last words included on that page.

Enrichment

Materials
- a desk dictionary for each student

Instruct each student to bring a dictionary to class. To help students practice finding words in the dictionary, read the following words aloud one at a time. The first student to find the word will stand and read its definition or definitions aloud.

- disparate
- superfluous
- plethora
- brogue
- flummox
- fisticuffs
- platitude

Understanding the Entry

The **pronunciation,** a respelling that indicates how to pronounce the word, usually appears right after the entry word itself. Some words have two or more different, acceptable pronunciations. The introduction to the dictionary will explain how to tell whether one pronunciation is preferred over another.

One entry word may be able to function as several different parts of speech. Each **part of speech label** is listed with the definition to which it applies. For example, the word *read* can function as a noun or as a verb. Dictionaries usually classify verb meanings into two groups. Transitive verb meanings are labeled *tr.* (or *v.tr.* or *vt*). Intransitive verb and linking verb meanings are both labeled *intr.* (or *v.intr.* or *vi*). Every verb has at least one of these labels along with its meanings.

The entry may also include **inflected forms,** words that differ from the main entry because of the addition of suffixes or because of other changes. Inflected forms include irregular plural forms of nouns, certain verb forms, and comparative and superlative forms of modifiers. Some dictionaries also include **related words** at the end of the entry, such as the adjective *botanical* at the end of the entry for the noun *botany*.

If a word can be spelled correctly more than one way, the entry will include the **variant spellings.** The correct **capitalization** will also be indicated.

If a word has more than one **definition,** each definition will be listed and numbered. The entry may also list **synonyms** (words with the same or similar meaning).

Most entries will include an **etymology.** An etymology is the history of the word, beginning with its recent past and ending with its earliest form or the language from which it came originally. The abbreviations for the languages are explained in the front of the dictionary.

Certain entry words will also have **usage labels.** Usage labels point out special areas of meaning. A **field label** points out a definition that applies to a particular field, such as music or biology. A **stylistic label** limits a word or a definition to a particular usage level, such as *informal* or *obsolete*.

Encyclopedias

Encyclopedias contain articles that give brief introductions to many subjects. Most major encyclopedias are available in both print and electronic formats. Some are even available on the Internet. Electronic versions usually offer keyword searching options.

Printed encyclopedias usually consist of several volumes, each labeled with one or more letters and a numeral. The articles are arranged alphabetically. Guide words at the top of the page tell you the topic of the first article on that page. Information on some subjects may be included in several different articles. The index lists all the pages that contain information on a particular subject. Some encyclopedias have an index in each volume; others have a separate volume (usually the last volume) that is the index for the entire set. Many encyclopedia articles list cross-references to related articles, under a heading such as "See also."

Indexes

Indexes are listings that make it easy to find information. Most useful are the periodical indexes. In addition to the *Readers' Guide,* useful indexes include *Book Review Index, Essays and General Literature Index,* and **books of quotations** such as *Bartlett's Familiar Quotations.* A book of quotations allows you to find a famous quotation by looking up its author, a keyword, or the topic. Most books of quotations also list each quotation's original source and date.

Thesauruses

A **thesaurus** is a treasury of synonyms and antonyms. Some thesauruses list the main words alphabetically, while others group all words by meaning, directing you to the meaning groups from a detailed index in the back. In either case, you choose a synonym included in the words you find listed. A dictionary and a thesaurus are often well used together—the thesaurus to help you think of a word and the dictionary to confirm that the word is in fact the one you need.

 **13-5** *P*RACTICE THE *S*KILL

Use the following entry to answer each question.

COMPUTER SOFTWARE

How to upgrade your computer software at low cost. Richard Gaverton. *Computer Weekly* v56 no6 p23-35 S 2001.

1. What is the title of the article?

   How to Upgrade Your Computer Software at Low Cost

2. When was the article published?

   September 2001

3. What is the subject heading under which the article is listed?

   Computer Software

4. On what page of the magazine does the article begin?

   23

5. What is the title of the magazine in which the article appears?

   Computer Weekly

6. What is the volume number in which the article appears?

   56

7. Who is the author of the article?

   Richard Gaverton

Reinforcement

Assign Teaching Help 13C (Book 2, p. 58) for more practice in using special reference tools.

Enrichment

Instruct students to choose a person from the past whom they would like to learn more about (e.g., a missionary, an author, a sports figure, a president, or an inventor). Write the following introductory question and related items for display:

Where would you find the following information?

- date of birth
- hometown
- local news at the time of birth
- current population of the person's native country
- news stories about the person
- books written by the person
- awards won by the person during his lifetime

Once the students have finished, choose a few volunteers to share whom they chose and where they would look to learn more about that person.

8. An article can be located in what two ways?

subject and author

9. How could you find other articles by the same author?

Search the Readers' Guide _by author, using Gaverton, Richard._

10. What is another subject heading that could be searched for related topics?

Answers will vary.

13-6 REVIEW THE SKILL

In the blank write the letter of the reference tool you would use to find the answer to each question. *(Answers may vary.)*

A. Almanac or yearbook	F. Desk dictionary
B. Atlas or gazetteer	G. Special-purpose dictionary
C. Bible commentary	H. Encyclopedia
D. Book of quotations	I. Index
E. Biographical dictionary	J. Thesaurus

_B or H_ 1. On which river in France is Paris located?

_A_ 2. How many pounds does a metric ton weigh?

_J_ 3. What is an antonym for the word *progress?*

_E or H_ 4. Where did Herman Melville attend school?

_G_ 5. What is the French equivalent of the English word *hello?*

_C_ 6. What did Paul mean by "another gospel" in Galatians 1:6?

_F_ 7. What is the definition of the word *calendar?*

_A or H_ 8. What is the national anthem of Russia?

_D_ 9. What did Shakespeare's Macbeth say in one of his famous soliloquies?

_I_ 10. Where can you find a magazine article about bacteria?

14 STUDY SKILLS

Lesson Support

Teacher's Edition, Book 1
Bulletin Boards—p. 451

Teacher's Edition, Book 2
Teaching Helps—pp. 59-60

"And Jesus increased in wisdom and stature, and in favour with God and man" (Luke 2:52).

For nine months each year, you are probably spending five days of each week and seven hours of each day in school. And you will most likely do this for at least twelve years of your life. If you are going to spend that much time in school, you no doubt want to know what you are supposed to be accomplishing there. The goal of your childhood and teenage years, in and out of school, is your development as a person. You are made in God's image. God designed you with special abilities (different from everyone else's and some that you may not yet even know that you have), and He intends for you to fulfill a specific purpose. Even our Lord, who was perfect, went through several years of training in which He developed many areas of His life. His public ministry began at age thirty and lasted only three years. Likewise, the disciples underwent three years of intense training before they could begin their ministries. Right now is your time of preparation. Luke 2:52 tells us that Christ grew in all areas; you need to be like Christ, developing your mind, your body, your character, and your social skills. Learning and practicing good study skills will help to develop your mind and your character.

One of the most important character qualities you need to develop is diligence. Diligence is your making every effort to complete a task well. Proverbs 22:29 says, "Seest thou a man diligent in his business? he shall stand before kings; he shall not stand before mean men." God promises rewards and success for the diligent. *How* you study is just as important as your grades. You all know those students who procrastinate, cram the night before a test, and still manage to get an A. But students who prepare ahead and study diligently develop good work habits regardless of what grade they receive. Don't be satisfied with just making a good grade. Be satisfied when you have done your best. If you make developing your character the goal, then you will certainly be successful. "He becometh poor that dealeth with a slack hand: but the hand of the diligent maketh rich" (Prov. 10:4).

Your character is most important, but another important focus in school is the development of your mind. The most important thing you will learn is *how* to learn. In the following years, you will forget many of the specific things that you are learning in class (no doubt you have been saying that to yourself all along), but in every subject, you are developing your mind. It is like sports training. It seems pointless to swing repeatedly at balls in a batting cage, but when you are actually in a real game, your performance depends on how well you swung at those balls in the batting cage. Your performance in life will depend on how well you prepared for it. Your life will constantly be changing, and you will need to know how to assimilate all the new information you will gather. Develop an alert and sharp mind that can learn in any situation.

Improving Your Study Time

Keeping in mind your goal, use these tips to develop great study habits.

Keep a good attitude. Having a negative attitude about school will make studying harder. If you have the right goals and avoid last-minute panic studying, you might be surprised how much you can enjoy school. Working hard and reaching your goals give a sense of satisfaction. No matter what your I.Q., you can be successful in school. A positive attitude will affect your grades and your personality as well.

Get plenty of sleep and exercise, and eat wisely. Yes, you have heard this one before, but it really is important. It is very hard to concentrate when you are tired, out of shape, or malnourished.

Be organized. If you are not naturally an organized person, read a book on organization or get a friend to help you. Always write down assignments and have a definite place in your notebook for completed work. Be sure to take home every book needed for that day's assignments. Make a weekly and monthly calendar that includes other activities such as sports events and trips. This allows you to know when you will have busy weeks and when you will have time to work on projects. Having your materials ready and organized will make your study time more profitable.

Be prepared for class. Reading the assignment the night before class will enable you to learn more during class time. Be on time and make sure you have your textbook, the assignments that are due, and the appropriate items for taking notes.

Make good use of class time. If you have read the assignment the night before, you are already ahead. Now listen carefully and ask good questions. Take notes and avoid daydreaming. Sit in your chair correctly; do not slouch.

Read over your notes each night. If you do this each night, your study time before the test will be considerably easier. If you go over your notes with a friend, you will both be able to share things that one of you missed during class. Begin with your hardest subject first. When you have finished, go back and review that subject.

Have a specific study time. Set aside a certain time each night to study. This will keep you from waiting until the last minute and enable you to get projects done ahead of time. Study in a comfortable (not too comfortable) and well-lighted place that is free from disturbing noise.

Get help from a teacher or a tutor. If you follow these steps and continue to struggle in any subject, you need to ask your teacher or a tutor for help. Everyone is different, and you may need more explanation than what is presented in class.

Master each concept. During your study time, be sure that you have mastered each concept presented that day. Don't just finish the exercise. Make sure you fully understand the concept.

Don't give up. Read over this chapter several times during the year. People often forget and need to be reminded. If you mess up, don't stop trying. Just start over again and keep going.

Now that you know the two most important goals and you have several valuable study tips, you can begin developing important skills to improve your study time.

Evaluation

Review the tips for developing good study habits. If your students struggle with several of these, you may wish to make an evaluation chart for them. List the study tips and then ask the students to rate themselves from one to four in these areas (with one being the lowest and four being the highest). Then help the students develop strategies for improving the areas in which they struggle.

Using the Parts of a Book

Organization is very important to most writers, especially writers of nonfiction works such as textbooks. Most nonfiction books include features to help you, the reader, follow the organization of the book easily. When you understand the parts of a book, you can find the information in it more quickly. Not all books contain all of these parts, nor are the parts arranged in the same order in all books.

Every book, though, begins with a **title page,** which gives the title of the book, the name of the author or editor, the name of the publisher, and the place of publication. On the back of this page is the **copyright page,** which lists, among other things, the year that the book was copyrighted. *Copyright* means that the author or publisher has the legal right to that book; no one else can reprint any part of it without permission.

A **table of contents** tells you two important things: the major topics in the book and the logical organization the author uses to discuss those topics. He may start with the simplest and go to the most difficult concept, or he may discuss the information in chronological order. The table of contents lists the chapter or unit divisions with page numbers in numerical order. A **list of illustrations** is similar to a table of contents; it lists the location and sequence of pictures in the text.

Contents

Some books also include **acknowledgments,** the names of people the author or editor wants to thank. Some books also have an **introduction** or **preface,** which states the purpose of the book.

The largest part of every book is the **text.** In both fiction and nonfiction books, the text is usually divided into units, sections, or chapters. Chapters in textbooks usually display clear organization. The chapter may have bold headings that introduce main topics and smaller bold headings to introduce smaller parts of the main subject. The rest of the information is usually in lists or paragraphs. Each paragraph will have a topic sentence and details that support the topic sentence. Pictures and illustrations, which may include captions with important information, further help to support the topic.

Many nonfiction books also contain additional sections of information that are placed after the text. One of these is the **bibliography,** which lists some additional books and articles about the same subject.

Extra helps, such as charts, diagrams, long lists, and notes of explanation, are included in the **appendix.** One kind of appendix is a **glossary,** which gives the definitions of special vocabulary words used in the text. Many textbooks have glossaries and other appendixes.

An **index** is an alphabetical listing of key words and phrases with all the page numbers where they appear in the text. Sometimes the index also lists the page numbers of the illustrations.

Index

You may notice that fiction books usually have only a title page, a copyright page, a table of contents, and the text. This is true because the main purpose of fictional writing is usually to entertain, not to inform.

Reinforcement

Remind the students that a bibliography is a great place to find additional sources on a particular topic.

Enrichment

Assign Teaching Help 14A (Book 2, p. 59) for more practice in using the parts of a book.

Use the sample table of contents (p. 339) and index (p. 340) to find the answer to each question. In the blank write the letter of the correct answer.

_A_ 1. Where is information about addition of integers?
A. Chapter 1
B. Chapter 2
C. Chapter 3

_B_ 2. Which page would tell you about the distributive property?
A. 6
B. 20
C. 118

_A_ 3. Which chapter discusses division by zero?
A. 1
B. 2
C. 3

_B_ 4. Common denominators are discussed in which chapter?
A. 1
B. 2
C. 3

_C_ 5. Which page defines the term *algebraic expression?*
A. 54
B. 62
C. 87

_B_ 6. The definition of coordinates on a number line is discussed in the same chapter as which topic?
A. abscissa
B. composite numbers
C. coin problems

_A_ 7. Which chapter includes teaching about the associative property of multiplication?
A. 1
B. 2
C. 3

_C_ 8. Which pages would tell you more about the Bernoulli family?
A. 54-57
B. 70-71
C. 118-19

_C_ 9. Which chapter includes the addition property of equality?
A. 1
B. 2
C. 3

_B_ 10. Addition of rational numbers can be found in the same chapter as which topic?
A. additive inverse
B. averages
C. combinations

In each blank write the letter of the correct book section that would give you the information requested.

A. title page   F. text
B. copyright page   G. bibliography
C. table of contents   H. appendix
D. list of illustrations   I. glossary
E. introduction or preface   J. index

__A__ 1. the name of the book

__G__ 2. listing of books that can give further information

__I__ 3. the definition of special vocabulary words

__B__ 4. the year the book was published

__C__ 5. chapter or unit divisions

__H__ 6. extra helps, such as charts, diagrams, long lists, and notes of explanation

__D__ 7. list of the pictures that are in the text

__J__ 8. the alphabetical listing of key words and phrases with all the page numbers where they appear in the text

__F__ 9. the largest portion of the book

__E__ 10. the explanation of the purpose of the book

Using Profitable Memory Techniques

After you complete your daily reading and written homework assignments, you will need to study for your tests and quizzes. Here are some techniques to improve your memory.

Read through the class notes for each class on a daily basis.

Pay attention as you study. Determine to remember, and remind yourself not to be mentally lazy.

Also, ask yourself questions about your notes and answer them aloud. Write down any questions regarding material that is unclear to you and then ask the teacher these questions when you return to class.

Make flash cards from your study notes. Write a question on one side and the answer on the other side.

Create your own written quizzes as you study. Put the quiz away for a day or two and then try to answer the questions. Those that you cannot answer correctly are the ones that need extra study time.

Ask a friend or family member to quiz you occasionally.

Cluster information that you are learning. When you are reviewing much information at one time, such as for a final exam, try to organize the material into related groups or clusters. Learn the information by category groups: the industrial products from New England, the industrial products from the Middle Atlantic states, the industrial products from the Southwest, and so forth.

Use memory devices to help you remember. Create rhymes, acronyms, acrostics, or other word games during your study times to help you remember detailed information. An acronym is a word in which each letter stands for another word. An acrostic is a phrase in which each initial letter stands for a different word or phrase.

ACRONYM   To remember the colors of the rainbow in order (red, orange, yellow, green, blue, indigo, violet), use this fictional name: *ROY G. BIV.*

ACROSTIC   To remember the names of the planets in order (Mercury, Venus, Earth, Mars, Jupiter, Saturn, Uranus, Neptune, Pluto), remember the following sentence: *My Very Earthly Mother Just Served Us Nine Pickles.*

Improving Your Reading Comprehension

Learning most often requires reading. Becoming an avid reader and improving your reading comprehension skills will increase your knowledge and ability to learn. You probably do not understand the meaning of every word that you read, and you do not always have time to look up every word. How can you discover the meanings of these words while you continue to read your assignments?

Context Clues

One method is defining a word from context clues. You discover enough clues from other words used around the word to guess its meaning. Look at the sentence below to understand by context what the word *plethora* means.

The overflowing party trays held a *plethora* of various kinds of desserts.

Plethora means an overabundance or excess. What other words in the sentence give you clues to the meaning?

Definitions

Sometimes the writer may write the definition of an unfamiliar word into the sentence. Keep reading, because the definition may be the sentence.

The frustrated travelers realized they were at an *impasse,* a road that does not continue and has no exit.

Here the sentence correctly defines the word.

Teaching Strategy: Motivation

Since many disciplines of study require good reading skills, use your classroom to encourage outside reading. You may want to have a time in class when students can discuss books or articles they have read. They may even want to recommend a certain work to other members of the class.

If students have trouble staying focused while reading nonfiction works, encourage them to summarize the work as they read, writing either a summary sentence for each paragraph or a summary paragraph for each chapter. Remind them that a little reading with understanding is better than extensive reading without understanding.

Restatements and Examples

If the text does not give a definition of the word, look for a restatement. Extra information may be included after the word that may explain the word.

Sometimes the meaning of a word may be given by using examples. The examples used may give enough information to enable you to guess the meaning of the unknown word in the sentence.

> As I approached, the evening's *persiflage* drifted from the room. The greetings, jokes, and exclamations at the party were a pleasant relief from the long day of lectures.

What does *persiflage* mean? From the second sentence, you may have guessed that persiflage is "light, good-natured talk."

> This year's *Alumnus* of the Year Award goes to Mr. Frank Devons, a 1995 graduate who used his political science degree to become actively involved in local politics.

What is an alumnus? From this example, you can guess that *alumnus* means "a graduate of a school."

Comparison and Contrast

Sometimes an unknown word may be compared or contrasted with another word. If you know the meaning of the second word, it can help you discover the meaning of the unknown word.

> **COMPARISON** Her behavior was *obnoxious,* like that of a small child who does not yet know how to behave in public.

> **CONTRAST** The rich man was surrounded by wealth, unlike the beggar who lived in *penury* at his gate.

From the comparison sentence, you can determine that obnoxious behavior is offensive or socially unacceptable. In the contrast sentence, penury is obviously the opposite of wealth. You will probably conclude that penury is extreme poverty.

14-3 *P*RACTICE THE *S*KILL

In the blank write a definition of the italicized word. Also identify the type of context clue used to determine the definition: *definition, restatement, example, comparison,* **or** *contrast.* (Answers will vary.)

1. Although my cupboard is completely empty, Aunt Denise's pantry is *replete* with homemade cookies, pastries, and other scrumptious treats.

   abundantly supplied (contrast)

2. Howard displayed a *cavalier* attitude in the meeting, making jokes about everything and carelessly dismissing the important issues.

   careless about important matters (example)

Enrichment

Assign Teaching Help 14B (Book 2, p. 60) for more practice in using context clues.

3. My overweight cat, Crosby, has a *voracious* appetite. Because he constantly craves food, he sits by his empty bowl, yowls as loudly as he can, and stares longingly at the closed doors of the pantry where his dinner is kept.

   having a strong craving for food (restatement)

4. The king was very *arrogant* as he strutted around the room like a peacock.

   proud, exaggerating one's own importance (comparison)

5. Friendly and engaging, Matthew is an *extrovert,* a person interested in others.

   a person interested in others (definition)

6. When Merilee called me last night, she was in a *loquacious* mood. She talked nonstop for almost two hours!

   very talkative (restatement)

7. Gabriel's dog, Frisky, has an extreme case of *lethargy;* like a bear in hibernation, he sleeps all day.

   dullness, abnormal drowsiness (comparison)

8. To stay healthy, Toni Marie became an *inveterate* runner, covering three miles four times every week.

   habitual (example)

9. A good team leader must possess *serendipity,* the gift of finding valuable or agreeable things not sought for.

   the gift of finding valuable or agreeable things not sought for (definition)

10. Though Athene now communicates her ideas clearly and with great precision, she produced nothing but *jabberwocky* when she was two.

    nonsense (contrast)

14-4 REVIEW THE SKILL

In the blank write a definition of the italicized word. Also identify the type of context clue used to determine the definition: *definition, restatement, example, comparison,* or *contrast.* (Answers will vary.)

1. The look on his face was *frigorific,* like a blast of cold air that chilled me to the bone.

   causing coldness, chilling (comparison)

2. Larry, a perfectionist preferring exact symmetry, will not leave his desk with papers scattered *askew.*

   crooked (contrast)

3. Charming and cheerful, the saleslady had a *winsome* personality.

   charming, attractive (restatement)

4. The new twenty-gallon fish tank was *cumbersome,* too bulky for me to carry upstairs by myself.

   bulky, hard to manage (definition)

5. The commanding officer's *valor* earned him the loyalty of his men, who were inspired by his example of courage.

   courage and boldness, as in battle (restatement)

6. As I watched her move, she seemed to be the very picture of *elegance,* gliding across the room like a swan.

   showing refined beauty of manner (comparison)

7. "May I help you with your luggage?" Bret asked the woman struggling with her bags, hoping to *alleviate* her burden.

   make lighter or more bearable (example)

8. Anna spoke *brusquely* to him, openly and forcefully stating the truth.

   abruptly, bluntly (restatement)

9. Jacquelyn found herself in a *precarious* situation, like a tightrope walker balancing her way over a deep chasm.

   dangerously lacking in stability (comparison)

10. Unlike the self-centered Ebenezer Scrooge, our new corporate executive officer demonstrated *altruism.*

    unselfish concern for others (contrast)

Word Parts

Sometimes certain parts of words give clues as to the word's meaning. If you understand the meaning of the root and the prefix or the suffix, you might be able to determine the meaning of the whole word. Look at the charts below to note the spelling and definition of several prefixes, suffixes, and roots.

Prefixes

A prefix is added to the beginning of a word.

PREFIX	MEANING	EXAMPLE
con	with, together	conform
pre	before	precede
post	after	postlude
de	down from, from; concerning	descend
se	apart	separate
extra/extro	outside of, beyond	extrovert
retro	back, backward	retroactive

Suffixes

A suffix is added to the end of a word.

SUFFIX	MEANING	EXAMPLE
ant/ent	performing or causing a particular action; being in a particular condition	informant
ance/ence	condition or state; act	performance
ous	having/possessing	famous

Roots

A root is the main part of the word.

ROOT	MEANING	EXAMPLE
rupt	break, burst	disrupt
sent/sens	feel, think	assent
lude (lud)/lus	play	interlude
scribe (scrib)/script	write	scribble
press	to press	impress
grade (grad)/gress	to step, go	degrade
cede (ced)/cess	go	concede
greg	herd, flock; company	segregate
terr	earth	terrace
voc/voke	call	vocation
spect	look at; watch	spectacle

USAGE

Chapter 10: Rules for Adding
Suffixes
pp. 240-41

14-5 PRACTICE THE SKILL

Using the definition of the prefixes, suffixes, and root words given above, guess the definitions for the words given below. Write your answer in the blank. *(Answers will vary.)*

1. consent *think together*

2. prelude *play before*

3. describe *write down from*

4. retrogress *step backward*

5. secede *go apart from*

6. depressant *causing a pressing down*

7. convoke _call together_

8. postscript _write after_

9. retrospect _look backward_

10. precedence _act of going before_

14-6 Review the Skill

In the blank write a sentence using the word as you defined it in Practice the Skill 14-5. *(Answers will vary.)*

1. consent _Do you have your parents' consent for the class trip?_

2. prelude _Marjorie played the prelude at church last Sunday._

3. describe _How would you describe your hometown?_

4. retrogress _My grandfather sometimes retrogresses to his childhood._

5. secede _If the rules continue to be broken, I will have to secede from the club._

6. depressant _Coffee is not a depressant._

7. convoke _The class president convoked the student council._

8. postscript _Sabrina adds a postscript to all of her letters._

9. retrospect _In retrospect, I don't think we should have eaten so much chocolate cake._

10. precedence _My older brother has claimed precedence when choosing household chores for the week._

Taking Tests

Studying and doing homework are part of learning, but they are also part of an organized plan to help you do well on tests and quizzes. You have no doubt learned that waiting to study until the night before a test is not a good way to earn good grades for a class. The more often you review material and the longer the period of time over which you review, the more information your memory will retain. Here are some other hints for taking tests.

How to Take Classroom Tests

1. Before you begin, look over the test to determine the number and type of questions there are.

2. Read all directions carefully.

3. Work through the entire test in one of two ways.

    • Start at the beginning of the test and keep going. Answer those questions about which you are confident and those about which you are 50 to 75 percent certain of the answers. In some way mark those questions to which you do not know the answer or that you need to spend more time thinking about. Come back to them later.

    • Start at the most difficult section of the test and do it first. (Be careful, however, not to spend too much time on that one section!) Again, mark questions with which you are having problems and come back to them later.

4. Try to answer all questions, even if you have to guess at some.

5. Think carefully and be selective about what you write for short answer and essay questions. It is better to write a little about what you do know than to write a lot about what you do not know.

6. Write neatly. Correct answers might not count if the teacher cannot read what you have written.

How to Answer Objective Test Questions

Multiple Choice

1. Read each question carefully. Formulate an answer before you look at the choices.

2. Read all the choices carefully. Eliminate those that you know are wrong.

3. Choose or guess the best answer from the choices left.

    Example: __B__   Which is the largest land animal?
    A.   raccoon
    B.   hippopotamus
    C.   whale
    D.   kangaroo

Matching

1. Read each question carefully. Formulate an answer before you look at the choices.

2. Match the questions and answers that you know are correct.

3. From the choices remaining, choose the best answer for each question.

Match each state with the body of water it borders. Write the letter of the correct answer in the blank.

__B__ 1. Georgia	A.	Lake Huron
__D__ 2. Texas	B.	Atlantic Ocean
__A__ 3. Michigan	C.	Pacific Ocean
__C__ 4. California	D.	Gulf of Mexico

True/False

1. Read each item carefully. If any word in the item is false, the entire item is false.

2. Look for words like *always* or *never;* these words often signal a false item.

Example: ___false___ The main character of a story is always the protagonist.

Short Answer

1. Accurately and completely answer the questions that you know.

2. If you do not know the answer, make the best guess you can. You may receive partial credit for your answer.

Example: ___denouement___ What is another name for the conclusion of a story?

How to Take Standardized Tests

Periodically you will be required to take standardized tests. You will have a better chance of doing well if you are familiar with the types of questions usually included on standardized tests.

Reading Comprehension

The reading comprehension section tests your ability to analyze a written passage. The questions may ask about the main ideas, details, or meaning of the passage. You may have to evaluate information or draw conclusions. The following strategies will help you on this part of the test.

1. Look at the questions briefly.

2. Read the paragraph and answer the questions you definitely know.

3. Read the other questions carefully as time allows, eliminating answers you know are incorrect.

4. Choose the most logical answer from those remaining.

Example: The president's popularity is unprecedented. Other presidents have stayed tucked away in their offices, dealing with only the highest company manager. Mr. Appleman regularly makes his rounds throughout the company. The people know him and appreciate his understanding of them.

   D   In this paragraph the word *unprecedented* means
- A. not necessary.
- B. without reason or cause.
- C. without appreciation.
- D. not occurring previously.

The paragraph has no information leading the reader to think that *unprecedented* means *unnecessary.* The remaining three sentences suggest that the president's popularity is a result of his availability and concern and that it is, in fact, appreciated. The correct answer is clearly letter *D,* "not occurring previously." No other president had ever been so popular.

Vocabulary

Standardized tests also contain a vocabulary section that tests your knowledge of common English words. This section may include two types of questions. One type gives a sentence (or part of a sentence) with a word in bold print. You must then choose the word or phrase that best matches the meaning of the word in bold print. Context clues will help you choose your answer.

Example: **C**   A **rendezvous** was planned for 9:00 at the doughnut shop on the corner.
- A. a debate
- B. a formal reception
- C. a prearranged meeting
- D. an initiation for an organization

The sentence states a specific time and place for the *rendezvous,* but it does not indicate the purpose of the occasion. The best answer is *C,* "a prearranged meeting."

Another type of question may list several sentences, each including the same underlined word. You must choose the sentence in which the word has the same meaning as in the original sentence.

Example: **C**   In Western culture, the heart is considered the <u>seat</u> of the emotions.
- A. In the election, the senator regained his <u>seat</u> in the House of Representatives.
- B. The concert hall will be renovated with new carpet and comfortable <u>seats</u>.
- C. The influential, yet corrupt institution is the <u>seat</u> of moral decay in that city.
- D. Ushers will <u>seat</u> the guests as they come in.

In the original sentence, *seat* means "the place where something is located or based." *Seat* in the first choice means "membership in an organization obtained through an election." In the second choice, *seat* means "a place where one may sit." In the fourth choice, *seat* means "to place in a seat." The correct answer is the third choice where *seat* means "the place where something is based," as in the example.

Reinforcement

Remind the students that although more than one answer may be technically correct, they must choose the best answer. Teach them to eliminate the wrong answers and then to evaluate the remaining possible answers. They must determine which choice best answers the question.

Analogy

Many standardized tests also contain an analogy section. An analogy is a comparison of one thing to another. Analogy questions on standardized tests ask you to compare the relationship of one pair of words to the relationship of another pair of words. Analogies are similar to vocabulary questions because they test your understanding of the meanings of words. But they are different from vocabulary questions because they ask you to think about the relationship between the words.

In an analogy question, you must choose the pair of words whose relationship most closely matches that of the original pair of words. The two words in a set are usually separated by a colon that stands for the phrase "is to"; and the two sets of words are separated by a double colon that means "as."

Example: __C__   MOTHER : DAUGHTER ::
    A.   mother : son
    B.   father : daughter
    C.   father : son
    D.   mother : father

First, read the question as an interrogative sentence. This question would be read as *"Mother* is to *daughter* as *what* is to *what?"* Then change that question into a statement that expresses the relationship between the two words: *A mother is the female parent of a daughter, a female child.* Now you are ready to compare the other sets of words to the original set. The original set expresses a relationship between a parent and a child, and the first three choices also express a parent-child relationship. But only choice *C* expresses a relationship between a parent and a child who are the same gender, just like the original pair of words. The question and answer together would be read as *"Mother* is to *daughter* as *father* is to *son."*

Grammar, Usage, and Mechanics

Standardized tests often combine questions about grammar, usage, and mechanics in one section. Other tests include several separate sections of questions. Depending on the test, the questions may appear in different formats. For example, the test may show a sentence with several words underlined and labeled, requiring you to choose the word that contains the error. If the sentence is correct, you choose the "no error" option.

Example: __B__   The <u>gymnasts</u> meet on <u>weekdayes</u> and <u>practice</u>
                 A   B   C
    their routines. <u>No error</u>
                    D

The correct choice is *B* because the correct spelling should be *weekdays.*

Another type of question may show you a sentence with part of the sentence underlined. You must choose one of the possible replacements for the underlined part. If the underlined part is correct, choose the answer that indicates no change is necessary.

Example: __A__   Either the back windows or the front door <u>need its</u>
    glass cleaned.
    A.   needs its
    B.   needs their
    C.   need their
    D.   correct as is

Teaching Strategy: Discussion

Before introducing the analogy section, discuss analogy with your students. An analogy explains (or actually makes an argument about) one situation by comparing it to a similar situation. For example, the Book of Proverbs makes an analogy between humans and ants. Just as the ants work hard and prepare their homes and food for the winter, so we should be diligent and prepare for the future. Also, how many times have you heard someone say, "It's like riding a bicycle: once you learn how, you'll never forget"? When someone says this, he is making an analogy between a particular situation and the process of learning to ride a bicycle. Ask the students to identify or create other analogies. Lead a discussion about the benefits and dangers of using analogy to support an argument.

Additional Resources

For further information about arguing from analogy, see pages 65-66 of *Better Thinking and Reasoning,* published by Bob Jones University Press.

Choice *A* is correct because the verb *needs* agrees with the singular subject. (The singular part of the compound subject is closer to the verb.) The pronoun *its* is also singular.

Other standardized tests have separate sections for mechanics (capitalization and punctuation). The question may divide one sentence into several parts. Each part is listed separately. You choose the part that contains an error. If the sentence is correct, choose the answer that indicates no change is necessary.

Example: _____B_____ A. When the apples are ripe,
　　　　　　　　　　　　 B. we pick them all day,
　　　　　　　　　　　　 C. and celebrate with a party in the evening.
　　　　　　　　　　　　 D. no mistakes

Choice *B* contains an error. A comma should not separate two verbs or predicates.

14-7 Practice the Skill

Reading Comprehension: Read the paragraph and answer the following questions. In the blank write the letter of the correct answer.

Germany is the birthplace of the Reformation. Martin Luther was born in northern Germany, studied in its schools, was converted, and spent the rest of his life preaching to and teaching the German people. Protestant leaders used the printing press, invented by another German, Johann Gutenberg, to spread the ideas of the Reformation around the world. Today, almost one-half of the German people are Lutherans. They constitute the largest population of non-Catholics in Continental Europe.

_____C_____ 1. The topic of the above paragraph is
　　　　　　　　　A. Martin Luther.
　　　　　　　　　B. Johann Gutenberg.
　　　　　　　　　C. Religion in Germany.
　　　　　　　　　D. Continental Europe.

_____D_____ 2. Martin Luther did not
　　　　　　　　　A. preach to the German people.
　　　　　　　　　B. study in German schools.
　　　　　　　　　C. teach the German people.
　　　　　　　　　D. invent the printing press.

Vocabulary: In the blank write the letter of the definition that most closely matches the word in bold print.

_____A_____ 3. Tina's **melancholy** personality often causes her to have a negative outlook on life.
　　　　　　　　　A. gloomy
　　　　　　　　　B. perceptive
　　　　　　　　　C. insightful
　　　　　　　　　D. sensitive

Scriptural Application

In the Gospels, Christ often uses analogy to teach spiritual truths. In Matthew 6, the disciples are told not to worry about food and clothing. Ask the students to identify the analogy Christ uses to help the disciples understand that such anxiety is futile. *(The birds and the flowers do not worry about food and clothing; their heavenly Father takes care of them.)* Later, Christ tells his disciples of a man who sold all his possessions to purchase one pearl of great value (Matt. 13:45-46). Relating this story to the kingdom of God, He explains that a person must forsake all to be a true partaker of God's kingdom. Once, the Pharisees accused Christ of spending too much time with sinful people of bad reputation. Christ responded with an analogy. He said that a doctor comes to heal the sick, not the healthy (Luke 5:29-32). This analogy explains that Christ came to save sinners, not those who believe themselves to be righteous already. Ask the students to look for more analogies in the Gospels. They may be able to find analogies in other parts of the Bible as well.

In the blank write the letter of the sentence in which the definition of the underlined word most closely matches that of the first sentence.

_B_ 4. Mr. Hansen always heads our departmental meetings.
A. My father always sits at the head of the table.
B. Alex headed the discussion on economics.
C. Neil really has a head for business.
D. The clown wore a funny hat on his head.

Analogy: In the blank write the letter of the pair of words whose relationship most closely matches the relationship of the original pair of words.

_C_ 5. PAGE : BOOK ::
A. chapter : index
B. picture : frame
C. slice : loaf
D. bookstore : library

_C_ 6. SHARP : KNIFE ::
A. wood : handle
B. knife : cut
C. rough : sandpaper
D. old : antique

Grammar, Usage, and Mechanics: In the blank write the letter that corresponds to the error in the sentence.

_B_ 7. The scarf of the Mayor is lying on the street. No error
         A   B   C   D

_B_ 8. A. In the late 1800s
B. my grandfather and grandmothers
C. house and barn were built.
D. no mistakes

In the blank write the letter of the correct replacement for the underlined section of the sentence. If the sentence is correct, choose D.

_D_ 9. One of the boys always drops his pen on the floor.
A. drop his
B. drop their
C. drops their
D. correct as is

_B_ 10. Neither of the girls has swam her required ten miles.
A. have swam their
B. has swum her
C. has swum their
D. correct as is

Reading Comprehension: Read the paragraph and answer the following questions. In the blank write the letter of the correct answer.

The island of Cyprus is almost twice the size of Delaware. Two mountain ranges cross Cyprus from east to west and rise as high as 6,406 feet. The plain between these forested mountains is called Mesaoria. The valley and the coasts have a typical Mediterranean climate—rainy, mild winters and hot, dry summers. Only the mountains get snow in winter. The climate supports grapefruit, lemons, oranges, grapes, and olives.

_____A_____ 1. According to the paragraph, two mountain ranges cross
Cyprus from
A. east to west.
B. north to south.
C. south to west.
D. east to north.

_____B_____ 2. Summer in Cyprus is
   A. cool.
   B. hot and dry.
   C. moderately warm.
   D. warm and moist.

Vocabulary: In the blank write the letter of the definition that most closely matches the word in bold print.

_____B_____ 3. The children in Jenna's kindergarten class always **flourish** under her watchful guidance.
   A. wither away
   B. grow well
   C. misbehave terribly
   D. wave dramatically

In the blank write the letter of the sentence in which the definition of the underlined word most closely matches that of the first sentence.

_____C_____ 4. My homework is rather <u>light</u> tonight.
   A. The <u>light</u> in my room is not working.
   B. If you are cold, you can <u>light</u> a fire.
   C. A <u>light</u> snow fell last night while you were sleeping.
   D. You need to <u>light</u> from the horse now.

Analogy: In the blank write the letter of the pair of words whose relationship most closely matches the relationship of the original pair of words.

_____B_____ 5. RUN : FAST ::
   A. skip : hop
   B. jump : high
   C. pace : walk
   D. drive : car

_____D_____ 6. AUTHOR : NOVEL ::
   A. doctor : patient
   B. teacher : teaching
   C. lawyer : courtroom
   D. artist : painting

Grammar, Usage, and Mechanics: In the blank write the letter that corresponds to the error in the sentence.

_____A_____ 7. Edgar <u>droped</u> the <u>lilies</u> as he <u>entered</u> the room. <u>No error</u>
                          A   B   C   D

_____B_____ 8. A. "Who wrote the song
   B. 'My wild Irish Rose'?"
   C. asked Margaret.
   D. no mistakes

In the blank write the letter of the correct replacement for the underlined section of the sentence. If the sentence is correct, choose *D*.

___D___ 9. Both of the kittens <u>are in their</u> basket.
      A. are in its
      B. is in their
      C. is in its
      D. correct as is

___A___ 10. Robert and I enjoy baseball. <u>He and me</u> have box seats for this Saturday's game.
      A. He and I
      B. Him and me
      C. Me and him
      D. correct as is

15 COMPOSITION SKILLS

Lesson Support

Teacher's Edition, Book 1
Bulletin Boards—p. 452

Teacher's Edition, Book 2
Teaching Helps—pp. 61-64

Whenever Frank Lloyd Wright, the famous architect, was asked to design a house, he did at least two things before he started drawing. He learned all he could about the people who would be living in the house—their interests, their preferences, their way of life. He also carefully studied the site where the house would be built so that he could harmonize the building with the natural world around it. In other words, he gathered information and considered it carefully as he made his plans.

Writing is much more than just putting words down on paper. Writers no less than architects need to do some things ahead of time. Following the right process can make writing a pleasure, especially as the results become better.

Writing Process Overview

Planning

Just as an architect's design involves careful planning, so a writer's work requires thoughtful preparation. What you do before you begin to write can be just as important as the actual writing. Without proper planning, your attempts at writing will prove frustrating for both you and your audience. Taking time to plan will save you time in the later stages of writing.

Choosing a Topic

Of course, the first step in planning will be to choose a topic. You may be assigned a writing topic, asked to choose from a list of topics, or asked to choose your own topic. Choose one that you already know something about or that you are interested in. The following strategies will help you find a topic that will work for you.

Making a List

Write down memories, experiences, or important events from your own life that you could write about. Read journal entries, look at scrapbooks and photograph albums, and observe everyday surroundings and routines. Think about hobbies and other interests. Here is an example of one student's list.

- books
- dogs
- vacation to Williamsburg
- soccer
- candles

Teaching Strategy: Motivation and Discussion

Explain to the students that knowing how to write effectively is a tool they can use for the rest of their lives. English class is not the only place where they will be asked to write. If any of them pursue a college education, they will be required to write papers in many classes. In addition, writing has been and continues to be a vital form of communication. Challenge the students to think about the importance of writing in our society today. Ask the class to suggest some contexts in which writing is used (e.g., print and broadcast journalism, print and broadcast advertising, instruction manuals, novels, biographies, and Bible commentaries) and then display the list.

Asking Questions

Ask yourself questions to get started. The answers to these questions may lead to more questions. Eventually you will have several ideas to explore. The following questions may help you think of other topics.

- What are my favorite hobbies or pastimes? Why?
- What books have I enjoyed reading? Why?
- What is my best (or most difficult) subject? Why?
- What is the funniest thing that ever happened to me?
- Whom do I admire?
- What would I like to do when I get older?

Brainstorming

Start by choosing one topic. Then list everything about that topic that you can remember. Write down every idea that you think about. When you have finished, you will have many topic possibilities, both general and specific. Here is an example based on one of the items from the sample list on page 359.

- vacation in Williamsburg
- colonial life
- blacksmith
- architecture
- tourist attraction
- candlemaking
- restoring homes
- College of William and Mary

Clustering

Clustering is similar to brainstorming but goes one step further. Instead of a simple list, clustering yields a diagram that shows relationships between ideas. Clustering will help you generate topic ideas and suggest ways of organizing your information. Write down the general topic and circle it. Then write down any related ideas and circle them. Next, draw lines connecting ideas to one another and to the main topic.

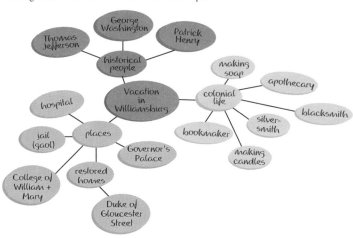

Teaching Strategy: Participation

With the students' help, develop and display a list of potential topics. Lead the class to select a topic from the list. Tell the students that the next step will be brainstorming. Remind them that participants in a brainstorming session list whatever comes to mind as they are thinking of the topic. Allow the students to list as many ideas as possible in five minutes. Next, divide the class into groups of three or four students. Instruct each group to pick a topic from the list. Then allow each group seven minutes for clustering. Ask a representative from each group to share the group's findings.

Freewriting

Freewriting can help spark your creativity. Choose a general topic. Then set yourself a time limit (five minutes, for example) and write about that topic for the entire time without stopping. When you finish, read what you have just written and look for ideas to explore further.

> Last winter I went to Williamsburg over Christmas vacation. We had an interesting time. It was really neat to see all of the reenactments of colonial life. The jail and the hospital were interesting. I wouldn't have wanted to get sick during that time in history! Anyway, I especially enjoyed the demonstrations of things made during colonial times. I especially enjoyed seeing silver and candles made. The governor's mansion was amazing. Well, the colonists didn't have electricity, so they had to make candles. Since I especially enjoy candles, I might write about candlemaking. I may focus on today's process for making candles.

Narrowing Your Topic

Students often think they need a broad, general topic because the writing assignment requires a lengthy paper. Remember, it is better to say more about less than to say less about more. Ask yourself these questions: *How long will my paper be? Is my topic too broad to be adequately covered in the assigned pages?* If the answer to the second question is yes, focus on one aspect of your topic. For example, the topic *Williamsburg* is too large for a paper of almost any length. In fact, books have been written on Williamsburg. Even a colonist's life in Williamsburg is fairly broad. Perhaps you could consider the process of candlemaking.

Considering Your Audience

After an architect gets his information, he still has to decide how he will use it and what is most important. A writer, too, still has some thinking to do before he can make specific plans. First decide who your audience will be. Your teacher only? Your family? Your whole class? The student body? The editor at the local newspaper? Good writers also consider their audience by asking *How large is my audience? How much do they know about my topic? What about my topic will interest my audience?* These factors affect the formality of a piece of writing.

Determining Purpose

Next, figure out what your purpose will be. Do you want to inform your audience or persuade them? Do you want to entertain or merely describe? As you answer these questions, think about what the main thrust of your paper will be. Include in your writing only that information that will achieve your purpose.

Gathering Information

First, list everything you already know about your topic. The methods you used to choose a topic can also be used to gather information. When you have finished, look at the information you have gathered. Do you have enough information to interest your audience and to achieve your purpose? After you have written down your ideas, you should look for additional information. Besides encyclopedias and books, remember to check magazines and electronic media.

Teaching Strategy: Modeling

Pick one of the general topics listed in the previous exercise. Write the selected topic for display and tell the students you are going to write a paper on that topic. Begin listing points you could cover under that topic. After making a fairly extensive list, ask the students how long your paper would have to be to cover all that material.

Read the following student example and answer the questions at the end. *(Answers will vary.)*

Once you arrive in America from England, you will need several basic necessities for your simple colonial home. First, you must be sure that you have plenty of firewood on hand to heat your house. Tallow candles will be essential for lighting your home, and buckets will hold your water. You will need wooden bowls and plates for your dishes, and you will use iron pots to cook your food. Barrels or stools will be your chairs, and your table will probably be made from wooden boards. A spinning wheel and loom will also be helpful items for making clothing since you will make most of your own clothes.

1. What is the purpose of this paragraph?

   to inform

2. Who is the intended audience for this paragraph?

   friends in England who are planning to move to colonial America

3. Who might the writer of this paragraph be?

   a colonial man or woman

Read the following student example and answer the questions at the end. *(Answers will vary.)*

In 1740, when I was fifteen years old, I became apprenticed to John Plumstead, the local blacksmith. I served Mr. Plumstead for the next six years, and, in exchange, he taught me his trade. Although I was not paid for my work, Mr. Plumstead allowed me to live with him and his family, and he also gave me my meals and provided me with clothes. My sister Nell also went to live with a family; however, she worked as a servant in the home of Peter Wyeth. Nell cooked, cleaned, and sewed for the Wyeth family, and she also learned how to do other everyday jobs that would prepare her for her future. Both Nell and I did our very best to be hard workers, and we also tried to be obedient to our masters. It was during this time of my apprenticeship that I learned to read and write, so I am ever grateful to my kind master, Mr. Plumstead. Your apprenticeship will also teach you many valuable things.

1. What is the purpose of this paragraph?

   to inform, to entertain

2. Who is the intended audience of this paragraph?

   a young friend; a person who is going to become an apprentice

3. Who is the writer of this paragraph?

   a man who lived during the colonial period in America

If someone had asked Frank Lloyd Wright to design a house without bothering to draw up a blueprint, Wright would have had a difficult time getting the builders to put up the structure he envisioned. Builders need plans to guide them. Writers need plans as well. A writer's blueprint is an outline.

Some people think outlining is a waste of time. Don't bother with planning, they say—just write. At first, this method may seem faster, but eventually a lack of planning will cost more time than it saves. A person might as well try to cut out a dress without a pattern or build an engine without a plan. Outlining your paper helps you to remember to cover all of your important points in a logical order. Use the ideas you wrote down earlier; then rearrange them in the best order for the paper, omitting any ideas that no longer seem to fit the main idea of your paper.

A Tentative Outline

A tentative outline is always helpful. Simply jot down the ideas you will include in your paper. After you have the ideas written down, you can rearrange them in the best order for the paper.

braiding cotton threads
making wicks
mixing paraffin
melting wax
trimming the candle
preparing the molds
letting wax harden
inserting the wicks
adding color with crayons
gathering materials
decorating candles

The next step is to group similar things together.

gathering materials
preparing molds
making wicks

melting wax
adding color with crayons
pouring the wax
letting the wax harden

decorating candles
inserting the wicks
trimming the wicks

Enrichment

Divide the class into teams of three or four students each. Assign the class a general topic. Instruct the teams to narrow the topic and then to construct a tentative outline, following the procedure on page 363.

Outline Forms

A well-organized outline can be a real help in writing a paper. Sometimes you will be asked to hand in an outline along with a paper. Any outline that others will see should follow one of the two forms given below.

A Topic Outline

A **topic outline** uses phrases only—no sentences and no verbs (verbals may be used). Points numbered or lettered in the same series should have the same grammatical form (nouns, adjectives, prepositional phrases, or participles, for instance).

   I. Organizing the supplies
      A. Gathering the materials
      B. Making the wicks
      C. Preparing the molds

  II. Making the candles
      A. Melting the wax and paraffin
      B. Adding color
      C. Pouring the wax
      D. Letting the wax harden

 III. Finishing the candles
      A. Inserting wicks
      B. Trimming wicks
      C. Decorating the candles

A Sentence Outline

A **sentence outline** includes more information than a topic outline does because every point in it is a complete sentence.

   I. The candlemaker organizes his supplies.
      A. First he gathers his materials.
      B. Then he makes the wicks.
      C. Just before he actually makes the candles, he prepares the candle molds.

  II. Making the candles is a matter of knowing about wax.
      A. He melts the wax and paraffin.
      B. Next he adds color with wax crayons.
      C. Then he pours the wax into the molds.
      D. Finally, the candlemaker lets the wax harden.

 III. Finishing the candles is a quick procedure.
      A. The wicks must be inserted.
      B. The wicks must be trimmed to the right length.
      C. The candles can be decorated.

Reinforcement

Assign Teaching Help 15A (Book 2, p. 61)
for more practice in outlining.

Read the following outline carefully. Then answer the questions. In each blank write the letter that corresponds to the correct answer.

Benjamin Franklin
I. Early life
  A. Birth
    1. January 17, 1706
    2. Boston, Massachusetts
  B. Education
    1. Formal education
    2. Self-education
II.
  A. Candlemaker
  B. Printer
    1. Apprenticeship
    2. Pseudonymous articles
  C. Publisher
    1. *Pennsylvania Gazette*
    2. *Poor Richard's Almanac*

III. Important inventions
  A. Lightning rod
  B. Stove
  C. Bifocal glasses

IV. Political activities
  A. Plan of Union
  B. Delegate to London
  C. Postmaster
  D. Stamp Act

_____B_____ 1. Where would the entry "Glass harmonica" be the most appropriate?
  A. II. D
  B. III. D
  C. II. B. 3
  D. I. C

_____C_____ 2. Which heading best fits II?
  A. Neighbors
  B. Businesses
  C. Occupations
  D. None of these

_____C_____ 3. Which entry does *not* belong in IV?
  A. Plan of Union
  B. Delegate to London
  C. Postmaster
  D. Stamp Act

<u>A</u> 4. In what position would your answer for number 3 fit more logically?
A. II. D
B. III. D
C. I. B. 3
D. I. C

<u>B</u> 5. In which section would electricity be discussed?
A. I. Early life
B. III. Important inventions
C. IV. Political activities
D. None of these

15-4 *R*EVIEW THE *S*KILL

Arrange the following list of topics into an outline with three main points. Be sure to group the items logically. One of the items will be the topic heading for the outline. *(Answers will vary.)*

Colonial America   William Penn
Early settling groups   Early colonial leaders
Rhode Island   Puritans
Virginia   Massachusetts Bay
Pilgrims   Roger Williams
John Winthrop   Pennsylvania
Early colonies   Captain John Smith

Colonial America

  I. Early settling groups

    A. Pilgrims

    B. Puritans

  II. Early colonial leaders

    A. John Winthrop

    B. William Penn

    C. Captain John Smith

    D. Roger Williams

  III. Early Colonies

    A. Massachusetts Bay

    B. Pennsylvania

    C. Virginia

    D. Rhode Island

Drafting

Once you have planned your paper, you are ready to write your rough draft. The rough draft is simply your first try at writing the paper. You will have a chance to improve it later, so you need not spend much time trying to find exactly the right word for something. It is generally better to write the entire first draft quickly and then go back to improve it later.

Paragraphs

The body of your paper should consist of well-developed paragraphs. A **paragraph** consists of a group of sentences closely related to one main idea. The main idea of the paragraph is usually stated in the **topic sentence.** Many times, the topic sentence begins the paragraph. Everything else in the paragraph relates to the subject matter of the topic sentence.

Once you have your main idea, you need to develop that idea with sentences that support your topic. Your **supporting sentences** may use details, examples, illustrations, or other methods to support the topic sentence.

A **concluding sentence** then joins all the ideas so that the paragraph will be complete. Often the concluding sentence restates the idea in the topic sentence.

> The clothing of wealthy colonial men consisted of lavish materials. — **topic sentence**
> Breeches were often silk or velvet. Fastening the breeches at the knee were silver buckles. With the breeches the men often wore fine linen shirts with lace ruffles at the neck and wrists. Over the shirt was a coat decorated with gold braids and fancy buttons. Completing the outfit, silk hose and shoes with silver buckles added to the wealthy appearance. — **supporting sentences**
> Expensive clothing was important to many colonial men. — **concluding sentence**

Writing a Topic Sentence

Once you have completed the planning stages, you are ready to write. First, write your **topic sentence.** A topic sentence embodies the main idea of the paragraph. The topic sentence is usually, but not always, the first sentence in a paragraph. Because it introduces the topic, putting the topic sentence first is often helpful to the writer as well as to the reader.

> Benjamin West and John Singleton Copley were two famous painters who were born in colonial America. West, a native of Pennsylvania, was a portrait painter who studied art in Philadelphia in the mid-1700s. Copley, who was born in Massachusetts, also painted portraits; he worked in Boston. Both of these artists later moved to Europe to test their skills, but they still greatly influenced future American painters.

If someone asked you right now what the above paragraph is about, you would probably say something like "colonial painters." And you would be correct. If you said only "colonial Americans," you would not be entirely accurate. The paragraph tells about two colonial Americans, but it more specifically tells about two colonial Americans who were painters.

You could also answer the question with the first sentence: "Benjamin West and John Singleton Copley were two famous painters who were born in colonial America." The first sentence is the topic sentence of the paragraph. It tells you both what the subject is and what will be said about the subject.

Reinforcement

Materials
- several examples of well-developed paragraphs

Read one of the paragraph examples to the students. Re-read the topic sentence. Then read the supporting sentences and ask the students how the sentences support or relate to the topic sentence. Read the next paragraph without the topic sentence. Ask the students to supply an appropriate topic sentence. Next, read the topic sentence of another paragraph. Ask the students to supply possible supporting sentences. For display, write the paragraph your students construct. Then read the actual paragraph.

Choose the best topic sentence for the following paragraph from the choices provided. In the blank write the letter that corresponds to your answer.

Colonial men often enjoyed foot races or wrestling contests. Plowing and corn husking competitions were also popular. The women gathered together to sew quilts. Children played typical children's games such as hopscotch and hide-and-seek. They also occupied themselves with balls and toys.

___B___ A. Colonial men were responsible for the entertainment of their families.
           B. Colonial Americans of all ages found many ways to entertain themselves.
           C. Colonial Americans were hard workers.

Write a good topic sentence for the following paragraph. The sentence should both tell the topic of the paragraph and indicate what will be said about the topic. Make the topic of the paragraph the grammatical subject of the sentence. *(Answers will vary.)*

He was a Puritan, and his church was located in Northampton, Massachusetts. He was also a well-known speaker outside of his church. In 1731 Edwards delivered a message entitled "God Glorified in the Work of Redemption," in which he spoke out against people's relying on their good works for salvation instead of upon God. Three years later, Edwards gave several messages on the theme of justification by faith alone, which in turn led to a revival among his own parishioners. Jonathan Edwards preached his most famous sermon, "Sinners in the Hands of an Angry God," during the Great Awakening, a period of great spiritual revival in America.

Jonathan Edwards was an influential preacher of colonial America.

Developing the Supporting Sentences

Now that you have the main idea, you need sentences that develop that idea. Your supporting sentences use the information that you have gathered in the planning stage. Remember your audience and your purpose: what kind of support will help you reach your goal?

Paragraphs may be developed in several ways. One obvious way is to back up the topic sentence with facts, examples, details, or reasons. Another way is to explain the topic further, perhaps even to define a key term. You may also compare or contrast two things or ideas. Many times, you will not adhere strictly to one method of development. Notice the example paragraph about the clothing of wealthy colonists. The paragraph is developed with examples of the different materials used for the clothes.

Enrichment

Materials
- several examples of good paragraphs
- strips of paper
- envelopes

Write each topic sentence on a separate strip of paper and label the topic sentences with a *T.* Then write each of the supporting sentences from each paragraph on a separate strip of paper. Label each supporting sentence with an *S.* Next, write each concluding sentence on a strip of paper and label the concluding sentences with a *C.*

Mix up the papers and insert them into the envelopes. Divide the class into teams of three or four students and give each team an envelope. Instruct the groups to form a correct paragraph with a topic sentence, supporting sentences, and a concluding sentence. Inform the teams that they may have to trade with each other to find sentences that will fit together logically. The first team to construct an appropriate paragraph wins.

Paragraph Development

Kind	Definition	Example
Fact	A statement that can be proved	Plymouth was the second permanent English settlement in America.
Example	A fact or an occurrence that illustrates a point	A group of men, women, and children established Plymouth in 1620.
Incident/Anecdote	A brief personal account that relates to the subject	My visit to Williamsburg helped me to understand colonial life.
Statistic	A fact expressed in numbers	The first settlers on Jamestown Island were about one hundred men and boys.
Sensory Details	The use of sense words—taste, touch, smell, etc.	Members of a farming family often wore garments made from coarse, scratchy materials like wool.
Reasons	Explanation of a truth	Because so many settlers died during the winter of 1609-10, the period became known as "the starving time."
Comparison/Contrast	Similarities and differences between two things	Many working colonists made their own furniture, but wealthy colonists often imported furniture from England.

15-7 PRACTICE THE SKILL

In the blank write the type of paragraph development the author uses in the following paragraph.

Although education has changed since colonial America, many things about it have remained the same. In colonial times, many children attended school in a one-room schoolhouse. These one-room schools were supported by the taxes of the public, and children were required to go to school unless they had a private tutor or their parents taught them at home. Similarly, many of today's children go to schools that are tax-supported. In addition, going to school is still a requirement for children unless their parents school them at home. One way that today's education differs from colonial education, however, is that most children no longer attend one-room schoolhouses. Today's students go to school in a building that is filled with rooms.

comparison/contrast

In the blank write the type(s) of paragraph development the author uses in the following paragraph.

In the seventeenth and eighteenth centuries, the population of the American colonies grew quickly. Babies were being born in the colonies that were already established, and new immigrants were finding their homes in America. In 1700 the population of the colonies was approximately 250,000, and by 1750 this number more than quadrupled to over a million. By 1770 more than two million people lived in the colonies, and five years later, the populace rose to almost 2.5 million.

statistic, fact, example

Organizing the Supporting Sentences

Now that you have your details, you must organize those details logically so that your reader can follow them easily. There are several ways in which you could construct your paragraph. Keeping your audience and purpose in mind, choose an organizational method that will best suit your needs and meet your goals.

Paragraph Organization		
Method	Definition	Good Places to Use
Chronological	A presentation of events in order of their occurrence	Stories, biographies, news reports, and process or historical writing
Spatial	A description according to how something is arranged in physical layout	Descriptive writing—especially descriptions of places or objects
Order of Importance	A move from least important to most important or vice versa	Persuasive or descriptive writing

Notice how the different organizational methods are used to achieve different purposes in these examples.

Chronological Order

What words indicate the order in which things happen?

Communication improved in the colonies. During early colonial times, news was spread by word of mouth. Often, a town crier read news to the people. Until 1700 mail service existed in only three colonies. However, by the mid-1700s Benjamin Franklin and William Hunter began developing post offices in all colonies. Later improvements included more widespread use of newspapers in the mid to late eighteenth century.

The words *during, until, by,* and *later,* as well as the dates themselves, show chronological order in this paragraph.

Spatial Order

What words indicate that this paragraph's development is spatial?

> Wealthy colonists were able to afford luxurious beds for their bedrooms. These beds had four posts, which held a canopy that covered the bed. From the border of the canopy hung curtains, which a person could pull around the edges of the bed. The mattress, filled with feathers, rested on a rope frame. Beneath the mattress was an open space that often housed a trundle bed. A trundle bed was a small movable bed that could be removed from underneath the four-poster bed at night. These canopied beds were an elegant addition to colonial bedrooms.

Some of the words that describe location are *from, on, beneath,* and *underneath.*

Order of Importance

What words indicate the relative importance of ideas?

> Many important discoveries and inventions are attributed to Benjamin Franklin. One of Franklin's first inventions was the lightning rod. The lightning rod protected buildings from harm if they were struck by lightning. Perhaps an even more significant invention was Franklin's stove. This invention allowed colonial Americans to keep their homes warmer without using as much fuel. Perhaps Franklin's greatest invention was bifocal glasses. A person can use them for reading as well as for seeing things at a distance. Bifocal glasses are still used by numerous people throughout the world.

The words *important, even more significant,* and *greatest* signal the order of importance.

15-9 PRACTICE THE SKILL

In the blank write the type of organization used in the paragraph.

Williamsburg was founded in 1633. At first this city was called Middle Plantation, but in 1699 its name was changed to Williamsburg in honor of William III, the king of England. From 1699 to 1776 Williamsburg served as the capital of the Virginia Colony, and from 1776 to 1780 this settlement was the capital of the Commonwealth of Virginia. Several historic events occurred in Williamsburg. For example, in 1765 Patrick Henry spoke out against the Stamp Act in Williamsburg's capitol building. Later, in 1776, the Virginia Declaration of Rights was accepted in Williamsburg.

chronological

15-10 REVIEW THE SKILL

In the blank write the type of organization used in the paragraph.

The early colonists often used "Betty lamps" to light their homes. A "Betty lamp" was a cast-iron lamp that held oil. The base of the lamp was bowl-like with a narrowing spout. Extending upward from the back of the base was a straight handle that curved near the top. At the top of the handle, a link connected a pointed hook, which allowed the lamp to be hung.

spatial

Coming to a Conclusion

A good paragraph usually contains a good conclusion. As you end your paragraph, you want your audience to have a sense of closure. There are several ways to conclude. One common method is to summarize your main idea. However, you could also give a solution to a problem or even ask your audience a question. The purpose of your paragraph will help determine how you end your paragraph.

Look at the sample paragraphs in the previous section. Each of the paragraphs uses the summary method to conclude. Compare the first sentence in each paragraph to the last sentence. Notice that the writer uses the same idea but states it in different words.

Now look at this example paragraph. Which method does this writer use to conclude the paragraph?

> The British army is posted here in America. The British Parliament wants us to support the army, so they have ordered us to buy stamps that will bring England income. However, this law is unfair. We Americans believe that there should be "no taxation without representation." What can we do to repeal this Stamp Act? I suggest that we stop buying these stamps and show the British government that we Americans will not be controlled by the king and Parliament.

The sample paragraph presents a problem to be solved; the conclusion gives one possible solution to that problem. The writer's purpose (to persuade colonists to repeal the Stamp Act) determined the type of conclusion that would be most effective. As you write your conclusion, remember to consider your audience and your purpose.

15-11 PRACTICE THE SKILL

Choose the best conclusion for the following paragraph from the choices provided. In the blank write the letter that corresponds to the correct answer.

In the 1600s the pillory and the stocks were two forms of punishment that deterred persons from breaking the law. These punishments were for persons who committed minor crimes such as drunkenness and lying. The pillory was a wooden structure with openings for the offender's head and hands. The criminal would stand for hours with his head and hands placed through these holes while townsfolk humiliated him. The stocks were a similar construction; however, they held the lawbreaker's legs. Although the pillory and the stocks were uncomfortable forms of discipline for crimes that may have seemed insignificant, they still served a respectable purpose.

_C___ A. The pillory and the stocks provided an opportunity for townspeople to make fun of their enemies.

B. The pillory and the stocks permitted the lawbreaker to defend himself openly.

C. The pillory and the stocks deterred both the offender and others from committing similar crimes.

Reinforcement

Assign Teaching Help 15B (Book 2, p. 62) for more practice with paragraphs.

Write a good conclusion for the following paragraph. Be sure to give your audience a sense of closure. *(Answers will vary.)*

A common form of punishment in seventeenth-century America was the ducking stool. The ducking stool was a wooden chair connected to a pole. This apparatus was used to punish a woman who liked to argue. The woman was tied to the seat, and then she was "ducked" into water several times. The woman's correction was carried out publicly; therefore it was very embarrassing.

Humiliation made the ducking stool effective.

Essays

An **essay** is a composition that consists of several paragraphs about one main idea. A typical essay structure has an introduction paragraph, several paragraphs of the body, and a conclusion paragraph. The main idea of the essay is stated in the essay's thesis statement, which usually appears at the end of the introduction. Each supporting paragraph develops the thesis statement in some way. The conclusion paragraph unites all the ideas in the essay. It may begin with a restatement of the thesis statement.

Thesis Statement

The **thesis statement** of an essay or paper is similar to the topic sentence in a paragraph: it states the main idea of your essay in one sentence. A good thesis statement includes the topic and suggests what you will say about that topic.

> **POOR** I would like to tell you about making candles.
> This paper is about making candles.

> **GOOD** A candlemaker organizes his materials, makes the candle, and finishes the candle.

Supporting Paragraphs

The body of your paper will consist of several paragraphs that support the thesis statement. Each paragraph will deal with a single division of the subject you have chosen. These divisions, of course, come from your outline.

Just as the supporting sentences in a paragraph follow a logical order, the supporting paragraphs in an essay should follow a logical order too. How can you organize your essay? Choose the method that will help you reach your goals. Consider the good thesis above and the sample sentence outline at the beginning of the chapter. The writer is following a process; therefore, the paper will be organized chronologically.

Each of the main points in your outline will furnish a paragraph for the essay. Notice the following rough draft of our essay:

The candlemaker first organizes his supplies. Only a few utensils are needed. He needs a pan, a double boiler, an ice pick, and a paring knife. He also needs wax. Paraffin is indispensable. If he wants colored candles, the candlemaker should select wax crayons or oil paints to add to the paraffin. To make a stronger candle, he can add beeswax also. Then he must get some braided cotton string for the wicks. This string he dips into wax so that it will burn evenly. Finally, he greases the metal or glass molds with vegetable oil.

The actual making of the candle is a matter of knowing about wax. Candles can be made entirely of paraffin, or they can be a combination of paraffin and beeswax. In either case, the candlemaker melts the paraffin in a double boiler, being careful not to heat it to the smoking point. After the wax is melted, he shaves crayons into the wax to produce the color he wants. For example, one red crayon and one yellow crayon will make about five pounds of light orange wax. Then he pours the hot wax into molds. Some molds are ornate metal forms, but an empty milk carton will also work. At last, the candlemaker lets the wax harden. It takes at least twelve hours for a candle to harden enough to remove it from the mold. Sometimes the candlemaker will take the candle out after it has hardened but is still warm. Then he can twist it or hand-form it as he wants.

Finishing the candle is a quick procedure. Wicks can be inserted in a finished candle. The candlemaker heats an ice pick and makes a hole in the candle. The hole should be large enough for the wick, stiffened with wax, to be passed through the candle from top to bottom. Then he threads the wick through the hole and melts the wax a little around the top of the wick. When the wax around the wick hardens again, he trims the wick. A wick that is too long will burn too high and melt the candle down. One that is too short will not give much light and will soon drown in melted wax. As the last touch, the candlemaker may want to decorate his candle. Some craftsmen carve beautiful designs on the hardened wax. Seals and sealing wax also make interesting designs on candles.

Introduction and Conclusion

Most papers begin with an introduction paragraph. A good introduction does three things: catches the reader's interest, introduces the topic, and draws attention to the main idea of the topic. You may want to begin with an interesting story, a compelling question, or a problem to solve. An introduction is like a funnel: it is wide at the beginning where it introduces the broad topic, and it narrows to a specific thesis statement at the end.

Usually the best plan is to begin the paragraph with an "interest-arouser" and then to tie it in to the subject of your paper. Do not say, "In this paper I will tell you about such-and-such"; instead simply mention your topic in the very last sentence of your paragraph. Look at the example below:

Before there were light bulbs, before there were oil lamps, there were candles. Who invented the candle? No one knows for sure. Nearly anyone, however, can make a candle, because the process is relatively simple. A candlemaker needs to gather a few materials. Then he organizes his materials, makes the candle, and finishes the candle.

A good conclusion draws the paper's many ideas together and leaves the reader thinking about the essay's topic. Your purpose will help determine how to conclude your essay. You may want to summarize your main

Teaching Strategy: Demonstration

When reviewing the material on introductory and concluding paragraphs, display a funnel shape for the introduction and an inverted funnel shape for the conclusion. Use this visual aid to help students understand that the introduction begins general and broad and continually narrows to the specific thesis; the conclusion merely inverts this process.

idea, give a solution to a problem, or ask your audience a question. Whichever method you use, be sure to leave your reader with something that he will remember. Think of the conclusion as an inverted funnel: it begins narrowly with a restatement of the thesis and broadens to a larger view of the topic.

> With simple materials and a careful plan, anyone can make a candle. A candle makes an appropriate gift, a pretty decoration, or a handy light. Moreover, a candlemaker becomes both a craftsman and an artist, creating something useful and timeless in its beauty.

Revising

Revision of the first draft should be *re-vision*—seeing the material again. Look at the rough draft again after a day or so to see whether you have said what you wanted to say and to see how you can improve the saying of it. The lapse of time helps you see it more objectively, as other people will see it.

No experienced writer skips the process of revision. Revision is the only way to improve whatever you are writing at the time, and it will gradually help you turn out better first drafts.

Revising for Ideas

Follow this revision checklist to check the logic and the logical flow of your piece.

Clarity of Purpose

Check your composition to see whether you have fulfilled your purpose in writing it. Is your purpose clear in your topic sentence? A paper that has not zeroed in on its purpose probably also lacks unity and clear organization.

Interest

Even the most lively piece of writing may seem dull after you have worked on it for a while. One solution is to let one or more friends read it for you and tell you their reactions. You can also try writing an alternate introduction or conclusion and ask a friend to help you decide which is more interesting and effective.

Unity of Ideas

Everything within a paragraph should relate to the topic sentence. Leave out any sentence that does not belong.

Coherence

The principle of coherence is that the parts should cohere (stick together) well. Logical, clear transitions are an important element in good writing. Use clear transitional and connecting words to show relationships. Look at these sample transitional expressions:

Reinforcement

Instruct the students to write a paragraph with at least six sentences. Collect the paragraphs and redistribute them the next day. Instruct the students to revise their paragraphs, checking for logical ideas, clarity, and correctness.

Time	first, after, before, finally, next
Space	behind, below, here, in front of
Degree	first, second, mainly, most important
Comparison	than, similarly, also
Contrast	on the contrary, however, on the other hand
Cause and Effect	because, therefore, since
Introductory	for example, in particular

Here is a sample paragraph. Notice how the revision corrects the problems of clarity, interest, unity, and coherence.

First draft

People made various types of clothing in colonial America. There was also a variety of furniture. Women planted flax, harvested the crop, and wove the flax into linen. Women also wove woolen cloth from sheep. They colored the fabrics with dyes made from barks, berries, roots, or walnut hulls. The colonists often made shoes or leggings from leather made from cows or deerskin.

Second draft

Making clothing was a normal and necessary process in colonial households. For example, women planted flax, harvested the crop, and wove it into linen cloth. They also wove woolen cloth from yarn spun from the fleece of sheep. For the coloring of fabrics, colonial people used dyes made from barks, berries, roots, or walnut hulls. Finally, many colonial men tanned cowhide and deerskin for leather for shoes and leggings.

15-13 *P*RACTICE THE *S*KILL

Read the paragraph carefully. Then answer the five questions. *(Answers may vary.)*

Colonists came to America in the 1600s. First, many settlers came to America to have freedom of worship. Harsh religious persecution caused them to long for a land with more freedom. Settlers wanted work. Making a good living was difficult in many European countries. A new world was waiting to be worked. Colonists wanted land ownership. Between 1607 and 1733 England established thirteen colonies on the North American coast. Many settlers were offered land at little or no cost. In their home countries, land ownership was more difficult and expensive.

1. Rewrite the topic sentence to provide a clearer purpose for the paragraph.

   Colonists came to America for a variety of reasons.

2. Which sentence in the paragraph does not belong?

   Between 1607 and 1733 England established thirteen colonies on the

   North American coast.

3. Identify a transitional expression in the paragraph.

First _____

_____

4. Add a transitional expression to the beginning of the following sentence in order to make the relationships clearer: "Settlers wanted work."

Furthermore _____

_____

5. Rewrite the sentence "Settlers wanted work" to make it more interesting.

Furthermore, many settlers came to America to find work because they

could not in their home countries.

Rewrite the following paragraph, adding interest and correcting any problems in clarity, unity, and coherence. *(Answers will vary.)*

Each of the original thirteen colonies was a proprietary, corporate, or royal colony. A proprietary colony was under the control of an important individual, or proprietor, who received a grant from the king of England. A corporate colony was chiefly operated under a charter that had been received from the king by a particular company's stockholders. All thirteen colonies were originally established either as proprietary or corporate colonies. By 1775 eight of the colonies had become royal colonies. The population of the colonies had grown to almost two and a half million people by 1775. A royal colony was under the direct control of the king.

A colony was a proprietary, corporate, or royal colony, based on the official

head of the colony. For example, a proprietary colony was under the dominance

of a powerful individual, or proprietor, who received a grant from the king of

England. A corporate colony was, however, one that chiefly operated under a

charter received from the king by a particular company's stockholders. All

thirteen colonies were originally established either as proprietary or as corporate

colonies. However, by 1775 eight of the colonies had become royal colonies,

which were directly controlled by the king.

_____

_____

_____

_____

Revising for Style

Emphasis

Good writers use emphasis to make important ideas stand out. The most effective way to attain emphasis is to put the important ideas in emphatic positions. The most important idea in a sentence or a paragraph usually appears at the beginning or the end—usually at the end.

POOR EMPHASIS   This is an essay about colonial farmers and their hardships.
IMPROVED   Colonial farmers endured many hardships.

Precise Words

As you revise, correct inaccurate or imprecise words. Precise words help you to state your message clearly. Some words may be general (like *town* or *wrote*), and some may be specific (like *Plymouth* or *scribbled*). A thesaurus may help you find the specific word you need.

Conciseness

Elimination of Obvious Redundancy

All writing contains some redundancy, but normally you should get rid of any that is noticeable. If fewer words will do the job, use fewer words.

REDUNDANT   Colonial farmers *repeated* the process *again*.
IMPROVED   Colonial farmers repeated the process.

Reduction of Clauses

You can often improve a problem sentence by reducing a dependent clause to a shorter, simpler element. Often the reduced clause is not only more concise but also more flexible in sentence position. Often, clauses can be reduced to the various types of phrases.

SENTENCE WITH DEPENDENT CLAUSE   Poets *who wrote during colonial times* wrote mainly about religious topics.

DEPENDENT CLAUSE TO PARTICIPLE   Poets *writing during colonial times* wrote mainly about religious topics.

DEPENDENT CLAUSE TO PREPOSITIONAL PHRASE   Poets *during colonial times* wrote mainly about religious topics.

Smoothness

A good way to judge the flow of your writing is to read your paper aloud or to listen while someone reads it aloud. If any sentence sounds awkward, rewrite it using language and expressions that sound natural.

Fresh Words

Find a fresh replacement for a word that is repeated too often in your paper. A thesaurus may help you find suitable synonyms. A similar problem is a cliché, a worn-out phrase that has lost its effectiveness. Substitute simpler expressions or new comparisons for clichés such as *cool as a cucumber, stick out like a sore thumb, first and foremost,* and *to the bitter end.*

Enrichment

Assign Teaching Help 15c (Book 2, p. 63) for more practice in revising. Be aware that the idiomatic language in this activity may prove difficult for ESL students to revise.

Rewrite the following paragraph, correcting any problems of emphasis, precise words, conciseness, smoothness, and fresh words. *(Answers will vary.)*

Transportation in early America was difficult and not easy. At first, the settlers walked along small paths. As time passed, however, the colonists made the paths into roads. These roads could be accessed by a large animal. Later, these paths were expanded so that a person could drive a cart or wagon down the path as easy as pie.

Ground transportation in early colonial America was difficult since the road

system was rather primitive. At first, the brave settlers had to travel by foot

along narrow, wooded paths. As time passed, however, the industrious

colonists broadened the small trails into roads that could be accessed by a

large animal such as a horse. Later, these widened paths were expanded

even more so that a person could drive a horse cart or a farm wagon down

the road.

Rewrite the following paragraph, correcting any problems in emphasis, precise words, conciseness, smoothness, and fresh words. *(Answers will vary.)*

The first written and published colonial American book, *The Bay Psalm Book,* was written and published in the mid-1600s in 1640. It was a book written in English that consisted of hymns. It was an English translation of the Hebrew Psalms from the Bible. Several colonists were responsible for its translation, and Stephen Day is the man who was responsible for actually printing the book. Last but not least, some men associated with Harvard College, Henry Dunster and Richard Lyon, were responsible for making some changes in *The Bay Psalm Book* several years later in 1651.

The first colonial American book, The Bay Psalm Book, *was written and*

published in 1640. It was a hymnal that was an English translation of the

Hebrew Psalms from the Bible. Several early colonists translated it, and

Stephen Day of the Massachusetts Bay Colony printed the book. Two

scholarly men associated with Harvard College, Henry Dunster and

Richard Lyon, revised The Bay Psalm Book *eleven years later in 1651.*

Proofreading your paper is just as important as revising. Make sure that no errors crept in as you wrote your final draft. Good proofreading takes practice, but you can learn to do it well. The most important principle is this: do not expect to find every error (or every kind of error) in a single reading. Read in different ways to find different things.

Follow a proofreading checklist.
- Sentence structure and grammatical forms

  Be sure that you correct fragments, comma splices, or fused sentences. Also be sure that the grammatical forms in the paper are correct.
- Usage

  Be sure that your subjects and verbs agree and that your pronouns and antecedents agree. Check for correct pronoun case and other correct usage too.
- Spelling, Punctuation, and Capitalization

  Check your final draft carefully for spelling. Use all tools at your disposal. However, always proofread because those tools cannot possibly catch every error. Be sure you have omitted any punctuation marks or used any marks incorrectly. Finally, check your capitalization.

Use these tactics to proofread your paragraph or paper.
- Slow your reading down by using a blank sheet of paper to cover the part you have not yet read.

- Read the paper aloud. You may hear an error that you did not see when you read the paper silently.

- Look at the words in reverse order; begin reading at the end of the paper and work toward the beginning. This tactic will force you to look at each word individually for spelling or capitalization errors.

- Finally, read the paper through quickly a few times, looking each time for some particular problem area that has been difficult for you in the past. For instance, it is fairly easy to spot comma problems when you read looking only for commas.

Careful proofreading does take some time. It is only a little more time, however, in comparison with what you have already invested in your paper. And it can make an important difference in people's impression of your work.

Publishing

Once you have revised and corrected your paper, you are ready to make a neat copy of the final draft, the copy to turn in. **Publishing** your paper simply means that you are sharing it with others.

Reinforcement

Distribute copies of Teaching Help 15D (Book 2, p. 64) for students to use as they revise their work.

Reinforcement

Distribute copies of several paragraphs containing errors in punctuation, spelling, and usage. Tell the students how many errors there are and allow them to proofread and correct the mistakes. Then read the selection aloud and correct the mistakes with the students.

Enrichment

Instruct each student to write an essay that describes a favorite place. The essay should attempt to persuade others to visit the location it describes. Once the essays are written, assign each student a proofreading partner. Tell the students to exchange papers and to proofread each other's work. Once students have made final corrections and have written their final drafts, post the papers for the class to read. Also, post a sheet of paper so that students can write their choices of which places they would like to visit based on what their classmates have written.

Title

Before you publish, you need to choose a title for your work. The title tells the reader what he is about to read. The title should generally be short, usually no more than five or six words. If possible, it should be interesting, inviting the audience to read on. Finally, a title should be specific. Rather than just the general subject area, it should suggest the specific subject and perhaps the approach of that particular paper. For example, "Colonial America" is not a good title. It is too broad; it does not let the reader know anything about the paper's specific topic. A better title is "Candlemaking Made Easy." This title lets the audience know the paper's topic. Choose a title for your paper that interests your readers and hints at your topic.

Neat Copy

If you publish for a class, know what form your teacher expects and follow that form carefully.

Handwritten papers usually must be written on $8\frac{1}{2}$-by-11-inch lined notebook paper, on one side only, in blue or black ink. The teacher may prefer that you use the standard wide-lined paper or that you write on every other line of the narrow-lined paper. Leave even margins on the right and left sides.

Word-processed or typewritten papers should be printed in black ink on standard-sized white paper. Double-space your paper, leaving at least one-inch margins on all four sides. Follow your teacher's instructions about the placement of your name, the date, and the name of the class.

Other Ideas for Publishing

You have many options for publishing your papers. Here are just a few ideas.

- Send it to your local newspaper.
- Put together a class collection.
- Use your work for programs.
- Read your work over your school's public address system.
- Share it with your English class.
- Read your work to someone at home.
- Mail a copy to a friend or relative.

Writing Folders

After you finish your composition, you may want to put it in a folder or notebook where you keep your writing. By the end of the year, you could have a complete collection of your work. Include your rough drafts and revisions or just the final papers. The folder allows you, your parents, and your teacher to see your progress over the weeks, semesters, or year. The folder also can help you see mistakes that you have made in the past so that you can avoid making them again in your future papers.

Choose the best title for the paragraph from the choices provided. In the blank write the letter that corresponds to your answer.

When settlers first moved to America, their homes were very primitive. However, as the years passed, well-to-do colonists were able to build houses that were more sizable and luxurious. When constructing their new homes, they often imitated the Georgian architectural designs of English residences. These two-story houses had a central chimney as well as a hall with a staircase. A chimney located in the middle of the home was very practical. It allowed each room to have a fireplace so that the entire house could be adequately heated. Along with practicality, balance was a very important element in the design of colonial homes. The first floor had two windows on either side of a door, and the second level had five windows. The early Americans often obtained their house plans from European books.

_____B_____ A. Colonial Homes: The Importance of Their Structure
B. Colonial Homes: Practical and Balanced
C. Colonial Homes: Primitive to Prominent

Write a good title for the following paragraph. Make your title both informative and interesting. *(Answers will vary.)*

When the Pilgrims first arrived in America, they endured some very difficult times. However, God was good to these early settlers, and He richly blessed them through a good harvest and friendship with the Indians. Governor William Bradford, recognizing God's wonderful provision, called for a celebration to give thanks to Him, and in 1621 the Pilgrims celebrated the first Thanksgiving in Plymouth Colony. The first Thanksgiving Day celebration lasted for three days, and to the Pilgrims, it was a festivity with the primary purpose of praising God.

The First Thanksgiving: A Day to Praise God

Writing Strategies

If you follow the writing process correctly, you will have a good paper, right? Not necessarily. Many strategies can help you state ideas with clarity and in an interesting fashion.

Sentence Variety

A boring voice is one that is always the same. It has the same tone, the same speed, the same loudness—the same everything. Nothing seems more important than anything else. As in speech, sameness in writing can be boring. Variety helps to create and maintain interest. In order to be effective, a writer must use a variety of sentence types. Clear, interesting sentences have variety.

Varying Length and Complexity of Sentences

The ideal combination of sentences is a mix of short, medium, and longer sentences. Most likely, some of these sentences would be simple, some would be compound, and still others would be complex or compound-complex. Here is a paragraph that needs improvement:

> Peter Cooper was an American inventor and manufacturer. He contributed much to American industry. He built the famous *Tom Thumb*. The *Tom Thumb* was a steam locomotive. It proved the ability of steam engines to pull railroad cars over track. Cooper developed an iron company. He supplied iron for major railroad companies. Peter Cooper was a social advocate. He advanced causes such as improved education and better police and fire protection. *(9 simple sentences)*

The style above is choppy; all ideas are treated as if they were equally important. Revised, the paragraph reads better:

> Peter Cooper was an inventor and manufacturer who contributed much to American industry. He built the famous *Tom Thumb*. The *Tom Thumb* was a steam locomotive, and it proved the ability of steam engines to pull railroad cars over track. Furthermore, Cooper developed an iron company that supplied iron for major railroad companies. Finally, Peter Cooper was a social advocate. He advanced causes such as improved education and better police and fire protection. *(6 sentences including simple, compound, and complex)*

Varying Sentence Patterns

Good writing should naturally include a variety of sentence patterns. In the process of revision, check your writing to see whether you have overused one or two of the sentence patterns. Work consciously for variety. Notice the following poor example:

> Many locomotives were famous or important in history (S-LV-PA). For example, the *General* was a Confederate locomotive (S-LV-PN), and it became famous during the Civil War after its capture by Union soldiers (S-LV-PA). The Confederates were successful in recovering it (S-LV-PA). Engine 382 was important because of the famous Casey Jones (S-LV-PA), who was its driver (S-LV-PN). Casey Jones grew notable after giving his life for his passengers in 1900 (S-LV-PA). Also, the *Big Boy* was the largest steam locomotive in history (S-LV-PN). It was instrumental in helping with freight traffic of World War II (S-LV-PA). Finally, the Burlington *Zephyr* became the first streamlined diesel locomotive for passengers in the United States (S-LV-PN). It became operative in 1934 (S-LV-PA).

Revision gives the paragraph greater variety:

> Many locomotives were famous or important in history (S-LV-PA). For example, the *General,* a Confederate locomotive, became famous during the Civil War (S-LV-PA). After Union soldiers captured the *General* (S-TrV-DO), the Confederates successfully recovered it (S-TrV-DO). Casey Jones drove another famous locomotive, Engine 382 (S-TrV-DO). The driver became famous (S-LV-PA) after he gave his life for his passengers in 1900 (S-TrV-DO). Also, the *Big Boy,* which helped with the freight traffic of World War II (S-InV), was the largest steam locomotive in history (S-LV-PN). Finally, the Burlington *Zephyr,* the first streamlined diesel locomotive for passengers in the United States, began operating in 1934 (S-TrV-DO).

Varying the Sentence Beginnings

Writing becomes monotonous when every sentence begins with a subject followed by a verb. To achieve variety, you can move phrases, modifiers, or clauses to the beginning of the sentence. (Of course, remember that overuse of one type of beginning is also monotonous!) Consider beginning sentences with the following: adverb, adjective, participle, participial phrase, infinitive, infinitive phrase, prepositional phrase, or dependent clause. Look at a few examples of varied sentence beginnings:

SUBJECT AND VERB	My father and I traveled extensively by train last summer.
ADJECTIVE	*Fast and comfortable,* today's trains are a convenient way to travel.
PARTICIPIAL PHRASE	*Hauling coal, grain, lumber, machinery, and other products,* trains are effective cargo carriers.
DEPENDENT CLAUSE	*Because other methods of transportation have developed,* trains have fierce competition.

15-19 PRACTICE THE SKILL

Rewrite the following paragraph, using different kinds of sentences and different types of sentence patterns. Also, vary the sentence beginnings. *(Answers will vary.)*

The wagon has been a popular form of transportation for more than two thousand years. The Egyptians were some of the earliest people to use wagons. The Romans later became recognized for their development of the chariot. The Romans' chariot was lighter and faster than the Egyptians'. A wagon of the Middle Ages was often a carrier of weapons. Wagons were continually developed for the purpose of transporting people. Stagecoaches were common in colonial America for transporting people. The Conestoga wagon is famous for carrying pioneers west in the eighteenth and early nineteenth centuries. People often used horse-drawn wagons to deliver goods during the early 1900s. Modern wagons are common on farms today. Modern wagons are haulers of grain and other harvested goods. The tractor-trailer is actually a kind of wagon. Wagons have been used throughout history and are still being used today.

For more than two thousand years, the wagon has been a popular form of

transportation. The Egyptians were some of the earliest people to use wagons.

Later, the Romans became recognized for developing a chariot that was lighter

and faster than the Egyptians'. In the Middle Ages wagons often carried

weapons. However, wagons were continually developed for the purpose of

transporting people. Common in colonial America, stagecoaches transported

people. In the eighteenth and early nineteenth centuries, the Conestoga wagon

carried pioneers west. To deliver goods during the early 1900s, people often

384   Chapter 15

Teaching Strategy: Participation

After reviewing the different ways to create sentence variety, display the following paragraph:

The cat was sitting in the sun. The cat saw the dog. The cat ran across the street. The cat was followed by the dog. The cat tried to jump into a tree. The cat did not make it. The cat and the dog got into a fight. The cat won.

Instruct the students to use the strategies they have learned to make this short paragraph flow better and sound more interesting. Ask several volunteers to read aloud their new versions.

384   Chapter 15

used horse-drawn wagons. Today, wagons are common on farms. Modern

wagons haul grain and other harvested goods. Actually, the tractor-trailer is a

kind of wagon. Wagons have been used throughout history and are still being

used today.

_____

_____

_____

_____

15-20 REVIEW THE SKILL

On your own paper, write an original paragraph of at least ten sentences. Work for sentence variety and try to avoid passive verbs. When you finish writing, answer these questions.

1. Write down the number of times you use the following sentence patterns:

_____ S-InV

_____ S-TrV-DO

_____ S-TrV-IO-DO

_____ S-LV-PA

_____ S-LV-PN

2. Write down the number of times you use the following sentence types:

_____ Simple

_____ Compound

_____ Complex

_____ Compound-Complex

3. List the types of structures that begin your sentences.

_____

_____

_____

_____

_____

_____

_____

_____

_____

G
GRAMMAR

Chapter 4: Active and Passive
Voice
p. 102

Expansion and Reduction of Sentences

Variety is important to the readability of your writing. What if every sentence were a bare-bones simple sentence? You would need to read many more sentences to gain the same information. You can join thoughts on an equal basis, making compound sentences. You can also join them on an unequal basis, pointing up certain ideas as more important. The ideas that are less important can be subordinated in a variety of ways. Reducing your sentences will also make your writing more concise.

Changing Sentences to Dependent Clauses

Sometimes you can show a relationship more clearly by combining two simple sentences into a complex one.

SIMPLE SENTENCES	Some areas lack modern roads. The people there often use pack animals for transporting goods.
COMBINED TO MAKE A DEPENDENT CLAUSE	Because some areas lack modern roads, the people there often use animals for transporting goods.

Reducing Dependent Clauses to Phrases

Often, dependent clauses can be reduced to verbal phrases, prepositional phrases, or appositive phrases.

DEPENDENT CLAUSE	People *who are avoiding traffic* often use public transportation.
REDUCED TO PARTICIPIAL PHRASE	People *avoiding traffic* often use public transportation.
DEPENDENT CLAUSE	Many people *who live in countries without good roads* ride bicycles to work.
REDUCED TO PREPOSITIONAL PHRASE	Many people *in countries without good roads* ride bicycles to work.
DEPENDENT CLAUSE	The first supersonic airliner, *which was the Concorde,* began service in 1976.
REDUCED TO APPOSITIVE PHRASE	The first supersonic airliner, *the Concorde,* began service in 1976.

Reducing Phrases and Clauses to Single Words

You can also reduce phrases and clauses to single words.

GERUND PHRASE	*Studying physics* is interesting.
REDUCED TO NOUN	*Physics* is interesting.
CLAUSE	A form of public transportation *that is common* is the bus.
REDUCED TO ADJECTIVE	A *common* form of public transportation is the bus.
CLAUSE	The lesson *that I am teaching today* is about ships.
REDUCED TO ADVERB	*Today,* the lesson is about ships.

Rewrite the following sentences on the blanks below. Make them more concise or emphatic by combining or reducing sentences to clauses, phrases, or simple modifiers. *(Answers will vary.)*

1. An elevator is a form of transportation; it carries people and freight to various floors of a building.

   An elevator is a form of transportation that carries people and freight

   to various floors of a building.

2. Most buildings that are tall need elevators.

   Most tall buildings need elevators.

3. Passengers inside the elevator push a button so that they can reach the floor they want.

   Passengers inside the elevator push a button to reach the floor they

   want.

4. Archimedes, who was an ancient Greek mathematician, invented a type of elevator before 230 B.C.

   Archimedes, an ancient Greek mathematician, invented a type of elevator

   before 230 B.C.

5. The world's first elevator that was specifically planned for human use was installed in New York City in 1857.

   The world's first elevator specifically planned for human use was installed

   in New York City in 1857.

6. In the 1890s automatic elevators were installed in buildings that were residential.

   In the 1890s automatic elevators were installed in residential buildings.

7. The elevators of today are regulated by safety codes.

   Today's elevators are regulated by safety codes.

8. Observation elevators have glass sides; passengers can get a spectacular view.

   Because observation elevators have glass sides, passengers can get a

   spectacular view.

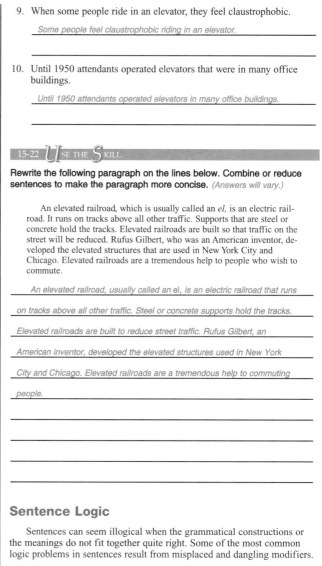

9. When some people ride in an elevator, they feel claustrophobic.

Some people feel claustrophobic riding in an elevator.

10. Until 1950 attendants operated elevators that were in many office buildings.

Until 1950 attendants operated elevators in many office buildings.

Rewrite the following paragraph on the lines below. Combine or reduce sentences to make the paragraph more concise. *(Answers will vary.)*

An elevated railroad, which is usually called an *el,* is an electric railroad. It runs on tracks above all other traffic. Supports that are steel or concrete hold the tracks. Elevated railroads are built so that traffic on the street will be reduced. Rufus Gilbert, who was an American inventor, developed the elevated structures that are used in New York City and Chicago. Elevated railroads are a tremendous help to people who wish to commute.

An elevated railroad, usually called an el, is an electric railroad that runs

on tracks above all other traffic. Steel or concrete supports hold the tracks.

Elevated railroads are built to reduce street traffic. Rufus Gilbert, an

American inventor, developed the elevated structures used in New York

City and Chicago. Elevated railroads are a tremendous help to commuting

people.

G

GRAMMAR

Chapter 5: Misplaced Modifiers
p. 134

Sentence Logic

Sentences can seem illogical when the grammatical constructions or the meanings do not fit together quite right. Some of the most common logic problems in sentences result from misplaced and dangling modifiers.

Misplaced Modifiers

If a modifier is not near what it modifies, confusion or unintended humor may be the result. A **misplaced modifier** is a modifier that seems to modify the wrong word in the sentence.

I saw a new car looking through my window.

Teaching Strategy: Demonstration

Write the following sentence for display: *He is watching the team play with his dad.* Ask the class whether the meaning of this sentence is clear. *(no)* Then ask what the sentence could mean. *(He is sitting with his father watching a team, or he is sitting alone watching his dad play with a team.)* Lead the students in rewriting the sentence to make the meaning clear.

In the example *looking through my window* is not intended to modify *car.* You can correct a misplaced modifier by moving it closer to the word it modifies.

> Looking through my window, I saw a new car.

Dangling Modifiers

A **dangling modifier** is a modifier (often a verbal or a verbal phrase) that does not logically modify any word in the sentence. Because the word that it should modify is not in the sentence, a dangling modifier cannot be corrected by just moving it. Dangling modifiers confuse the reader and create unclear sentences.

> Driving in heavy traffic, the cup of water spilled onto the seat.

Who or what was driving? The modifier is "dangling" because the implied subject of *driving* (some unnamed person) is not the same as the actual subject of the sentence *(the cup of water)*.

One way to correct a dangling modifier is to change the rest of the sentence so that the missing element is supplied right next to the modifier:

> While driving in heavy traffic, I spilled a cup of water onto the seat.

Another way to correct a dangling modifier is to change the modifier into a complete clause that includes the missing element:

> While I was driving in heavy traffic, a cup of water spilled onto the seat.

Here is an example of a dangling infinitive and a correction of the sentence.

> UNCLEAR   To wash the car, good soap is necessary.
> CLEAR   To wash the car, you need good soap.

15-23 PRACTICE THE SKILL

Rewrite the following sentences, correcting any misplaced or dangling modifiers. *(Answers may vary.)*

1. Known as one of the most scenic drives in America, we enjoy driving the Blue Ridge Parkway.

   We enjoy driving the Blue Ridge Parkway, known as one of the most

   scenic drives in America.

2. The Blue Ridge Parkway headquarters tells of the parkway's history located in Asheville, North Carolina.

   Located in Asheville, North Carolina, the Blue Ridge Parkway

   headquarters tells of the parkway's history.

3. The parkway has many scenic overlooks winding through two states and several mountain ranges.

   Winding through two states and several mountain ranges, the parkway

   has many scenic overlooks.

4. Driving along the parkway, many hiking trails appear on both sides.

    While driving along the parkway, we see many hiking trails on both

    sides.

5. By hiking the trails, your health will improve.

    By hiking the trails, you can improve your health.

6. We enjoyed the various mountains traveling the 469 miles of the parkway.

    Traveling the 469 miles of the parkway, we enjoyed the various

    mountains.

7. To enjoy camping along the parkway, a good knowledge of various campgrounds is necessary.

    To enjoy camping along the parkway, you need a good knowledge of

    the various campgrounds.

8. For safe bicycling, a helmet should be worn.

    For safe bicycling, you should wear a helmet.

9. By not picking flowers, the parks can be preserved.

    By not picking flowers, visitors can preserve the parks.

10. You can appreciate God's wonderful creation traveling down the parkway.

    Traveling down the parkway, you can appreciate God's wonderful creation.

15-24 Review the Skill

Rewrite the following sentences, correcting any misplaced or dangling modifiers. If the sentence is correct, write *C* in the blank. *(Answers may vary.)*

1. By being careful in a car, many accidents could be avoided.

    By being careful in a car, people can avoid many accidents.

2. Driving too quickly or too slowly, the chance of an accident increases.

    When a motorist drives too quickly or too slowly, the chance of an

    accident increases.

3. A driver can prevent accidents watching the road.

   Watching the road, a driver can prevent accidents.

4. To help ensure safety, seat belts should be buckled.

   To help ensure safety, passengers should buckle their seat belts.

5. A motorist creates danger talking on a car phone.

   A motorist talking on a car phone creates danger.

6. A road is a threat to a driver glazed with rain.

   A road glazed with rain is a threat to a driver.

7. By slowing down, the danger is decreased.

   By slowing down, a driver decreases the danger.

8. Damaging concentration, drowsiness causes instability in a driver.

   C

9. Many people become safer in a car taking a driver's education course.

   Taking a driver's education course, many people become safer in a car.

10. Starting in an empty parking lot, a teenage driver can become acquainted with driving a car.

    C

Parallelism

Parallel structures are used when items are joined by a coordinating conjunction. The structures are **parallel** when they have the same grammatical form.

Advantages of Parallel Structures

Parallelism helps writing to flow more smoothly and shows relationships between ideas. Here are some acceptable sentences:

> This past year Lola had good success in winning many bicycle races. She also won several track meets and several swim meets.

Notice the improvements through use of parallelism:

> This past year Lola had great success in winning many bicycle races and even in winning several track and swim meets.

Because the second version puts similar things together, it is both shorter and easier to read. The occasional use of parallel structures improves the clarity and even the rhythm of your writing. Here is another example:

> To Kyle the bicycle seemed perfect. However, his brother thought the bicycle was too large.

Revision produces a single sentence with parallel structures:

> The bicycle seemed perfect to Kyle but too large to his brother.

Using Parallelism Only for Parallel Ideas

Parallelism is a very useful device, but it should be used only for ideas that are truly of the same type.

ILLOGICAL PARALLELISM	People often ride bikes for exercise, pleasure, and long periods of time.
CORRECTED	People often ride bikes for exercise and pleasure.

The detail about people riding bikes for long periods of time does not fit with the reasons that people often ride bikes, and so it is removed from the parallel construction.

Using the Same Part of Speech

Sentence parts joined by a coordinating conjunction must be of the same grammatical type. Most important, they must be of the same part of speech.

NOT PARALLEL	Adj N Bike riding is enjoyable and good exercise.
CORRECTION	Adj Adj Bike riding is enjoyable and good for the body.
NOT PARALLEL	TrV DO PA A reliable bike has a sturdy frame and easy to maneuver.
CORRECTION	TrV DO DO A reliable bike has a sturdy frame and easy maneuverability.

Using the Same Type of Structure

Not only should parallel elements be of the same part of speech, but when possible they should also be of the same general type of structure. Make sure that types of phrases, types of verbals, and types of clauses are the same. For example, join two prepositional phrases or two participial phrases. Avoid joining different types of words, phrases, or clauses.

NOT PARALLEL	Ger. phrase Inf. phrase Obeying traffic signs and to keep to the right are important rules for bicyclists.
CORRECTION	Ger. phrase Ger. phrase Obeying traffic signs and keeping to the right are important rules for bicyclists.

Placing Correlative Conjunctions Correctly

Correlative conjunctions are pairs like *both—and, either—or, neither—nor,* and *not only—but also.* The sentence element that immediately follows the first correlative conjunction must be of the same grammatical form as the element that immediately follows the second correlative conjunction.

                                           V   Ger.

NOT PARALLEL   Bicycle touring *both* includes traveling *and* sightseeing.

                                                 Ger.   Ger.

CORRECTION   Bicycle touring includes *both* traveling *and* sightseeing.

The incorrect sentence has different elements after the two conjunctions. The problem can be corrected by moving the first conjunction.

                                         V

NOT PARALLEL   In the 1980s, bicycles *either* had a small seat *or* a long

             DO

        "banana" seat.

                                               DO

CORRECTION   In the 1980s, bicycles had *either* a small seat *or* a long

             DO

        "banana" seat.

15-25 PRACTICE THE SKILL

Rewrite the following sentences, correcting any illogical or incorrect parallelism. If the sentence is correct, write *C* in the blank. *(Answers may vary.)*

1. Learning to ride a bike can be difficult and a challenge.

    Learning to ride a bike can be difficult and challenging.

2. Kai's bike is equipped with a basket, a bell, and a light.

    C

3. Baron Karl de Drais de Sauerbrun is the inventor of the draisienne and exhibited it in Paris in 1818.

    Baron Karl de Drais de Sauerbrun invented the draisienne and exhibited it

    in Paris in 1818.

4. The draisienne had a wooden frame and was awkward to ride.

    The draisienne was wooden and awkward to ride.

5. Last summer Trixie both rode a tandem and a recumbent bicycle.

    Last summer Trixie rode both a tandem and a recumbent bicycle.

6. A tricycle's frame is small, sturdy, and suits a child.

   A tricycle's frame is small, sturdy, and suitable for a child.

7. Utility bikes neither are costly nor difficult to care for.

   Utility bikes are neither costly nor difficult to care for.

8. Mountain bikes both have wide tires that are heavy treaded and gears that range up to twenty-one speeds.

   Mountain bikes have both wide tires that are heavy treaded and gears that

   range up to twenty-one speeds.

9. Not only did bicycle motocross racing become popular in America, but also became well liked in Europe.

   Not only did bicycle motocross racing become popular in America, but it

   also became well liked in Europe.

10. James Moore won both the first bicycle race in 1868 and the first road race in 1869.

    _C_

15-26 ℝEVIEW THE 𝕊KILL

Rewrite the following sentences, correcting any illogical or incorrect parallelism. If the sentence is correct, write _C_ in the blank. *(Answers may vary.)*

1. My bicycle has reliable brakes, a comfortable seat, and a hard time getting up hills.

   My bicycle has reliable brakes and a comfortable seat.

2. When Lori buys a new bike, it will either be a touring bike or a mountain bike.

   When Lori buys a new bike, it will be either a touring bike or a mountain

   bike.

3. Not only does the bike shop open in the morning but also does not close until the late evening.

   Not only does the bike shop open in the morning, but it also does not

   close until the late evening.

4. Many cyclists want a bike that both rides smoothly and fast.

    Many cyclists want a bike that rides both smoothly and fast.

5. When we looked at the wheels of the old bike, we noticed that the tires were thin, worn, and deflated.

    C

6. When Phil first learned to ride a bike, he neither wanted training wheels nor help from his parents.

    When Phil first learned to ride a bike, he wanted neither training wheels

    nor help from his parents.

7. Taking proper precaution and to ride carefully are two things a cyclist should do when riding in heavy traffic.

    Taking proper precaution and riding carefully are two things a cyclist should

    do when riding in heavy traffic.

8. Early bicycles designed especially for women were the safety bicycle and the tandem bicycle.

    C

9. Europeans ride their bikes to their place of work and to go shopping.

    Europeans ride their bikes to get to their place of work and to go shopping.

10. Not only does a stationary bike measure your speed, but also shows the number of miles you have ridden.

    Not only does a stationary bike measure your speed, but it also shows

    the number of miles you have ridden.

Biased Language

The Christian writer must be especially careful to avoid giving unnecessary offense. The most common offense in writing is the stereotype. A **stereotype** is an oversimplified generalization usually founded on either ignorance or malice. Generalizations based solely on gender, race, cultural background, age, or physical characteristics have no place in a Christian's speaking or writing.

Chapter 1: Sentences

Four Types of Sentences

In the blank, label the sentence *declarative, interrogative, imperative,* or *exclamatory.* Insert the correct punctuation mark at the end of the sentence.

_____declarative_____ 1. Israel is located in southwestern Asia.

_____interrogative_____ 2. Did you know that Israel was declared a country in 1948?

_____imperative_____ 3. Look at the Knesset building.

_____declarative_____ 4. The Knesset building is the home of the Israeli parliament.

_____exclamatory_____ 5. How beautiful the Star of David is!

Subjects and Predicates

Find the simple subject and the simple predicate (the verb). Underline the simple subject once and the verb twice.

6. Hebrew and Arabic are the official languages of Israel.

7. Approximately 80 percent of the population of Israel is Jewish.

8. Have you heard of Zionism?

9. Many Jews arrived in Palestine.

10. They wanted a Jewish state in Palestine.

Find the complete subject and the complete predicate. Underline the complete subject once and the complete predicate twice.

11. Israel has a democratic republic with a parliament-cabinet form of government.

12. Israel's parliament is called the Knesset.

13. Israelis vote for a party, not an individual.

14. The prime minister maintains the support of a majority and leads the policy-making group.

15. Does the Knesset have to approve the cabinet appointments?

Sentence Patterns

Label the sentence patterns *S-InV, S-TrV-DO, S-TrV-IO-DO, S-LV-PN,* or *S-LV-PA*. Above each word of the sentence pattern, write its label.

16. The president of Israel functions as the head of state.
    S ... *InV*

17. The president serves a five-year term.
    S ... *TrV* ... *DO*

18. Elected councils are the local government in Israel.
    S ... *LV* ... *PN*

19. Regional councils are larger than elected councils.
    S ... *LV* *PA*

20. The minister of interior assigns officials different sections of Israel.
    S ... *TrV* ... *IO* ... *DO*

Phrases and Clauses

In the blank, label each italicized group of words *P* (phrase), *IC* (independent clause), or *DC* (dependent clause).

___P___ 21. Israel was created as a homeland *for the Jews.*

___DC___ 22. *Even though the Ashkenazim and the Sephardim come from two different sections of the world,* they are now the two main Jewish cultural groups in Israel.

___P___ 23. The Ashkenazim come *from the Jews of Europe and North America.*

___IC___ 24. *The Sephardim come from the Mediterranean and the Middle East.*

___IC___ 25. *Israel has been greatly influenced by Western pressure.*

Sentence Problems

In the blank, label each group of words *S* (sentence), *F* (fragment), *FS* (fused sentence), or *CS* (comma splice).

___F___ 26. Hebrew, the Israelis' main language.

___S___ 27. Most of the Arabs in Israel speak Arabic.

___FS___ 28. Yiddish is a Germanic language it developed in Jewish communities in Europe.

___CS___ 29. Most of the Arabs live in communities separate from the Jews, they also speak a different language.

___S___ 30. The Jewish way of life is different from that of the Arabs.

Chapter 2: Nouns

Identifying Nouns
Questions 1-5: Underline each common noun once and each proper noun twice in the following paragraph.

The childhood of a writer often greatly influences his work, as in the case of Joseph Rudyard Kipling, producer of many poems, stories, and novels. Born in a British colony in Bombay, India, in the mid-nineteenth century to John Lockwood Kipling and Alice Macdonald, Kipling lived with his parents for six years. Early in his childhood, he was sent to Southsea, England, near Portsmouth, to live at a boarding school. There in England, Kipling spent five unhappy years, feeling deserted by his parents. Kipling later recalled this experience in a bitter story and a novel.

Forms of Nouns
Identify the form of each underlined noun. In the blank write the letter that corresponds to the correct answer.

        A. singular
        B. singular possessive
        C. plural
        D. plural possessive

___C___ 6. When he was twelve, Kipling enrolled in the United Services College, an inexpensive school for the sons of army officers.

___A___ 7. The hard experience of the years spent in that deplorable establishment is discussed in a collection of short stories entitled *Stalky and Co.*

___B___ 8. Because of his family's limited finances, Kipling could not attend a university, and so he returned to India in 1882.

___C___ 9. Once back in India, he joined the staff of the *Civil and Military Gazette* and worked for seven years as a journalist.

___D___ 10. His stories' subjects were mostly local events, and while writing these stories, he learned much about the region where he lived.

Forming Possessive Nouns

Identify the correct possessive form of each phrase. In the blank write the letter that corresponds to the correct answer.

___B___ 11. the experience of the author
A. the authors experience
B. the author's experience
C. the authors' experience

___A___ 12. the parents of Kipling
A. Kipling's parents
B. Kiplings parent's
C. Kiplings parents

___C___ 13. the imagination of a writer
A. a writers imagination
B. a writers' imagination
C. a writer's imagination

___C___ 14. the hot weather in India
A. Indias' hot weather
B. Indias hot weather
C. India's hot weather

___A___ 15. the success of stories
A. stories' success
B. storie's success
C. stories's success

Count and Noncount Nouns

Identify each underlined noun as count or noncount. Write your answer in the blank.

Kipling's early <u>stories</u> and poems were published in newspapers. His first book of <u>fiction</u>, *Plain Tales from the Hills,* contains forty stories, thirty-two of which had been written for the *Civil and Military Gazette.* Kipling's other early stories were collected into a <u>set</u> of six paperback books, which were sold in railway stations. This collection, popular for <u>travelers,</u> spread his <u>fame</u> far outside India.

___count___ 16. stories

___noncount___ 17. fiction

___count___ 18. set

___count___ 19. travelers

___noncount___ 20. fame

Collective and Compound Nouns

In the blank, label the underlined noun *Col* (collective) or *Cd* (compound).

_Cd_ 21. Kipling had also written for an Indian <u>newspaper</u> called the *Pioneer.*

Col 22. After he returned to England in 1889, the <u>collection</u> from the Indian Railway Library, stories originally printed in the *Pioneer,* was reprinted as *Soldiers Three* and *Wee Willie Winkie.*

Col 23. When Kipling published the *Barrack-Room Ballads,* a <u>group</u> of poems including "Fuzzy Wuzzy" and "Gunga Din," his popularity grew tremendously.

_Cd_ 24. In 1892 the <u>newlywed</u> Kipling moved to Vermont with his wife, Carrie.

Col 25. Soon after relocating, he published *The Jungle Book* and *The Second Jungle Book,* gaining an <u>audience</u> scattered around the world.

Functions of Nouns

Identify the function of each underlined noun. In the blank write the letter that corresponds to the correct answer.

  A. subject
  B. predicate noun
  C. indirect object
  D. object of preposition
  E. noun of direct address
  F. appositive
  G. direct object

_D_ 26. Kipling returned to England once more in 1896 and continued his career by writing poems for the <u>*Times*</u> of London.

_A_ 27. His <u>writings</u> took on a political tone as he made bold political judgments and urged the transfer of power from colonial government to native populations in parts of the British Empire.

_G_ 28. Drawing on his earlier experience, Kipling's masterpiece, a novel titled *Kim,* tells the <u>story</u> of an Irish orphan adopting Indian ways.

_G_ 29. Many troubles, including the loss of two children, darkened Kipling's later <u>works</u>.

_F_ 30. His last work, an <u>autobiography</u> entitled *Something of Myself,* was printed in its unfinished form shortly after his death in 1936.

Chapter 3: Pronouns

Personal Pronoun Usage

Underline the correct pronoun from the choices in parentheses. In the blank, label the function of the pronoun S (subject), DO (direct object), IO (indirect object), PN (predicate noun), or OP (object of the preposition).

__S__ 1. Flags are universal symbols of identity. (They, Them) usually have a design that stands for something.

__IO__ 2. The flag of the United States symbolizes America's ideas and beliefs, and the stars and stripes give (it, its) a unique pattern that shows our country's heritage.

__PN__ 3. We are proud that the flag is (our, ours).

__OP__ 4. The flag inspires a feeling of patriotism in (we, us).

__DO__ 5. I love (it, they).

Appositives, Archaic Second-Person Pronouns, Courtesy Order

Underline the correct pronoun from the choices in parentheses.

6. (We, Us) Americans celebrate our freedom with the flag.

7. (Melanie and I, I and Melanie) pledge allegiance to the flag every morning in homeroom.

8. Some of our class—Eileen, Kurt, Larry, and (I, me)—are researching the history of our country's founding.

9. "My country, 'Tis of (Thee, Thou)" is a patriotic hymn that we enjoy.

10. (Your classmates and you, You and your classmates) should research the history of the flag and other important symbols of our country's heritage.

Demonstrative and Interrogative Pronouns

Underline the demonstrative and interrogative pronouns. In the blank, label them D (demonstrative) or I (interrogative).

__I__ 11. Who designed the first American flag?

__I__ 12. Francis Hopkinson made the flag for whom?

__D__ 13. That is the flag that represented the thirteen original colonies.

__D__ 14. This is the first time I have seen someone fold the flag correctly.

__I__ 15. What is the proper way to dispose of a flag?

Reflexive and Intensive Pronouns

Underline the reflexive and intensive pronouns. In the blank, label them *R* (reflexive) or *I* (intensive).

___*I*___ 16. The flag <u>itself</u> is used to show victory in battle and prestige for casualties of war.

___*R*___ 17. I remind <u>myself</u> that many ordinary people used extraordinary courage to protect this country.

___*R*___ 18. My sister made <u>herself</u> a collage of war photographs and memorabilia.

___*I*___ 19. My grandfather <u>himself</u> was at Pearl Harbor when it was bombed.

___*R*___ 20. The soldiers protected <u>themselves</u> by using other ships as protection.

Indefinite Pronouns

Underline the indefinite pronouns. In the blank, label the pronoun *singular* or *plural*.

___*singular*___ 21. <u>Each</u> of the parts of the flag has a special meaning.

___*plural*___ 22. The stars represent the states in the union. <u>Most</u> of our first national flags included stars.

___*plural*___ 23. <u>All</u> of the colors portray a different attribute of early Americans. For instance, red symbolizes hardiness and courage, and white symbolizes purity and innocence.

___*plural*___ 24. The blue also represents <u>several</u> of the desired attributes: vigilance, perseverance, and justice.

___*plural*___ 25. A <u>few</u> of the first flags included the British cross in the blue square.

Relative Pronouns

Underline each relative pronoun and write its antecedent in the blank.

___*flag*___ 26. The American flag is the flag with <u>which</u> I am most familiar.

___*He*___ 27. He <u>who</u> uses the flag must remember certain rules.

___*rules*___ 28. To follow all of the rules <u>that</u> accompany the flag requires diligence and concentration.

___*person*___ 29. A person <u>who</u> is careful will keep the flag from touching the ground.

___*Anyone*___ 30. Anyone <u>who</u> wishes to discard his flag should burn it, not throw it into the trash.

Unclear Reference
Describe the pronoun reference in each sentence as *clear* or *unclear*.

‗‗‗‗‗‗*clear*‗‗‗‗‗‗ 31. During a battle in the War of 1812, the British captured Francis Scott Key and one of his colleagues; from the ship, Key saw the American flag still flying.

‗‗‗‗‗‗*clear*‗‗‗‗‗‗ 32. Key, inspired by the sight, penned the words to his famous song, "The Star-Spangled Banner."

‗‗‗‗‗‗*unclear*‗‗‗‗‗‗ 33. He wrote the words, "O say can you see by the dawn's early light / What so proudly we hailed at the twilight's last gleaming. / Whose broad stripes and bright stars / Through the perilous fight / O'er the ramparts we watched were so gallantly streaming"; it became part of the first verse of our national anthem.

‗‗‗‗‗‗*unclear*‗‗‗‗‗‗ 34. Another famous name for the flag is *Old Glory,* but it is not as popular as *Stars and Stripes.*

‗‗‗‗‗‗*unclear*‗‗‗‗‗‗ 35. The flag Key saw in 1812 is displayed in the Smithsonian Institution; it is fifty feet long.

Chapter 4: Verbs

Linking Verbs
Underline the complete verbs once and the complements twice. Label the sentence patterns *S-LV-PA* or *S-LV-PN*. Above each word of the sentence pattern, write its label.

1. The mockingbird has been the official state bird of Florida and Texas since 1927.

2. Thirty species of mockingbirds are native to the Western Hemisphere.

3. The northern mockingbird, or the common mockingbird, has become simply the mockingbird.

4. This particular bird grows large quickly.

5. Mockingbirds appear gray in color with white patches on the wings.

Transitive and Intransitive Verbs
Underline the verb in each sentence. Label the sentence patterns *S-InV*, *S-TrV-DO*, or *S-TrV-IO-DO*. Above each word of the sentence pattern, write its label.

6. The scientific name of the mockingbird, *Mimus polyglottos,* translates as "many-tongued animal."

7. This little creature can mimic the songs of at least thirty other birds.

8. This talent gives the mockingbird his name.

9. In addition, these "mockers" can reproduce the sounds of animals and man-made devices, such as musical instruments, chainsaws, and creaky hinges.

10. One mockingbird imitated the songs of thirty-two birds in ten minutes.

Regular and Irregular Verbs
Underline the correct verb from the choices in the parentheses.

11. These gifted songbirds usually *(choose, chose)* thickets, low trees, and bushes for their nest locations.

12. They *(lie, lay)* from four to six greenish-blue or whitish-blue, brown-flecked eggs that take about fourteen days to hatch.

13. Each mockingbird *(eaten, eats)* different foods.

14. The basic mockingbird meal *(consisting, consists)* of spiders, grasshoppers, ants, and berries.

15. Some of these birds *(is, are)* carnivorous, feeding on small insects, other animals, and even eggs.

Verb Tenses

In the following sentences, fill in the blank with the correct form of the verb in parentheses. In the blank to the left, label the tense *Present, Past, Future, Present Perfect, Past Perfect, Future Perfect, Present Progressive, Past Progressive, Future Progressive, Present Perfect Progressive, Past Perfect Progressive,* or *Future Perfect Progressive.* Some answers may vary.

_____*Present*_____ 16. The carnivorous mockingbirds ____*are*____ good hunters with their long, hard beaks and powerful legs. *(be)*

_____*Past Progressive*_____ 17. Ellis ____*was watching*____ a mockingbird hunt its dinner when it began to rain torrentially. *(watch)*

_____*Past Perfect*_____ 18. The bird ____*had pried*____ a centipede from its crevice. *(pry)*

_____*Past*_____ 19. The bird then whipped the insect about, ____*threw*____ it down, and pierced it with its sharp beak. *(throw)*

_____*Past Perfect*_____ 20. After several minutes of this, the bird ____*had disarmed*____ the poisonous centipede satisfactorily. *(disarm)*

_____*Past Progressive*_____ 21. Ellis ____*was shooting*____ pictures as this fascinating scene unfolded. *(shoot)*

_____*Future Perfect*_____ 22. When he finishes this role of film, Ellis ____*will have taken*____ over a hundred pictures of his favorite bird, the *Mimus polyglottos.* *(take)*

_____*Present Perfect Progressive*_____ 23. Ellis ____*has been studying*____ the mockingbird for two years now. *(study)*

_____*Past Perfect*_____ 24. Because of his careful research and fascinating photographs, Ellis ____*had published*____ three articles on robins before he began this project. *(publish)*

_____*Future Progressive*_____ 25. By this time next spring, Ellis ____*will be writing*____ a book based on his research on the multitalented mockingbird. *(write)*

Name_____

Auxiliaries

Underline the complete verb. If the sentence contains *do* or *will* as an auxiliary, label it according to its use: *E* (emphasis), *Q* (question), or *N* (negative).

___Q___ 26. Will the mockingbird defend his home fiercely?

___Q___ 27. Did you know that they swoop down on dogs and even cats?

___E___ 28. Mockingbirds do have their own song, a long sequence of greatly varied notes with each phrase repeated several times in succession.

___N___ 29. They do not just copy other birds.

___Q___ 30. Do you know how to mimic other birdcalls?

Active and Passive Voice

Underline each complete verb and label it *A* (active) or *P* (passive).

___P___ 31. Farmers are helped by mockingbirds' eating harmful insects.

___A___ 32. These pest controllers will also eat weed seed.

___P___ 33. However, they have been known to damage fruit crops.

___A___ 34. A flock of mockingbirds once ate a grape farmer's entire crop.

___A, A___ 35. In anger, he shot a thousand of these birds and buried them in his field!

Mood

Underline the complete verb and in the blank, label the mood *indicative* or *imperative.*

___Indicative___ 36. Can you tell me where to find these interesting creatures?

___Indicative___ 37. Mockingbirds live throughout North America and in parts of Canada and Mexico.

___Indicative___ 38. This songbird often sings at night, especially on bright moonlit nights.

___Indicative___ 39. The mockingbird fools many hunters.

___Imperative___ 40. Don't be fooled by the king of the mimickers!

Chapter 5: Adjectives and Adverbs

Position of Adjectives

Underline the adjectives once. Underline all proper adjectives twice. Draw an arrow from each adjective to the noun or pronoun it modifies.

1. Nathan Hale was an American patriot during the Revolutionary War.

2. He was only twenty-one when an officer in the British army hanged him for spying.

3. Hale will always be known for his bravery and courage.

4. He remains one of America's most-remembered heroes.

5. Hale's famous statement, "I only regret that I have but one life to lose for my country," has long inspired patriotism in students of American history.

Position of Adverbs

Underline the adverbs. Draw an arrow from each adverb to the word it modifies.

6. As a young person, Hale was mostly known for his calm and pious spirit.

7. He thoroughly enjoyed sports, and his friends said he played soccer very well.

8. Hale also took advantage of many education opportunities during his teen years.

9. He rigorously studied under the tutelage of Joseph Huntington and later at Yale College.

10. After his graduation from Yale, he successfully worked as a teacher for a year in Connecticut.

Using Modifiers Correctly

Underline the correct adjective or adverb from the choices in parentheses.

11. Nathan Hale was *(concerned, more concerned)* than most of his peers about American rights.

12. He became a lieutenant and *(greatly, greatlier)* helped in the siege of Boston.

13. The British had the *(largest, most largest)* organized army in the world at that time.

14. His courage was *(greater, greatest)* than many others'.

15. He *(openly, more openly)* displayed his bravery by following the British to New York.

Distinguishing Between Adverbs and Predicate Adjectives
Underline the correct word from the choices in parentheses.

16. Hale's superior seemed *(unwilling, unwillingly)* to ask for anyone to cross enemy lines.

17. Hale appeared *(eager, eagerly)* about assuming this responsibility.

18. He looked *(deceptive, deceptively)* like a Dutch businessman in his disguise.

19. Hale felt *(devoted, devotedly)* to his duty, even after his capture.

20. In the face of death, he remained *(faithful, faithfully)* to his belief in American rights.

Good or *Well? Bad* or *Badly?* and Avoiding Double Negatives
Underline the correct word from the choices in parentheses.

21. Hale performed *(good, well)* as a soldier.

22. He wasn't afraid of *(anything, nothing)*.

23. Hale's behavior was never *(bad, badly)*, even in extreme danger.

24. He was a *(good, well)* strategist.

25. Hale didn't have *(any, no)* fears about facing the enemy.

Problems with Modifier Positions
Rewrite the following sentences, correcting or improving modifier positions.

26. Hale even knew that he could help save the American army from defeat.

   Hale knew that even he could help save the American army from defeat.

27. He only volunteered because he felt it was his duty as a soldier to protect his country.

   He volunteered only because he felt it was his duty as a soldier to protect his country.

28. The soldiers who waited for his return expectantly hoped that he would not be caught.

   The soldiers who expectantly waited for his return hoped that he would not be caught.

29. All of the soldiers were not as brave as Hale.

   Not all of the soldiers were as brave as Hale.

30. Instead of only serving himself, Hale sacrificed for the good of the nation.

   Instead of serving only himself, Hale sacrificed for the good of the nation.

Chapter 6: Prepositions, Conjunctions, and Interjections

Prepositional Phrases

Place parentheses around the prepositional phrase in each sentence, and underline the word or words it modifies. In the blank, label the function of the phrase *Adj* (adjectival) or *Adv* (adverbial).

Adj 1. The ancient Egyptian pyramids are the oldest and largest stone <u>structures</u> (in the world.)

Adv 2. Thirty-five major ruins still <u>stand</u> (along the Nile River.)

Adv 3. Giza's three impressively large pyramids are <u>listed</u> (among the world's seven wonders.)

Adj 4. The largest pyramid is the <u>Great Pyramid</u> (at Giza,) standing 450 feet high.

Adj 5. The <u>base</u> (of this pyramid) covers thirteen acres.

Troublesome Prepositions

In each sentence, underline the correct preposition in parentheses.

6. Over two million limestone blocks went *(in, <u>into</u>)* the building of the Great Pyramid of Giza.

7. *(Beside, <u>Besides</u>)* the large number of blocks, consider their tremendous weight as they averaged about two and a half tons apiece!

8. Over the years, the Egyptian pyramids have been the subject of much research and debate *(<u>among</u>, between)* scholars.

9. Oftentimes, the pharaoh constructed smaller pyramids that lay *(<u>beside</u>, besides)* his own pyramid.

10. The king's wives or daughters were sometimes buried *(<u>in</u>, into)* these pyramids.

Prepositions and Adverbs

Identify each italicized word as a preposition or an adverb. In the blank write the letter that corresponds to the correct answer. Underline the objects of the prepositions.

    A. Preposition
    B. Adverb

_A_ 11. The first pyramid was built *over* two thousand <u>years</u> before Christ.

_A_ 12. It was designed *for* the Pharaoh <u>Djoser</u>, but the architect, Imhotep, is now better known.

_B_ 13. A structure like this step pyramid had never been seen *before*.

_A_ 14. *Beneath* the stone structure lies a burial chamber for the Pharaoh and five members of his family.

_B_ 15. A portrait of the king lies *inside*.

Misplaced Prepositions

Correct each misplaced prepositional phrase by rewriting the sentence correctly in the blank. If the sentence is correct, write *C* in the blank.

16. Around it, Djoser's pyramid had a complex consisting of courtyards and ceremonial buildings built.

    Djoser's pyramid had a complex consisting of courtyards and ceremonial buildings built

    around it.

17. Some of the courts were used for special feasts and celebrations.

    _C_

18. Djoser within one of these courtyards once ran a special course, and crowds traveled long distances to observe this event.

    Djoser once ran a special course within one of these courtyards, and crowds traveled long

    distances to observe this event.

19. By completing the course, the Pharaoh symbolically renewed his power.

    _C_

20. Djoser was then recrowned according to history as king of Upper and Lower Egypt.

    According to history, Djoser was then recrowned as king of Upper and Lower Egypt.

Conjunctions

Underline the conjunction in each sentence and identify it as coordinating, correlative, or subordinating. In the blank write the letter that corresponds to the correct answer.

    A. Coordinating
    B. Correlative
    C. Subordinating

_B_ 21. The true pyramid, introduced around 2575 B.C., is not only a development from the step pyramid but also an improvement in the appearance of the structure.

_C_ 22. While the outside looks different with smooth, triangular walls, the inside support is basically a step pyramid.

_A_ 23. Packing blocks fill in the spaces of the steps, <u>and</u> casting blocks, usually lime-stone, create the finishing touch.

_C_ 24. <u>Before</u> actual construction began, the Egyptian architects made careful prepara-tions.

_A_ 25. The location had to be on a solid rock base, <u>or</u> the ground would crack under the tremendous weight.

Prepositions, Conjunctions, and Interjections
In the blank, label the italicized word *preposition*, *conjunction*, or *interjection*.

___interjection___ 26. *Unbelievable!* The sides of the pyramids line up with almost exact precision to the compass points, true north, south, east, and west!

___conjunction___ 27. *Although* these structures are mostly all limestone, some granite was used for internal chambers and passageways.

___conjunction___ 28. The Egyptian tools were simple *yet* highly effective and well developed.

___preposition___ 29. The Egyptian pyramids fascinated people of the ancient world, and they continue to draw admirers *from* all over the world.

___preposition___ 30. An Arab proverb says, "Time laughs *at* all things, but the pyramids laugh at time."

Chapter 7: Verbals

Participles

Underline the participles in each sentence. Draw an arrow from each underlined participle to the noun it modifies. In the blank, label each underlined participle *past* or *present*.

_____*past*_____ 1. The renowned Parthenon is an ancient temple in Athens.

_____*present*_____ 2. This standing temple sits on Acropolis, a hill in Athens.

_____*past*_____ 3. The committed builders wanted to build the best temple possible.

_____*past*_____ 4. The finished temple was dedicated to the patron goddess, Athena.

_____*present*_____ 5. The Parthenon is an amazing example of Greek architecture.

Gerunds

Underline the gerunds. Place parentheses around the gerund phrases. In the blank, label each gerund or gerund phrase *S* (subject), *DO* (direct object), *IO* (indirect object), or *OP* (object of the preposition).

__*S*__ 6. (Building the Parthenon) took fifteen years.

__*OP*__ 7. Ictinus and Callicrates were responsible for (designing the Parthenon.)

__*DO*__ 8. With the help of the Greek sculptor Phidias, the temple decorations began (arriving.)

__*S*__ 9. (Sculpting) became an important part of his work.

__*OP*__ 10. After (capturing the city,) the Turks used the Parthenon as a mosque.

Infinitives

Underline the infinitive phrases. In the blank, label the function of each infinitive phrase *noun* (noun), *adj* (adjective), or *adv* (adverb). Some sentences may not have an infinitive phrase.

_____*noun*_____ 11. The Parthenon was badly damaged when the Venetians tried to conquer Athens.

_____*adv*_____ 12. The Parthenon was being used by the Turks to store gunpowder.

_____ 13. This gunpowder exploded, bringing harm to part of the temple.

_____*adj*_____ 14. Because the Athenians desired to protect them from further harm, they moved the sculptures to Athens and London.

_____ 15. The ruins of the Parthenon remain in Athens to this day.

Cumulative Review

Underline the verbals in the following sentences. In the blank, label each verbal *P* (participle), *G* (gerund), or *I* (infinitive).

__G__ 16. Creating the entire Parthenon out of marble gave the structure a look of grandeur.

__P__ 17. It has an enclosed space called a cella, which is separated into two rooms.

__I__ 18. One room housed a huge gold and ivory statue, used to remind people of the patron goddess, Athena.

__P__ 19. Painted sculptures gave the spectacular structure some color and vibrancy.

__I__ 20. Sculptures were used to fill the pediments, the triangular ends of the roof.

Questions 21-25: Underline each verbal in the following paragraph.

The Parthenon includes small sculpted panels (metopes). The mythological background of the temple is reflected by these panels, showing battles between the Lapiths and the centaurs. Scenes from the Trojan War also lined the painted walls of the Parthenon. All of the artwork was painted to honor Athena. Christians understand that the Athenians were not blessed for revering a pagan god.

Chapter 8: Clauses

Phrases and Clauses

In the blank, label the italicized group of words *P* (phrase) or *Cl* (clause).

_P_ 1. Called "nature's masterpieces," elephants are *the largest living land animals.*

_Cl_ 2. They have the longest noses and front teeth in the entire animal kingdom, and *they might also have the longest memories.*

_Cl_ 3. *The elephant is one of the tallest animals,* second only to the giraffe.

_P_ 4. These creatures, *having a high level of intelligence,* are one of the world's best known animals.

_P_ 5. Elephants live in organized social frameworks, *using sophisticated communication calls.*

Dependent and Independent Clauses

Identify each italicized clause as dependent or independent. In the blank, write the letter that corresponds to the correct answer.

A. Dependent
B. Independent

_A_ 6. Together with over 160 other species, the elephant family belongs to the order Proboscidea, *which means animals with a trunk.*

_B_ 7. *There are two chief kinds of elephants living today,* the African elephant and the Indian elephant.

_A_ 8. African elephants can be found only in Africa south of the Sahara, *whereas Indian elephants live in parts of India and Southeast Asia.*

_A_ 9. Larger than the Indian elephant, the African elephant male and female both grow tusks *that reach extreme lengths.*

_B_ 10. *The Indian elephant is commonly trained for forestry wor*k.

Using Independent and Dependent Clauses

Label each sentence *S* (simple), *Cd* (compound), *Cx* (complex), or *Cd-Cx* (compound-complex).

_S_ 11. Because of their incredible strength and trainability, elephants have been used in many ways: instruments of war, bulldozers in the logging industry, entertainment in circuses and zoos.

_S_ 12. The earliest recorded use of elephants dates back to 331 B.C.

_Cd-Cx_ 13. Alexander the Great led a Macedonian army into battle, and under his leadership they defeated Persian troops, who were riding on elephants.

_Cx_ 14. In 218 B.C., Hannibal of Carthage, leading an army that were mounted on elephants, crossed the Alps and invaded Italy.

_Cd_ 15. Working elephants have long been common in Asia, and they are still used today in the logging industry.

_S_ 16. An elephant can haul a log weighing up to four tons.

_Cd-Cx_ 17. When the British ruled in India, Burma, and Siam, large-scale logging developed, and thousands of elephants were employed to fell teak trees.

_S_ 18. An African elephant featured in the London Zoo in the 1800s fascinated visitors from all over the world.

_Cd_ 19. Jumbo was the largest animal in captivity at that time, and now the word *jumbo* has become an adjective describing excessively large objects.

_Cd_ 20. P. T. Barnum bought Jumbo in 1882, and this fascinating creature soon took center stage in his circus.

Adjective and Adverb Clauses

Place parentheses around each adjective clause. Underline the relative pronouns once and the relative adverbs twice. Draw arrows from each adjective clause to the word or words it modifies.

21. Adventurous tourists should visit Africa and Asia, (where they can take safaris on elephants' backs.)

22. Elephant herds, consisting of all females, have from twenty to forty members (that are part of the same extended family.)

23. This social group follows the oldest female (who is responsible for the herd's safety.)

24. After reaching their midteens, male elephants leave the herd and join a loosely bonded pack of males, (where they will vie for the top position.)

25. Elephants spend time in the water drinking and bathing, time (which often turns into playtime as they roll in the mud and splash around.)

Underline the adverb clause in each sentence once. Underline the word it modifies twice.

26. Because they are so massive, adult elephants consume about three hundred pounds of food in one day.

27. The elephant's trunk functions as though it were a hand.

28. Although the elephant's trunk is really his nose, it serves as a windshield wiper for his eyes, a forklift to pick up food, and a water hose to soak any innocent bystander.

29. Elephants with tusks use them as tools and weapons, and whenever their trunk muscles tire, they can rest the weary limb on their ivory shelves.

30. Although elephants appear intimidating with their great size and fierce-looking tusks, they are generally easygoing and peaceful creatures.

Chapter 9: Agreement

Subjects and Predicates

Underline the simple subject in each sentence. Underline the correct verb from the choices in parentheses.

1. Pittsburgh, Pennsylvania, *(is, are)* one of the largest makers of steel in the world.

2. The Pittsburgh area *(provides, provide)* about 10 percent of the United States' steel.

3. In our technological age, service industries *(grows, grow)* more rapidly than steel.

4. In Pittsburgh, the economy still *(depends, depend)* on the steel industry.

5. The city also *(has, have)* important health and computer centers.

Auxiliaries and Special Rules for *Be*

Underline the simple subject in each sentence. In the blank, label the italicized verb *V* (main verb) or *Aux* (auxiliary).

___Aux___ 6. Pittsburgh *is* located in southwestern Pennsylvania.

___V___ 7. The Allegheny and the Monongahela *join* to form the Ohio River.

___Aux___ 8. These rivers *have* helped to make the city the core of the state's inland waterway system.

___V___ 9. Only Philadelphia *has* more people than Pittsburgh.

___Aux___ 10. Pittsburgh *was* named after William Pitt, a former prime minister of Britain.

Compound Subjects, Finding the Subject, and Indefinite Pronouns as Subjects

Underline the simple subject or subjects in each sentence. Underline the correct verb from the choices in parentheses.

11. The area between the Allegheny and Monongahela Rivers *(forms, form)* the Golden Triangle.

12. Most of the major headquarters for many businesses *(resides, reside)* in the Golden Triangle.

13. There *(is, are)* large skyscrapers in this wedge-shaped business section.

14. The United States Steel Building, not the other skyscrapers, *(stands, stand)* highest at sixty-four stories high.

15. Neither the residential areas nor the manufacturing district *(contributes, contribute)* as much to the Pittsburgh economy as the steel industry.

Problem Nouns
Underline the simple subject. Underline the correct verb from the choices in parentheses.

16. The <u>riches</u> of Pittsburgh *(is, <u>are</u>)* found in the steel business.

17. A large <u>group</u> of people *(<u>works</u>, work)* in the business district.

18. The <u>Gateway Center</u> *(<u>takes</u>, take)* up about twenty-three acres.

19. <u>Two dollars</u> *(<u>is</u>, are)* required to ride the cable car into downtown Pittsburgh.

20. The <u>Benedum Center for Performing Arts</u> *(<u>serves</u>, serve)* as the home of the Pittsburgh Ballet Theater.

Nouns as Antecedents: Compound and Indefinite Pronouns
Underline the correct answer from the choices in parentheses.

21. Andrew Carnegie was a famous Pittsburgh steel manufacturer. *(<u>He</u>, They)* founded the Carnegie Library of Pittsburgh.

22. Richard and Andrew Mellon began the industrial research branch of the Carnegie Mellon University. *(He, <u>They</u>)* established this institute in 1913.

23. Neither the baseball team nor the Pittsburgh Penguins play *(its, <u>their</u>)* games in Schenley Park.

24. Each of the teams has *(<u>its</u>, their)* own stadium or arena.

25. Both the Museum of Natural History and the Museum of Art contain *(its, <u>their</u>)* own outstanding collections of important artifacts.

Chapter 10: Spelling and Troublesome Words

Formation of Plurals
In the blank write the correct plural form of the word in parentheses.

_____lenses_____ 1. My sister Deanna and I wear contact _?_. *(lens)*

_____forms_____ 2. Because he has perfect eyesight, my brother does not need any _?_ of corrective lens. *(form)*

_____children_____ 3. Aunt Megan's two _?_ needed glasses when they were two years old. *(child)*

_____brothers-in-law_____ 4. Her two _?_ research and develop new technology for making glasses. *(brother-in-law)*

_____1200s_____ 5. The date when glasses were first used is not known, but Europeans began to wear them in the _?_. *(1200)*

Spelling with *ie* or *ei*
In the blank write the letter that corresponds to the correctly spelled word.

6. __A__ A. receive
   B. recieve

7. __B__ A. feif
   B. fief

8. __B__ A. beleive
   B. believe

9. __A__ A. reign
   B. riegn

10. __B__ A. theif
    B. thief

Adding Final Suffixes
Add a suffix to the italicized word in each sentence. Then write the new, correctly spelled word in the blank.

_____reported_____ 11. In 1275, Marco Polo *report* + *ed* seeing people in China wearing glasses.

_____accompanied_____ 12. The demand for reading glasses *accompany* + *ed* the increasing availability of printed books in the late 1400s.

_____beginning_____ 13. By the 1500s, people were *begin* + *ing* to use glasses for cleared distance vision.

_____resourceful_____ 14. The *resource* + *ful* Benjamin Franklin wore bifocals in 1784.

_____putting_____ 15. Bifocals are made by *put* + *ing* together part of a lens for focusing up close and part of a lens for distance vision.

Troublesome Verbs
Underline the correct word from the choices in parentheses.

16. Alfredo, did you see where I *(sat, set)* my glasses?

17. I need those reading glasses so that I *(can, may)* read my book without getting a headache.

18. Perhaps they are *(lying, laying)* on my desk.

19. Maybe I had *(lay, laid)* my glasses on the kitchen table.

20. *(Will, Shall)* we look in the study?

21. Can we *(rise, raise)* the shade to let a little light into this dark room?

22. Wait! Don't *(sit, set)* in that chair!

23. I thought I saw my glasses *(lying, laying)* there.

24. Oh! I just remembered that I left them *(sitting, setting)* on the top of the television with my book.

25. I immediately *(rose, raised)* to get them.

More Troublesome Words
Underline the correct word from the choices in parentheses.

26. Glasses *(affect, effect)* the way the eye focuses on light rays.

27. The light must focus on the retina; *(than, then)* a clear image is seen.

28. The *(principal, principle)* purpose of the single-focus lens is to focus the light before it enters the eye and hits the retina.

29. *(Their, There)* are many different kinds of lenses that help correct a variety of eyesight problems.

30. Now, because of modern technology, *(its, it's)* much easier to see clearly.

Chapter 11: Capitalization

Personal Names, Religions, and Nationalities
Underline each capitalization error.

1. My <u>Mother</u> told me that Poland is a beautiful country.

2. My teacher, H. M. <u>wallace</u>, used to live in Poland.

3. He told us many things about <u>polish</u> culture.

4. Many Poles have a strong affiliation with <u>roman catholicism</u>.

5. The name *pole* comes from the Slavic word for a plain or field.

Place Names and Transportation
Underline each capitalization error.

6. Poland is located in central <u>europe</u>.

7. It borders the Baltic <u>sea</u>.

8. To the <u>East</u> of Poland lie Belarus and Ukraine.

9. *Gift of youth,* a Polish ship, has participated in many races throughout the world.

10. Rysy <u>peak</u> is the highest elevation above sea level in Poland.

Astronomical Terms
Underline each capitalization error and write the correction in the blank. If the sentence is correct, write *C* in the blank.

_____*earth*_____ 11. Nicolaus Copernicus was a Polish scientist who believed that the universe did not revolve around the <u>Earth</u>.

_____*C*_____ 12. Most of the scientists in Copernicus's time believed that the universe revolved around the earth.

_____*sun*_____ 13. Copernicus asserted that the earth revolved around the <u>Sun</u>.

_____*C*_____ 14. Even though people mocked his theory then, he is remembered today as a great scientist because of his observations.

_____*Way*_____ 15. The sun is the central point for all of the planets in our galaxy, the Milky <u>way</u>.

Businesses and Organizations, Cultural and Historical Terms
Underline each capitalization error. If the sentence is correct, write *C* in the blank.

_____ 16. In Poland, the National government is separated into two houses.

___C___ 17. The lower house of government in Poland is called the *Sejm*.

_____ 18. The Communist party dissolved itself in 1990.

_____ 19. Education is very important to the Polish people; most students attend Government-operated schools.

_____ 20. The first Polish University was established in Kraków.

Titles and First Words
Underline each capitalization error. If the sentence is correct, write *C* in the blank.

_____ 21. In my History class, I learned that Poland has produced many writers, painters, and composers.

_____ 22. Wladyslaw Reymont wrote *The peasants* and other novels.

_____ 23. Tadeusz Makowski painted *The shoemaker*.

___C___ 24. Stanislaw Moniuszko, a Polish composer, wrote the opera entitled *The Countess*.

_____ 25. My grade on the quiz over Polish artists was an a.

Chapter 12: Punctuation

End Marks and Initials and Abbreviations
Insert the correct end mark for each sentence. Insert any missing periods or decimal points in the following sentences. If the sentence is correct, write *C* in the blank.

_____ 1. Have you ever been to Finland?

_____ 2. At 4,344 ft. Mount Haltia rises above every other mountain in Finland.

_____ 3. In the Land of the Midnight Sun, one can see the sun shining even at 2:30 A.M.

_____ 4. Our science professor, Michael Bowen, Ph.D., believes that the aurora borealis is most beautiful in Finland.

_____ 5. Russia controlled Finland from A.D. 1809 to 1917.

Commas: In a Series, After Introductory Elements, to Set Off Certain Sentence Elements
Insert any missing commas in the following sentences. If the sentence is correct, write *C* in the blank.

_____ 6. After the writing of the Constitution in 1919, all Finns who were eighteen and older could vote.

_____ 7. Finnish farmers produce beets, sugar, potatoes, and oats.

_____ 8. The huge, thriving forests increase Finland's wealth.

___C___ 9. During the 1000s Sweden and Russia fought for control of Finland.

_____ 10. The Finns, as you may know, regained control of their country in 1917.

Appositives and Restrictive and Nonrestrictive Elements
Insert any missing commas in the following sentences. If the sentence is correct, write *C* in the blank.

_____ 11. The president, Finland's head of state, is also the chief executive officer.

_____ 12. The parliament of Finland, a one-house legislature, is called the *Eduskunta*.

___C___ 13. An official who wants to govern one of Finland's twelve provinces must be appointed by the president.

_____ 14. The party that usually receives the most votes, the Social Democrat Party, is supported mostly by the working class and the middle class.

___C___ 15. Another party that receives many votes is the National Coalition Party.

Commas with Quotations, Dates, and Addresses; Commas in Letters

Insert any missing commas. If the phrase is correct, write *C* in the blank.

_____ 16. Dear Kirsten₍ᵥ₎

_____ 17. I am leaving Helsinki on May 26,ᵥ2001.

_____ 18. I will be landing in Chicago,ᵥ Illinois,ᵥ on Saturday.

_____ 19. Could you please send my sweater to 36 Woodlawn Ave.,ᵥ Marietta?

__*C*__ 20. Love, Helga

Incorrect Commas

Cross out any incorrect commas in the following sentences. If the sentence is correct, write *C* in the blank.

_____ 21. Most of Finland's population✗ live in the southern part of Finland.

_____ 22. The Finnish✗ and the Swedish people often look alike.

_____ 23. In the cities most Finnish people rent apartments, but✗ in the country most people live on farms.

_____ 24. My grandparents✗ and my uncle own a cattle farm in the middle part of Finland.

_____ 25. My parents will visit my grandparents in July✗ 2003.

Semicolon and Colon

Insert any missing semicolons or colons in the following sentences. If the sentence is correct, write *C* in the blank.

_____ 26. Northern Finland is sometimes called the Land of the Midnight Sun because the sun shines even at 12ᵥ00 A.M. during part of the year.

_____ 27. The Finns enjoy many outdoor sports;ᵥ ice hockey, skiing, boating, and hiking.

_____ 28. The Finns attend many concerts and ballets;ᵥ they also enjoy plays and operas.

__*C*__ 29. Finland has four major land regions, including the Coastal Lowlands, the Lake District, the Upland District, and the Coastal Islands.

_____ 30. Finland has many hills and plateaus;ᵥ many lakes also are scattered along the countryside.

Quotation Marks and Underlining for Italics

Insert any missing quotation marks and underlining for italics in the following sentences. If the sentence is correct, write *C* in the blank.

_C_ 31. The sauna is the most famous feature of Finnish life.

_____ 32. Henry Wadsworth Longfellow's poem *The Song of Hiawatha* is based on the Kalevala, a huge collection of Finnish folklore that became Finland's national epic.

_____ 33. A popular summer sport includes pesäpallo, a Finnish form of baseball.

_____ 34. Finland's national anthem is "Maamme," meaning "Our Land."

_____ 35. The first line is "Our land, our land, our fatherland."

Apostrophes, Hyphens, Dashes, and Parentheses

Insert any missing apostrophes, hyphens, dashes, and parentheses in the following sentences. If the sentence is correct, write *C* in the blank. *(Answers may vary.)*

_____ 36. Simplicity of line and shape can be seen in the works of Finland's best-known architects Eliel Saarinen and Alvar Aalto.

_____ 37. Johan Ludvig Runeberg became known as Finland's national poet.

_____ 38. Finland has thirteen universities and twenty-six other institutions of higher learning.

_____ 39. Aleksis Kivi and Minna Canth (writers of the nineteenth century) championed women's rights.

_C_ 40. Akseli Gallen-Kallela's paintings use themes from the *Kalevala*.

Chapter 12 Review   429

A

a/an 117
accept/except 245
adjective
  adjective clause 199
  article 117-18
  comparing with 127-28
  correct usage of 127-28
  definition of 114-15
  determiner 117-18
    article 117-18
    demonstrative 118
    indefinite 118
    interrogative 118
    possessive 117-18
  irregular, regular 127-28
  modifying noun 120-21
  positions of 114-15
  possessive noun 17
  possessive pronoun 117
  prepositional phrase as 144
  proper 120-21
  test frame for 114
adjective order (ESL) 120
adjectives, no plurals of (ESL) 128
adjective vs. adverb 130
adverb
  adverb clause 202-3
  comparing with 127-28
  correct usage of 127-28
  definition of 122-23
  forming 123
  irregular, regular 127-28
  positions of 122-23
  prepositional phrase as 144-45
  qualifier 125
  relative 200
adverbs, forming of (ESL) 123
affect/effect 246
agreement
  pronoun-antecedent 224-30
  subject-verb 209-23
almanac 331
antecedent
  agreement of pronoun with 224-25
  compound 227
  definition of 46
apostrophe 27-28, 251, 306-8
appositive 38, 55, 62
archaic second-person pronouns 56
archaic second-person pronouns, chart 56
article
  definite *(the)* 117
  definition of 117-18
  indefinite *(a/an)* 117
atlas 331
auxiliaries in subject-verb agreement (ESL) 211
auxiliaries, modal (ESL) 82
auxiliary
  definition of 82-83
  examples of 82

B

bad/badly 132
be (ESL) 85
be, forms of 8, 82, 98, 102-3, 210-12
beside/besides 147
between/among 146
biased language 358
biographical sources 331-32
book of quotations 334
book, parts of
  acknowledgments 340
  appendix 340
  bibliography 340
  glossary 340
  index 340
  introduction 340
  list of illustrations 339
  preface 340
  table of contents 339
  text 340
  title page 339
borrow/lend/loan 246
brainstorming 254, 360

C

call number 324, 326-27
capital/capitol/Capitol 248
capitalization
  of proper adjectives 120-21
  of proper nouns 30
    astronomical terms 260
    businesses and organizations 262
    cultural and historical terms 262-63
    nationalities 258
    personal names 257
    place names 260
    religions 258
    transportation 260
  of titles and first words 265-66
card catalog
  author card 326-27
  subject card 326-27
  title card 326-27

TEACHING
SCHEDULES

Suggested Teaching Schedule: One Semester

Week	Day One	Day Two	Day Three	Day Four	Day Five
1	1: Sentences (xi-4)	1: Sentences (4-7) 1: *Notes (20)**	1: Sentences (7-10)	1: Sentences (10-15)	1: *Essay Answers (21)*
2	1: Sentences (15-19)	Test 1	2: Nouns (23-27)	2: Nouns (27-31)	2: Nouns (31-35) 2: *Paragraphs (40-42)*
3	2: Nouns (35-38) 2: *Paragraphs (42-43)*	2: Nouns (38-40)	Test 2	3: Pronouns (45-52)	3: Pronouns (52-56)
4	3: Pronouns (57-65)	3: *Definitions (78-79)*	3: Pronouns (66-70)	3: Pronouns (71-78)	Test 3
5	4: Verbs (81-86)	4: Verbs (86-93)	4: Verbs (93-97)	4: *Compar. & Contrast (110-11)*	4: *Compar. & Contrast (110-11)*
6	4: Verbs (98-100)	4: Verbs (100-102)	4: Verbs (102-6)	4: Verbs (107-10)	Test 4
7	5: Adjectives & Adverbs (113-22) 5: *Personal Exper. (138-39)*	5: Adjectives & Adverbs (122-26) 5: *Personal Exper. (138-39)*	5: Adjectives & Adverbs (127-33) 5: *Personal Exper. (138-39)*	5: Adjectives & Adverbs (134-38)	Test 5
8	6: Prep., Conj., & Interj. (141-46)	6: Prep., Conj., & Interj. (146-52)	6: Prep., Conj., & Interj. (152-59)	6: Prep., Conj., & Interj. (160-63)	Test 6
9	MIDTERM REVIEW AND MIDTERM EXAMINATION				
10	6: *Research Essay (163-67)*	6: *Research Essay (163-67)*	6: *Research Essay (163-67)*	7: Verbals (173-77) 6: *Research Essay (163-67)*	6: *Research Essay (163-67)*
11	7: Verbals (177-81) 6: *Research Essay (163-67)*	7: Verbals (181-82)	7: Verbals (183-87)	Review of Verbals (168-87) 7: *Poetry (187-89)*	Test 7
12	8: Clauses (191-94)	8: Clauses (194-99) 8: *Devotional (206-7)*	8: Clauses (199-202) 8: *Devotional (206-7)*	8: Clauses (202-6)	Test 8
13	9: Agreement (209-13)	9: Agreement (213-15) 9: *Response to Lit. (232-33)*	9: Agreement (215-18) 9: *Response to Lit. (232-33)*	9: Agreement (218-22)	9: Agreement (222-26)
14	9: Agreement (227-31)	Test 9	10: Spelling & Troublesome Words (235-40) 10: *Storyboard (253-55)*	10: Spelling & Troublesome Words (240-45) 10: *Storyboard (253-55)*	10: Spelling & Troublesome Words (245-51) 10: *Storyboard (253-55)*
15	10: Spelling & Troublesome Words (251-53)	Test 10	11: Capitalization (257-60)** 11: *Oral History (269-71)*	11: Capitalization (260-61) 11: *Oral History (269-71)*	11: Capitalization (262-64) 11: *Oral History (269-71)*
16	11: Capitalization (265-68) 11: *Oral History (269-71)*	Test 11	12: Punctuation (273-78)** 12: *Letter (316-17)*	12: Punctuation (278-83) 12: *Letter (316-17)*	12: Punctuation (283-93)
17	12: Punctuation (294-97)	12: Punctuation (298-306)	12: Punctuation (306-10) 12: *E-mail (317-19)*	12: Punctuation (310-15) 12: *E-mail (317-19)*	Test 12
18	FINAL REVIEW AND FINAL EXAMINATION				

Chapters 13-15 are reference chapters. Teach material from these chapters throughout the semester whenever it is appropriate for your students.
*The topics in italics refer to writing lessons and assignments within the chapter.
**If necessary, adjust the schedule to teach Chapter 11 (Capitalization) and Chapter 12 (Punctuation) before your students take any standardized achievement tests.

Suggested Teaching Schedule
(First Semester)

Week	Day One	Day Two	Day Three	Day Four	Day Five
1	1: Sentences (xi-1)	1: Sentences (2-4)	1: Sentences (4-7)	1: Sentences (7-11) 1: Notes (20)*	1: Sentences (11-13)
2	1: Sentences (13-15)	1: Sentences (15-19)	Test 1	1: Essay Answers (21)	1: Essay Answers (21)
3	2: Nouns (23-27)	2: Nouns (27-31)	2: Nouns (31-33)	2: Nouns (33-35)	2: Nouns (35-37)
4	2: Nouns (38-40)	Review	Test 2	2: Paragraphs (40-42)	2: Paragraphs (40-42)
5	2: Paragraphs (42-43)	2: Paragraphs (42-43)	3: Pronouns (45-48)	3: Pronouns (48-52)	3: Pronouns (52-56)
6	3: Pronouns (57-65)	3: Pronouns (66-70)	3: Pronouns (71-74)	3: Pronouns (75-78)	Test 3
7	3: Definitions (78-79)	3: Definitions (78-79)	3: Definitions (78-79)	3: Definitions (78-79)	
8	4: Verbs (84-86)	4: Verbs (86-88)	4: Verbs (88-93)	4: Verbs (93-97)	4: Verbs (98-100)
9	4: Compar. & Contrast (110-11)	4: Compar. & Contrast (110-11)	4: Verbs (100-102)	4: Compar. & Contrast (110-11)	4: Verbs (102-6)
10	4: Verbs (107-10)	Review	Test 4	5: Adjectives & Adverbs (113-20)	5: Adjectives & Adverbs (120-22)
11	5: Personal Exper.(138-39)	5: Personal Exper.(138-39)	5: Personal Exper. (138-39)	5: Personal Exper.(138-39)	5: Adjectives & Adverbs(127-29)
12	5: Adjectives & Adverbs (122-26)	5: Adjectives & Adverbs (130-33)	5: Adjectives & Adverbs (134-38)	Review	Test 5
13	6: Research Essay (163-67)	6: Research Essay (163-67)	6: Research Essay (163-67)	6: Research Essay (163-67)	6: Research Essay (163-67)
14	6: Research Essay (163-67)	6: Research Essay (163-67)	6: Research Essay (163-67)	6: Research Essay (163-67)	6: Research Essay (163-67)
15	6: Prep., Conj., & Inter. (141-46)	6: Prep., Conj., & Inter. (146-52)	6: Prep., Conj., & Inter. (152-56)	6: Prep., Conj., & Inter. (157-59)	6: Prep., Conj., & Inter. (160-63)
16	Review	Test 6	6: Research Essay (163-67)	6: Research Essay (163-67)	6: Research Essay (163-67)
17	MIDTERM REVIEW AND MIDTERM EXAMINATION				
18					

Suggested Teaching Schedule
(Second Semester)

Week	Day One	Day Two	Day Three	Day Four	Day Five
19	7: Verbals (169-72)	7: Verbals (173-75)	7: Poetry (187-89)	7: Poetry (187-89)	7: Verbals (175-77)
20	7: Verbals (177-79)	7: Poetry (187-89)	7: Poetry (187-89)	7: Verbals (179-81)	7: Verbals (181-82)
21	7: Verbals (183-87)	Review	Test 7	8: Clauses (191-94)	8: Clauses (194-96)
22	8: Clauses (197-99)	Review	8: Clauses (199-200)	8: Clauses (199-200)	8: Clauses (200-202)
23	8: Clauses (202-6)	Review	Test 8	8: Devotional (206-7)	8: Devotional (206-7)
24	8: Devotional (206-7)	8: Devotional (206-7)	9: Agreement (209-13)	9: Agreement (213-15)	9: Response to Lit. (232-33)
25	9: Response to Lit. (232-33)	9: Response to Lit. (232-33)	9: Response to Lit. (232-33)	9: Agreement (215-18)	9: Agreement (218-22)
26	9: Agreement (222-24)	9: Agreement (224-26)	9: Agreement (227-31)	Review	Test 9
27	10: Storyboard (253-55)	10: Storyboard (253-55)	10: Spelling & Troublesome Words (235-40)	10: Spelling & Troublesome Words (240-45)	10: Spelling & Troublesome Words (245-51)
28	10: Spelling & Troublesome Words (251-53)	Review	Test 10	10: Storyboard (253-55)	10: Storyboard (253-55)
29	11: Capitalization (257-60)**	11: Capitalization (260-61)	11: Capitalization (262-64)	11: Capitalization (265-68)	Test 11
30	11: Oral History (269-71)	11: Oral History (269-71)	11: Oral History (269-71)	11: Oral History (269-71)	12: Punctuation (273-78)
31	11: Oral History (269-71)	11: Oral History (269-71)	11: Oral History (269-71)	12: Punctuation (278-83)**	12: Punctuation (283-88)
32	12: Letter (316-17)	12: Letter (316-17)	12: Punctuation (288-91)	12: Punctuation (291-93)	12: Letter (316-17)
33	12: Punctuation (294-97)	12: E-mail (317-19)	12: E-mail (317-19)	12: Punctuation (298-300)	12: E-mail (317-19)
34	12: Punctuation (300-306)	12: Punctuation (306-9)	12: Punctuation (310-15)	Review	Test 12
35	FINAL REVIEW AND FINAL EXAMINATION				
36					

Chapters 13-15 are reference chapters. Teach material from these chapters throughout the semester whenever it is appropriate for your students.
*The topics in italics refer to writing lessons and assignments within the chapter.
**If necessary, adjust the schedule to teach Chapter 11 (Capitalization) and Chapter 12 (Punctuation) before your students take any standardized achievement tests.

BULLETIN BOARDS

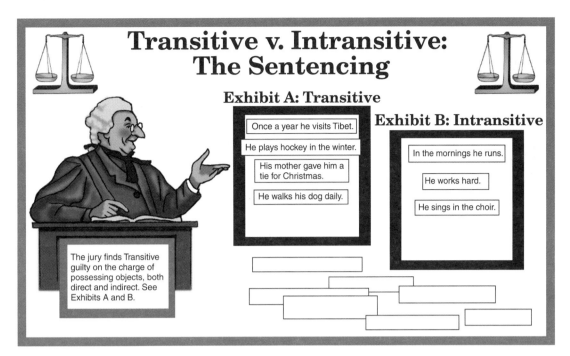

Chapter 1: Transitive v. Intransitive: The Sentencing

Use a white background, a red border, and red letters for the heading. Draw the judge wearing a black robe. Write the verdict on white paper and mount it on red construction paper. For Exhibits A and B, laminate two pieces of white paper or poster board and mount them on black paper. Prepare sentences on strips of paper and laminate. Allow students to place the sentences in the correct exhibit.

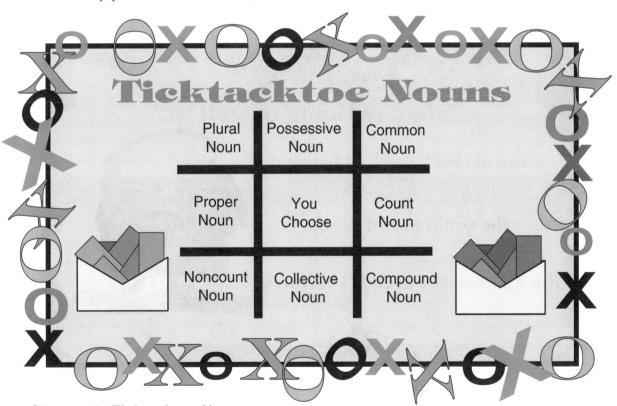

Chapter 2: Ticktacktoe Nouns

Create a grid using black construction paper. Create nine cards to place in the grid. Eight should represent different types of nouns, and one card should be entitled "You Choose." Prepare two envelopes filled with color-coded cards (e.g., blue cards for one team and red cards for the other) which represent each kind of noun in the grid. Students will take turns choosing cards from their team's envelope and matching the noun to its proper category. (Some nouns may fit in more than one category.) If a student chooses a card from an occupied category, he may choose another card. If the student chooses a card that says "You Choose," he must name a noun and identify the type of noun he has named. The team that colors three squares in a row wins. (There might not be a winning team for some games.)

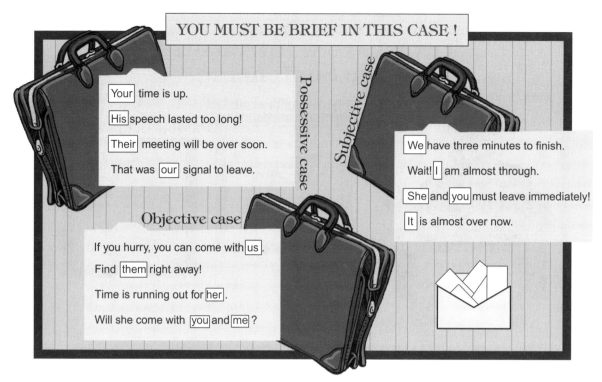

Chapter 3: You Must Be Brief in This Case

Cover the board with a light-colored fabric and use a dark border. Create three large brown briefcases. Cut out three manila folder shapes and several cards from tag board or white paper. Write the sentences on the folders and the missing pronouns on the cards. Encourage the students to place the cards in the correct sentences.

Chapter 4: State-of-Being or Action?

Write various verbs (both state-of-being and action) on pieces of colored construction paper. Use these pieces of paper for the border. Display several sentences with verbs that can be considered state-of-being verbs or action verbs depending on their use in a sentence. Personify the subject of a sentence that contains a state-of-being verb and explain to students that this personification is what they are expressing if they use the state-of-being verb as an action verb.

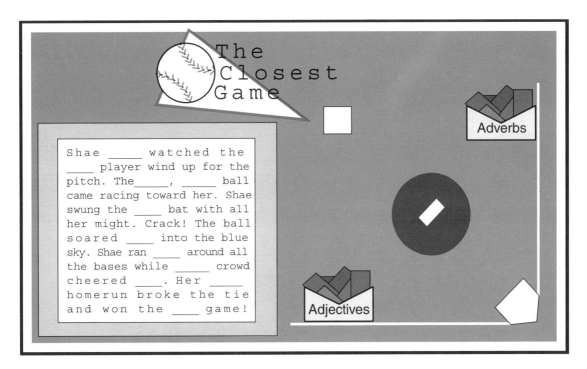

Chapter 5: The Closest Game

On a green background, use white chalk to draw sidelines and a pitcher's mound. Make bases from white construction paper and place two envelopes labeled "Adverbs" and "Adjectives" on first and third base respectively. Write the paragraph, with blanks for the missing words, on white or gray poster board. Use newspaper as a background for the poster. Put cards with the missing adjectives and adverbs in the appropriate envelopes. Instruct students to add the modifiers to the paragraph.

Chapter 6: Conjunctions

Use light blue paper for the background of the board and create a "pond" of a darker blue to mount on the board. Prepare several lily pads from green construction paper and write coordinating conjunctions on some of them. Write at least one compound sentence on the light blue background. (Each sentence should be missing a conjunction.) Allow students to complete the sentences by adding a lily pad with an appropriate conjunction written on it.

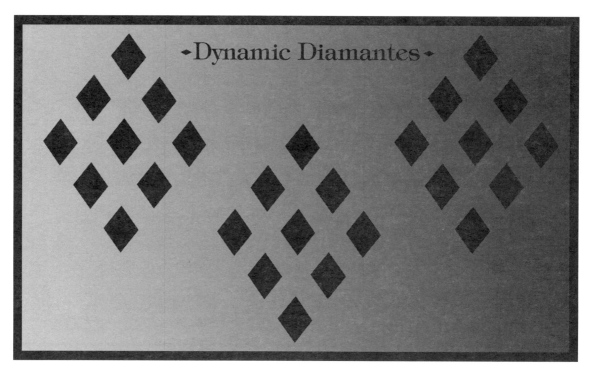

Chapter 7: Dynamic Diamantes

Cover the board with plain silver wrapping paper. Use a solid black border. Make the title and diamonds out of black construction paper. Display the students' diamantes from the "Your Turn" exercise at the end of the chapter.

Derek and Adam enjoy playing soccer.
Derek is the sweeper, and Adam is the goalie.
Derek is the one who is wearing the blue jersey.
Whenever Derek and Adam play together, they
  use good teamwork, and both play their best.

SCORE	
Ind.	Dep.
1	0
2	0
1	1
2	1

Chapter 8: What's the Score?

Use green paper for the background of the board. Mount a figure playing soccer in the center of the board. On light yellow poster board, prepare four sentences, one of each sentence type. Create a scoreboard from white poster board, color-coding the "Ind." and "Dep." labels. (Indicate that they are two different "teams.") Explain to the students that the "score" indicates how many independent and dependent clauses are found in each sentence type. Explain that complex and compound-complex sentences have *at least* one dependent clause.

AGREEMENT

Would you agree that these sentences are correct?

1. Each of the boys remembered to complete their homework.
2. All of the girls wants to receive a good grade on her paper.
3. The students or the teacher open the class with prayer.
4. Here is my completed assignments.
5. Everyone in the class should do his best.

Chapter 9: Agreement

Display five sentences. Each should contain an error in subject-verb agreement or pronoun-antecedent agreement. You may choose to leave one sentence correct. Prepare cards that contain the correct pronouns and verbs so that students can correct the incorrect sentences.

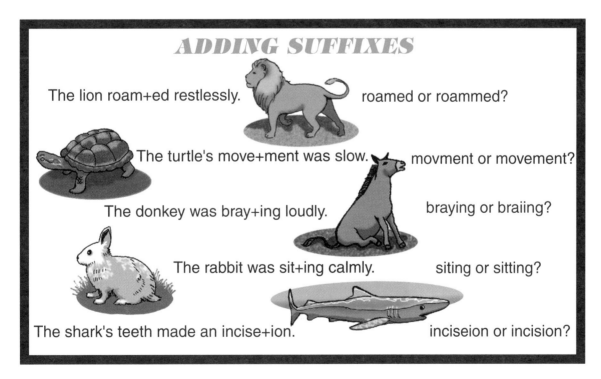

ADDING SUFFIXES

The lion roam+ed restlessly.   roamed or roammed?

The turtle's move+ment was slow.   movment or movement?

The donkey was bray+ing loudly.   braying or braiing?

The rabbit was sit+ing calmly.   siting or sitting?

The shark's teeth made an incise+ion.   inciseion or incision?

Chapter 10: Adding Suffixes

Use a light-colored background to cover the board. Prepare several sentences that contain words with suffixes. Join the base of the word to the suffix with a plus sign. Add figures that will illustrate each sentence. On the right side of the board, write out the base of the word with its added suffix. Ask students which choice is correct. Discuss the rules for adding suffixes to words.

Chapter 11: Oral Histories

Use dark fabric for the background of the board. Display the students' oral histories mounted on different colors of construction paper. Display photographs that accompany the students' histories. The photographs may be mounted on construction paper as well.

Chapter 12: *X* Marks the Punctuation?

Create a treasure map using light brown paper or grocery bags. To give the map an old look, you may want to crumple the paper and burn the edges. Write several sentences, leaving out various punctuation marks. Use an *X* to mark each missing punctuation mark. Be sure to include some *X*s where the punctuation is not necessary for the sentence. Read through the sentences and allow students to decide how each sentence should be punctuated. Prepare cards that include the correct punctuation marks. Place these cards in a treasure chest mounted at the bottom of the map. Explain to students that each *X* represents a clue that leads to the treasure chest. Students may use a thick felt-tipped marker to draw dashed lines from each sentence that requires punctuation to the next.

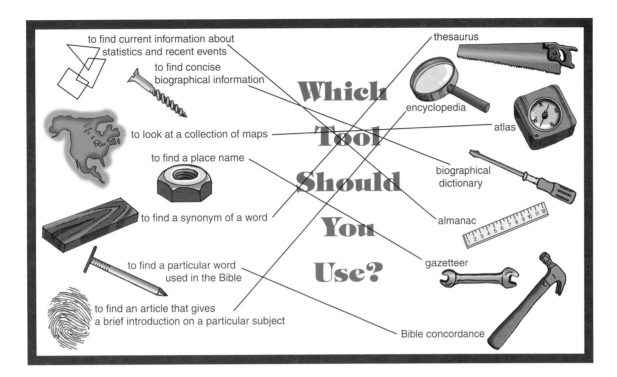

Chapter 13: Which Tool Should You Use?

On the left side of the board, display pictures of objects that correspond to pictures of tools on the right side of the board. (Do not arrange all of the objects and tools directly across from one another.) Prepare labels for each object. Each object label should include an activity that a student would perform using a particular reference tool. In like manner, create labels for each tool. Each of these labels should include a different kind of reference tool. Allow students to use pushpins and string or yarn to match each activity with the proper reference tool.

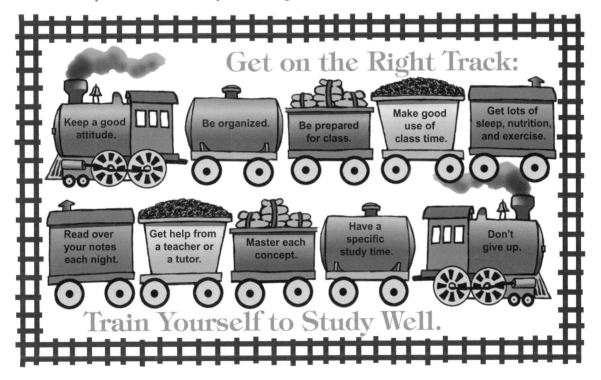

Chapter 14: Get on the Right Track

Using black poster board or construction paper, create a border that looks like a train track. Out of poster board, create two train engines and eight different train cars. On each engine and car, include one tip from the list "Improving Your Study Time" (p. 338). (You may choose to start with one engine and add a different part of the train each day.)

Chapter 15: Proofreading

Construct a list of proofreading checks from the proofreading checklist (p. 380). In each sentence on the board, include an error that is discussed in that particular sentence. On the left side of the board, display a figure of a man looking at the list through a magnifying glass. Discuss the sentences with the students and challenge them to find the errors.

DIAGRAM
ANSWERS

Chapter 1

1-6

1.
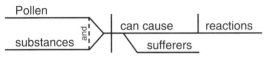

Changes | give | symptoms
people

2.

people | react

3.

Pollen / substances [and] can cause | reactions / sufferers

4.
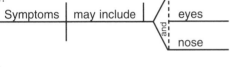

Symptoms | may include | sneezes [and] eyes / nose

5.

Hay fever | affects | Americans

6.

sufferers | should go

7.

weather | relieves | symptoms

8.
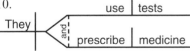

doctors | can give | help
people

9.

Doctors | can help

10.
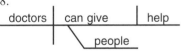

They [and] use | tests / prescribe | medicine

1-7

1.

day | feels \ beautiful

2.
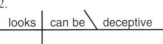

looks | can be \ deceptive

3.
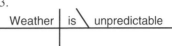

Weather | is \ unpredictable

4.

forecast | Does sound \ favorable

5.
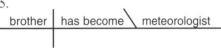

brother | has become \ meteorologist

6.

Computers | remain \ source

7.

forecast | can be \ accurate

8.
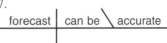

forecasts | seem \ difficult

9.

instruments | have become \ necessities

10.

Weather | is \ phenomenon

1-8

1.
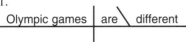
Olympic games | are \ different

2.

Olympics | had | events

3.

game | was \ pankration

4.

Pankration | was \ combination

5.

pankration | was \ dangerous

6.
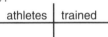
competitors | did wear | gloves

7.
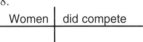
athletes | trained

8.

Women | did compete

9.
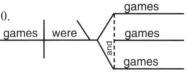
winner | gave | fame
city

10.
games | were \ games / and / games / games

Chapter 2

2-5

1.

number | is \ incredible

2.

Zack | pampers | dog

3.
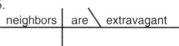
Zack | purchased | box
Aldo

4.
He | gave | Frisbees
Aldo

5.
Zack | finds | toys

6.
neighbors | are \ extravagant

7.

Mrs. Danton | sews | clothes

8.
Mrs. Danton | dressed | poodle

9.
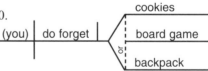
it | is \ winter

10.
(you) | do forget | cookies / or / board game / backpack

456 Diagram Answers

2-13

1.

Class

you | do know | anything

2.

Soviet Union | sent | satellite

3.

dog (Laika) | was \ stray

4.

Laika | was \ creature

5.

Technology | did permit | return

6.

Laika | could stay \ calm

7.

Sputnik II | carried | dog

she | died

8.

Russians | built | memorial
\ Laika

9.

Soviet Union | launched | dogs

10.

use | was \ preparation

Chapter 3

3-6

1.

People | amaze | me

2.

Many | have heard

3.

All | were \ protesters

4.

Some — taught | people / and \ gave | Bible / \ them
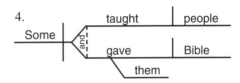

5.

John Huss | was \ priest

he | preached

6.

friends | came

cardinal | would listen

7.

instigator | was \ he

8.

leaders — imprisoned | Huss / and \ sentenced | him

9.

God | worked

reformers | used | life

10.

boldness | has given | courage
\ me

3-19

1.

person | may think

2.

Kathryn Forbes | wrote | story

3.

family (itself) | did have | money

4.

father (himself) | was recuperating

5.

Kathryn
and
friends | wanted | presents

6.

mother (herself) | did have | money

She | offered | brooch
\ Kathryn

7.

Kathryn | did want | brooch

She | wanted | set

8.

set | could bring | joy

9.

mother (herself) | had sold | brooch

10.

Kathryn | understood | herself

Chapter 4

4-4

1.

Meteorology | is \ branch

2.

Meteorologists | are \ students

3.

types | are \ important

4.

weather balloons
Some | are < hygrometers
and
satellites

5.

atmosphere | is \ divisible

6.

region | feels \ different

7.

troposphere | is \ region

8.

Air | is \ static

9.

troposphere
and
waters | are \ home

10.

interesting
study | has become < and
important

4-5

1.
ozone layer | blocks | rays

2.
increases | cause | smog

3.
ozone layer | gives | protection
    humans

4.
M. J. Molina / F. S. Rowland (and) | showed | decrease
    people

5.
eye | can see | changes

6.
scientists | argue

7.
levels | had decreased

8.
countries | have reduced | use

9.
eruptions | can decrease | level

10.
investigation | has given | information
    researchers

Chapter 5

5-7

1.
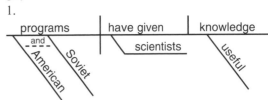
programs (and) American / Soviet | have given | knowledge
    scientists | useful

2.
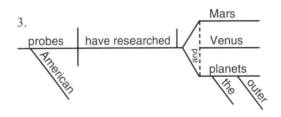
exploration / Planet | has been | result | a / valuable

3.
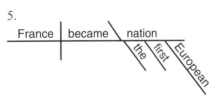
probes / American | have researched | Mars / Venus / planets (and) the / outer

4.
nations / Many / other | have developed | programs / space

5.
France | became | nation / the / first / European

6.
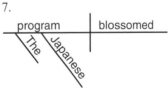
probes / two / German | flew

7.
program / The / Japanese | blossomed

8.
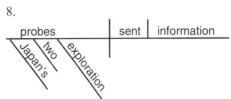
probes / Japan's / two / exploration | sent | information

9.

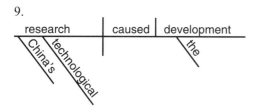
research | caused | development
China's technological
the

10.

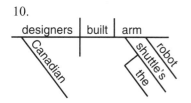
designers | built | arm
Canadian
robot
shuttle's
the

5-9

1.

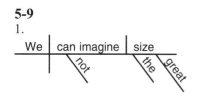
We | can imagine | size
not
the great

2.

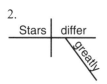
Stars | differ
greatly

3.

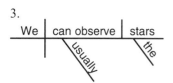
We | can observe | stars
usually
the

4.

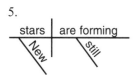
star | consists
A mainly

5.

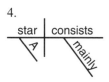
stars | are forming
New still

6.

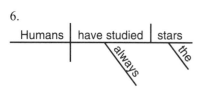
Humans | have studied | stars
always
the

7.

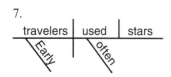
travelers | used | stars
Early often

8.

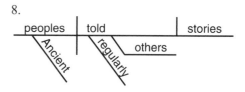
peoples | told | stories
Ancient
regularly
others

9.

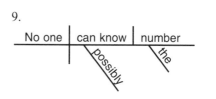
No one | can know | number
possibly
the

10.

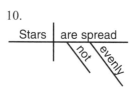
Stars | are spread
not evenly

Chapter 6

6-1

1.

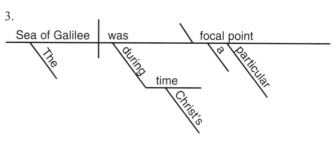
Much | was located
of
ministry
Jesus'
in
Galilee

2.

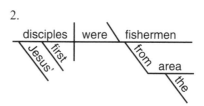
disciples | were \ fishermen
Jesus' first
from
area
the

3.

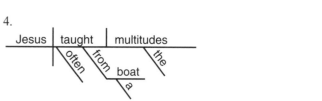
Sea of Galilee | was | focal point
The
during
a particular
time
Christ's

4.

Jesus | taught | multitudes
often from
boat
a
the

5.

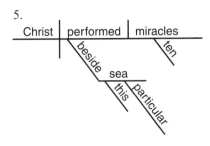

6.

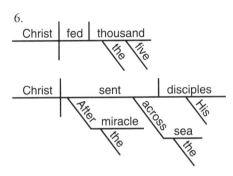

7.

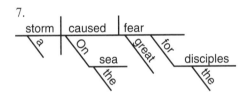

8.

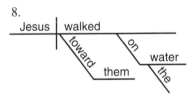

9.

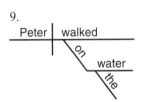

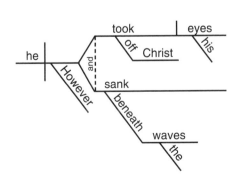

10.

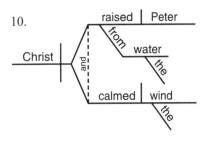

6-13

1.

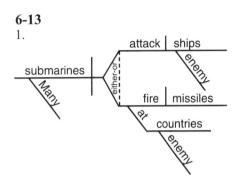

2.

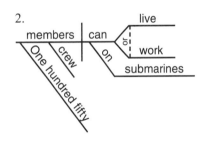

3.

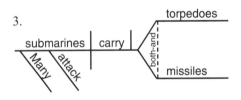

4.

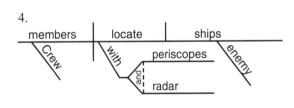

5.

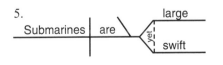

6.

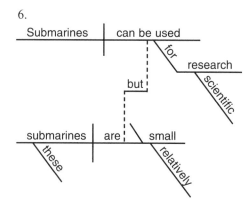

7.

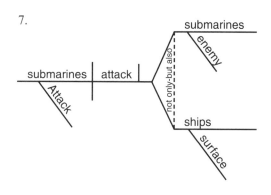

8.

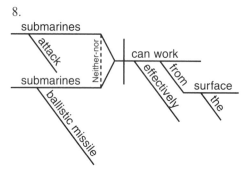

9.

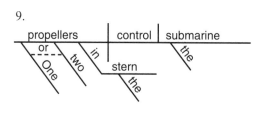

10.

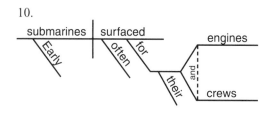

1.

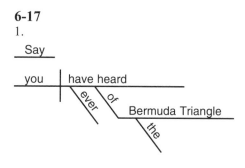

2.

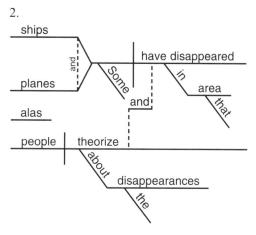

3.

4.

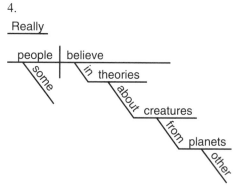

5.

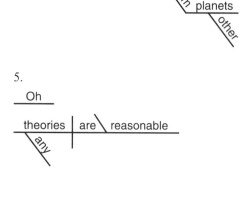

6.

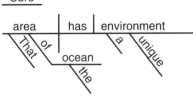

Sure

That area of the ocean has a unique environment

7.

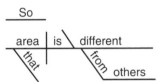

See

a compass points normally toward magnetic north

8.

So

that area is different from others

9.

Yes

a compass in the Bermuda Triangle points to the true north

10.

Wow

The difference definitely could cause some serious problems captain a ship's or pilot a

7-5

1.

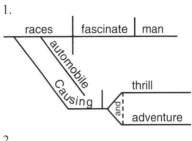

automobile races fascinate man Causing thrill and adventure

2.

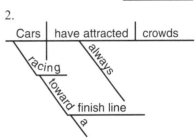

Cars racing have always attracted crowds toward a finish line

3.

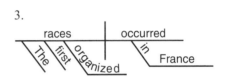

The first races organized occurred in France

4.

roads France's Developed largely by Napoleon were equipped better for races

5.

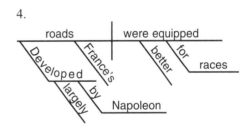

Early races consisted of types many different of vehicles racing from one city to another

6.

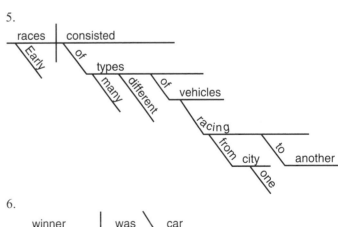

The winner of the first auto race in France was a car steam driven by Count De Dion

7.

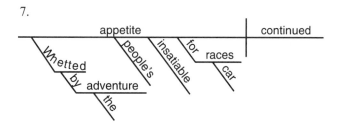

8.

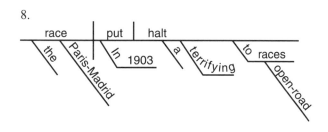

9.

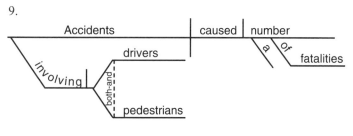

10.

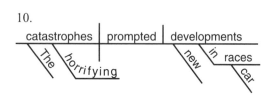

7-9

1.

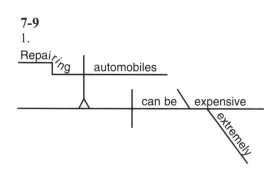

2.

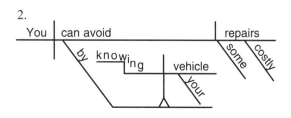

3.

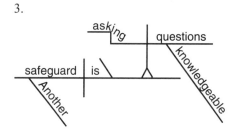

4.

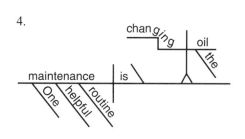

5.

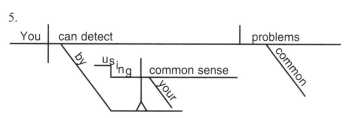

6.

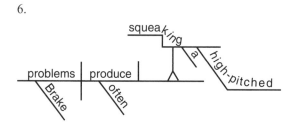

7.

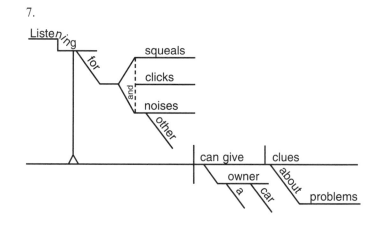

8.

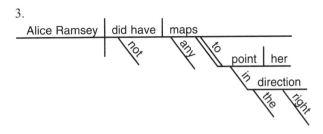

3.

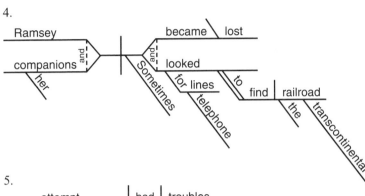

9.

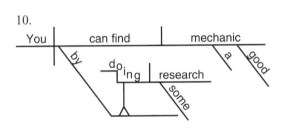

4.

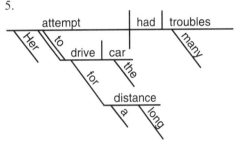

5.

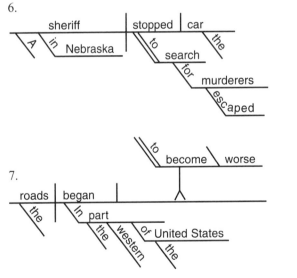

10.

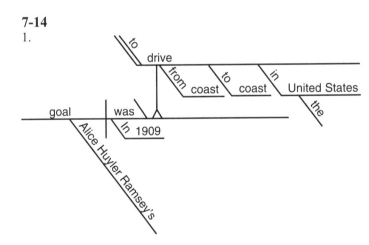

6.

7-14

1.

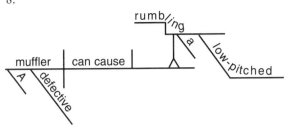

7.

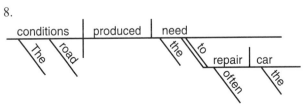

8.

2.

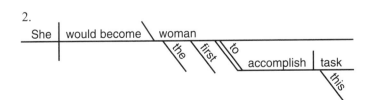

9.

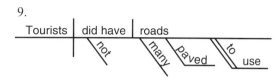

10.

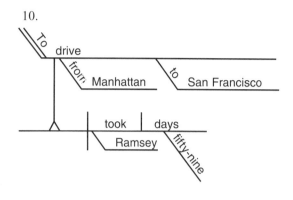

3.

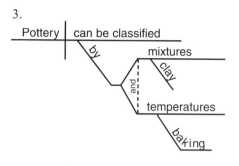

4.

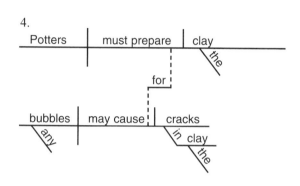

Chapter 8

8-5

1.

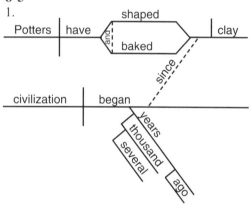

2.

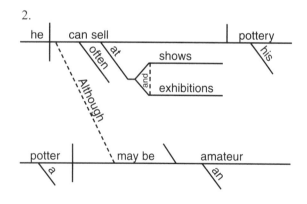

5.

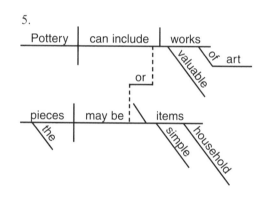

6.

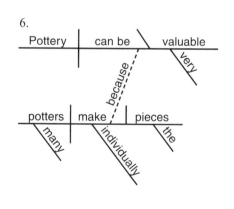

7.

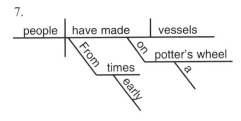

8.

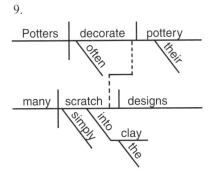

9.

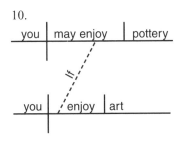

10.

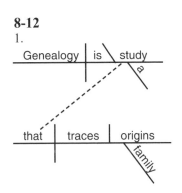

8-12

1.

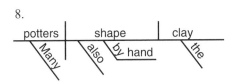

2.

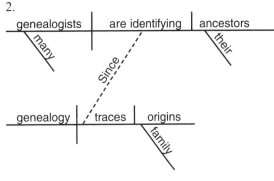

3.

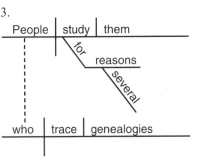

4.

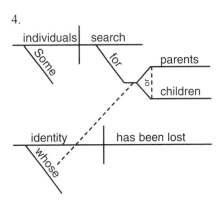

5.

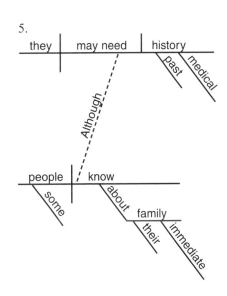

6.

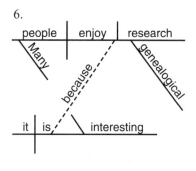

7.

8.

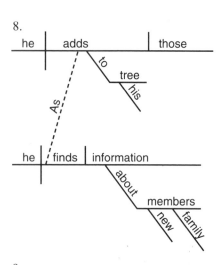

9.

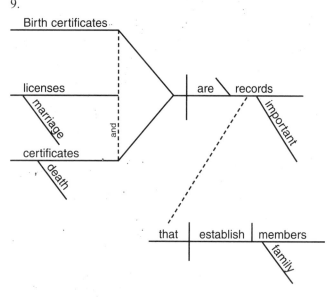

10.

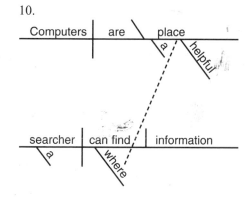